CHINA REVIEW 1997

Related titles already published

China Review (1991)
Edited by Kuan Hsin-chi
and Maurice Brosseau

China Review 1992
Edited by Kuan Hsin-chi
and Maurice Brosseau

China Review 1993
Edited by Joseph Cheng Yu-shek
and Maurice Brosseau

China Review 1994
Edited by Maurice Brosseau
and Lo Chi Kin

China Review 1995
Edited by Lo Chi Kin, Suzanne Pepper
and Tsui Kai Yuen

China Review 1996
Edited by Maurice Brosseau, Suzanne Pepper
and Tsang Shu-ki

China Review 1997

EDITED BY

Maurice Brosseau,

Kuan Hsin-chi

AND

Y. Y. Kueh

The Chinese University Press

ISBN 962–201–774–6

THE CHINESE UNIVERSITY PRESS
The Chinese University of Hong Kong
SHA TIN, N.T., HONG KONG
Fax: +852 2603 6692
+852 2603 7355
E-mail: cup@cuhk.edu.hk
Web-site: http://www.cuhk.edu.hk/cupress/w1.htm

Printed in Hong Kong

Steering Committee

Maurice Brosseau
Joseph Y. S. Cheng
Hsi-sheng Ch'i (on leave)
Kuan Hsin-chi
Y. Y. Kueh
Yun-wing Sung
Paul S. L. Wong

Contents

Preface

This is the seventh volume of *China Review* since its introduction in 1991. Like *China Review 1996*, *China Review 1997* has been subjected to a system of quality control different from the past volumes. Instead of a workshop where draft chapters were discussed and revisions suggested, a system of double blind review has been adopted. The new procedure has considerably tightened up an already tight schedule of publication. It has also led to the rejection of a few manuscripts which were submitted by invitation for consideration of publication. We wish to thank all authors who have kindly accepted our request to make a contribution. Special thanks should also be extended to our reviewers and contributors. Without their cooperation in adhering to the deadlines for the submission of drafts, assessment reports, and revised papers, *China Review 1997* would not have been published in time, as planned.

As convenor of the Steering Committee for *China Review*, I have to acknowledge a deep gratitude to two persons in the team. Dr Maurice Brosseau, one of the editors for this volume and many previous ones, has, as usual, generously given his time in ensuring the language standard of the volume and in compiling the index. Mr Tse Wai Keung, an assistant editor of The Chinese University Press, has, in a professional way, performed the duties of an executive editor since the birth of *China Review*. There are indeed many people behind the scene who have made possible the continuance and improvement of this annual publication.

Kuan Hsin-chi
April 1997

Contributors

ROBERT F. ASH works in the Department of Economics at the School of Oriental and African Studies (SOAS), where from 1986 to 1995 he was also Director of the Contemporary China Institute. He is currently Director of the EU–China Academic Network, based at SOAS. He has published widely on various aspects of economic change in China, focusing especially on the agricultural sector.

BRIAN BRIDGES is Associate Professor in the Department of Politics and Sociology at Lingnan College, Hong Kong. He received his BA and Ph.D. from the University of Wales, studied at Waseda University, Tokyo, and worked for the BBC and the Royal Institute of International Affairs, London. His research interests include Northeast Asian politics and international relations as well as European relations with Asia. His publications include *Korea and the West* (1987), *Japan and Korea in the 1990s* (1993) and, as co-author, *Pacific Asia in the 1990s* (1991).

MAURICE BROSSEAU is Research Officer at the Hong Kong Institute of Asia-Pacific Studies, The Chinese University of Hong Kong. He co-edited several volumes of *China Review*.

JOSEPH C. H. CHAI is Senior Lecturer in Economics at the University of Queensland, Brisbane, Australia. He has written extensively on the Chinese economy. His publications include *Development and Distribution in China* (with C. K. Leung, 1986), *China's Economic Reforms* (with C. K. Leung, 1987) and *China: Transition to a Market Economy* (1997).

HIM CHUNG is a Ph.D. candidate at the Department of Geography, Research School of Pacific and Asia Studies, the Australian National University.

GEORGE DOCWRA is Reader in Economics at the University of Queensland. He was Senior Economic Adviser to the Interstate Commission (1985–1987) and is a member of the Chartered Institute of Transport. He specializes in applied micro-economics, regulation of industry, public enterprise economics, and has published extensively in these areas.

JOSEPH FEWSMITH is the Director of the East Asian Interdisciplinary Studies Program and Associate Chairman of the Department of International Relations at Boston University. He is the author of *Dilemmas of Reform in China: Political Conflict and Economic Debate* (Armonk, NY: M. E. Sharpe, 1994) and *Party, State, and Local Elites in Republican China* (Honolulu: University of Hawaii Press, 1985). He has written numerous articles on the politics and economics of contemporary China and is editor of *Chinese Economic Studies*, a journal of translations.

K. C. FUNG is Associate Professor of Economics, University of California, Santa Cruz; Associate Director, Hong Kong Centre for Economic Research, University of Hong Kong; and Visiting Scholar, Asia/Pacific Research Center, Stanford University. He was consultant to the World Bank (Summer 1993 and Summer 1995). His most recent publications on trade and investment include "Accounting for Chinese Trade: Some National and Regional Considerations," in *Geography and Ownership as a Basis for Economic Accounting*, edited by Robert Baldwin, J. David Richardson and Robert Lipsey (1997); *Trade and Investment: Mainland China, Hong Kong and Taiwan*, HKCER Monograph (1997); and "Mainland Chinese Investment in Hong Kong: How Much, Why and So What?," *Journal of Asian Business* (1996).

HUA LINSHAN is a member of the Centre of Studies on Modern and Contemporary China (EHESS, Paris). Among his publications, besides the book co-authored with Isabelle Thireau which is a study of his own lineage, he has published a book relating the events of the Cultural Revolution in Guangxi province, *Les années rouges* (Paris: Seuil, 1987). He is currently doing research on the present evolution of his native lineage.

HIROYUKI IMAI is an Assistant Professor in Economics at Lingnan College, Hong Kong. His current main research area is macroeconomic aspects of the Chinese economy. He has written several papers on economic cycles and inflation in China.

KUAN HSIN-CHI is Professor of Government and Public Administration, The Chinese University of Hong Kong, and concurrently the Director of its Universities Service Centre. His area of research interest and publication is political development in Hong Kong and China, with special emphasis on political culture, participation, and constitutional change.

Y. Y. KUEH is Chair Professor of Economics and Dean of Faculty of Social Sciences, Lingnan College. His publications include: *The Chinese Economy under Deng Xiaoping* (1996), *Agricultural Instability in China, 1931–1991: Weather, Technology and Institutions* (1995), *Economic Trends in Chinese Agriculture* (1993) (all by Oxford Clarendon Press) and *The Political Economy of Sino-American Relations: A Greater China Perspective* (Hong Kong University Press, 1997), and numerous articles on various aspects and policy issues of the Chinese economy.

LAWRENCE J. LAU received his BS degree in physics and economics, with great distinction, from Stanford university in 1964, and his Ph.D. degree in economics from the University of California at Berkeley in 1969. He joined the faculty of the Department Economics, Stanford University, in 1966 and was promoted to Professor of Economics in 1976. In 1992, he was named the first Kwok-ting Li Professor of Economic Development at Stanford University. His specialized fields include economic theory, economic development, economic growth, applied microeconomics, econometrics, agricultural economics, industrial economics and the economies of East Asia, including China. Dr Lau has been elected a member of Phi Beta Kappa, a member of Phi Beta Kappa, a fellow of the Econometric Society, a member of the Academic Sinica, a member of the Conference for Research in income and Wealth, and an Overseas Fellow of Churchill College, Cambridge, England.

PETER NAN-SHONG LEE presently teaches at the Department of Government and Public Administration at The Chinese University of Hong Kong and concurrently serves as Programme Director of the China's Reform and Development Programme of Hong Kong Institute of Asia-Pacific Studies. In addition to his research interest in China's industrial policy, he has been lately working on public policy studies in reform China. His recent publications include "Reforming the Social Security System in China" (1996) and "Housing Privatisation with Chinese Characteristics" (1995).

MELANIE MANION is Associate Professor of Political Science at the University of Rochester. Recent publications include "The Electoral Connection in the Chinese Countryside," *American Political Science Review* (1996) and "Corruption by Design: Bribery in Chinese Enterprise Licensing," *Journal of Law, Economics, and Organization* (1996). She is currently working on a book on corruption and corruption control in post-Mao China.

HELMUT MARTIN is, since 1979, Professor of Chinese Language and Literature with the Ruhr University Bochum, Germany. He has published several books on Maoist ideology and Chinese literary problems. During the 1980s, his interest was focused on introducing contemporary Chinese literature to the Western public; his articles were published in six volumes as *ChinaBilder* (China Perspectives) in 1996. He also edited, with Qi Mo, *Dalu dangdai wenhua mingren zhuan, gongmin shehui de kaichuang zhe* (Biographies of Famous Cultural Personalities from China Mainland — Creators of a Civil Society) (Taipei: Chungcheng shuchü, 1995). Since the early 1990s, Dr Martin has been working on Taiwan's cultural regionalism and literary history.

BARRY NAUGHTON is Associate Professor at the Graduate School of International Relations and Pacific Studies of the University of California at San Diego. He is the author of numerous articles on the Chinese economy and the book *Growing Out of the Plan: Chinese Economic Reform, 1978–1993* (1995). Research interests include the economics of transition, as well as Chinese industry and macro-economics in China. His most recent work has been on China's system of foreign investment, which has resulted in the article "China's Emergence and Future as a Trading Nations," in *Brookings Papers on Economic Activity* (1996) and the forthcoming edited volume *The China Circle: Economics and Technology in the PRC, Taiwan, and Hong Kong*.

ISABELLE THIREAU is currently Lecturer in the Department of Sociology of The Chinese University. She has recently published with Hua Linshan a book relating the changes in a Guangdong lineage from 1911 to 1949, *Enquête sociologique sur la Chine, 1911–1949* (Paris: PUF, 1996). She is now focusing on the study of informal disputes and mediation processes in the Chinese countryside, as well as legal disputes.

TSANG SHU-KI is a Professor of Economics at the Hong Kong Baptist University. He holds a Ph.D. degree from the University of Manchester. Before joining the academe in 1985, he had worked in the financial field and was a bank economist during the Hong Kong dollar crisis in 1982–1983. He has published four books on Hong Kong and China and a number of journal papers and book chapters on comparative economics, econometrics, monetary economics and the Chinese economy.

ANDREW G. WALDER is Professor and Head, Division of Social Science, Hong Kong University of Science and Technology. He is the author of *Communist Neo-traditionalism: Work and Authority in Chinese Industry* (California, 1986) and editor of *The Waning of the Communist State: Economic Origins of Political Decline in China and Hungary* (California, 1995), *China's Transitional Economy* (Oxford, 1996), and *Zouping in Transition: The Process of Reform in Rural North China* (Harvard, 1998).

GUOGUANG WU, an Assistant Professor in the Department of Government and Public Administration at The Chinese University of Hong Kong, received his Ph.D. in political science from Princeton University in 1995. Apart from contribution to journals like *The China Quarterly*, he has also published five books in Chinese. His current research interests cover China's political change in the reform years and Sino-US relations in the post-Cold War era.

Abbreviations

APEC	Asia Pacific Economic Cooperation
ASEAN	Association of Southeast Asian Nations
BOC	Bank of China
CASS	Chinese Academy of Social Sciences
CCP	Chinese Communist Party
CDIC	Central Discipline Inspection Commission
CFETS	China Foreign Exchange Trade System
CMC	Central Military Commission
CPI	consumer price index
CRS	contract responsibility system
DPP	Democratic Progessive Party (Taiwan)
EU	European Union
FDI	foreign direct investment
FFE	foreign funded enterprise
FIE	foreign invested enterprise
FYP	Five-year Plan
GATT	General Agreement on Tariffs and Trade
GDP	gross domestic product
HDTV	high definition television
HKSAR	Hong Kong Special Administrative Region
ICAC	Independent Commission Against Corruption (Hong Kong)
IMF	International Monetary Fund
KEDO	Korean Energy Development Organization
KMT	Kuomintang
LMSOE	large and medium state enterprise
MFN	most-favoured-nation
MISOA	managing institutions of state-owned assets
NCNA	New China (Xinhua) News Agency
NPC	National People's Congress
OECF	Overseas Economic Cooperation Fund (Japan)
PBOC	People's Bank of China

PLA	People's Liberation Army
PRC	People's Republic of China
RMB	*Renminbi* (Chinese currency)
RMRB	*Renmin ribao* (People's Daily)
ROC	Republic of China
RPI	rate of inflation
SAAB	State Asset Administrative Bureau
SAEC	State Administration of Exchange Control
SAIC	State Asset Investment Company
SASC	State Asset Supervisory Council
SEZ	special economic zone
SOE	state-owned enterprise
SSTC	State Science and Technology Commission
TFP	total factor productivity
TVE	township and village enterprise
UK	United Kingdom
UNDP	United Nations Development Programme
US	United States
USSR	Union of Soviet Socialist Republics
VAT	value-added tax
WTO	World Trade Organization
ZGTJNJ	*Zhongguo tongji nianjian* (Statistical Yearbook of China)

Major Statistics of the PRC, 1996

	Unit	1996	Growth rate (%)
(1) Year-end total population	million persons	1223.89	1.047
(2) Gross domestic product (GDP)	billion RMB	6779.5	9.7*
GDP — primary sector	billion RMB	1335.0	5.1*
GDP — secondary sector	billion RMB	3314.8	12.3*
GDP — tertiary sector	billion RMB	2109.7	8.0*
(3) Grain production	million tonnes	490.0	5.0
(4) Cotton production	million tonnes	4.2	−11.7
(5) Industrial value added	billion RMB	2858.0	12.7*
(6) Total State revenue	billion RMB	736.6	18**
(7) Total State expenditure	billion RMB	791.4	16**
(8) Total investment in fixed assets	billion RMB	2366.0	12.7**
State sector		1235.9	13.4**
Collective sector		349.0	6.1**
Urban and rural residents		333.0	30.1**
Others		448.1	37.0**
(9) Growth of money supply (M2)	% change		25.3
(10) Consumer price index (CPI)	% change		8.3
Urban CPI			8.8
Rural CPI			7.9
(11) Total value of exports	billion US dollars	151.1	1.5**
(12) Total value of imports	billion US dollars	138.8	5.1**
(13) Foreign Exchange reserves by year-end	billion US dollars	105.0	42.66**
(14) Foreign capital actually utilized	billion US dollars	55.27	14.2**
(15) Primary school net enrolment rate	%	98.8	
(16) Drop-out rate of primary school students	%	1.3	
(17) Hospital beds	thousand beds	3100.0	9.3
(18) Per-capita expenditure of residents in cities and towns	RMB	4377.0	3.3*
(19) Per-capita net income of peasants	RMB	1926.0	9*
(20) Retail sale value of consumer goods	billion RMB	2461.4	12.5*
(21) Unemployment rate in cities and towns	%	3.0	

Notes: * The growth rate is in real terms.
** The growth rate is in nominal terms.

Sources: "1996 nian guomin jingji he shehui fazhan de tongji gongbao" (1996 Statistical Communiqué of Economic and Social Development of the PRC), *Renmin ribao* (People's Daily), domestic edition, 5 April 1997.

"1996 nian zhongyang he difang yusuan zhixing qingkuang ji 1997 nian zhongyang he difang yusuan caoan de baogao" (Report on the Implementation of the 1996 Budget and the 1997 Draft Budget of the Central and Local Governments of the PRC), *Renmin ribao* (People's Daily), domestic edition, 17 March 1997.

(Compiled by Raymond C. W. Ng and checked by Y. Y. Kueh)

Chronology of 1996

Him Chung

January

On the **18th**, New China (Xinhua) News Agency announced that a centralized management over the release of economic information in China would be implemented. Under the new system, foreign news agencies and their affiliated information organs should apply to have any economic information released. Relevant authorities would take action if the information was considered detrimental to China's national interest. According to the spokesperson, this requirement was an international practice which helped to establish a standardized information market.

The Preparatory Committee for the Hong Kong Special Administrative Region (HKSAR) was officially established on the **26th**. The Committee was composed of 150 members, 94 from Hong Kong and 56 from China. Its main task was to prepare the establishment of the first government and the legislature of the HKSAR. Although the Chinese government claimed that the Committee included people from all sectors of Hong Kong, members of the Democratic Party which had received the largest public support in the Legislative Council election were excluded.

The State Council and the Central Military Commission (CMC) of the People's Republic of China on the **28th** announced that the formation of the HKSAR Garrison had been completed. The garrison was composed of People's Liberation Army (PLA) ground, naval and air force and was placed directly under the leadership of the CMC. It was headed by Major General Liu Zhenwu, with Xiong Ziren as the political commissar. The garrison to be stationed in Hong Kong in July 1997 would be responsible for defence affairs only. Its size would be smaller than that of the British force now in Hong Kong. A close control of these units was also emphasized in order to gain the confidence of Hong Kong people.

February

Security surrounding senior officials in Beijing was tightened when Li Peiyao, one of the vice-chairpersons of the National People's Congress (NPC) and the chairperson of the Revolutionary Committee of the Chinese Kuomintang (KMT), was murdered by a robber in his residence on the **2nd**. Two days later, a young policeman, who had been one of Li's bodyguards, was arrested. Later, on the **27th**, the commander of the paramilitary People's Armed Police Force, Ba Zhongtan, announced retirement. Observers generally believed his removal was related to the killing of Li. The murderer was executed in December.

At least 233 people were killed and 3,702 seriously injured in a strong earthquake in Yunnan province on the **3rd**. According to the National Seismological

Bureau, a strong quake measuring 7 on the Richter scale was recorded in the evening of the day, followed by a strong aftershock of 6 on the Richter scale. Another 200 more small aftershocks were also recorded. Two northwest counties, Lijiang and Zhongdian, were severely damaged. In Lijiang, 330,000 people had been affected and over one million houses had collapsed. This had been the third earthquake measuring above 6 on the Richter scale in that area since 1930.

A series of personnel arrangements were made in various provinces this month. On the **6th**, Wang Yunshen was selected as the governor of Jilin province. On the **9th**, Sung Baorui and Zuo Huanshen were selected as the governor and vice-governor of Sichuan province and Shanghai city, respectively. In Shanxi province on the **10th**, Wang Shoushen was elected as the new governor. Finally, in Jiangxi, Xu Xinyou was elected as the new governor on the **11th**.

The State Statistical Bureau on the **14th** announced the result of 1996's nationwide one percent population census. This was the second survey of its kind, with more than ten state departments involved. According to the census, China's population totalled 1.20778 billion on the 1st October 1995. Male constituted 51.03%. The annual growth rate had slowed down to 0.34%. The number of illiterate and semi-illiterate had decreased from 15.88% to 12.01% from 1990 to 1996. In terms of urbanization, about 28.85% of the population lived in towns and cities, 2.62% higher than in 1990.

New China News Agency on the **21st** reported that there were about 70 million people in China living in poverty. Most of them resided in arid areas of Ningxia, Gansu and Shanxi, and other remote areas in Guangdong, Guangxi, Yunnan and Guizhou.

March

Cross-straits tension reached its apex this month. The People's Liberation Army conducted a series of military exercises, seemingly as a warning against the independence movement in Taiwan. This included two missile tests, from **8th** to **20th**, and one large scale joint ground, naval and air exercise, from **18th** to **25th**. The latter took place in Pingtan, some 30km south of Matsu (Mazu), one of Taiwan's most important outlying islands. Although the Chinese government claimed that the exercises did not constitute "an act of war," pro-China Hong Kong newspapers reported that the exercises were to prepare for a blockade or assault on Taiwan or its small islands. The United States (US) intervened by sending two aircraft carriers, the Nimitz and the Independence, and their battle groups to the straits. It was the largest American armada assembled since the Vietnam war.

On the **19th**, the State Science and Technology Commission (SSTC) announced that a hundred counties had been selected for their outstanding development of science and technology. This was the first ever such move made by the country's science and technology authority. Its objective was to strengthen the awareness among government leaders at different levels and encourage labourers to improve their skill by learning more. Among the 100 counties commended, 32 of them were in Jiangsu province, 30 in Shandong, 10 in Zhejiang, 6 in Liaoning and 5 in Guangdong. This result demonstrated an unequal spatial distribution of high technology industries.

Taiwan's first fully democratic polls to elect its president was conducted on the **23rd**. The incumbent, Lee Teng-hui, was successfully reelected and became the ninth, and the first democratically elected, president under the Kuomintang. Lee and his partner, Lien Chan, candidate for the vice-presidency, gained 53.42% of the votes. Their closest challenger, P'eng Ming-min of the Democratic Progressive Party, obtained only 20.9% of the votes.

The Information Office of the State Council on the **28th** published a 7,000-word report in response to the "1995 Human Rights Report" published by the United States on the 5th. The commentary, entitled "Safeguarding Human Rights or Interfering in Internal Affairs," criticized the US for imposing power politics, practicing hegemonism and interfering in China's internal affairs. A series of facts were also listed to show China's progress in human rights over recent years.

April

A new regulation on foreign exchange was implemented on the **1st**. The "Regulations of the People's Republic of China on Foreign Exchange Control," which consisted of seven chapters and 54 articles, replaced the "Interim Regulations of the People's Republic of China on Foreign Exchange Control" that had been promulgated by the State Council in 1980. The new regulations specified strict measures to control financial institutions with foreign exchange operations. To coordinate with the new regulations, the State Administration of Exchange Control (SAEC) also reviewed rules and documents which had been issued by the People's Bank of China and itself since the 1980s. As a result, 72 sets of rules were abolished and 39 others amended.

A couple of personnel changes were made in Guangdong. On the **5th**, Tong Bingquan was appointed as the vice-governor of the province. Shen Bainian was appointed as the new vice-mayor of Guangzhou city on the **29th**. Later, on the 27th of August, Li Ziliu, the current mayor of Guangzhou city, was to resign, and Lin Shushen to be appointed as acting mayor.

The State Administration of Exchange Control announced on the **16th** that China's foreign debt had reached US$106.59 billion by the end of 1995, an increase of US$13.78 billion over a year earlier. Eighty-eight percent of the amount was in medium and long-term debts. The foreign debt ratio was 69.9%, which was below the international warning level.

The Ninth Five-year Plan (1996–2000) and long-term development plan for education were officially announced by the State Education Commission on the **21st**. Two of its major goals were to make nine-year compulsory education more available and eliminate illiteracy among the young and middle-aged people. Accordingly, by the end of the Ninth Five-year Plan, compulsory education would cover 85% of China's population. Illiteracy rate among people aged 15 or above would drop to 5% or less. Moreover, a "pay-to-learn" system would be launched. University, college and vocational school students would have to pay their own tuition fees. Grants, loans and free admission, however, would be granted to hardworking students and those under financial difficulties.

May

On the **1st**, the People's Bank of China reduced interest rates on deposits and loans. This was the first downwards adjustment of interest rates since 1993. The action implied that state macroeconomic control had succeeded in checking inflation and bringing soaring prices down. State-owned enterprises, the major borrower, would benefit from this adjustment.

A new regulation on governing the employment of foreigners in China took effect on the **1st**. The new regulation was more concrete and transparent than the previous one. Hong Kong, Macau and Taiwan people who sought jobs in China, however, would be subject to another regulation.

China on the **7th** announced a RMB10 billion educational programme for poverty-stricken areas in the next five years. This was the country's largest educational project since 1949. According to the State Education Commission, the programme covered poverty areas in 21 provinces and autonomous regions to improve primary and secondary education. Funds would be injected into these areas under earmarked education projects. The central authorities would provide RMB3.9 billion by the year 2000, with local governments making up the remainder.

On the **27th**, Bao Tong, Zhao Ziyang's former secretary and the most senior Chinese official to be imprisoned after the 1989 pro-democracy movement, was released. Bao, now 73, had been arrested in May 1989 and sentenced to a seven-year imprisonment after being found guilty of disclosing state secrets and spreading counter-revolutionary propaganda. In spite of his release, Bao was sent immediately to Xishan, west of Beijing, and placed under house arrest. China watchers said that the Chinese government was concerned that Bao would disclose some "secret" to the foreign press that might embarrass the authorities.

A book entitled *China Can Say No,* which was published **in this month**, led to heated discussions in both China and abroad. The authors made bold comments on Sino-American relations, Sino-Japanese relations and the Taiwan issue. Some observers regarded the publication and its aftermath as indicators of rising nationalism.

June

China on the **4th** released her first white paper on the environment. The paper, entitled "Environmental Protection in China," consisted of seven sections. According to Xie Zhenhua, director of the Environmental Protection Bureau, the paper aimed to help the international community understand environmental protection in China and strengthen active international cooperation on the issue.

Formal talks on the protection of intellectual property rights (IPR) started on the **13th** in Beijing. Before the talks, both the US and China had issued their lists of trade sanction and counter-retaliation in May. A trade war was averted when an agreement was finally reached on the **17th**. China promised to tighten up IPR legislation and law enforcement, and closed down 15 factories that illegally manufactured laser video disks.

China took another big step to promote the free convertibility of the *Renminbi* (RMB) when the People's Bank of China promulgated the "Regulations Controlling the Settlement of Exchange and the Sale and Payment of Foreign Exchange" on the **20th**. Starting on the 1st July, enterprises with foreign investors could convert and sell foreign exchange at foreign exchange designated banks. They could also open foreign exchange accounts in foreign exchange designated banks as needed. At the same time, old regulations on the control of exchange conversions, exchange sales and payments would be revised, and new regulations would be issued. The objective was to make the RMB convertible in current accounts by the end of 1996.

The People's Bank of China on the **25th** promulgated ten measures for all financial services to promote reform and development in state-owned enterprises. The ten measures included: (1) amassing funds to support key enterprises; (2) easing commodity circulation channels to support enterprises in expanding exports; (3) applying the credit lever to improve enterprises technological level;

(4) optimizing enterprises' capital structure so as to lower their debt level; (5) establishing a system under which a bank unit is responsible for certain enterprises; (6) enhancing accounts settlement and funds clearance; (7) using the interest lever to improve management and operation; (8) helping enterprises widen the channel of funds accommodation; (9) opening new services to meet the various needs of modern enterprises; and, (10) strengthening the control over credit funds.

July

On the **12th**, China published its first specific newspaper on state assets. The newspaper, entitled "China Assets News," was to be a leading publication of the State Assets Department. According to Zhang Youcai, director of the National State-Property Administration, the newspaper would play an important role in spreading information on the importance of state assets management and arousing people's awareness in managing state assets.

A work conference on the reform of judicial procedures was held on the **15th** in Beijing. The conference decided to reform people's courts at all levels across the nation. The objective was to raise the judicial standard of the people's court and thus better serve China's development and stability. According to Ren Jianxin, president of the Supreme People's Court, the guiding ideology of the reform was to ensure fair and public trials.

Torrential rainfall this month caused flood disasters in Hunan, Jiangsu, Zhejiang, Anhui, Jiangxi, Guangxi, Guizhou and other provinces. On the **17th**, a rainstorm in Guangxi trapped 20,000 people. Five thousand houses were destroyed, 60 bridges broken, 38 roads blocked, 6 power stations and 130 schools flooded, and 21,000 hectares of paddy field severely affected. Similar conditions were reported in other provinces. In Hunan, 10,000 people were believed to have died in the disaster.

On the **29th**, after a nuclear test conducted on the same day, the Chinese government announced that the country would stop nuclear testing effective from the **30th**. It claimed that the decision was a response to the appeal of non-nuclear states and a positive step to promote nuclear power usage. A previous test had been conducted on the 6th of June.

August

The Ministry of Foreign Trade and Economic Cooperation on the **21st** published *Management Methods on Goods Transportation Factorage between the Two Sides of the Taiwan Strait.* Two pilot ports, Xiamen and Fuzhou, would be open for direct shipping. Taiwan responded by saying that direct shipping was a political issue which affected the island's security. Direct shipping would not be implemented until security problems were solved.

Dai Houying, a well-known Chinese woman writer, and her niece were murdered on the **25th** at their home in Shanghai. The murderer was a friend of Dai. He was later arrested in Anhui province and sentenced to death by the Shanghai Municipal Intermediate People's Court on the 18th of October.

September

The Beijing-Kowloon Railway, the largest railway construction project in China's history, was opened to traffic on the **1st**. The RMB 40 billion project was 2,381 km long and covered 11,000 ha of land. Travelling time was reduced from 72 to 48 hours and would be further reduced to 38 hours next year.

Taiwan's attempt to "re-enter" the United Nations (UN) faced another failure when the issue was excluded from the agenda of the UN General Assembly General Affairs Committee on the **18th**. Although the "re-entry" proposal was supported by some 16 countries this year, this was the fourth consecutive year that the UN had rejected Taiwan's request.

The Defend Diaoyu Islands campaign in Hong Kong met disaster when an activist, David Chan Yuk-cheung, drowned during a demonstration near the Diaoyu Islands on the **27th**. This wave of protests had been prompted by the installation of a lighthouse by right-wing Japanese Youth Federation in July. Mass demonstrations were also held in Taipei and overseas Chinese communities. The reaction of the Chinese government was confined to verbal attack. Demonstrations in the country were blocked.

The State Council Information Office on the **27th** reported on the development of Chinese children during the mid-1990s. Xu Zhijian, deputy secretary general of the State Council and vice-chairperson of the State Council Committee for Women's and Children's Work, said that both the mortality rates of infants and pregnant women decreased over the period. Regarding children's education, enrolment rates for primary school children and girls were 98.5% and 82.8%, respectively. Enrolment rate in junior middle school was 78.4%.

October

The Beijing No. 1 Intermediate People's Court on the **14th** sentenced Zhou Beifang, former assistant general manager of Shougang Corporation and former president of Shougang Concord (HK) Ltd., to death with a two year reprieve. Zhou's case was one of the 1,277 cases of corruption and bribery uncovered under the "strike hard" drive. Until August, a total of 40 cadres above the county level had been prosecuted for bribery. Seven of them had been bureau-level cadres, including Li Min, former deputy chief of the State Security Bureau, and Chen Jian, secretary of the former Beijing municipal party secretary, Chen Xitong.

Liu Xiaobo, the dissident who co-authored the "10th October Declaration," was sentenced to three years of re-education. Wang Xizhe, another author of the declaration, fled to the United States via Hong Kong, on the **16th**.

The State Council on the **24th** issued a white paper on China's grain production and food issues. The 12,000-word paper, entitled "White Paper: The Grain Issue in China," pointed out that total grain output in China had recorded an annual average increase of 3.1%. It was the largest grain producer in the world and was able to feed 22% of the world's population on about 7% of the world's cultivated land. The white paper claimed China's per capita share of grain had reached the global average. Its population would not cause any threat to world food demand.

On the **24th**, the European Parliament awarded the 1996 Sakharov Prize for Human Rights to Wei Jingsheng, China's famous dissident who was still in prison. Foreign Ministry spokesperson, Shen Guofang, criticized the decision for its encouraging activists to oppose the Chinese government.

Beijing student movement leader, Wang Dan, was formally charged by the Chinese government for the crime of counter-revolutionary demagogy after having been detained by the government for 17 months. This was the second time that Wang had been charged with the same offence. On the **30th**, the Beijing No. 1 Intermediate People's Court sentenced Wang to another 11 years imprisonment and to be deprived of political rights for two years. Wang appealed in vain against sentence on the 2nd of November; the hearing took only ten minutes.

November

On the **6th**, Chen Ziming, China's famous dissident, was released on medical parole. Chen, 44, suffering from cancer, was serving a 13-year sentence for attempting to overthrow the government. He, however, was put under house arrest after his release.

Hong Kong newspapers on the **14th** reported that the Chinese media were facing a new round of rectification. About one-third of China's 3,600 or more provincial and municipal newspapers/periodicals, as well as internal newspapers/ periodicals that had not registered with the State Press and Publications

Administration would be closed down. The decision was taken by the 6th plenary session of the 14th CCP Central Committee in order to enhance macroscopic regulation and control.

The Chinese and the Philippines governments reached an important consensus on the South China Sea issue on the **26th**. The two countries decided to shelve their disputes on the issue and draw up plans to jointly exploit the resources. A consultation mechanism was established to study development plans. The question of sovereignty was put aside. Both countries claimed that they owned the Spratly Islands in the area.

Taiwan's diplomatic work registered a major failure when South Africa, the largest of the few countries that have diplomatic relations with the island, announced on the **27th** to switch diplomatic recognition from Taiwan to China. According to Nelson Mandela, president of South Africa, diplomatic relations with Taiwan would be severed by the end of December 1997.

The Town and Village Enterprise Law was adopted at the 22nd meeting of the 8th NPC Standing Committee on the **29th**. The law clearly defined basic guidelines, important principles and main tasks for the development of town and village enterprises. Their property rights and management structure were also clarified. This new law would take effect on the 1st of January 1997.

New China News Agency on the **29th** announced that China's foreign exchange reserves had reached US$100.45 billion. The figure was second to Japan only, which had the largest foreign exchange reserves in the world.

December

On the **9th**, New China News Agency reported that China would build a new medical insurance system to cover all urban employees by the year 2000. The system separated the overall fund into a social insurance fund and personal accounts. Medical expenses for minor illnesses would be paid from the personal accounts while serious ailments would be taken care of by the social insurance fund. The system was implemented in some pilot cities in Jiangxi and proved to be successful.

The first Chief Executive of the HKSAR was selected on the **11th** by a 400-member Selection Committee which had been formed by the Beijing-appointed Preparatory Committee of the HKSAR. Tung Chee-hwa, a shipping magnate, received 320 votes and became Hong Kong's first Chief Executive–designate. His appointment was officially confirmed on the **18th** by Premier Li Peng, in Beijing.

New China News Agency on the **13th** released statistics on savings deposits. By the end of November, savings deposits of China's urban and rural residents had reached RMB 3,791.7 billion, a 31.5% increase over the level at the beginning of the year. On the **17th**, China also released figures on tax revenues. Up to November, China had collected RMB 564 billion in industrial and commercial taxes, and RMB 29.7 billion in agricultural tax revenues. Total tax revenues for the year was expected to reach RMB 695 billion, a 13.6% increase over the last year.

Despite the strong protests from the British government and the democratic parties in Hong Kong, the Provisional Legislature of the HKSAR was elected by the Selection Committee on the **21st** in Shenzhen. It would replace the existing popularly elected Legislative Council on the 1st of July 1997 and would be the legislature until the first formal legislature would be elected in 1998. The Provisional Legislature was composed of 60 members and would be responsible for the passing of the 1997/1998 budget, endorsing the appointment of the Chief Justice of the High Court and the passing of laws in the HKSAR.

1

Chinese Politics on the Eve of the 15th Party Congress

Joseph Fewsmith

When the 14th Party Congress met five years ago, it marked, ironically, both the highpoint of Deng Xiaoping's career and the opening of a new, and distinctly less "Dengist" era in Chinese politics. The 14th Party Congress was the culmination of a nearly year-long Dengist assault on the conservative policies and politics that had dominated most of the post-Tiananmen period. Following Deng's dramatic "southern tour" to Shenzhen at the beginning of the year, a trip memorable for the bluntness of Deng's criticism of the left (which he told to "go to sleep"), the 14th Party Congress endorsed an unambiguous declaration on building a "socialist market economy" — a theoretical breakthrough that had been unattainable even during the hightide of reform in the late 1980s. At the same time, Deng and his thought were enshrined as never before. The resolution adopted by the Congress lauded Deng for his "tremendous political courage in opening up a new paths in socialist construction and a tremendous theoretical courage in opening up a new realm in Marxism."[1] Chinese politics had come a long way from the autumn of 1989 when Jiang Zemin, then the newly anointed general secretary of the Chinese Communist Party (CCP), had declared virtual fealty to Chen Yun, asserting that the "greatest lesson" to be derived from the People's Republic of China (PRC) economic history was that the country not "depart from its national conditions, exceed its national strength, be anxious for success, or a have great ups and downs" — all well-known theses of the conservative party elder.[2] In only three years, Deng appeared to have finally vanquished Chen and his conservative brand of economic and political thinking.

Precisely at this apogee of Deng's thought and influence, however, the basis was being laid for a new era in Chinese politics, one that would have a considerably more conservative tone, at least for the remaining years of Deng's life. Although Jiang Zemin was Deng's third and final choice to succeed him, Deng aided Jiang's effort to secure power more than he had ever helped Hu Yaobang or Zhao Ziyang. Whatever doubts Deng may have had about Jiang's leadership (Deng had criticized him only the previous spring for his caution), the ageing patriarch dramatically supported Jiang in his conflict with Yang Shangkun and Yang Baibing. Although other factors were involved in the shakeup of the military command, it is apparent that the removal of Yang Baibing as vice-chairman of the Central Military Commission (CMC) put Jiang in a position to cultivate support in the military — something that he has done assiduously ever since. In addition to the purge of Yang Baibing and the consequently diminished influence of his reform-oriented older half brother Yang Shangkun, there were other signs that the Dengist assault on leftists in the party was being curtailed. Although conservatives, such as Yao Yilin and Song Ping, were removed from the Politburo, conservative ideologue Wang Renzhi, despite being removed as head of the Propaganda Department, was nevertheless appointed party secretary of the Chinese Academy of Social Sciences, and conservative leader Deng Liqun was allowed to organize many leftist leaders into a PRC Historical Society.

The apparent intent of such manoeuvres was to bolster Jiang's influence by preventing reform leaders associated with Hu Yaobang or Zhao Ziyang from taking advantage of Deng's attack on leftism to regain their influence. Thus, the power of leftist leaders was reduced, not ended, and Jiang would rely on their continuing influence to fend off any new wave of "bourgeois liberalization." This pattern has continued and come into focus ever more sharply in the years since then.

At least until the time of Deng's death in February 1997 (discussed below), Chinese politics took an increasingly conservative tone as Deng's health faded, as the successor generation manoeuvred for power, and as the problems of governance in the wake of reform have come more clearly into focus. Jiang, whom Western commentators used to compare frequently to the hapless Hua Guofeng, has increased continuously his hold on power and taken to define himself as the upholder of the party and the defender of ideological purity.

An important turning point in Jiang's drive for power came at the 4th plenum of 1994. After economic issues were dropped from the agenda, the plenum concentrated on party-building issues. Commentary at the time repeatedly called for the subordination of lower levels to higher levels, the part to the whole, and everything to the party centre, of which, of course, Jiang was the "core." *People's Daily* signalled Jiang's victory at the session by declaring that "the second generation central leading collective has been successfully relieved by its third generation leading collective."[3] The following year, Jiang implicitly compared himself with Mao Zedong by giving a major speech on twelve critical relationships that called for development and marketization on the one hand and for stability and enhancing state capabilities, on the other. He also introduced a heightened sense of danger by warning of the efforts of "hostile forces" to "Westernize" and "divide" China.

When the 15th Congress of the CCP meets later this year the generational transition signalled at the 4th plenum and given yet greater weight by Deng's death will be completed. One might say that this change is, not simply a generational transition, but indeed the generational transition, for the transition from Mao to Deng did not really represent a generational transition; both were members of the generation that had won the revolution. Now, there will be a real generational transition as the first post-revolutionary generation will come to power. The implications of this for Chinese politics are profound.

Manoeuvring for Power

Jiang has proven himself a more capable, if not necessarily a more visionary, politician than most observers, whether Chinese or foreign, were willing to grant. In his quest for power, Jiang has no doubt built alliances and relied on the support of others, but increasingly in recent years he has shown considerable political skill in picking his battles and defeating his adversaries. In 1994, Jiang was able to secure the promotion of two protégés from Shanghai, Huang Ju and Wu Bangguo (who were promoted to the Politburo and Secretariat, respectively) and of Jiang Chunyun from Shandong (who joined the Secretariat and then became vice-premier in charge of agriculture). Moreover, as Deng's health faded in late 1994 and early 1995, Jiang managed to oust Chen Xitong, a close Deng ally, thereby both extending his influence into the nation's capital and sending a strong message to provincial leaders throughout China.[4] The recent reshuffle of the Beijing municipal party committee suggests that Jiang is increasing his influence in the city.[5]

Jiang has also been surprisingly successful in exerting influence, if not control, in the military, an area in which he had no experience before being promoted to general secretary. Not only was the removal of Yang Baibing followed by the removal or reassignment of some 300 senior military officials, in June 1993, Jiang promoted 19 People's Liberation Army (PLA) officers to the rank of general. More recently, as the 15th Party Congress approaches, Jiang has apparently strengthened his hand *vis-à-vis* the military by enforcing the retirement age. This stand forced five high-ranking military leaders, including the heads of the navy and air force, to step down. Thus, through a combination of rotation, retirement, and promotion, it appears that Jiang has secured the support of most of the military brass. This does not mean that the military will not be able to influence policy. On the contrary, Jiang's continuing need to cultivate this national security community may very well give the military considerable influence in such matters as foreign policy, but it seems unlikely that the military will seek to replace Jiang.[6]

Despite this and other evidence that Jiang has been successfully negotiating the treacherous tides of Chinese politics, his power is hardly unchallenged. Indeed, even as Jiang looks increasingly certain to be confirmed in his power at the 15th Party Congress, he continues to face an ideological vacuum and the consequent polarization of thinking within China. This ideological vacuum has much to do with Jiang's efforts to shape and defend a new ideological orthodoxy.

Pressures from the Left

China's conservatives have long seen the Dengist reforms as undermining the authority of the party and threatening its leadership. Following Tiananmen, conservatives declared that "bourgeois liberalization" emerged with the beginning of reform, increasing over time as efforts to curtail it were repeatedly cut short.[7] In 1991, after the famous "Huangfu Ping" commentaries supporting a reinvigoration of reform appeared in the Shanghai press, Premier Li Peng turned to Zhu Rongji, who had helped supervise the preparation of the articles, and said, "[t]he influence of the 'Huangfu Ping' articles is terrible. It caused the unified thinking that the centre had expended a great deal of effort to bring about to become chaotic again."[8]

This ideological "chaos" — in the opinion of conservatives — was exacerbated by Deng Xiaoping's 1992 trip to Shenzhen and the subsequent adoption at the 14th Party Congress of the decision to create a "socialist market economy." These actions inaugurated a major upsurge in China's economy, one that has attracted intense international attention, but they also increased the role of the township and village enterprises, of joint ventures, and of the private economy. In short, as the economy as a whole boomed, the role of the state-owned enterprises decreased relatively.

These and other conservative ("leftist") criticisms of reform were vented in a sharply worded document entitled "Several Factors Influencing China's National Security" ("*Yingxiang woguo guojia anquan de ruogan yinsu*") that was circulated internally in late 1995. Although no name is attached to the document, it was reportedly written by a researcher at the Chinese Academy of Social Sciences and endorsed by conservative ideologue Deng Liqun. The article warned that the proportion of state-owned enterprises in China's aggregate industrial output value had fallen from 76% in 1980 to 48.3% in June 1994, that there are now 328,000 registered private enterprises with over five million employees and RMB 100 billion of capital, and that a "new bourgeoisie" had already taken shape as a class in itself. As if this were not enough, the document warned that the nature of the party was changing as more and more technically trained specialists were promoted to leadership positions, that the sovereignty of the country was being undermined by increasing economic dependence on the West, and that "bourgeois liberal" thinking was once again on the rise and been linking up with private entrepreneurs to form a threat to the party. Although the document explicitly or implicitly questioned the whole reform enterprise since the 3rd plenum of 1978, it reserved special venom for Deng Xiaoping's 1992 trip to Shenzhen. Not only did it state that bourgeois liberalization had gained the upper hand "since 1992," it also argued that bourgeois liberalization had "spread unchecked under the 'anti-left' signboard" — an apparent reference to Deng's statement during his trip to Shenzhen that the left was the "main danger."

It is worth noting in passing exactly how different the author's evaluation of China's domestic situation is compared to the recent and widespread emphasis on the rise of Chinese nationalism. According to the author, the spread of "money worship," "hedonism," "individualism," and Western values, means that if the Chinese government somehow finds itself in opposition to the United States, it will not be able to count on the support of a large percentage of its own people; indeed, those who subscribe to Western-oriented values "are very likely to betray and sell-out the interests of the fatherland, and directly harm our country's security."[9]

According to some reports, this letter was sent to the CCP leadership in September 1995, just prior to the 5th plenary session of the 14th Central Committee (which convened on 25 September). Whatever, the details of the document's circulation and its precise impact, Jiang Zemin in his report to the 5th plenum certainly responded to the political concerns raised by the document. In an apparent effort both to respond to conservative admonitions and to solidify his own position against potential challengers, Jiang repeatedly emphasized the need to "talk politics." This admonition, which built self-consciously if not self-confidently on a reference Deng Xiaoping made to "talking politics" in 1986,[10] continued Jiang's long-standing courting of China's political conservatives and sharply rebuked those who demurred from central policy. Jiang told the plenum:[11]

> I also want to underscore one issue here. Our senior cadres — especially provincial party committee secretaries, provincial governors, ministers, Central Committee members, and members of the CCP Central Committee Politburo — must pay attention to politics. By politics, I mean political direction, political stand, political viewpoints, political discipline, political perception, and political sensitivity.... Can we afford not to pay attention to politics, or can we afford to lower our guard and stop fighting when hostile forces in the West want to "Westernize" and "divide" us, and impose their "democracy" and "freedom" on us; and when Lee Teng-hui is bent on promoting "Taiwan independence"?

This frank statement suggests the difficulty Jiang Zemin has had in securing the compliance of many of his colleagues as well as Jiang's need to play the nationalistic card in his warnings of foreign (primarily American) efforts to "Westernize" and "divide" China.

There is, of course, a danger in Jiang's stress on "talking politics," namely that the "left" is far better than any other political element in talking politics. For instance, shortly after Jiang raised the slogan of "talking politics," the *People's Daily* ran a pseudonymous article that implied that reform had gone off course and that the most important task at the present was to defend the central authorities.[12] Lost in the emphasis on "politics" and centralization is a sense of how reform is supposed to proceed.

Pressures from the Right

At the same time that Jiang has been pressured from the left, he has also faced considerable pressures, both economic and ideological, from the "right." Particularly noteworthy is the publication of *Farewell to Revolution* by prominent philosopher Li Zehou and leading literary critic Liu Zaifu. *Farewell to Revolution* argues that the most debilitating characteristic of Chinese politics has been the marked tendency for political struggles which degenerate into all-or-nothing battles in which "you die, I live" (*nisi wohuo*). Li and Liu argue that this characteristic of Chinese politics is a feature of its "revolutionary" politics (although it can be argued that its roots lie deeper in Chinese history and polity). Accordingly, they trace the development of this type of destructive political struggle to the emergence of political radicalism and revolutionary activity that developed in the late 19th century (particularly with Tan Sitong) and came to the fore with the Revolution of 1911. This intellectual exploration leads them to the conclusion that the 1911 Revolution was "not necessarily necessary."[13]

The conclusion that China might have been better off following a non-revolutionary course of development flies in the face of contemporary Chinese historiography and the long-standing claim of the Chinese Communist Party that it and its revolution "saved" China. This implication has stirred considerable anger in Beijing, as conservatives accuse Li and Liu of negating the value and meaning of China's revolutionary history and all the sacrifices that that entailed. The publication of their work (in Hong Kong, not the PRC) has been taken as evidence that the forces of "bourgeois liberalization" are on the rise again. Articles critical of *Farewell to Revolution* have appeared in journals, including the party journal *Qiu shi*, and Wang Renzhi, party secretary of Chinese Academy of Social Sciences (CASS), denounced the book in an internal meeting in October 1996.[14]

Qiao Shi's Role

The pressure from the right comes not only from diffuse (but important) economic pressures and the thinking of liberal intellectuals; it comes as well from those seeking to accommodate the pressures China faces by emphasizing the role of law and the limited opening up of public discourse. Such people are being championed by Qiao Shi, the former security official who currently heads the National People's Congress (NPC). Over the last several years, as Jiang Zemin emphasized the role of the party "core," Qiao has continuously emphasized the rule of law. On assuming his position as head of the NPC in 1993, Qiao immediately declared that "democracy must be institutionalized and codified into laws so that this system and its laws will not change with a change in leadership, nor with changes in [individual leader's] viewpoints and attention." Such views echoed the perspectives, often forgotten, that Deng Xiaoping put forth in his remarkable speech, "On Reform of the Party and State Leadership System" in August 1980. Similarly, Qiao's close associate at the NPC, Vice-Chairman Tian Jiyun, has repeatedly emphasized the role of the NPC and its right to supervise the government.[15]

In 1996, as Jiang has continued to move to the left ideologically, Qiao has remained one of the few voices in the top level of the party publicly urging a more moderate course.[16] At the Beidaihe conference in August, Qiao reportedly criticized the resurgence of leftist thinking.[17] In September, Qiao went public with his concerns. Echoing Deng Xiaoping's famous remark during his 1992 trip to Shenzhen, Qiao told the German newspaper *Handelsblatt* that, while it was important to guard again the right, the main danger was on the left.[18] This warning had completely disappeared from the Chinese press over the preceding years.

In December, Qiao had a lengthy interview with *Philadelphia Inquirer* correspondent Trudy Rubin. In his remarks, Qiao laid out in some detail the functioning and importance of the NPC. Emphasizing the rule of law, Qiao quoted the stipulation from the party charter that says that "the party should conduct activities within the limits permitted by the constitution and the law" as well as the parallel statement in the state constitution that says that "no organization or individual may enjoy the privilege of being above the constitution or the law." Qiao also emphasized Deng Xiaoping's bedrock principle that "practice is the sole criterion for testing truth," a principle that is not cited frequently these days.[19]

Qiao also appeared to take on Jiang Zemin over the pace of economic growth and reform. Touring Jiangsu province in January 1997, Qiao told cadres that they "must have a sense of urgency" regarding the reform of state-owned enterprises and that "local governments should take bolder and speedier steps in reform."[20] Similarly, during his December tour of Guangdong province, NPC Vice-Chairman Tian Jiyun emphasized the need to continue to criticize leftism and stresses the Dengist doctrine of "putting development first."[21]

Seeking a Middle Ground

The circulation of the leftist manifesto "Several Factors Influencing China's National Security" on the one hand and the publication of Li Zehou and Liu Zaifu's *Farewell to Revolution* on the other suggest that the ideological gulf separating the "left" and the "right" in Chinese politics is as great, if not greater, than ever. They also suggest that Jiang Zemin has so-far failed to establish an ideological orthodoxy that is either persuasive or authoritative.

Given this conspicuous gap between left and right, Jiang Zemin has set about the difficult task of defining and shoring up the centre. This effort was plainly visible in an article by Xing Fensi, deputy head of the Central

Party School, that was published in *People's Daily* in June 1996. The difficulty Xing had in trying to define and defend a middle ground between the left and the right speaks volumes about the dilemmas facing the current regime. What Xing's article tried to do was to distinguish between Marxism and anti-Marxism. As Xing admitted, this is something that is no longer easy to do. A lot has changed since the birth of Marx 150 years ago. Although "some" of the "fundamental principles" (*jiben yuanli*) of Marxism are still applicable, he said, "indeed a considerable portion of the principles" of Marxism have changed. Xing argued that there were parts of Marxism that contained universal truth and were still applicable, parts that needed to be supplemented, and parts that were "completely unsuitable for use, which should not be continued and upheld in the present day."

One has to note in passing the difficulty Xing has in even writing this. He says that the "fundamental principles" (*jiben yuanli*) of Marxism are still applicable but that a "considerable portion of the principles (*yuanli*)" are not. Obviously, he does not want to say that even some "fundamental" (*jiben*) principles are no longer applicable, even if that is what he means. Drawing a distinction between *jiben yuanli* and *yuanli*, however, is difficult at best.

Xing thus had to argue that "The criterion for determining the border dividing Marxism and anti-Marxism has to rest on developed Marxism"; in present day China, the "only correct" criterion for distinguishing Marxism and anti-Marxism was the "theory of socialism with Chinese characteristics established by Deng Xiaoping." Xing defined Deng's thought — redundantly — as, first, "liberating thought, seeking truth from facts," secondly, "liberating production, developing the productive forces, eliminating exploitation, eliminating polarization, and finally attaining common prosperity," and thirdly, "one centre (economic construction) and two basic points [the four cardinal principles and emancipating the mind]."

On the one hand, in clear reference to the "10,000 character letter," Xing criticized as "leftist," those who had "doubts about some new things that have emerged in the course of reform and opening up." On the other hand, with equally clear reference to Li Zehou and Liu Zaifu, Xing criticized those who sought to use "cultural conservatism to replace political radicalism" and "to eliminate the ideological mainstream, namely Marxism."

Xing's article was an obvious effort to define a middle ground against the increasingly disparate ideological tendencies that were appearing as the Dengist era was coming to an end.

The 6th Plenum of the 14th Central Committee

The 6th plenary session of the 14th Central Committee was held on 7–10 October. Jiang Zemin made a speech, which has not yet been disseminated, and the session adopted a 14,000 character resolution entitled, "Resolution of the CCP Central Committee concerning Several Important Issues on Strengthening the Building of Socialist Spiritual Civilization." According to the Communiqué, the "mainstream" of reform, development, and stability must be recognized, but it should be seen that the problems of "neglecting ideological education and building spiritual civilization" and of "being strong in one, while weak in the other" have still not been solved. It warned that "At no time should we achieve short-term economic growth at the expense of spiritual civilization."[22] It also announced that a special committee for guiding the building of spiritual civilization was being set up, reportedly with Jiang Zemin as head and Ding Guan'gen as the deputy head.[23]

The plenum received the full media treatment, including a *People's Daily* editorial extolling it as sending a "strong gust of east wind to further strengthen the building of socialist spiritual civilization," and an endorsement by the Central Discipline Inspection Commission, which held its 7th plenary session on 11 October and stressed that "Under the situation arising from the development of a socialist market economy and opening to the outside world, it is especially important to strengthen the conviction in communism, to earnestly practice communist ethics, and to uphold political steadfastness and ideological and ethical purity." New books, including *Deng Xiaoping on the Promotion of Socialist Ethical and Cultural Progress* and *Selected Documents on the Construction of Socialist Spiritual Civilization*, were published in conjunction with the plenum.[24]

The 6th plenum was only the second party conclave in the 18 years since Deng Xiaoping came to power to devote itself to ideological issues. The first was the 6th plenary session of the 12th Central Committee, which had been held exactly 10 years before. The difference between the resolutions of the two sessions suggests just how much China has changed in a decade. Ten years ago, Hu Yaobang was general secretary, and he and other reformers were trying to loosen up the ideological atmosphere to provide more room for reform. The resolution passed ten years ago was notable for several things. It dropped the phrase, incorporated in the 12th Party Congress document, that declared that the party took "communism as the core," replacing it with the weaker statement that said that the party took "Marxism-Leninism as its guidance." In accordance with this downplaying of Communist ideology, the document also stressed the "common ideal." The idea of the "common ideal" was that all Chinese, Communist party members or not, could agree on developing China, making it more open and democratic. It appealed to a patriotic (not nationalist) sentiment, rather than to Communist ideology.[25] The current resolution also speaks of the "common ideal" of building socialism with Chinese characteristics for the whole nation, but it does not develop the notion of a common ideal or make it seem like a vital concept.

The most controversial part of the document ten years ago, of course, was the sentence that declared that "bourgeois liberalization" was aimed at the overthrow of socialism. It was a sentence, coming three years after the campaign against spiritual pollution, that Hu Yaobang did not want inserted, but that Deng Xiaoping insisted on.[26] Hu's opposition no doubt helped grease the skids for his ouster just a few months later.

Although the document adopted a decade ago was quite limited, it represented an effort by a reform-minded élite to push ahead. Although under attack by conservatives, reformers at the time were still self-confident and idealistic. The current document reflects the very different atmosphere of the mid-1990s. There was no sense a decade ago that too much reform might bring down the whole system; today, there seems to be a fear that even the current amount of reform presents a danger to political stability. The loss of ideological legitimacy and political self-confidence is palpable.

One might think, given the generational transition under way, that Jiang Zemin and his colleagues might seize the opportunity to define themselves and to present a vision for the future. Instead, the document defines spiritual civilization in almost wholly negative terms. Thus, in language reminiscent of Mao Zedong's "Yen'an Forum on Literature and Art," the plenum resolution calls on writers and artists to "immerse themselves among the masses" and to "earnestly and seriously consider what social effects (*shehui xiaoguo*) their works may produce." Similarly, it calls for strengthening control over press and publishing circles and for keeping the propaganda front and public opinion "firmly" in the hands of "those comrades who are loyal to Marxism, Leninism, and Mao Zedong Thought."[27]

The plenum resolution suggests that such ideological vigilance is necessary because reform has allowed social morality and loyalty to decline. Thus, the document states that "The standard of moral conduct has been lowered in some spheres, and the practices of worshipping money, seeking pleasure, and individualism have grown," and that "a number of people have a weak concept of the state, and doubt and waver over the future of socialism." It also urges people to "carry forward the cream of our traditional culture, prevent and eliminate the spread of cultural garbage, [and] resist the conspiracy by hostile forces to 'Westernize' and 'split' our country."[28]

Campaign to Build Spiritual Civilization

Although the plenum resolution was not likely to inspire great faith, it was meant to be taken seriously. The day after the plenum concluded, on 30 October, Wang Dan, who had been under detention since the previous May, was suddenly and harshly sentenced to 11 years in prison. Other efforts showed that the latest effort to tighten ideological controls would not be limited to political dissidents. A four-volume collection of Wang Shuo's writings, then at the printers, was stopped from publication, the outspoken editor of *Beijing Youth News* was removed, and *Jiao dian* (Focus), a current affairs monthly in Guangdong, was shut down.[29]

It soon became apparent that the 6th plenum marked the beginning of a new effort to tighten control over ideology. In December, party leaders convened the "Third National Symposium on Deng Xiaoping Theory of Building Socialism with Chinese Characteristics." This symposium was part of what to an outsider can only be taken as an awkward and artificial effort to give philosophical content and structure to the thought of a leader whose leadership was best known for breaking out of precisely such philosophical constructs. Indeed, just as Deng was able to dispose of the greater part of Mao's thought by calling on people to understand it "comprehensively and accurately," Ding Guan'gen told the symposium that Jiang Zemin has "comprehensively, correctly, and enthusiastically" upheld "Deng Xiaoping theory." Not only is Deng's "theory" to be understood comprehensively and correctly, but it is now also to be forced into a Procrustean bed with Mao Zedong Thought so that there is a systematic development of a single philosophical system running from Mao through Deng. Imposing such coherence on the Chinese past surely breaks with Deng's injunction to "seek truth from facts."

The effort to tighten ideology was also apparent at the 6th National Congress of the China Federation of Literary and Art Circles and the

5th National Congress of the Chinese Writers' Association that met in December. Speaking to the inaugural session of the meeting on 16 December, Jiang Zemin declared that "Marxism-Leninism, Mao Zedong Thought and Deng Xiaoping theory of building socialism with Chinese characteristics form a direct line of succession to become a unified scientific system." More importantly from the perspective of China's art circles, Jiang went on to declare that literature and art must "serve the people and socialism" and to call on artists, just as Mao did in the Yan'an Forum 54 years ago, to "go deeper into the realities of life and mingle with the masses ...." Reflecting a cultural insecurity that seems unnecessary, Jiang called on writers and artists to "resist the infiltration of colonial culture," lest China copy Western capitalist values and "become dependent."[30]

The message of these meetings was reiterated for guidance of the party's propaganda departments at a national meeting in January, and at CASS party secretary Wang Renzhi warned that the research institute "will not allow theories and opinions that are against Marxism, the leadership of the party and the people's democratic dictatorship to spread unchecked."[31] In February, the State Council issued new regulations to tighten control over the media.[32]

Although the tone of Chinese politics has become progressively more conservative over the last three years, such a campaign against unorthodox thinking is unprecedented since Deng's southern tour in 1992 and perhaps since the campaign against bourgeois liberalization following Tiananmen. Moreover, it is not just China's intellectual circles that are bearing the brunt of the latest campaign, it is also directed against dissident activities in minority areas, particularly Tibet and Xinjiang. It is difficult to talk about a new "crackdown" in a place that has been subject to so much repression since 1987; nevertheless, the tone adopted at the plenary session of the Tibetan CCP in early November was unusually harsh. Regional party secretary Chen Kuiyuan, after conveying the spirit of the 6th plenum, called for a "strategic, powerful, and sustained offensive in the spiritual field" in Tibet. "Religious idealism," Chen declared, was a "striking hindrance" to efforts to build spiritual civilization in the region. The relative religious tolerance that had prevailed in the region during the 1980s, Chen said, had given rise to a region-wide "religious fanaticism" and "narrow nationalism" that were being used by the Dalai Lama to destabilize the area and promote "splittism."[33] A hard-hitting article that appeared in the *Tibet Daily* the same day the regional party plenum opened declared, "Some temples are directly or indirectly controlled by the Dalai clique and have become strongholds and command posts for separatist forces at home and abroad to engage in separatist activities." It would therefore be necessary to strengthen management over temples and to make "large-scale readjustments and reforms" in Tibetan Buddhism, so that it could "accommodate itself to the brand new social system of socialism."[34]

Similarly, Wang Lequan, the CCP secretary of Xinjiang, called on people to "ride on the strong east wind brought by the 6th plenary session of the 14th Central Committee" and fight against decadent ideas and culture, religious fanaticism, bourgeois values, and ethnic separatism. Xinjiang, Wang declared, was on the "front line of the struggle against the attempt of the international reactionary forces to 'Westernize' or 'divide' our country."[35] Wang's comments hardly stilled tensions in the northwestern province as riots broke out in Yining and a series of bombs exploded in Urumqi.[36]

There are several (non-exclusive) explanations that account for the conservative drift in Chinese politics over the past three years, culminating in the adoption of the recent document on spiritual civilization. The first and most obvious explanation was the overriding concern of the regime to prevent any social disorder as Deng's death approached. There was obviously a concern that people might try to take the opportunity of Deng's death, as they did Hu Yaobang's, to voice complaints or to press for more radical change. The government obviously wants to forestall any such outburst. One reason that the government is concerned about the possibility of protests is because of the pressures it is under to lay off workers from deficit incurring state-owned enterprises.

Economic Difficulties

In some ways, the Chinese economy has performed extremely well in recent years. In 1996, the economy again grew impressively, 9.7%, while inflation — which had run as high as 25% in 1994 — was brought down to 6%. The "soft landing" that Chinese policy makers had tried to engineer appeared to be successful. At the same time, foreign investment was continuing to pour into China, and foreign reserves reached US $100 billion.

At the same time, however, the economy is facing serious difficulties as losses of state-owned enterprises continue to mount. According to official figures, 43.7% of state-owned industrial enterprises lost money in 1996 — five percentage points higher than in 1995 — while the amount of their losses surged almost 30% to RMB 61.6 billion (US$ 7.4 billion). At the same time, RMB 150 billion (US$ 18.1 billion) was tied up in excessive stockpiles.[37]

Although the difficulties of the state-owned enterprises are long-standing, there is a sense that the situation is reaching a crisis point. Over the past several years, China has turned increasingly to the banking system to support the state-owned enterprise sector, but the result has been that over three-quarters of China's "investment" (much of which should be seen not as investment but as subsidy) goes to state-owned enterprises, but much of this money is never repaid. Approximately one-third of outstanding bank loans are said to be non-performing, suggesting that the size of China's internal debt could, under certain circumstances, lead to a major financial crisis.[38]

In response, the state has looked, generally slowly, for new approaches to solve the crisis in state-owned enterprises. The effort to reform 100 large state-owned enterprises led by Wu Bangguo has been very unsuccessful, not only casting doubt on the ability of China to revive these enterprises within the broad framework of the "socialist economy," but perhaps on Wu Bangguo's hopes to become premier as well.[39] Current policy calls for "grasping the large and letting go of the small" state-owned enterprises, but it is far from clear that such a policy can cope with the size of the problem. Clearly, ideological and political factors remain important in preventing the government from taking more radical steps. For instance, party elder Song Ping has said that, in light of the difficulties of the large- and medium-sized SOEs, some people have given up the "Marxist stand, viewpoints, and methods" and looked for a way out through privatization — something that Song and like-minded conservatives obviously oppose.[40] Similarly, Premier Li Peng warned that China could not use "capitalist" methods, such as bankruptcies and layoffs, to deal with the problems of state-owned enterprises.[41] More recently, Premier Li, during a trip to Anshan Iron and Steel in Liaoning province, declared, "State-owned enterprises are the socialist system's economic base. We should understand the importance of improving state-owned enterprises from the high plane of the socialist system's life and death."[42]

Despite such reluctance to take major steps to overhaul the economy, workers are being laid off. Although some estimates are considerably higher, Qiu Xiaohua, spokesman of the State Statistical Bureau, recently stated that 4 million urban workers, approximately 5% of the total, had been laid off. Perhaps more important than the overall numbers is the impact in specific areas. For instance, in the old industrial city of Shenyang in the northeast, it is said that as many as 60% of workers at state-owned enterprises have not been paid in recent months.[43] Given the pressures facing state-owned enterprises, yet more will have to be done to restructure industry and layoff redundant workers. Protests and strikes seem inevitable.[44] The conservative tone of recent party documents is no doubt in part intended to discourage the public expression of such discontent.

Nationalism

The palpable rise of nationalism is another force fuelling China's current political direction. Much has been said about the rise of Chinese nationalism in recent months, some of it quite exaggerated. It is true that nationalism has become an important force, but then this is not new in the context of modern Chinese politics. Indeed, over the last century, nationalism has been the most potent force in Chinese politics; viewed in this context, it is the ebbing of nationalism in the Dengist period that seems anomalous. No doubt the rise of nationalism in recent years has been prompted by the government's efforts to rally support as faith in Marxism-Leninism-Mao Zedong Thought has waned, but the question is: Why have the government's propaganda efforts been so successful in this regard, whereas they have been quite unsuccessful in whipping up support for socialism?

In thinking about nationalism in contemporary China, it is useful to distinguish between "official nationalism" and "popular nationalism." While there is an interaction between these two phenomena, they are by no means identical. Popular nationalism frequently touches on passions and raises issues that the government would prefer not to deal with. Thus, while nationalism tends to redound to the government's benefit, it also causes difficulties for the government.

Having said this, it is useful to try to reconstruct the origins of the most recent wave of nationalist sentiment. There is a wide variety of nationalist sentiments prevalent in China at present, so different people have undergone different experiences, but broadly speaking, the primary sources of contemporary nationalism appear to lie in the following.

First, the film *River Elegy* (*He shang*), which captivated audiences in the summer of 1988 and encapsulated a wide-spread urge for reform and Westernization at the time, also offended the nationalist sentiments of some. While some sympathized with the film's message of reform and opening up, they could not accept its cosmopolitanism and apparent disdain for China's cultural heritage. The film seemed needlessly to heap scorn on the symbols of China's past and suggest that there was nothing of value in that cultural heritage. Not unlike the turn from cosmopolitanism in the 1920s, contemporary nationalists find a search for modernization that does not inherit and treasure the past discomforting. Although some of the sharpest criticisms of the film, voiced following the Tiananmen crackdown, were part of a highly partisan effort to smear Zhao Ziyang and the reform effort he had led, others shared the nationalist sentiments of the critics if not always their conservatism.

Secondly, the disintegration of the Soviet Union and the collapse of the Russian economy had a tremendous impact on China, both among officialdom and among the people. By 1991, as the Soviet Union was lurching towards dissolution, China's economy was pulling out of the slowdown that had followed the imposition of retrenchment polices and Chinese society was beginning to recover from the shock of Tiananmen. The socialist states of Eastern Europe had collapsed, and their economies were suffering badly. By comparison, the performance of the Chinese government was quite credible. The disintegration of the Soviet Union confirmed this impression, as the one-time superpower collapsed into a decidedly second tier power (or rather powers) and as the standard of living declined drastically. Indeed, there was a pride, perhaps even a smugness, as Russians came to China to look for work in Chinese restaurants.

The impact of this collapse should not be underestimated. Nothing did more to undermine the credibility of Western economics, particularly those who advocated a "big bang" approach to reform, than the collapse of the Russian economy. It was not long before the Chinese approach to reform, which ironically had itself been so sharply questioned by its practitioners in the late 1980s, came to be viewed as a unique, and wise, approach to reform. Chinese economists could argue whether the "Chinese model" was limited in applicability to China or whether it had universal characteristics. Young Chinese economists who had championed Western economics in China found themselves denounced as believers in "utopian capitalism."

Incrementalism had won the day, and the lesson of incrementalism was extended from economics to government. Even those who favoured the liberalization and democratization of China nevertheless accepted the idea that such changes would take a long time. The lesson on the collapse of the Soviet Union was that economic reform required government authority. Without a sufficiently strong central government, it would be impossible either to develop the economy or carry out reform. Indeed, reform-minded economists came to believe that the reforms had undermined the "state capacity" of the central government and called for a variety of measures, including tax reform, to strengthen the "state capacity" of the central government.[45] Such sentiments can be seen as expressing a certain type of nationalist sentiment, although certainly not of an aggressive or expansionist type, and they found futile ground in the wake of the disintegration of the Soviet Union — in sharp contrast to the way similar arguments had been rejected in the mid- and late-1980s.

A third factor contributing to the recent wave of nationalism was, of course, the very heavy handed diplomacy of the United States. One of the apparent intents behind the American criticism of China's human rights — in addition to moral indignation, which was real enough — was the belief that in expressing such sentiments the United States would be placing itself on the side of history. There was a shallow and simplistic reading of the events of 1989 that held that Tiananmen was the precursor of similar movements in the future and the near-term democratization of China, and that in expressing support for the student leaders of the Tiananmen demonstrations the United States would be making common cause with the future leaders of China. But, the heavy-handed approach adopted by the American government soon turned an expression of moral indignation against the actions of the Chinese government into what appeared to many to be an effort to oppose China as a country. The reckless statements of some members of Congress and commentary in the press certainly added to the impression.

The summer of 1993 marked an important turning point in this regard. This was just after President Clinton, in an effort to square the circle between the criticisms the Democratic Party had made of President Bush's China policy and the realities of dealing with China, renewed China's most-favoured-nation (MFN) trade status but conditioned that renewal on improvements in China's human rights record. Although the Clinton administration would have settled for a fig leaf, the Chinese government had a very strong interest in resisting any linkage at all — especially after the ill-fated meeting between John Shattuck and Wei Jingsheng. In the summer of 1993, relations soured badly as the US chose to oppose China's bid to host the 2000 Olympics in Beijing. No doubt, propagandists in Beijing played the issue brilliantly, but the fact remains that the US underestimated how easily an action intended to underscore its continuing dissatisfaction with China's human rights record could be perceived as an anti-China campaign. The rise of anti-American sentiment in China was palpable as the decision to bypass Beijing in favour of Sydney was announced.

Overlapping with the rift on China's Olympic bid was the *Yin He* ("Milky Way") incident. Accepting the intelligence community's strong belief that chemical agents for making nerve gas were on board the *Yin He*, the non-proliferation community in Washington demanded that the *Yin He* be followed and, if it did not turn back, stopped and inspected. Ignoring assurances from the highest levels in China that there were no such agents on board, Washington pursued a highly public policy of confrontation with China.[46] When the cargo of the *Yin He* was finally inspected outside the Persian Gulf, no contraband was found. The American government offered no apology or compensation for Chinese losses. The high-handedness of American statements and actions left a residue of bitterness that can still be felt in Beijing.

Finally, there is simple fact that China has, somewhat to its own surprise, emerged as an economic powerhouse. From 1978 through 1988, China had an average annual growth rate of about 9.5%. No other country the size of China has ever sustained such high-speed growth. China's century long quest for "wealth and power" is finally within reach. What has caught the attention of Americans is the broad issue of: How do you deal with a rising power like China? How can China be integrated into the world economic system? What has generally escaped attention is the degree of uncertainty within China over what to make of its own economic growth. After a century of striving for "wealth and power," many Chinese have difficulty believing that the country has attained considerable prosperity and that, at least in aggregate terms, the country is a world economic power. Some wish to discount reports of China's success, believing the country still far from its goals, while others seem to glory in the country's new-found wealth, seeing in it verification of China's greatness. In general, economic success has fed into a feeling of national self-confidence, which has, in turn, provided futile ground for nationalism.

If such factors have led to a new wave of nationalism, the question is what type of nationalism and what impact will it have on China's foreign policy. Although many critics in the West have depicted the rise of Chinese nationalism in ominous terms, even comparing it to the xenophobia of the Boxers, it is not yet clear that Chinese nationalism is such a malevolent force.

The book that has attracted the most attention is *China Can Say No*. Written by five young (in their 20s and 30s), mostly unemployed people, *China Can Say No* is a shallow work, reflecting little sophistication about either China or the West. As far as can be determined, the authors have no relations with political circles (indeed they seem curiously uninformed about many of the arguments swirling about them), and they do not appear to have been encouraged to write the book. Indeed, the chief motivation, though the authors deny it, appears to have been to make money, and perhaps to make a splash on the social scene. One of the authors, who has run a very successful private enterprise, put up the money for publication.[47]

The authors claim that their book is intended to express a sense of "patriotism" and the feelings of the common people, and the sales figures for the book suggest that they are right. Although hastily and not particularly well written, the sale of the book certainly exceeded whatever expectations the authors might have had. The authors claim that a million copies of the book have been sold. Even intellectuals who are far more sophisticated than the authors bought and praised the book for expressing emotions that they share.

The government's reaction to the publication of *China Can Say No* appears to be ambivalent. On the one hand, those in charge of managing China's relationship with the United States no doubt find that the book, and the popular sentiment that it expresses, complicates their task. The Ministry of Foreign Affairs, in particular, often comes under fire from within China for being too weak *vis-à-vis* the United States, and the publication of *China Can Say No* does not make their job any easier.[48] On the other hand, there are many within the government who find this expression of nationalist sentiment comforting; in some parts of the government, it has become difficult to say anything critical about the book. "It's not possible to contradict *China Can Say No* line now," one Beijing foreign policy expert was quoted as saying.[49]

The sort of popular, unofficial nationalism expressed by *China Can Say No* appears, for the moment at least, to be as superficial as it is widespread. Of more concern over the long run, are the less virulent but more profound expressions of anti-Americanism found either in the halls of government or among intellectuals closely related to policy circles. In this regard, the publication of *Why China Can Say No* by three young scholars of international relations is more disturbing than the publication of *China Can Say No* by five authors, none of whom had visited the United States prior to writing the book. Also of concern is the publication of *A Test of Strength between China and the US*, a two-volume work that covers the history of Sino-US relations since the founding of the People's Republic of China. Published with a preface by Chai Zemin, *A Test of Strength between China and the US* has a semi-official flavour; its implication that the current tensions between China and the US are a continuation of those that existed in the 1950s and 1960s seems unwarranted.[50]

Such feelings of nationalism no doubt bolster the tendency to look inward for models of governance and to try to define a "Chinese" model of economic and political development. As such, they reinforce the conservative trend reflected in the recent document on spiritual civilization.

Jiang's Strategy and Deng's Death

After his sudden elevation to general secretary in 1989, Jiang Zemin faced the problem of securing his own authority without offending his patron — a task at which neither Hu Yaobang nor Zhao Ziyang had succeeded.[51] No doubt reflecting both his own inclinations and his assessment of the balance of forces in Chinese politics, Jiang Zemin adopted a different tack than his predecessors. Unlike Hu and Zhao, both of whom pushed the limits of Deng Xiaoping's thinking on the right, Jiang curried favour with the conservative wing of the party. Over the past three years, stretching from the 4th plenary session of the 14th Central Committee to the 6th plenum in 1996, Jiang Zemin worked to consolidate his position by emphasizing party discipline ("democratic centralism") and ideology ("talking politics" and "spiritual civilization"). Indeed, Jiang has seemed intensely conscious both of the requisites of power (particularly personnel changes) and of the need to articulate an ideological vision, however vague. As Jiang was once reported to have said, Mao Zedong's generation had the theory of revolutionary socialism and Deng Xiaoping's generation had the theory of building socialism with Chinese characteristics, but the third generation (i.e., Jiang Zemin's generation) had not yet put its ideological stamp on politics.[52] Obviously, the 6th plenum resolution on building spiritual civilization was intended as a step in this direction, albeit one that seems directed more at mollifying conservatives and protecting himself from potential attack than at inspiring either party members or the people at large.

Overall, Jiang's tactics of distancing himself gently from the policies of Deng Xiaoping (even while enshrining "Deng Xiaoping theory of building socialism with Chinese characteristics" as a new orthodoxy), building alliances with conservatives, articulating a neo-conservative political and ideological agenda, and making strategic personnel changes appear to have been generally successful. Up until early 1997, Jiang appeared to be headed for an important, if not necessarily overwhelming victory, at the 15th Party Congress.[53] Then, Deng died.

The early speculation immediately following Deng's death was that life, within China and within the party, would go on as usual.[54] After all, Jiang had been general secretary for more than seven years, and Deng had faded from the political scene some two years before his death. Moreover, the leadership appeared unusually well prepared for Deng's death. On 1 January, China Central Television began broadcasting a twelve-part series on the life of Deng Xiaoping. Introduced by Jiang Zemin, the film appeared designed to prepare the Chinese public for Deng's death and for Jiang's emergence from Deng's shadow.[55] When Deng did die on the evening of 19 February, Xinhua reported the death only five hours after its occurrence, an unusually rapid response time for announcing the deaths of major leaders. Only two hours later, the press agency released a long letter to the Chinese people recounting Deng's life and eulogizing the late leader.[56] Thus, the early indications were that Deng's death had caused no confusion or infighting.

Despite such initial calmness and the continued likelihood that Jiang would prevail at the 15th Party Congress, there were soon indications that Jiang may have to navigate some unusually difficult waters on the way to the congress. His enemies on both the left and the right perceive the passing of Deng as the time to press their agendas, and, at a minimum, these challenges are likely to affect the compromises struck at the party congress and thus the evolution of Chinese politics over the next several years.

The first salvo of the post-Deng era came from the left. No sooner had the patriarch died than leftists, apparently associated with Deng Liqun, circulated a 20,000 character document entitled, "Certain Theories and Policies on Upholding the Primary Status of the Public Ownership System." The document harshly criticized the direction of party policy and emphasized the need to "grasp the 'contradiction' between state ownership and privatization."[57] Even before this salvo was fired, the conservative journal *Zhongliu* (Mainstream) in its February issue had published an article sharply criticizing the book *Heart to Heart Talks with the General Secretary*, which was published in 1996 in an apparent effort to boost Jiang Zemin's prestige. The book carried a preface written by Liu Ji, a vice-president of the Chinese Academy of Social Sciences who is reportedly close to Jiang.[58]

What is interesting, given this pressure from the left and Jiang's own tendencies over the last three years, is that Jiang decided to tack to the right in the wake of Deng's death. Jiang's eulogy of Deng was perhaps the most reformist speech Jiang had given since 1992. While great praise of Deng was to be expected at such an occasion, Jiang appeared to go out of his way to emphasize Deng's bold leadership and his pragmatic economic policies. For instance, Jiang quoted Deng as saying at the time he was restored to his posts in 1977 that there were two attitudes towards work: "One is to act as a bureaucrat, the other is to work." This appears to be a risky quotation for the cautious Jiang to cite. Jiang went on to endorse the still controversial 13th Party Congress of 1987, which had elaborated on the idea of the initial stage of socialism, and highlighted Deng's 1992 tour of Shenzhen. Given Jiang's own reservations at the time, it is remarkable that Jiang chose to call Deng's remarks then a "scientific summing up of the party's basic practices and experiences" since the inauguration of reform.[59] The editorial that ran in *People's Daily* the following day likewise endorsed Deng's controversial definition of socialism, given during his 1992 Shenzhen visit, as consisting of all things that can raise "productive forces" (the economy), increase the country's "comprehensive national strength," and boost people's standard of living.[60] Deng gave this "definition" of socialism in response to the deep controversies that had flared within the party following Tiananmen. It was precisely such pragmatism that had launched China's economic reforms and roused the ire of party leftists.

Also significant in the battle to claim Deng's legacy was the decision to cast Deng's ashes into the sea. As MacFarquhar points out, Deng's decision contrasted with that of Zhou Enlai, who had his ashes scattered over the rivers and land of China. Like the controversial TV series *River Elegy*, Deng final act emphasized that China's future lay with the sea and opening up.[61] MacFarquhar's interpretation is reinforced by a Xinhua newsletter on scattering Deng's ashes. According to the report, "All his life, Deng Xiaoping was enchanted with the vast ocean and forged an indissoluble bond with ridges of waves.... The boundlessness of the vast ocean broadened his breadth of mind."[62]

It remains to be seen whether the more liberal tack that Jiang took in his eulogy of Deng marks a temporary shift or a possible realignment of China's political hierarchy. Certainly, the more liberal wing of the party hardly seems more welcoming to Jiang than the left. As various officials made ritualistic expressions of support for Jiang as the "core" of the party, Qiao Shi yielded only during his third public speech following Deng's death. At the closing session of the NPC Standing Committee meeting on 23 February, Qiao called for three minutes of silent tribute in memory of Deng but said nothing about Jiang. It was only at the opening of the NPC session on 1 March that Qiao finally made the ritual statement.[63]

Despite Qiao's apparently reluctant endorsement of Jiang, a number of intriguing rumours have surfaced in the days following Deng's death which might explain Jiang's tacking to the right and which could presage important shifts in Chinese politics. A copy of what purported to be Deng's will circulated quickly. The document, which took responsibility and expressed remorse for Tiananmen, was quickly denounced as a forgery by the CCP, but others viewed the document as possibly legitimate.[64] At the same time, there were rumours in Beijing that the party might undertake a substantial reevaluation of Tiananmen, an effort that presumably would have adverse consequences for Li Peng who is closely associated with that event. At the same time, it appears that Sino-US relations may improve greatly if an agreement can be worked out for Chinese improvement of human rights and some political reform in exchange for the US dropping its annual criticism of China at the United Nations Human Rights Commission and willingness to admit China into the World Trade Organization (WTO).[65] Such a major improvement in Sino-US relations might indeed provide the stimulus for the Chinese leadership to consider a new round of reforms.

The 15th Party Congress and the Politics of Succession

The various rumours swirling in the aftermath of Deng's death underscore what was already known, namely, that the 15th Party Congress will be critical, both for Jiang Zemin and the CCP. Despite the political manoeuvring that has surfaced following Deng's death, it still seems quite likely that Jiang will prevail at the fall congress. The question is: How successful will he be and what trade-offs will he have to make? The odds are that Jiang will be quite successful, but that he will have to retain both Li Peng and Qiao Shi, both of whom are potential adversaries, at least in some capacity.

Having served two terms as premier, Li Peng must retire, but few expect him to leave politics. Li is widely regarded as the representative of conservatives and central bureaucrats, and this has continued to make him a powerful figure at the highest levels. Putting Li as head of the NPC is impossible; his unpopularity there was reflected in his election as premier in 1993 when 210 NPC delegates casts votes against him and another 120 abstained (and one cast a vote for Zhao Ziyang).[66] Although it was widely rumoured that Jiang would yield the largely ceremonial role of PRC President to Li, doing so would hardly help China's diplomatic efforts and it would prevent Jiang from playing the role on the world stage that he obviously relishes.[67]

It thus seems likely, as has been rumoured recently, that the position of party chairman will be restored, that Jiang will become CCP chairman, and that Li will become vice-chairman. This arrangement is rumoured to have been first bruited by Yuan Mu on behalf of Li Peng. The condition, however, was that there would be only one vice-chairman. Quickly, however, others within the leadership noted that in the Maoist era there were several vice-chairmen and that the vice-chairmen plus chairman made up the Politburo Standing Committee. Thus, the debate as this article goes to print revolves around how many vice-chairmen there will be. It seems highly unlikely that Jiang will yield to Li Peng's request that there be only one vice-chairman; after all, Jiang removed Li as deputy head of the powerful Central Finance and Economics Leadership Small Group, suggesting that relations between the two leaders are less than harmonious.[68] Most people anticipate that there will be two vice-chairmen, the second one being Qiao Shi. This would provide balance if not necessarily stability.

Assuming that Li vacates the premiership, the question is who will replace him. Zhu Rongji allegedly took himself out of the running by offering to become president of Tsinghua (Qinghua) University, but he should not be counted out. Presumably, Jiang hoped to promote his former Shanghai associate, Wu Bangguo, to be premier, but Wu's efforts to reform state-owned enterprises have been so unsuccessful that this seems unlikely. Li Lanqing is widely regarded as the compromise candidate. Well educated and amiable, Li offends few. Moreover, his relationship with Jiang Zemin goes back a long way. But, whether such a personality can guide the economy through a period of important changes in which the centre may have to make unpopular decisions is uncertain. Zhu Rongji, despite having offended many local leaders, may yet emerge as the choice for premier.

The other high-level position that is being watched closely is that of head of the NPC. Qiao Shi may continue in this capacity, but he recently told an interviewer that his position in the new leadership was still "under discussion." Undoubtedly, Jiang Zemin would like to remove Qiao; Qiao has been a constant thorn in Jiang's side. But, removing Qiao would be difficult and would come at a high price. No doubt, like Deng, Jiang will be sensitive to the importance of balancing different constituencies in the party, and removing Qiao would force Jiang to rely on conservatives.

As this chapter goes to press, the 15th Party Congress is still some months away. There will undoubtedly be surprises along the way, but it appears highly likely that Jiang will emerge from the congress strengthened. Allies, such as Ding Guan'gen, appear certain to enter the Politburo Standing Committee, and, as the recent changes in the military high command suggest, Jiang appears poised to bring his military backers into top leadership positions as senior officials, such as Politburo Standing Committee member Liu Huaqing and Central Military Commission vice-chairman Zhang Zhen, retire from office. At the same time, Jiang will not emerge so strong that he will not have to balance the disparate wings of the party. Li Peng and Qiao Shi appear positioned to stay as the voices of the conservative and reformist forces, respectively. One also hopes that the political report that Jiang will deliver will set out a more positive vision than did the recent 6th plenum. Only by doing so, can Jiang hope to put his own ideological stamp on the current era.

Conclusion

Although in many ways the post-Deng era has already begun, the 15th Party Congress seems destined to mark the opening of a new era. The three plenums from 1994 to 1996 appear as preparatory to this formal unveiling of the third generation of leadership. As this landmark approaches, the disparate tendencies within the party appear to be as great as ever. Jiang Zemin has set himself the task of holding the centre, but as Xing Fensi's effort to define the centre suggests, this is not an easy task. Indeed, the centre is holding in part because the alternatives seem either unpalatable (returning to neo-Maoist orthodoxy) or dangerous (opening up the system).

Clearly, Jiang has decided that his first order of business is to secure power, and both personnel moves and the content of party resolutions suggests that he is succeeding. It is also clear that he has succeeded by shifting to the left — at least up until Deng's death. As suggested above, Jiang sought a position significantly to the left of Deng Xiaoping in the wake of Tiananmen, and, as the enthusiasm surrounding Deng's 1992 southern sojourn has dissipated, Jiang has gradually returned to that position. Such tendencies suggest not only Jiang Zemin's cautious personality but also the conservative thinking of much of the top party leadership. The growth of nationalistic thinking among top leaders, including in the military, reinforces such trends.

Assuming that Jiang emerges from the party congress with his power enhanced, if not necessarily secure, the question is: How will he use his power to address the problems facing China? The answer to this question is by no means certain. To date, Jiang has shown little inclination to adopt bold moves to address such issues as the serious conditions of state-owned enterprises, but that appears to be an issue that cannot be delayed indefinitely. Will Jiang have the authority and vision to move more decisively on such issues, and how will he incorporate such reform measures, if he adopts them, into his vision of a socialist China? The answers to such questions will have to wait until after the 15th Party Congress.

Notes

1. "Political Report" to the 14th Party Congress, Beijing Television, trans. in Foreign Broadcast Information Service, *China Daily Report* (hereafter, FBIS), 13 October 1992.
2. Joseph Fewsmith, "Reaction, Resurgence, and Succession: Chinese Politics Since Tiananmen," in *The Politics of China: The Eras of Mao and Deng*, edited by Roderick MacFarquhar (2nd ed.; Cambridge: Cambridge University Press, 1997), p. 479.
3. Joseph Fewsmith, "Jockeying for Position in the Post-Deng Era," *Current History*, Vol. 94, No. 2 (September 1995), pp. 252–58.
4. Yang Zhongmei, *Jiang Zemin zhuan* (Biography of Jiang Zemin) (Taipei: Shih pao wen hua, 1996).
5. *South China Morning Post*, 13 October 1996.
6. On military influence, see Michael D. Swaine, *The Role of the Chinese Military in National Security Policymaking* (Santa Monica: Rand, 1996).
7. See, in particular, Wang Renzhi, "Guanyu fandui zichan jieji ziyouhua" (On Opposing Bourgeois Liberalization), *Renmin ribao* (People's Daily), 22 February 1990, pp. 1–3.

8. Gao Xin and He Pin, *Zhu Rongji zhuan* (Biography of Zhu Rongji) (Hong Kong: Xinxinwen, 1993), p. 232.
9. "Yingxiang woguo guojia anquan de ruogan yinsu" (document circulated internally), p. 14.
10. This remark is not contained in the three volume compendium of Deng Xiaoping's selected works but is contained in a recent volume published in conjunction with the 6th plenum of the 14th Central Committee. Deng's remark was made during an inspection tour of Tianjin. The volume editors acknowledge that the selection contained in the volume was only an excerpt of Deng's remarks and that the title, "Always Talk Politics" had been selected by the editors. See Zhonggong zhongyang wenxuan yanjiushi (ed.), *Shehui zhuyi jingshen wenming jianshe wenxian xuanbian* (Selected Documents on Building Socialist Spiritual Civilization) (Beijing: Zhonggong zhongyang wenxuan yanjiushi, 1996), p. 235.
11. "Leading Cadres Must Pay Attention to Politics," excerpted from Jiang Zemin's speech to the 5th plenum of the 14th Central Committee, Xinhua, 17 January 1996, trans. FBIS, 17 January 1996.
12. Ren Zhongping, *Renmin ribao*, 1 April 1996.
13. Li Zehou and Liu Zaifu, *Gaobie geming: Huiwang ershi shiji Zhongguo* (Farewell to Revolution: Looking Back on Twentieth Century China) (Hong Kong: Cosmos Books, Ltd., 1995).
14. Author's interview.
15. Joseph Fewsmith (Note 3), pp. 252–58.
16. Another has been Yang Shangkun, whose political profile appears to have risen somewhat in the four years since his half-brother was dismissed as vice-chairman of the CMC. Recently Yang Shangkun reiterated his calls for greater boldness and openness in reform. See Fong Tak-ho, "Veteran Yang Calls for Bold Reforms in Zhuhai Visit," *Hong Kong Standard*, 4 February 1997.
17. "Senior Leader Qiao Shi Reiterates Deng Xiaoping's Stance on 'Leftism'," *Ching Pao*, No. 231 (1 October 1996), pp. 29–31, trans. *BBC Summary of World Broadcasts*, 5 November 1996.
18. Xinhua, 4 September 1996, trans. *BBC Summary of World Broadcasts*, 5 September 1996.
19. Xinhua, 14 December 1996, trans. *BBC Summary of World Broadcasts*, 16 December 1996. See also Trudy Rubin, "Bringing China under the Rule of Law," *Philadelphia Inquirer*, 18 December 1996.
20. *South China Morning Post*, 13 January 1997.
21. *South China Morning Post*, 31 December 1996.
22. "Resolutions of the CPC Central Committee Regarding Important Questions on Promoting Socialist Ethical and Cultural Progress," *Beijing Review*, 4–10 November 1996, pp. 20–31.

23. Ibid. See also Willy Wo-lap Lam, *South China Morning Post*, 18 October 1996.
24. Xinhua, 27 October 1996, trans. *BBC Summary of World Broadcasts*, 29 October 1997.
25. "Resolution of the Central Committee of the Communist Party of China on the Guiding Principles for Building a Socialist Society with Advanced Culture and Ideology," Xinhua, 26 September 1986, trans. FBIS, 29 September 1986, pp. K2–13.
26. Ruan Ming, *Deng Xiaoping diguo* (The Empire of Deng Xiaoping) (Taipei: Shih-pao ch'u-pan kung-ssu, 1991), pp. 183–85.
27. See Note 22.
28. Ibid.
29. Jiang An, "China Tightens Cultural Grip, Gives Jiang a Boost," *The Straits Times*, 8 November 1996.
30. Xinhua, 16 December 1996, trans. *BBC Summary of World Broadcasts*, 18 December 1996.
31. *China Daily*, 15 January 1997.
32. *The Straits Times*, 17 January 1997.
33. Tibet TV, 4 November 1996, trans. *BBC Summary of World Broadcasts*, 7 November 1996; *Xizang ribao*, 6 November 1996, trans. *BBC Summary of World Broadcasts*, 6 November 1996; and *Xizang ribao*, 12 November 1996, trans. *BBC Summary of World Broadcasts*, 27 November 1996.
34. Shen Kaiyun, "Actively Guide Religion to Accommodate Itself to Socialist Society," *Xizang ribao*, 4 November 1996, trans. *BBC Summary of World Broadcasts*, 19 November 1996.
35. *Xinjiang ribao*, 31 October 1996, trans. *BBC Summary of World Broadcasts*, 30 November 1996.
36. Patrick E. Tyler, "In China's Far West, Tensions with Ethnic Muslims Boil over in Riots and Bombings," *The New York Times*, 28 February 1997.
37. Benjamin Kang Lim, "Four Million of China State Firm Workers Jobless," *Reuters*, 27 January 1997. Agence France Presse, 27 January 1997.
38. Nicholas Lardy, "Testimony: Statement Before the Committee on Banking and Financial Services, U.S. House of Representatives," 20 March 1996.
39. Author's interview.
40. Song Ping, "Vigorously Advocate Practice and Investigation and Study — Speech Delivered at Forum on Mao Zedong Thought on Investigation and Study on 23 December 1995," *Renmin ribao*, 4 January 1996, p. 4, trans. FBIS, 19 January 1996.
41. Reuter, 5 February 1996.
42. Xinhua, 28 January 1997.
43. *Business Week*, 10 March 1997, p. 48.
44. Recently, 3,000 workers from the Acheng Textile Mill in Heilongjiang gathered at the Acheng railway station to protest the failure of the mill to pay

even the subsidies these workers, placed on "long leaves," were owed. See *Hsin Pao*, 21 January 1997, trans. *BBC Summary of World Broadcasts*, 25 January 1997.

45. See Wang Shaoguang and Hu Angang, *Jiaqiang zhongyang zhengfu zai shichang jingji zhuanxing zhong de zhudao zuoyong: Guangyu Zhongguo guojia nengli de yanjiu baogao* (Strengthen the Guiding Role of the Central Government during the Transition to a Market Economy: A Research Report on China's State Capacity) (Beijing: The Chinese Academy of Sciences, 1993), trans. *Chinese Economic Studies*, Vol. 28, Nos. 3 and 4 (May–June and July–August 1995).
46. Current rumours suggest that the contraband cargo either did not get loaded for reasons unrelated to American protests or was unloaded before the ship left Chinese waters. Author's interviews.
47. Author's interviews.
48. Author's interview.
49. Trudy Rubin, "In China, America as the Enemy," *Philadelphia Inquirer*, 27 December 1996.
50. *ZhongMei jiaoliang* (A Test of Strength between China and America) (Beijing: Zhongguo renmin chuban she, 1996).
51. This is no doubt in part because Jiang Zemin was supported at least as much by other leaders, particularly Li Xiannian, as Deng. Thus, it is not accurate to consider Jiang to be Deng's protégé, though Deng obviously could have rejected Jiang.
52. Joseph Fewsmith (Note 3), pp. 252–58.
53. The *Far Eastern Economic Review* reported that Jiang Zemin was in overall control of organizing preparations for the congress.
54. Not everyone agreed with this assessment. A number of Chinese dissidents believed that Deng's death would set off a power struggle and new demands for democracy. See, for instance, Harry Wu's comments cited in *USA Today*, 20 February 1997.
55. He Ping and Liu Siyang, "The Footsteps of a Giant and a Magnificent Scroll of Picture — Interview with Producers of the Large-scale TV Documentary 'Deng Xiaoping'," Xinhua, 12 January 1997, trans. *BBC Summary of World Broadcasts*, 15 January 1997.
56. Xinhua, 19 February 1997, trans. *BBC Summary of World Broadcasts*, 21 February 1997.
57. Willy Wo-lap Lam, *South China Morning Post*, 23 February 1997, p. 1.
58. Ibid. See also *Asia Times*, 24 February 1997, p. 4.
59. Xinhua, 25 February 1997.
60. Ibid.
61. Roderick MacFarquhar, "Demolition Man," *New York Review of Books*, 27 March 1997, p. 16.

62. He Ping and Liu Siyang, "Live Forever in the Boundless Seas: Notes on Scattering the Remains of Comrade Deng Xiaoping," Xinhua, 2 March 1997. This article had not been published at the time MacFarquhar wrote his article.
63. Xinhua, 23 February 1997, and Xinhua, 1 March 1997.
64. *The New York Times*, 27 February 1997.
65. *The New York Times*, 28 February 1997. See also *The Guardian*, 28 February 1997.
66. Joseph Fewsmith, "Notes on the First Session of the Eighth National People's Congress," *The Journal of Contemporary China*, No. 3 (Summer 1993), pp. 81–86.
67. The rumour is that Li might succeed to the Presidency resurfaced in the autumn. See Willy Wo-lap Lam, "Li Peng's Path to the Presidency," *South China Morning Post*, 9 October 1996.
68. Author's interview.

2

Corruption and Corruption Control: More of the Same in 1996

Melanie Manion

Of the 54 countries ranked by the Berlin-based public interest organization, Transparency International, according to the prevalence of corruption in 1996, China ranked 50th: corruption was judged more pervasive only in Bangladesh, Kenya, Pakistan, and Nigeria.[1] When corruption is as widespread as it has been in China for more than a decade now, it constitutes an "informal political system," which, if ignored, results in a seriously misleading description of the Chinese political economy.[2] In some countries, widespread corruption extends from the lowest level to the very top, in a "kleptocracy" in which official power is simply an opportunity for plunder.[3] At the same time, widespread corruption can produce clear discomfort, if not always unambiguous intolerance, among top political leaders for any number of reasons. For example, leaders may find flagrant venality in public office morally unacceptable; too many corrupt officials can deprive the state of significant revenues; foreign corporations are often reluctant to invest in an economy with an obviously weak legal infrastructure; and, corruption virtually invites opponents to dispute regime legitimacy.

China is one of many countries in which top political leaders have made efforts to control corruption, but without evident success. The prospects for the disappearance of corruption as a fairly regular feature of government and economic activity in China were about as distant at the close of 1996 as ever. Moreover, as most ordinary Chinese citizens seem to prefer "clean government" to widespread official corruption, which public opinion polls (and, indeed, social unrest) have consistently indicated, then the tenacity of corruption there piques our scholarly interest all the more. What explains the robustness of corruption in China, considering that it provokes apparent disaffection in society and coexists with repeated regime efforts to stop its growth, reduce its scope, and lessen its severity?

This chapter argues that both the efforts and the generally acknowledged failure of the regime to make a significant impact on rampant corruption in 1996 reflect the fundamental dilemmas of corruption and corruption control that have existed in more or less unchanging form in China since the early 1980s. An analysis of corruption and efforts to control corruption in 1996 reveals contextually specific but not essentially new features of a problem that has challenged economic and political claims to legitimate rule by the Chinese Communist Party (CCP) for more than a decade, the sort of problem that has hastened the collapse of regimes throughout history the world over, in China not so long ago.

The chapter proceeds as follows. The first section sets out a framework for considering corruption in China, including the problem of defining corruption in the context of post-Mao China. The next two sections provide an overview of corruption and specific measures adopted to control corruption in 1996. In both, the general situation described does not differ essentially from that obtaining for the past several years in China. Both corruption and the approach to controlling corruption in 1996 can be described as "more of the same," compared to previous years. The descriptive accounts in these two sections are followed by an analysis elaborating the argument that fundamental dilemmas of the post-Mao era continue to sustain corruption as an equilibrium, although by no means a necessary, unique, or superior equilibrium. The conclusion reflects on the prospects for major change.

What Is Corruption in China?

Since the time of Aristotle, scholars exploring the question of corruption have adopted a variety of different definitions, associated with different sorts of research questions and normative concerns. In the past half-century, political scientists have most typically adopted a formal-legal perspective, which basically reduces the notion of corruption to a particular relationship between the actions of public officials and rules designed to constrain those actions.[4] Corruption, according to this perspective, is the use of public office to pursue private gain in ways that violate laws or other formal rules. Clearly, laws and other rules designed to constrain officials embody a normative theory of the state reflecting some evaluative notion of where the line between market and non-market allocation of goods and services is appropriately drawn.[5] For example, in a liberal democracy, laws designed to promote a competitive capitalist economy are not generally assumed to legally sanction a comparable role for market forces in the allocation of votes or political favours. The formal-legal perspective on corruption implies a choice not to explore such normative issues; rather, it takes the formally resolved evaluative questions (reflected in laws and other formal rules) as a point of departure, without proposing an independent position on those questions. Political scientists have adopted a formal-legal definition of corruption mainly because it is more tractable than other perspectives, such as views that treat "the public interest" or "public opinion" as standards by which to categorize actions as corrupt.[6] A formal-legal perspective implies that a comparative study of corruption across countries is a comparison not of similar actions necessarily but of a similar relationship between formal rules and actions of public officials, a relationship of incongruence between those rules and actions.

Is a formal-legal perspective on corruption suited to the analysis of corruption in China? Certainly, despite significant advances in the past decade, the Chinese system is by no means characterized by the rule of law, nor can it be so long as its rulers remain committed to a Leninist version of political organization.[7] Analysing corruption in China as a particular relationship between formal rules and actions of public officials does, however, capture the essence of the problem of corruption there. Chinese political leaders do not tolerate challenges to their monopoly of political organization. The claims of regime legitimacy rest on the premise that the CCP-dominated state is uniquely qualified to provide the public goods that rationalize the existence of states and the legitimacy of governments everywhere. These public goods are delivered by Chinese officials. Yet, a significant number of public officials from top to bottom flout the rules established by the regime they ostensibly embody, by using their authority over the delivery of public goods to provide themselves with private goods. Through its public officials, the Chinese state supplies a "public bad": in public policy terms, there is a government failure. This government failure has both distributive and efficiency implications in the supply of particular public goods and services. While corruption is not always inconsistent with economic growth, particularly in contexts featuring a high degree of government intervention, corruption is inconsistent with the most fundamental role of government to supply public goods, which by definition are unlikely to be supplied through private actions.[8] For this reason, corruption calls into question the legitimacy of those in power who monopolize control over coercive resources, in theory to guarantee the delivery of public goods. Indeed, "clean government" is itself a public good more vital to the operation of government than any other, because the delivery of other public goods depends on it.

While in principle the formal-legal perspective on corruption is not unsuited to the study of corruption in China, operationalizing a formal-legal definition in the Chinese context is not completely straightforward, for a number of reasons.

First, corrupt actions may be violations of any of three different sorts of formal rules. A strict (or narrow) definition might consider only criminal corruption, violations of law that fall in the category of corruption. Chinese officials are also, however, subject to the organizational discipline of the Communist Party (as most officials are party members) and the standards of professional ethics elaborated by the Ministry of Supervision and various departments of government. Each category of violations is addressed in hundreds of formal rules, enforced by procuratorates in the criminal justice system, discipline inspection committees that work under the leadership of Communist Party committees, and government supervisory departments. If corruption is the violation of formal rules that are designed to constrain officials to be "clean," then this requires a choice about which sorts of rules to consider (as well as a familiarity with the rules considered).

It makes good sense to consider relevant violations of party discipline when examining corruption in China. A simple reason is that interpretations of the law provide for some violations of law to be punished by party or government enforcement agencies, outside the criminal justice system if, for example, the amounts involved are not big and other circumstances not serious.[9] Another reason to take violations of party discipline into account in examining corruption in China has to do with the organizational mechanism through which party committees exercise leadership over efforts to control corruption. This is discussed at greater length below. Simply put, political-legal committees (*zheng fa weiyuanhui*) of party committees at the various levels act as coordinating agencies, determining the assignment of investigation of cases to one or another of the specialized enforcement agencies. By channelling cases to party discipline inspection committees, the political-legal committees can certainly postpone and influence the disposition of cases by the procuracy. In practice, it also appears that cases can be kept out of the criminal justice system altogether, and that party penalties imposed by the discipline inspection committees often substitute for more severe criminal punishment.[10]

The implication of both sorts of situations described above is that cases of corruption, in the strict sense of violations of law, may not in fact appear among cases of corruption investigated by the procuracy. This has implications, of course, for any assessment of the amount of corruption in China. The most regularly reported statistics are those on cases of "corruption" and bribery (*tanwu huilu*) handled by the procuracy.[11] In addition to all the usual problems of measurement posed by a crime that (unlike normal theft, for example) may not have a victim and thus tends to be underreported, there is the additional problem in China that the rate of corruption revealed through enforcement in the criminal justice system understates even the amount of corruption detected and punished.

Secondly, even within what is apparently the least problematic category, violations of law, there has been lack of clarity about particular violations. For example, "corruption" is the usual English-language translation of the Chinese *tanwu*. The legal notion of *tanwu* refers to a situation when a public official exploits official position to appropriate public property illegally. This notion was not clarified until 1985, despite the introduction of the crime of "corruption" in the Criminal Law passed in 1979.[12] "Corruption" is distinguished from other sorts of theft by the conditions that the property be public (or collective, as clarified in 1989), and that the act be committed by a public official directly exploiting the circumstances produced by official position.[13] Thus, for example, a financial officer in a state organization who steals public funds that her position entrusts to her care engages in "corruption," but if she takes advantage of her familiarity with the financial operations of the organization to steal public funds entrusted to the care of another official then it is not a case of "corruption." Further, the misappropriation of public funds (*nuoyong gongkuan*) may or may not be considered a case of "corruption," depending on circumstances, such as how quickly the funds are returned and for what sort of activity the funds are taken.[14] In sum, corruption has a legal reference point that has changed over time and, depending on particular circumstances, may not include some apparent violations of law.

Corruption in 1996

Figures on cases of corruption filed by the procuracy are commonly used to support generalizations about the incidence of corruption in China. Yet, this revealed rate of corruption cannot be disentangled from enforcement. If enforcement is roughly constant over time, then changes in the revealed rate may be useful as a crude measure of changes in the pattern of corruption, although estimating the actual incidence of corruption remains problematic. In China, however, the pattern of enforcement over the past decade and a half has fluctuated between routine and intense bursts of enforcement. Increased enforcement predictably results in a higher revealed rate of corruption. If a systematic relationship exists between enforcement and actual corruption, so that increased enforcement constitutes an organizational response to increases in corruption (discovered through intelligence, for example), then the enforcement effort itself can be a rough indicator of changes in the incidence of corruption. In China, however, increased enforcement has often been a highly publicized political response to real or anticipated social unrest provoked by official corruption.[15] For example, less than two months after the June 1989 military suppression of demonstrations against the regime, Chinese leaders responded politically to the charges of widespread official corruption that had fuelled the popular unrest.[16] The Central Committee and State Council issued a Decision on Actions in the Near Future to Address Some Matters of Concern to the Masses, setting in motion a major campaign to enforce laws and other standards proscribing official venality.[17] The anti-corruption campaign of autumn 1989 was itself an intensification of corruption control efforts that had begun in 1982 with the party rectification campaign. The April 1995 suicide of Wang Baosen, deputy mayor of Beijing, and the subsequent resignation of Chen Xitong from his position as secretary of the Beijing Municipal Party Committee was accompanied by another highly publicized increase in enforcement, in no small part due to concerns about the possibility of renewed public unrest. The corruption campaign that began in spring 1995 continued throughout 1996. With the other major anti-corruption campaigns launched in autumn 1989 and autumn 1993, the current campaign is the third intensified effort to control corruption since China began on its road to economic reform in 1978. The three periods of increased enforcement roughly coincide with significant increases in the revealed rate of corruption.[18] Clearly, the changes in enforcement over the past decade and a half seriously complicate attempts to generalize about the pattern of corruption over time in China.

Enforcement in 1996 was an extension of the campaign launched in spring 1995. Thc figures available indicate increases in a particular areas of enforcement emphasis in 1996 and a roughly steady state or small reduction in other areas. In this context, it is worth noting that many 1995 enforcement figures were peaks. In 1995 the procuracy filed 63,953 cases of "corruption" and bribery (as well as 19,732 cases of dereliction of duty and various sorts of irregularities amounting to abuse of official authority). Official action on these cases resulted in the recovery of RMB 4.8 billion for the state and collective workplaces. In his report to the 5th session of the 8th National People's Congress, Procurator General Zhang Siqing lumped together cases of "corruption" and bribery filed by the procuratorates in 1996 with cases of misappropriation of public funds and cases of huge unexplained assets. The total number of such cases filed in 1996 was 61,099, a reduction over the 1995 figure. Official action on these cases resulted in the recovery of RMB 6.8 billion. In addition, the procuratorates filed 21,257 cases of dereliction of duty and various sorts of irregularities amounting to abuse of official authority in 1996, a small increase over the comparable 1995 figure. The number of "major" and "serious" cases (*da yao an*) filed by the procuracy in 1996 also registered a small increase over the 1995 figure. In 1995, the procuracy filed 2,262 cases of "corruption," bribery, and embezzlement involving cadres at and above the county level (a 28% increase over 1994, previously a record year for such cases). In 1996, the number of such cases filed by the procuracy was slightly higher yet, at 2,699 cases. In 1995, the procuracy had filed 29,419 "major" cases (that is, cases involving over RMB 10,000) of "corruption," bribery, and embezzlement. In 1996, nearly half of all such cases filed by the procuratorates were "major" cases, a significant increase over 1995.[19]

Figures on the number of cases filed in 1996 by the party discipline inspection committees and government supervisory departments have not yet been made public, but we can expect the total number of cases to easily exceed 100,000. The number of such cases filed in 1995 (122,476 cases) was more than twice the number of cases of "corruption" and bribery filed by the procuratorates in that year. On average, in 1993 through 1995, cases of corruption filed by the procuratorates (about 135,000 cases) amounted to less than a third of the cases filed by the discipline inspection committees and government supervisory departments (about 422,000 cases).[20]

In sum, to the extent that data are available, the pattern of corruption in 1996 appears to have been one of continuity, with the same forms of corruption found in earlier years. Compared to those years, for the most part 1996 featured essentially more of the same, with perhaps more corruption among leading officials and more cases of corruption involving big amounts of money.

Corruption Control in 1996

Corruption control in 1996 also featured more continuity than basic change. Leaders continued to acknowledge corruption as a serious problem, a challenge to regime legitimacy, and threat to social and political stability. The regime continued efforts to build up a system of corruption control featuring more rules and higher standards, greater adherence to international legal norms, increased specialization in existing organizations, and the extension of corruption control to new areas. Continued systematization proceeded without change to other key features of corruption control in the post-Mao period, however. There continued to be a division of responsibility for enforcing different standards among party discipline inspection committees, government supervisory departments, and the procuratorates, under the overall political leadership and coordination of the party committees through their political-legal committees. Finally, the regime continued to affirm the method of periodic bursts of enforcement, with the intensification of the third major campaign against corruption, which had begun in 1995. This section provides a descriptive review of the pattern of corruption control in 1996, focusing on these four main features.

Acknowledgement of a Serious Problem

Top Chinese leaders continued in 1996, as in years before, to air publically their view of corruption as a serious problem. In an interview printed in the Chinese journal *Liaowang* in April, Premier Li Peng discussed the importance of understanding corruption "from the high plane of the rise or fall of the party and the state." He presented the effort to control corruption as a long-term task and acknowledged: "Contradictions in the deep layers of the anti-corruption struggle have not been fundamentally resolved, and some corrupt practices are still spreading and prominent in certain fields. Cases of economic crime, degeneration, and dereliction of duty have occurred one after another, and the proportion of major and serious cases has increased somewhat, particularly over the past two years."[21] A month later, Hou Zongbin, deputy secretary of the Central Discipline Inspection Commission (CDIC), noted at a conference: "The situation remains grim, and the tasks are extremely arduous." He stated that trends in corruption were a cause for serious concern, citing overall increases in cases of corruption and violation of discipline, yearly increases in cases of corruption involving cadres at or above the county level, recent increases in cases involving cadres at the provincial (or ministerial) level, and ever larger amounts of money involved in cases of corruption.[22] In December 1996, General Secretary Jiang Zemin complained to participants at a conference on law enforcement about "lawlessness, indiscipline, power abuse for personal gain, favouritism, bending the law, corruption, bribery, and other corrupt phenomena" among law enforcers. Jiang voiced a view consistent with those presented by him and other top Chinese leaders over the past decade or so: offenders constitute only a small minority of "rotten apples" among Chinese officials, but the regime "must absolutely not take it lightly but approach it seriously because of its enormous pernicious influence."[23]

The unremitting and very public acknowledgement by China's top leaders of the problem of corruption is by no means a trivial matter. It is a necessary and integral part of the regime's response to two problems: corruption is widespread and on the rise, and the mass public consistently views corruption as one of the most serious (if not the most serious) problems of the current regime. In 1996, as in years past, the Chinese publicized results of various public opinion surveys that revealed mass public concern. For example, the Institute of Opinion Research attached to People's University in Beijing surveyed urban workers on matters of concern in 1996 and reported that corruption was at the top of most lists.[24] The Anhui Provincial Discipline Inspection Commission published results of a survey conducted in that province, indicating similar mass dissatisfaction: 96% of respondents reported that corruption remains very severe (38%) or quite severe (58%), 65% of respondents reported the spread of corruption as the issue of most concern to them, and 78% of respondents reported corruption as the main factor determining stability in China. Respondents overwhelmingly viewed the problem of corruption as essentially a problem of corrupt officials (i.e., rather than ordinary citizens participating in corrupt acts): 80% defined the key problem of corruption as the abuse of public office to pursue private gain.[25] As corruption is indeed widespread and ordinary citizens seem to have direct and indirect experience with it, the official acknowledgement of the problem does not introduce new information about corruption, only information relating to regime response. A failure to acknowledge the problem might contribute to inferences about a lack of real concern by top leaders, perhaps inferences of corruption at the very top. These and other inferences about unwillingness to act (which, I argue below, are common among the mass public) are undoubtedly more costly to the regime than inferences about the inability to achieve success in controlling corruption, particularly when top leaders can point to important policy successes in other areas that have affected the daily lives of ordinary citizens over the past decade.

Whether or not China's leaders have adopted appropriate measures to achieve success in controlling corruption and mobilized the energies of the mass public in the most effective way is another matter, of course. There can be little doubt that success in controlling corruption requires cooperation of ordinary citizens. Unless the community believes the regime is indeed engaged in a sincere effort, there is little incentive to cooperate. Thus, the public acknowledgement of a serious problem is consistent with the publicity attached to figures reflecting community cooperation. Political leaders and high officials in the procuracy often note (in an obviously positive light) figures on public reports to the authorities about violations of the law and other irregularities. For example, Jiang Liyou, who directs the centre that collects reports of corruption for the Supreme People's Procuratorate, noted that the newly established anti-"corruption" departments in procuratorates throughout the country had received over 200,000 reports of economic crimes in the first eight months of 1996 and that, compared to previous years, more reports had been non-anonymous. While he gave no indication of the proportion of non-anonymous reports, Jiang concluded that increases in non-anonymous reports indicated growing public confidence in the regime's efforts to control corruption.[26] Similarly, Wei Jianxing, secretary of the Central Discipline Inspection Commission, noted in early 1996 that discipline inspection committees nationwide had received more than 200,000 reports of corruption involving officials at and above the county level in the first 11 months of 1995. Of these reports, 27% were non-anonymous.[27] To put this in perspective, it is useful to consider that about 65% of reports of corruption to the Hong Kong Independent Commission Against Corruption (ICAC) are non-anonymous. Indeed, in its very first year of operation over a decade ago, 35% of reports of corruption to the ICAC were non-anonymous.[28] This issue will be discussed again in sections below, but it is worth noting here that while Chinese leaders publicize such figures to indicate the extent of community cooperation, a comparative perspective suggests the mass public is not especially cooperative, probably because citizens anticipate high costs for "voluntary enforcement" by cooperating with criminal justice, party, or government corruption control agencies. As a Chinese scholar observed in one of the country's most prominent law journals, ordinary citizens continue to "fear retaliation" and "dare not exercise supervision" over corrupt officials.[29]

Systematization of Corruption Control

In 1996, efforts to strengthen and further develop the system of corruption control continued. These efforts took on a few different forms. The main elements of continuity with 1995 were concrete measures to implement and enforce rules introduced in that year. A main focus was rules governing the lifestyle of leading officials, rules designed to constrain the abuse of office to indulge in the sort of conspicuous consumption that the regime recognized as particularly provocative to ordinary citizens. The party's discipline inspection committees were to be responsible for enforcement of these sorts of rules. In January 1996, the 6th plenary session of the CDIC set as its key tasks for the year the continued implementation and monitoring of rules prohibiting the use of public funds for feasting and leisure activities, rules establishing standards for automobile use by leading officials and restricting the use of luxury automobiles, and rules designed to prevent abuses of power in housing matters (i.e., the abuse of official position or public funds to build new houses, renovate existing houses, or acquire better housing). A fourth task for the year was to implement the system introduced in April 1995 requiring leading officials in party and government organizations to report their income, including gifts.

In order to ensure that rules on feasting at public expense, use of automobiles and housing were being implemented, the CDIC and the Ministry of Supervision sent out inspection teams to 10 provinces and 15 ministries to investigate the conduct of leading officials. As well, in the first eight months of 1996 the CDIC vetted over 172,000 applications to accept gifts and ordered nearly 80,000 officials to turn over to the state some RMB 44 million worth of gifts deemed too lavish or in excess of the stipulated monetary limits.[30] The system of income reporting for leading officials began to be implemented too. By the end of August, all state organizations at the centre, more than 80% of local party and government organizations at and above the country level, and 60% of state enterprises had reportedly established an income declaration system.[31]

A second element of continuity in systematization in 1996 was specialization of functions in existing organizations. At the end of 1995, an Anti-"Corruption" and Anti-Bribery General Office had been established under the Supreme People's Procuratorate. Similar offices had been established at the provincial level in 28 provincial procuratorates and at the municipal level in nearly 300 municipal procuratorates. In 1996, the process of building specialized anti-"corruption" departments in the local procuratorates continued. The specialization was designed to strengthen the procuracy in controlling corruption through the criminal justice system. Amendments to the Criminal Procedure Law, adopted by the 8th National People's Congress in March 1996 and in effect beginning this year, introduced another measure of systematization that also will more than likely strengthen the procuracy in its role in corruption control. The amended Article 18 reduces the scope of cases that the procuratorates are authorized to investigate directly. For example, the procuratorates will no longer directly investigate cases of tax evasion or refusal to pay taxes, and the provision allowing the procuratorates to investigate other cases they "consider necessary to accept directly" has been deleted in the amended law.[32] This reduction in scope of investigatory power does not affect the procuracy's jurisdiction over cases of criminal "corruption" and bribery and other cases that fall under the general category of corruption. The reduction in scope should enable the procuratorates to focus on the sorts of criminal violations that the anti-"corruption" and anti-bribery departments were established in 1995 to investigate, and it takes into account the very real shortages of personnel and other resources in the procuracy.

In 1996, the Central Committee and State Council initiated the effort to clean up and inspect extra-budgetary funds as part of the struggle against corruption.[33] This extension of monitoring to the management and use of extra-budgetary funds and the concomitant greater involvement of departments of finance, auditing, and the banks in corruption control was a new component of corruption control. In April 1996, Premier Li Peng clarified the two-pronged content of the effort. The ban on the practice of concealing financial income by transferring budgetary funds to extra-budgetary areas (setting up "books outside the books" and "small treasuries") was to be strictly enforced; at the same time, legal extra-budgetary funds were to be more strictly managed, with special accounts set up. By some estimates, extra-budgetary funds exceeded RMB 300 billion in 1996. The Ministry of Finance, the State Auditing Administration, and the People's Bank of China were assigned responsibility for getting the new work underway.[34]

Party Leadership and Campaign-style Enforcement

Continued systematization in corruption control in 1996, including the increased specialization and clarification of responsibilities in the criminal justice system, did not imply change in the most fundamental principle of organization: the leadership of the Communist Party, with party committee coordination of corruption control through the political-legal committees. Relatedly, systematization was not evidently considered contradictory to the continuation of intensive enforcement through campaigns against corruption. Continuity in both of these features implied that corruption control in 1996, as in previous years, was essentially "political" rather than essentially a matter of standard enforcement of existing rules by the criminal justice system.

The Central Committee reaffirmed the principle of generalized party leadership over corruption control. It rejected proposals that would have liberated the party's discipline inspection committees from the leadership of party committees at the same level, committees whose members the party's specialized corruption control agencies are to monitor and investigate. The structural problem of party control within the party apparatus itself thus remained unresolved. Rules introduced at the 6th plenary session of the CDIC in January 1996 acknowledge structural problems but do not change the essential principle of generalized leadership of party committees. For example, the rules give party discipline inspection committees in localities and departments new authority to conduct preliminary investigations and report findings directly to the immediately superior discipline inspection committee when they have information suggesting that members of the party committees at the same level have violated party discipline. But, the decision to file charges against an ordinary party committee member, which precedes investigation leading to party penalties and an eventual criminal investigation and punishment in some cases, remains a decision in the hands of the party committee at the same level. The new rules also give the party discipline inspection committees a formal role in personnel matters: before submitting information to their party committees, party organization departments vetting candidates for positions of leadership in localities and departments are to solicit the views of discipline inspection committees at the same level; party organization departments and government personnel departments vetting candidates for positions of leadership in discipline inspection committees or government supervisory departments are to obtain the prior consent of the discipline inspection committee or supervisory department at the next level up.[35] The new rules by no means represent the introduction of a highly centralized and autonomous hierarchy of party corruption control agencies. They acknowledge concerns about ineffectiveness expressed by those in the party discipline inspection hierarchy but do not change the fundamental principle of generalized party leadership through the party committees.

The leadership of the party committees over corruption control can have important consequences for how particular cases are handled. Communist Party members, in principle held to higher standards than non-party members, can be routinely protected from the more serious sanctioning through the criminal justice system by an initial assignment of a case to the party committee's discipline inspection committee. The case may or may not be ultimately handed over to the procuracy to be investigated as a crime. In principle, if in the course of investigation the discipline inspection committee discovers that the case appears to be one of criminal corruption or other violations of the law, then the procuratorate at the appropriate level has jurisdiction over the criminal aspects of the case. In practice, however, turning the case over to the procuracy is by no means so automatic. More than one Chinese commentator have observed that: "Too often, disciplining by the party or the government [supervisory departments] takes the place of criminal prosecution." Sanctions may be especially lenient if the offender cooperates in the recovery of assets obtained corruptly, a practice of "letting the loot atone for the crime."[36]

The case of Chen Xitong, implicated in 1995 in the biggest corruption scandal of the post-Mao period, is an example of this delicate political handling of corruption cases. At the close of 1996, the Chen Xitong case, investigated for months by the CDIC, was still officially an instance of "serious mistakes" rather than crimes, a label that kept the case out of the criminal justice system for the year. By mid-1996, the Ministry of Finance and the State Auditing Administration had verified that Chen Xitong, Wang Baosen, and others implicated in the case had concealed or illegally transferred funds amounting to RMB 18.3 billion since 1988. More likely than not, the high profile of the case, due in no small part to the Wang Baosen suicide, will ultimately result in criminal prosecution. But, top political leaders are clearly ambivalent about how to handle it. On the one hand, important political decisions have already been made, as Chen has been dismissed from his positions of leadership in the party and government. A criminal prosecution can serve to demonstrate regime commitment to cleaning up corruption. On the other, top leaders are concerned not to take actions that might be seen to substantiate inferences of corruption at high levels of leadership more generally and weaken the Communist Party's already fragile political legitimacy. Thus, Chen Zuolin, deputy secretary of the CDIC, called in February 1996 for increased media coverage to support the battle against corruption, but only four months later Ding Guan'gen, head of the Central Propaganda Department, warned that over-zealousness of the media in reporting corruption in the Beijing party apparatus could seriously damage the Communist Party's authority.[37]

A second political sensitive case of corruption in 1995 was that of Zhou Beifang, former vice-president of Shougang Corporation and president of Shougang's Hong Kong subsidiaries, Shougang Concord International and Shougang Concord Grand. In November, Zhou was given a suspended death sentence for economic crimes that apparently included bribery in huge amounts. The death sentence with two-year suspension is normally followed by a commutation to a sentence of life imprisonment. Although few details of the crimes have been made officially available, the punishment is the heaviest meted out yet to a "princeling": Zhou Guanwu, president of Shougang until his abrupt retirement after the arrest of his son, Zhou Beifang, in February, was a close associate of Deng Xiaoping.[38] While the case is important and the sentence signals that an association with the Deng family no longer necessarily affords protection to those who blatantly abuse official position, it does not signal what top leaders might want ordinary citizens to read in it, namely, that no official, however high ranking, is above the law. Politically savvy Chinese will read a more nuanced message in the timing of the sentence, coming as it does in a period of seriously waning health and influence of Deng. Indeed, there are some indications that an inquiry into corrupt activities of Zhou Beifang was conducted in 1991, but that a full investigation met with obstruction from the senior Zhou.[39] If such allegations are widely publicized, the November sentencing will be interpreted all the more as power politics rather than a demonstration of top leaders' commitment to cleaning up government.

As is evident from the discussion above, political leadership over corruption control can be exercised through the party committees on a case-by-case basis, if desired. Political leadership is also evident in the continued resort to campaigns to enforce rules against corruption. A campaign is not simply an overall intensification of enforcement. Rather, each campaign has a specific focus, and this focus is a political decision. Thus, in 1996 top political leaders called for an emphasis on cases of corruption involving officials at the ministerial level. The 6th plenary session of the CDIC reflected this, calling for "breakthroughs" in a number of serious and influential corruption cases.[40] Given the limited personnel and other resources in the agencies responsible for corruption control, the identification of a particular focus and its formulation as a key task imply that enforcement will unevenly concentrate on targets that fit the current politically-defined priorities. This brings the discussion of corruption control full circle, to the description of corruption in 1996 presented in an earlier section. The picture of corruption in 1996 reflects in no small part the priorities that political leaders had identified for corruption control agencies. These priorities reflect one component of political leadership over corruption control.

Fundamental Dilemmas

The efforts to control corruption in 1996 differed very little from those adopted in China over the past decade or so. Despite these efforts (and problems of measurement notwithstanding), most observers of Chinese politics agree that corruption in the post-Mao period is not simply different from the forms of corruption found in previous decades of Chinese Communist rule, but that there is also more of it, involving greater amounts of money, greater numbers of high-ranking officials, and more officials in leading organizations of the party and government as well as law enforcement organizations. In sum, over the past decade or so there has been a virtual explosion of corruption in China.

Explanations of the rise of corruption in China have focused quite sensibly on changes that distinguish the current period from the Maoist era. New opportunities appeared: the two-track pricing mechanism, the increased economic contact with foreign business, the new toleration of private entrepreneurial activity, for example. Standards of propriety became blurred: norms that defined what was permissible were redefined, the gap between norms for Communist Party members and norms for ordinary citizens widened, and the proliferation of different sets of rules (none very clear) confounded the identification of what was important. All in all, the policies and practices associated with "reform and opening" produced major and fairly sudden changes that led to increased corruption in many areas.[41]

Taken together, the particular changes outlined above can be described as a "shock" to the various parameters that previously defined the framework within which Chinese officials made daily choices about how to exercise discretionary power over the allocation of many different sorts of specific goods and services. Two important features of this shock are that it was sudden and that it affected many areas more or less simultaneously. Efforts to control corruption with the establishment or revival of various sorts of enforcement agencies and the introduction of countless new rules in the 1980s and 1990s were no match for the rapid rise in corrupt activity. Very quickly, given real constraints on resources for increased enforcement, the rise in corruption produced increasing safety in numbers for corrupt officials "competing" for limited enforcement attention: the more corrupt activity, the lower the likelihood of detection and punishment for any given official.[42] Once corruption became widespread, enforcement resources were insufficient to detect and punish the large number of corrupt officials. The inherent difficulty in bringing about a decrease in corrupt activity after it had become widespread was all the greater as a rise in corruption in law enforcement itself introduced another sort of constraint on increased enforcement.[43]

Further, as the new corruption appears in many different areas of official activity, among officials in different sorts of public office, inferences about the scope of corruption that ordinary citizens make from interaction with officials in one area of official activity are reinforced in interactions in other areas. Thus, the view of the Chinese mass public that corruption is widespread is confirmed repeatedly. This view helps to sustain widespread corruption: to the extent that ordinary citizens observe flagrant violations of rules by public officials pursuing their own gain, they do not believe the state adjudicates in favour of the rules. Top Chinese leaders have proclaimed their commitment to cleaning up corruption, but the commitment is not credible when corruption is widespread because corruption is widespread. Thus, ordinary citizens cannot be expected to contribute much voluntarily to enforcement, even if corruption discriminates against them.[44] Cooperation in enforcement is not costless: indeed, as noted above, citizens fear retribution for reporting corrupt officials. Moreover, so long as the regime obviously has not enforced rules successfully, citizens have little basis to believe that reporting violations will result in adjudication in favour of the rules. The regime appears unreliable as rule enforcer. Instead of supplying a public good of "clean government," the regime appears to be the source of a "public bad": widespread corruption among its officials.

In the Maoist era, of course, there were selective incentives for contributing to enforcement in rectification campaigns and other bursts of enforcement activity that mobilized mass passions. Campaigns identified and rewarded activists, providing a channel for "voluntary enforcers" to move along and ahead in politics. Through mass campaigns, the regime engaged in "enforcement swamping" to bring about a fairly rapid decrease in specified improprieties.[45] Not surprisingly, the post-Mao regime is unwilling to mobilize mass energies in a similar way, for at least two reasons. First, as the protests of spring 1989 demonstrated, mass passions are not easily constrained: resentments about official corruption and other particular policy issues can turn into an implicit or explicit critique of communist rule *per se*. Secondly, the post-Mao regime has placed economic growth at the top of its policy priorities: mass campaigns that disturb the public order and political stability are detrimental to economic advances. Recent campaigns against corruption are managed mainly through corruption control agencies, with mass participation restricted to individual-level input through reporting centres, in keeping with the particular blend of politics and systematization in the post-Mao period.

Conclusion

What are the prospects for major change? In the 1990s, post-Mao politics is essentially "succession politics." No leader in the generation of successors to Deng Xiaoping and Chen Yun has sufficient resources to reject coalitional politics and ignore other contenders or the interests of important regional and bureaucratic constituencies.[46] A major crackdown on corruption thus appears unlikely. Top political leaders will continue routine efforts to clean up corruption, but routine corruption will continue to be tolerated as a feature of government and economic activity.

More generally, once corruption has become as widespread as it is in China now, any scenario featuring the gradual disappearance of corruption as a regular feature of government and economic activity is unlikely. Barring a different sort of "shock" to the system, corruption is likely to continue to flourish. The experience of Hong Kong in the 1970s suggests that change is feasible, however. There, the key feature that transformed a situation of routine corruption in the economy and in government departments, especially the police department, to one in which corruption is unusual was the creation of the ICAC, a credible signal of the government's commitment to transform the situation.[47]

Can the post-Mao regime send a credible anti-corruption signal to corrupt officials and ordinary citizens alike? The essence of the problem here is the contradiction between the sort of political leadership required for a signal to be credible and the sort of political leadership that defines the post-Mao regime as essentially Leninist, the sort of leadership that all contenders in succession politics can be expected to uphold. Clarke and Feinerman point out in their survey of post-Mao criminal law that the complaint of many Chinese that "China has no law" is not in the least inconsistent with the growth of a legal infrastructure of organizations and rules since 1979. Rather, the complaint refers to something very specific: "The government is not restrained by its own rules, *and it should be*."[48] A credible signal that corruption is no longer to be tolerated must be a signal that rules matter, in this most fundamental sense. This appears unlikely in the context of what remains still an essentially Leninist system.

Notes

1. Transparency International rankings are scores for countries on perceived levels of corruption, using a ten-point scale, with lower scores signifying more corruption. The scores are country averages from at least four separate surveys. Averaging results from nine separate surveys, China's score in 1996 was 2.43. To compare, New Zealand ranked the least corrupt, with a score of 9.43, and Hong Kong ranked 18th, with a score of 7.01. See http://www.gwdg.de/~uwvw.
2. On corruption as an informal political system, see James C. Scott, *Comparative Political Corruption* (Englewood Cliffs, NJ: Prentice-Hall, 1972).
3. The concept of "kleptocracy" was introduced by Stanislav Andreski in *The African Predicament: A Study in the Pathology of Modernization* (London: Michael Joseph, 1968).
4. For good discussions tracing or analysing different approaches to defining corruption, see Arnold J. Heidenheimer, Michael Johnston, and Victor T. Levine (eds), *Political Corruption: A Handbook* (New Brunswick, NJ: Transaction Publishers, 1990), and John A. Gardiner, "Defining Corruption," *Corruption and Reform*, Vol. 7, No. 2 (1993) pp. 111–24.
5. This view is elaborated best by Susan Rose-Ackerman in *Political Corruption: A Study in Political Economy* (New York: Academic Press, 1978).
6. See Gardiner (Note 4) and Michael Johnston, "Right and Wrong in American Politics: Popular Conceptions of Corruption," *Polity*, Vol. 18, No. 3 (1986) pp. 367–91.
7. See especially "Concepts of Law in the Chinese Anti-Crime Campaign," *Harvard Law Review*, Vol. 98, No. 8 (1985), pp. 1890–1908; Timothy A. Gelatt, "The People's Republic of China and the Presumption of Innocence," *Journal of Criminal Law and Criminology*, Vol. 73, No. 1 (1982) pp. 259–316; Donald C. Clarke and James V. Feinerman, "Antagonistic Contradictions: Criminal Law and Human Rights in China," *The China Quarterly*, No. 141 (1995), pp. 135–54.
8. A public good is characterized by non-rivalry in consumption (i.e., more than one person can consume the good at a given level of supply at the same time) and non-excludability in ownership and use (i.e., no one is able to consume

the good exclusively). National defence is a good example of a public good. Typically, public goods are not supplied by private actions, but pose a classic problem of collective action: if contribution to supply is voluntary, individuals generally have no incentive to contribute because they can consume the benefits once others have contributed to the supply of the good; if no one contributes, the good will not be supplied.

9. See, for example, Supreme People's Court and Supreme People's Procuratorate, "Reply to Certain Questions about the Concrete Application of the Law in the Current Handling of Cases of Economic Crime (for Trial Implementation), 18 July 1985," in *Xin Zhongguo fan fubai tongjian* (Survey of Corruption Control in New China), edited by Li Xueqin et al. (Tianjin: Tianjin renmin chubanshe, 1993), pp. 811–16. See also the discussion in "Concepts of Law in the Chinese Anti-Crime Campaign" (Note 7).
10. Regarding the effect on the disposition of cases, Gong and others note that, when the party discipline inspection committees or government supervisory departments investigate a case, first they often fail to turn it over to the procuratorates in a timely way, even when it has become clear that it constitutes a criminal case. As a result, by the time the case reaches the procuracy, the criminals have had sufficient time to destroy evidence and cover up tracks of their crimes, and the procuracy is left with an unresolved case. See Gong Xiaobing et al., *Tanwu huilu fanzui duice lun* (Policy Measures to Counter Crimes of "Corruption" and Bribery) (Beijing: Falü chubanshe, 1991), p. 16. Regarding the substitution of party penalties for criminal punishment, see Liao Zengyun and Feng Rui, "An Analysis of the Phenomena of Corruption and Efforts and Talks of Constructing an Honest Government," *Faxue yanjiu*, No. 101 (1995), pp. 23–28, in Foreign Broadcast Information Service, *Daily Report: China* (hereafter cited as FBIS), 20 March 1996. See also "Concepts of Law in the Chinese Anti-Crime Campaign" (Note 7) and Clarke and Feinerman (Note 7).
11. In this chapter "corruption" (in quotation marks) refers to the crime of *tanwu*, which has a very specific legal content. See below.
12. See Supreme People's Courts and Supreme People's Procuratorate (Note 9).
13. See the discussion in Sun Qian, *Jiancha lilun yanjiu zongshu (1979–1989)* (A Summary of Theoretical Studies on Procuratorial Work [1979–1989]) (Beijing: Zhongguo jiancha chubanshe, 1990), pp. 29–46.
14. See Supreme People's Courts and Supreme People's Procuratorate (Note 9).
15. We could assume that public unrest reflects real increases in the incidence of corruption. Given the high cost of this sort of collective action in China and the lack of independent monitoring and reporting agencies, public unrest is probably not nuanced enough to be a reliable gauge.
16. On corruption as a key issue in the 1989 protests, see Clemens Stubbe Ostergaard and Christina Peterson, "Official Profiteering and the Tiananmen

Square Demonstrations in China," *Corruption and Reform*, Vol. 6, No. 2 (1991), pp. 87–107, and Yan Sun, "The Chinese Protests of 1989: The Issue of Corruption," *Asian Survey*, Vol. 31, No. 8 (1991), pp. 762–82.

17. The Decision was issued on 28 July 1989. It is found in Ministry of Supervision, Policy and Legislation Bureau (ed.), *Jiaqiang lianzheng jianshe jiuzheng hangye bu zheng zhi feng zhengce fagui huibian* (Compilation of Laws and Regulations on Strengthening Clean Government and Correcting Unhealthy Tendencies in Professional Work) (Beijing: Falü chubanshe, 1991), pp. 54–56.
18. See Andrew Wedeman, "Corruption and Politics," in *China Review 1995*, edited by Lo Chi Kin, Suzanne Pepper and Tsui Kai Yuen (Hong Kong: The Chinese University Press, 1996).
19. Report on the work of the Supreme People's Procuratorate, 4th session of the 8th National People's Congress, 12 March 1996, *Xinhua* (Beijing), 21 March 1996, in FBIS, 29 March 1996; *Xinhua* (Beijing), 26 September 1996, in FBIS, 26 September 1996; "Top Law Enforcers to Speak on Corruption, Commercial Crime," *South China Morning Post*, 10 March 1997, in FBIS, 10 March 1997; NPC Session Hears Court, Procuratorial Work Reports, Beijing Central People's Radio, 11 March 1997, in FBIS, 11 March 1997; *Xinhua* (Beijing), 11 March 1997, in FBIS, 11 March 1997.
20. *Xinhua* (Beijing), 24 January 1996, in FBIS, 26 January 1996; *Xinhua* (Beijing), 15 May 1996, in FBIS, 15 May 1996.
21. "Anti-Corruption Struggle Is a Basic Task in Building State Power: Premier Li Peng Answers *Liaowang* Staff Reporter's Questions," *Liaowang*, 18 March 1996, pp. 4–7, in FBIS, 1 April 1996.
22. "National Conference of Provincial, Regional, and Municipal Discipline Inspection and Supervision Organs to Exchange Case-Handling Experiences Ends, Calling for Making a Breakthrough in Handling Major or Serious Cases Within This Year," *Xinhua ribao* (Nanjing), 16 May 1996, pp. 1, 3, in FBIS, 16 May 1996.
23. *Xinhua* (Beijing), 18 December 1996, in FBIS, 18 December 1996.
24. *Zhongguo xinwen she* (Beijing), 10 June 1996, in FBIS, 10 June 1996.
25. Shen Jiyan, "The Public Perceptions of the Anticorruption Campaign," *Anhui ribao* (Hefei), 17 June 1996, p. 2, in FBIS, 17 June 1996.
26. Jen Hui-wen, "CPC Corruption Erodes Hong Kong People's Confidence," *Hsin Pao* (Hong Kong Economic Journal), 6 December 1996, p. 18, in FBIS, 6 December 1996.
27. *Xinhua* (Beijing), 24 January 1996, in FBIS, 24 January 1996.
28. See Melanie Manion, "Policy Instruments and Political Context: Transforming a Culture of Corruption in Hong Kong," presented at the 48th Annual Meeting of the Association for Asian Studies, in Honolulu, Hawaii, 11–14 April 1996.

29. Liao and Feng (Note 10). See also Gong, et al. (Note 10), pp. 95–96.
30. *Zhongguo xinwen she* (Beijing), 16 August 1996, in FBIS, 16 August 1996.
31. Ibid.
32. See the discussion in "Principal Officials from Public Security, Procuratorate, Legal and Judicial Departments on the Amended Criminal Procedural Law," *Liaowang*, 20 May 1996, pp. 10–13, in FBIS, 20 May 1996.
33. Extra-budgetary funds refers to those funds collected and used by localities, departments, and workplaces that are not entered into the national budget. The main components are the funds levied by different levels of government and administrative charges levied by different administrative departments and workplaces. Before 1993, the depreciation funds and after-tax retained funds of state enterprises also were counted as extra-budgetary funds. Based on the old definition, extra-budgetary funds in China increased from about RMB 35 billion in 1978 to 386 billion in 1992. See Sun Yong, "Manage Well and Make Good Use of Extra-Budgetary Funds," *Jingji ribao* (Economic Daily, Beijing), 20 May 1996, in FBIS, 20 May 1996.
34. Ibid.
35. Li Demin and Zheng Hongfan, "Carry Out Anti-Corruption Campaigns in a More Solid, Thoroughgoing, and Effective Way: Interviewing Fan Xinde, Press Spokesman of Central Discipline Inspection Commission," *Renmin ribao* (People's Daily, Beijing), 24 January 1996, p. 3, in FBIS, 9 February 1996.
36. Liao and Feng (Note 10).
37. *Xinhua* (Beijing), 8 February 1996, in FBIS, 9 February 1996; Cary Huang, *Hong Kong Standard*, 4 June 1996, p. 7, in FBIS, 4 June 1996.
38. See Agence France Presse (Beijing), 8 November 1995 in FBIS, 8 November 1996.
39. Ibid.
40. *Xinhua* (Beijing), 27 January 1996, in FBIS, 29 January 1996.
41. See, for example, Helena Kolenda, "One Party, Two Systems: Corruption in the People's Republic of China and Attempts to Control It," *Journal of Chinese Law*, Vol. 4, No. 2 (1990), pp. 187–232; Peter Nan-shong Lee, "Bureaucratic Corruption during the Deng Xiaoping Era," *Corruption and Reform*, Vol. 5, No. 5 (1990), pp. 19–47; Leong H. Liew, "Rent-seeking and the Two-track Price System in China," *Public Choice*, Vol. 77, No. 2 (1993), pp. 359–75; James T. Myers, "China: Modernization and 'Unhealthy Tendencies'," *Comparative Politics*, Vol. 21, No. 2 (1989), pp. 193–213; Clemens Stubbe Ostergaard, "Explaining China's Recent Political Corruption," *Corruption and Reform*, Vol. 1, No. 1 (1986), pp. 209–33.
42. For a formal elaboration in a Schelling-type tipping model, see Melanie Manion, "Corruption as an Equilibrium," mimeo, University of Rochester (September 1996).

43. In 1995, the procuracy filed more than 6,000 cases of "corruption," bribery, and other crimes involving abuse of official authority for private gain in organizations of law enforcement and the judiciary alone. *Report on the Work of the Supreme People's Procuratorate*, 4th session of the 8th National People's Congress.
44. For greater elaboration of the collective action problem when corruption is widespread, see Manion (Note 42).
45. The term is applied to suggest methods to control illegal drugs in the United States in Mark A. R. Kleiman, "Enforcement Swamping: A Positive-Feedback Mechanism in Rates of Illicit Activity," *Mathematical Computer Modelling*, Vol. 17, No. 2 (1993), pp. 65–75.
46. See the discussion in David Bachman, "The Limits on Leadership in China," *Asian Survey*, Vol. 32, No. 11 (1992), pp. 1046–62.
47. See Manion (Note 28).
48. Clarke and Feinerman (Note 7), p. 153. Emphasis in original.

3

Conducting Dialogue under Strategic Conflict: Sino-American Relations in Flux

Wu Guoguang

Introduction

In regard of the "fragile" relationship between the People's Republic of China (PRC) and the United States of America (US), the year of 1996 was remarkable.[1] However, it also demonstrated how the capable leaders of the two countries were to manage this strategically significant relationship for the post-Cold War world. This chapter will try to provide an overview of Sino-American relations in the past year through two research lines: first, it will document the major events of this relationship in 1996; secondly, it will present some analytical viewpoints to help understand these events and, further, the development of Sino-American relations in the post-Cold War era.

From the very beginning, the year of 1996 witnessed to the fact that Sino-American relations were mired in numerous disputes, ranging from China's huge bilateral trade surplus, its nuclear testing programme and alleged arms exports in violation of non-proliferation pledges, to the criticism of China's human rights records by the US and the US's sale of missiles to Taiwan. In the spring, this relationship faced the most challenging crisis since it had been normalized in 1972. It was to be the third Taiwan Straits crisis since 1949, when the PRC was established, during which the US military was to experience a potential confrontation with the People's Liberation Army (PLA), the first time since the Vietnam War. The coldest spring between the two countries since the end of the Cold War could be detected from the unusual warning by a Beijing-controlled Hong Kong newspaper that the PLA would "bury" American naval forces in the Pacific if they came too close to China's coastline along the Taiwan Straits.[2] In the summer, the two countries went to the brink of a trade war.

Fortunately, this tension did not last for the whole year; the end of 1996 saw a warming of relations between Beijing and Washington. When US President Bill Clinton met his Chinese counterpart, Jiang Zemin, in Manila, the Philippines, at the occasion of the summit of the Asian Pacific Economic Cooperation (APEC) in late November, he concluded that they had had the best meeting ever. It was reported that the two presidents had

* The author wishes to thank Professor Hsin-chi Kuan for his advice and careful reading of a draft. Thanks also go to Chau Ho Wai and Li Jiehui for their research assistance and to two anonymous reviewers for their comments. However, the author bears responsibility for errors and interpretation.

agreed to exchange state visits in the next one or two years, and they had both stressed cooperation rather than conflict.

How could the two countries manage to do like this? How could they be able to avoid the damaging effects of the crises and the storms in the relationship? In reviewing the experience of the Sino-American relationship in 1996, this author submits that between the PRC and the United States a pattern of interaction in the post-Cold War era is being shaped. Its most prominent feature is the combination of continuing strategic conflicts and skilful diplomatic negotiations. While conflicts are determined by the differences and, sometimes, confrontations between the two countries' political systems, economic status and cultural heritages, diplomatic negotiations, sometimes, result in successful cooperation and more often in alleviation of disputes, or *détente*.

Conflicts between the two countries are undeniable; while the United States has become the single power as the *status quo* hegemonic power in the post-Cold War world politics, the PRC is widely seen as a potential challenger to the current international system.[3] However, a critical problem for both sides is how to manage these conflicts. Traditionally, political disputes, cultural differences, and strategic frictions often lead countries to confrontations, as the PRC and the United States already experienced in the early years of the Cold War.[4] Since the 1970s, the two countries have developed an interacting pattern of "negotiating cooperation," as Robert Ross summarized, to manage their disputes and realize their strategic goals.[5] How do the two countries now conduct their difficult relationship? Many observers have noticed that a new framework in Sino-American relations has emerged in the post-Cold War era,[6] but what the framework is and how it works remain to be conceptualized. By examining the major events in Sino-American relations of a single but significant year, this chapter argues that both strategic conflicts and diplomatic dialogue are critical factors to understand the new framework and its dynamics. Today, Sino-American cooperation still exists, but not overall and strategically. Instead, structurally strategic conflicts become a dominating factor in shaping the background of the two countries' relationship. But, the leaders in both countries are trying hard to avoid the confrontations they experienced in the 1950s and the 1960s; they are struggling not to be enemies in the post-Cold War world. Dialogue is the major way they depend on to construct this new relationship.

The development of Sino-American relations in 1996 vividly demonstrated this combination of inevitable conflicts and the efforts to manage them through dialogue. In retrospect, Sino-American relations in 1996 could be divided into four stages, each of which offered many splendid samples to illustrate how conflicts and negotiations coexisted to dominate this crucial relationship for both countries and for the world. These four stages happened to be in accordance with the four seasons of the year: In the spring, we saw the Taiwan Straits crisis; the summer came with the storm of a trade war between China and the United States; the Beijing trip of the American National Security Adviser, Anthony Lake, in the early autumn marked alleviation of tension and the modification of the relationship, which eventually brought positive fruits at the summit meeting of the two countries in December. In the following sections, I shall review the critical events at these different stages and sketch the whole picture of Sino-American relations in the year of 1996, then try to summarize their implications for future interaction. The final paragraphs will be devoted to the analysis of the factors in domestic politics of the United States and China, respectively, and the factors in international relations that contributed to explicating the dramatic change in Sino-American relations and the shape of the new interacting pattern of instruction.

The Spring Crisis in the Taiwan Straits

The year of 1996 began with a series of disputes. In early January, an old problem on the agenda of bilateral relations since 1989, the problem of China's human rights record, developed a new momentum after a Chinese physician of the Shanghai Children's Welfare Institute, Zhang Shuyun, had fled China the previous year. Based on Zhang's report and the medical records which she smuggled out, Human Rights Watch, a New York-based organization, asserted that thousands of children had died in China's state-run orphanages from deliberate starvation, medical malpractice and staff abuse. The group concluded in a news release on 5 January that "there is compelling evidence that these astonishing death rates are the result of a deliberate policy to minimize China's population of abandoned children, many of whom have been born in violation of the country's family planning regulations and are sometimes physically or mentally handicapped."[7]

Another news report which caught the eyes of the American public about Sino-American relations in January was also negative: according to the US State Department, China had detained an American military attaché, Lieutenant-Colonel Bradley Gerdes, for 19 hours and had demanded his recall. As *The New York Times* correctly understood, since those caught spying normally are quietly ejected, "China's arrest, detention and request for the recall on an attaché who had notified the authorities of his travel plans is an indication of the tension between Beijing and Washington."[8]

Meanwhile, more importantly, two continuing disputes remained on the Sino-American diplomatic agenda. One was about intellectual property rights, which was to become a central issue in later months, which we will discuss in the next section.[9] Another was about China's supply of nuclear materials to Pakistan, which prompted Washington to threaten the use of sanctions against Beijing.

All of these were but small troubles for both China and the United States in comparison with their confrontation in the Taiwan Straits in the Spring of 1996. Since the historical trip to Beijing in 1972 by President Richard Nixon, the Taiwan issue had always occupied a central place in Sino-American relations and had frequently caused disputes and conflicts between the two countries.[10] But, it had never burst into a crisis. Things seemed to be worse this time. When President Lee Teng-hui of Taiwan visited in June 1995 Cornell University in the United States, where he had earlier obtained his doctoral degree in agriculture, the crisis began. It was first indicated by the cancellation of a series of planned visits to Washington by high-level officials from China. Then, came the military confrontation in the form of a series of war games in the Straits. In addition, Taiwan's first direct election of the President was scheduled for March 1996. It seemed to eventually legitimize the claim for the island's independence, which was absolutely unacceptable to Beijing.

In March, the month of Taiwan's presidential election, China conducted a series of missile tests and live ammunition military exercises off Taiwan, including staged M-9 surface-to-surface missiles targeting at the watery zones a few dozen miles off Kaohsiung and Keelung, two major seaports of Taiwan in south and northeast, respectively, and launched three landing war games in an arrow shape.

The United States did not play the outsider in the game despite Beijing's claim that the Taiwan issue was China's internal affairs.

Taiwan has been regarded as strategically significant by the United States. It is America's 7th-largest trading partner, with a population of 21 million people, a vibrant American-style democracy, and occupies a crucial location in the west Pacific. To show its posture of defending Taiwan's democracy, the US sent two battle groups to the area, first led by the aircraft carrier Independence, then another carrier, the Nimitz, which had passed through the Taiwan Straits on its way to the Persian Gulf in December 1995 and now was being called back to the waters off Taiwan in time for Taiwan's first direct presidential election in March. The tension climbed to a higher level, with the United States for the first time assembling its largest battle group in the Far East since the Vietnam War had ended in the mid-1970s.

Beijing stressed, as always, that "Taiwan remains the most sensitive and important issue in Sino-American relations and will determine whether the relationship will develop smoothly this year," according to the official New China (Xinhua) News Agency.[11] As China failed to keep the United States protests out of Taiwan, the protests from the Chinese government became rasping. The Chinese Foreign Minister, Qian Qichen, commented: "Taiwan is a part of China and not a protectorate of the United States." He reacted with indignation to American State Secretary Warren Christopher's statement that China's recent military threats against Taiwan were "reckless" and "irresponsible." "When I meet him," Qian said of Christopher, "I would ask him if the United States has made a decision to criticize China on its military exercises as 'reckless' and 'erroneous' move. I would also ask the United States if their decision is reckless and erroneous."[12]

The Chinese Premier, Li Peng, even clearly spotted the possible military "use of force against China" by "somebody," that is, the United States, in this Taiwan Straits crisis. He warned that "we have a powerful military force to help us carry that national interest, and we have the freedom to move around anywhere in international waters that we want to preserve. If somebody threatens the use of force against China, this, as has been shown by past experience, will not spell any good results."[13]

The Chinese official media showed a more aggressive attitude than the political leaders. To respond to American Defence Secretary William Perry's comment that "America has the best damned navy in the world" and the United States was the most powerful country in the Pacific area, a Hong Kong-based Communist newspaper, *Wen Wei Po*, whose commentaries are often used to float Beijing's opinion, sternly issued the same warning but in an unusually harsh way:

> With a concentrated fire of guided missiles and artillery, the People's Liberation Army can bury an enemy intruder in a sea of fire. Don't forget that the Taiwan Straits is just off-shore China and within the scope of naval and air war-making operations.[14]

It was said that no one wanted a war in the Taiwan Straits in 1996, since Lee Teng-hui's hope for re-election on March 23 depended on convincing the voters that he could still manage relations with Beijing to the island's advantage. Only a year ago, Jiang Zemin had emphasized China's patience in pursuing peaceful reunification, and Bill Clinton did not want his handling of China to become an issue in his presidential campaign. But, as an American commentator analysed, "Taiwan's miscalculations, China's emotional reactions and the United States' inattention have created tensions that could escalate into combat soon after Taiwan's election. Such a war would not only threaten Taiwan's democracy but also finish any hopes of America's building a constructive relationship with China."[15]

But, Sino-American relations were not destroyed by this crisis. One major reason was behind the screen communication and negotiations between the two countries. This time, according to the American media, the two countries conducted in secret a series of visits of senior officials. This was quite different from the situations during two previous Taiwan Straits crises, which had happened in 1954–1955 and 1958, respectively. While the Chinese military began live ammunition exercises off Taiwan in early March, mainland Chinese officials tried to send unambiguous signals to the United States that China did not intend to invade or attack Taiwan.[16] While his colleagues in Beijing at the news conferences condemned the voyage of the American carrier Nimitz, Liu Huaqiu, the deputy foreign minister of the PRC, visited the US as a special messenger of Beijing and met privately with the US national security adviser, Anthony Lake, at American Ambassador to France Pamela Harriman's farm in Middleburg, Virginia. It was reported that Liu assured his American hosts that China would not take real military action towards Taiwan in this crisis.[17] The conclusion of their day long meeting was an "understanding" that went like this: The US would use its influence to restrain Taiwan from any further far-reaching moves towards independence, and in return Beijing would not use military force to resolve its current dispute with Taipei.[18]

The Summer Storm of a Trade War

As the crisis in the Taiwan Straits eased after the presidential election in Taiwan on 24 March, Sino-American relations still faced a series of difficulties. The issues which had emerged at the beginning of the year remained unresolved, and they were now moved up the agenda, after both countries had tried to play down the issues during the spring crisis.

These issues were about nuclear weapon technology proliferation, trade, and human rights.

At the beginning of the year, the United States accused China of selling Pakistan nuclear weapons technology. It was detected and reported by the Central Intelligence Agency (CIA) that China had sold 5,000 special ring magnets to Pakistan, which could be used to refine bomb-grade uranium, and the deal violated an American law designed to limit the spread of nuclear weapon technology. The Clinton Administration also faced a difficult decision in punishing China with economic sanctions, which could hurt American business. On the other hand, the Chinese side had refused to admit any wrong doing; they said the magnets were not on any list of forbidden products and refused to promise to refrain from such behaviour in the future.

"Sanction" eventually became a word most frequently used in negotiating Sino-American relations in the summer of 1996. The most prominent trouble for Washington and Beijing in the summer was about bilateral trade problems, especially the issue of intellectual property rights. In April, the Clinton Administration delivered a sharp warning in private to Chinese leaders. It stated that China's failure to comply with a 1995 agreement on copyright piracy of American products was undercutting the Administration's credibility in Congress and would force tariff sanctions on up to $2 billion in Chinese imports.[19]

In an early-May report to Congress, the Clinton Administration concluded that Beijing had failed to rein in the piracy of American video cassettes, compact disks, computer softwares and other products, and still designated China as the most egregious violator of agreements intended to combat the piracy. Meanwhile, the annual discussion about the renewal of China's most-favoured-nation (MFN) status in the trade with the United States got into the final stage in Washington, which always stirs up concerns with China's human rights record.

To that point, the question of how to deal with China on a range of issues including trade, human rights and the spread of nuclear technology became the Clinton Administration's most sensitive policies and political concerns. The storm moment finally came on 15 May. After months of issuing warnings to China, the Clinton Administration published a list of $3 billion worth of Chinese goods that could be subject to the largest trade sanctions ever imposed by Washington if Beijing refused to close factories that pirated American softwares and music.[20]

Unlike the behaviour about the nuclear weapon technology export,

China responded to this warning with a positive and cooperative posture. It undertook a nationwide crackdown against compact disc piracy and all other forms of copyright theft. Clearly, China was trying to send the United States a message that it was serious about stamping out the piracy of intellectual property. The Foreign Ministry spokesman, Shen Guofang, stressed that "the Chinese side has taken earnest measures." According to a Chinese official report, in the first five months of the year customs officials had seized about 80,000 pirate CDs and video discs that had been destined for export.[21]

When US officials talked about imposing trade sanctions on China, however, Beijing showed that it had prepared to retaliate heavily. According to the message sent by the Chinese Foreign Ministry spokesman, China would respond immediately with a list of its own sanctions, amounting to even more than the American penalty, if Washington proceeded with its threat to impose 100% tariffs on a long list of China-made goods. Therefore, upon the announcement of the sanction list by the United States, the Chinese government confirmed that it would retaliate within minutes by threatening to block new American investments and to place enormous tariffs on American automobiles, telecommunication equipment and other goods.[22]

The general ongoing background of the bilateral trade between China and the United States also contributed to intensify their trade disputes in the summer. In June 1996, for the first time on record, China surpassed Japan as the largest source of the American trade deficit, according to a report by the US Commerce Department. This development was seen to further strain relations between Washington and Beijing. The deficit with China climbed in June to US$ 3.3 billion, or 40% of the total American imbalance, which was driven mainly by American imports of toys, apparels, footwear and household goods.

But, the publishing of the sanction list by both sides did not mean Beijing and Washington were giving up their last-ditch negotiations on the issues of intellectual property rights and bilateral trade; rather, it could be interpreted as a strategy for strengthening each side's own position in the trade negotiations. Actually, at the last moment before the US deadline set for sanction went into force, the negotiators of the two countries sped up their negotiating work. They engaged in marathon talks in Beijing in mid-June, even spending the weekend bargaining. They finally avoided a trade war at the last moment by reaching a broad agreement on fighting the piracy of music, movies and computer softwares.[23]

Another example at that time also demonstrated the positive attitudes taken by both Beijing and Washington at constructing their relationship free of friction. Just during the intensive days of trade negotiations, an arms smuggling action conducted by China's state-owned companies was revealed in media reports; it was likely to further complicate Washington's quickly deteriorating relations with Beijing. In late May, US federal agents charged the China North Industrial Corporation and Poly Technologies, both owned by the PLA, of smuggling 2,000 AK-47 fully automatic rifles into the United States. The president of Poly Technologies was He Ping, a son-in-law of Deng Xiaoping's, China's paramount leader.[24] Washington could have used the event to embarrass Chinese leaders, but it did not do so, and both the Chinese and the American governments took a low profile in this scandal despite the pressure from the public and the media.

Certainly, both Beijing and Washington well understood that a trade war between the United States and China could prove costly to both countries. Unlike Washington's threatened tariff spike on Japanese luxury cars in 1995, the American victims of a trade conflict with China would not be the most affluent consumers. Low-income families, especially those that relied on inexpensive clothes, would be forced to pay higher prices. In fact, the National Retail Federation, an American organization representing businesses around the country, complained in a statement that the administration was protecting Hollywood at the expense of middle-class wage earners who bought their clothes at discount stores.[25]

The Modification in the Autumn

During the months of tension between Washington and Beijing, US President Clinton was preparing to send some positive signals to Beijing, which finally led to the modification of the relationship in the autumn. The visit to Beijing in July by Anthony Lake, the national security adviser to the US President, was decisive. It was the highest ranking administration visit to China in two years, since Secretary of State Warren Christopher and Secretary of Defence William J. Perry had visited Beijing in 1994.

Lake's Beijing trip aimed at trying to ease continuing and growing frictions between the two countries. Before his departure, the American media sounded positive towards China, which had not been the case for a long time. For example, a former Undersecretary of State in the Bush Administration, Robert Zoellick, suggested in the OP-ED page of

The Washington Post to "let China join the club" at the G-7 Economic Summit.[26] More importantly, President Clinton "delinked" China's MFN status in its trade with the United States from its human rights record in June, settling the continuing dispute on MFN since the Tiananmen massacre in 1989, once again to the advantage of American business.[27]

On this side of the Pacific, China also reciprocated with the coming modification. It promised to drop its insistence on carrying out "peaceful nuclear explosions." The move meant that for the first time all five nuclear powers — the United States, Russia, Britain, France, and China — were on record as supporting a ban on all nuclear explosions, without loopholes, thus removing a major obstacle to the signing of a comprehensive nuclear test ban treaty with a deadline of 28 June, a key priority of the Clinton Administration.

In Beijing, Lake spent two days in meetings with his Chinese counterpart, Liu Huaqiu, director of the PRC State Council's Foreign Affairs Office. After working out the details, Lake met with President Jiang Zemin, discussed economic cooperation and trade with Prime Minister Li Peng, and talked about Taiwan with Defence Minister Chi Haotian. In general, Lake stressed that "it's very important that China understand that the US does want to see China sharing world leadership," while his associates described the main purpose of this visit as a means to construct a bond of "mutual expectations." According to senior American officials, Lake's main approach to the talks was "the need precisely to anticipate problems, or at least figure out how to manage them jointly, or to contain any damage that might be caused."[28]

Similarly, the Chinese side thought that "common interests between China and the United States are far more numerous than our differences," according to a Foreign Ministry spokesman. In his meeting with Lake, Chinese President Jiang suggested the "16-characters principles" for the Sino-American relationship: "increase trust, reduce troubles, develop cooperation, and do not make confrontation."[29]

The major fruit of the Lake trip was the tentative arrangements for the mutual visits by the presidents. Now, both China and the United States expected President Clinton to visit China in 1997. In return, President Jiang Zemin would visit Washington, though no final decisions were made. Also, Vice-President Al Gore of the United States accepted in principle a long-standing invitation to attend a conference on sustainable development in Beijing, which was scheduled in early 1997. All of these arrangements attested to an apparent warming in relations.

However, all three issues had only receded, but remained unresolved. In fact, not only all three issues but all other difficulties were not settled after Lake's visit. For example, the sale of missiles by the US to Taiwan remained a major dispute in the relationship. In addition, China was critical to US's action in Iraq.

As we have found of the experience of Sino-American relations in the previous months, the difficulties did not prevent officials of the two countries from contacting each other and having intensive negotiations. Following Lake's Beijing trip, another meeting of high-ranking officials of the two countries was conducted. This was the meeting of Qian Qichen, the Chinese Foreign Minister, and his American counterpart, Warren Christopher, in Jakarta, Indonesia, during an international conference. They emphasized the positive aspects of the difficult relationship, while touching only generally on areas of intense disagreement, including the Taiwan issue and China's human rights record. More importantly, the two sides agreed on an ambitious schedule of high-level meetings that could lead to the first Chinese-American summit meeting since 1992. According to an American senior official, this meeting outlined a series of cabinet-level meetings planned before the end of the year on trade, the economy, the military, national security, and science and technology.[30] Based on progress in recent months, including the extension of China's MFN trade status, the easing of the tensions over Taiwan, the agreement on intellectual property rights, discussions on nuclear proliferation, and China's continued cooperation with the United States regarding North Korea, Sino-American relations entered a "constructive and productive" stage.

The Warm Winter of Beijing-Washington Relations

On 6 November, Bill Clinton was re-elected President, which greatly strengthened his internal political position and, correspondingly, his bargaining power in foreign policies. China congratulated Clinton. "We are ready to work with the US side for further progress," said the spokesman of the Chinese Foreign Ministry, Cui Tiankai, "now a good opportunity has presented itself for improving and expanding Sino-American relations."[31]

In Clinton's second term, adjusting his policy towards China and maintaining a good relationship with China were now a priority on his foreign policy agenda. As an editorial of *The Washington Post* expressed, now the United States needed a "fair and firm" approach towards China. The article said:

> A prime candidate for reassessment as President Clinton approaches his second term is policy toward China. In this area, the president does not have the luxury of waiting until a secretary of state was in place, for Mr. Clinton travels to Asia this week for meetings with his Chinese counterpart and other regional leaders. Making Asia his first post-election destination properly conveys the importance of cross-Pacific relations, but it also increases the pressure to think strategically about China.[32]

Only two days after the editorial had been published, American Secretary of State Christopher arrived in Beijing, and this trip was regarded as "strategic," as it was to bring a *détente* in Sino-American relations. The last time he had visited China, in March 1994, the Secretary had got into a dispute with his hosts over human rights. This time, human rights were still on the agenda but carefully managed. Before Christopher's arrival in Beijing, the Chinese government had just finished another wave of crackdown on leading dissidents, including Wang Dan, a student leader in the 1989 Tiananmen movement. But, the Clinton Administration intended to build a relationship with China that would not be hostile to any particular issue, according to State Department officials, although they denied that they were playing down human rights problems. Now, the United States stressed a "more constructive attitude" for the politically sensitive issue through "more structured channels," and "in a productive way."[33]

Michael McCurry, President Clinton's spokesman, talked about the similar point with a higher authoritativeness. He said:

> It's been very tough going in the area of human rights. There has not been progress that the President would see as sufficient. But the struggle for human rights, for freedom and for democracy is clearly one that is a long-term struggle when it comes to societies that are having a hard time adjusting to the realities of the world we now live in.[34]

This "long-term struggle" approach could be interpreted as one aspect of the strategic thinking. Thus, the two sides now made "useful progress" with respect to nuclear nonproliferation and other important issues. On the nuclear issue, China agreed to establish a comprehensive, nationwide system for tracking exports of nuclear materials. The decision marked a step towards the implementation of a 1985 agreement on nuclear cooperation designed to enable US companies to participate in nuclear energy projects in China.[35]

As the Beijing-Washington relationship was being mended, China also sent some high-ranking officials to the United States. Such prominent figures included Xu Kuangdi, mayor of Shanghai, and Defence Minister Chi Haotian, whose visit had been postponed again and again due to tensions between the two countries before it was finally to be realized in December.

The summit meeting between Chinese President Jiang Zemin and American President Bill Clinton in Manila on 24 November pushed the healing Sino-American relations to a culmination in the zigzag year of 1996. They confirmed the tentative arrangements to exchange state visits between Jiang and Clinton in the following two years. Mr Clinton said the session "went very well" and they engaged in "a real conversation." Furthermore, he thought this meeting with Jiang had been the best one among their four meetings. While disclaiming "any euphoria or *naïveté*," Winston Lord, American Assistant Secretary of State for East Asian and Pacific Affairs, concluded that "clearly, the relationship has stabilized and gained momentum from where we were last spring."[36]

Conducting Dialogue under Conflict: The Strategy to Manage the Relationship

Sino-American relations in 1996 demonstrated that dialogue was the major method through which the leaders of the two countries pursued to manage the conflicts they faced.

This phenomenon is much different from the interactions between the two countries in the 1950s and the 1960s, when conflicts had led them to confrontation. Also, the pattern of "strategic cooperation" that had characterized the relationship between the United States and the Soviet Union in the 1970s and the 1980s seems not to apply in the Sino-American case.[37] Now the situation is featured with such a combination: the structural conflicts continue to create tension, storms, and crises in the relationship; both the PRC and the United States prefer to negotiate rather than confront each other; and, negotiations always have a high priority on the agenda of the leaders of the two countries.

As we have seen, although the relationship between China and the United States echoed certain scenarios from the Cold War years, such as the Taiwan Straits crisis, however, the top leaders of the two sides had frequent meetings (Table 1). Furthermore, even though arranging these

Table 1: Some Meetings between China and US High-ranking Officials in 1996

12–15 February	Lee Sands, assistant US trade representative, visited Beijing for negotiations on intellectual property rights;
8 March	Liu Huaqiu, director of the Foreign Affairs Office of the State Council, visited Washington and met Anthony Lake, American President's national security advisor;
16 March	Chinese and American Treasury Ministers, Liu Zhongli and Rubin, had a meeting in Tokyo;
around 20 March	deputy secretary of State for Non-proliferation, Robert Einhorn, visited Beijing;
26–28 March	in Beijing, three-day talks between Chinese and American officials on textiles import;
early April	Charlene Barshefsky, acting US trade representative, visited Beijing for negotiations;
19 April	Chinese Foreign Minister Qian Qichen had a meeting with US State Secretary Warren Christopher in the Hague;
13–14 May	in Beijing, Lee Sands had talks with his Chinese counterparts on piracy;
20 May	US President Clinton announced that he would renew China's MFN status;
early June	Lee Sands visited Beijing for talks on intellectual property rights;
17 June	Chinese President Jiang Zemin met Charlene Barshefsky;
25–28 June	an American Deputy Defence Secretary visited Beijing and met Chinese defence Minister Chi Haotian;
Around 25 June	George Bush, former US President, visited China;
early July	an American Deputy National Security Advisor visited China;
6–10 July	Anthony Lake visited China, met Jiang Zemin, Li Peng, Qian Qichen, and Chi Haotian;
24 July	Qian Qichen met Christopher in Jakarta, Indonesia;
mid-September	a PLA general, Zhou Youliang, visited the US;
late September	a Chinese official responsible for Taiwan affairs, Tang Shubei, visited the US;
25 September	in New York, Qian Qichen had his third meeting with Christopher in 1996;
early November	mayor of Shanghai, Xu Kuangdi, visited the US;
20 November	Christopher visited China;
24 November	Presidents Jiang and Clinton met in Manila;
early December	Chinese Defence Minister Chi Haotian visited the US;

Sources: *The New York Times*, *The Washington Post*, *South China Morning Post*, *Ming Pao*, and *People's Daily*; various issues in 1996.

meetings were sometimes difficult, plagued by cancellations and postponements, the meetings bore substantive fruits.

Both the Taiwan Straits crisis and the intellectual property rights dispute can be used to illustrate the argument. For the first event, we have already discussed the secret talks between senior Chinese diplomat Liu Huaqiu and American national security adviser Anthony Lake in an earlier section of this chapter. It should be stressed that such communication was not conducted along a single line. For example, while the American navy was in danger of confronting the PLA during the crisis off the Taiwan Straits, the Clinton Administration released information that it would like to renew China's MFN status, which should be finally decided in June each year, as early as March through a television interview with Mr Lake.[38] Just after the crisis, on 20 April, American Secretary of State Warren Christopher had a meeting with Chinese Foreign Minister Qian Qichen in The Hague. This was their 16th meeting in the last four years. In the single year of 1996 alone, they had four meetings.

Also, both sides could cooperate in some minor events. For example, even during the days of tense relations in spring and summer, the US and China could reach agreement to address problems like rapid urbanization, pollution, energy consumption, and changing agricultural patterns.[39]

Sino-American negotiations about intellectual property rights also vividly exemplified the argument advanced in this chapter. Charlene Barshefsky, the acting United States trade representative and a tough negotiator in the eyes of Beijing, visited China twice for trade talks in 1996. In addition, her associates travelled to Beijing many times in 1996. They made these efforts not for the final trade sanctions on China, but for the dialogue aiming to resolve problems. To help get to this end, the US government showed its willingness to compromise. For example, just between Barshefsky's trips, the Clinton Administration called for the unconditional renewal of MFN status for China. In a similar vein, China wanted the US to continue the trade talks. Now, it was China which condemned the "Cold War thinking" and called for downgrading "political factors."[40]

When Chinese President Jiang stressed his "16-characters principle," US President Clinton also tried to make an U-turn in his policy towards China. Four years before, when governor of Arkansas Bill Clinton had run for President in 1992, he had accused George Bush of "coddling dictators" to promote trade with China, and had announced that he would fight the dictatorships "from Baghdad to Beijing." The year of 1996 was another election year, and Clinton was seeking re-election. This time, however, he conceded that he did not understand the complexity of America's relationship with the world's most populous nation. *The New*

York Times commented: "Mr. Clinton is unashamed of his learning curve, however steep. He admits to an early mistake on China, and came to believe that revoking Beijing's trading status with the United States would do nothing to improve its record on human rights or enhance Asian stability."[41]

According to the same source, the President's national security adviser, Anthony Lake, now stressed "an atmosphere of mutual respect and confidence, within which we can pursue issues of interest to us and to them."[42] Clinton himself put the points in this way:

> I concluded that if we were to revoke MFN we might cause serious short-term damage to them economically, but that they would not change their human rights policies — if anything, they would become more repressive — and that we would risk creating a new, I hesitate to say, cold war, but a very long-term fissure with a country that I think we still have some chance to influencing in a very positive way, to be a constructive partner in the 21st century.[43]

Here we need to note that, even though President Clinton mentioned the word "partner" and the US was eager to improve relations with China, the American governmental policy toward China was still cautious to avoid a close "partnership" with the communist country. After the summer when Christopher met Qian in Jakarta and the relationship was slowly mended, one of his senior associates stressed that "we are realistic and we know that this relationship, because of conflicting perspectives and cultures and ideologies, is always going to be difficult to manage."[44] In mid-November, when Christopher visited China and prepared to deliver a speech at Fudan University, he removed the word "partnership" from the speech title and replaced it with "cooperation," even though the previous edition of the speech draft had already been sent to his Chinese sponsor and even though President Clinton had talked about "a partnership with China" in Canberra in his trip to Australia at the same time. The American Ambassador to China, James Sasser, explained this change in this way: "I don't think we're in a position yet to say we're partners. But there's increasing understanding and cooperation between the two countries."[45]

In light of the above, the increasing cooperation cannot mean that the entire relationship between China and the United States in 1996 and the previous years had reached the level of a "strategic cooperation," as it had been witnessed between the US and the former Soviet Union during the late Cold War era. As Christopher carefully defined in his speech, "distance and differences have blinded us to our common hopes and interests, creating distorted images of each other that drive us apart." There was now an "opportunity to build a new era of cooperation for a new century."[46] Yes, the era of cooperation could emerge in the future, but not right now.

American Election and Chinese Nationalism: Domestic Constraints

When examining Sino-American relations in 1996, we must not neglect some domestic factors in both China and the United States, or international factors, such as Japan and Russia. All of them had substantial impacts on the relationship under discussion in 1996. First, I will discuss the effects of the presidential elections in the United States and the rise of nationalism in China as domestic political constraints on Sino-American relations; secondly, I will turn to examine how Japan and Russia influenced Sino-American relations in the year of 1996.

In discussing Lake's Beijing visit and the tentative exchange of state visits between Clinton and Jiang Zemin, *The New York Times* said, "the timing works for both sides. Mr. Clinton has his eye on the November election, and wants the Chinese to help avoid any diplomatic blow-ups beforehand. President Jiang Zemin has his eye on the Communist Party Congress in October 1997."[47] As Jiang cut deals and tried to sideline domestic rivals, welcoming an American President would, as the Chinese would say, give Jiang a lot of face.

Clinton's campaign for re-election and, later, his triumph played a critical part in the United States' policy on China in 1996. An editorial in *The Washington Post* observed during the campaign season, "it isn't true that foreign policy rarely counts in presidential campaigns. Even when no wars or crises take center stage, as now, a candidate's ability to earn the world's respect provides an important subtext to every presidential debate."[48] Only in this sense, can we understand Clinton's decision to send the carriers to the Taiwan Straits in the spring, which was followed by another similar, but much bolder, order to attack Iraq in the summer.

To show his maturity in foreign affairs as well as courage, Clinton paid a great deal of attention to American economic interests in dealing with international relations. One observer found that one of Mr Clinton's proudest achievements "is his success in linking American foreign policy with the domestic economy and jobs."[49] Similarly to Richard Nixon's elevation of the National Security Council as a counterweight to the State

Department and the Pentagon, Mr Clinton created the National Economic Council to coordinate domestic and foreign economic policy. In one of the biggest policy arguments, that is, confronting China on its piracy of intellectual property, it was reported that the Departments of Treasury and Commerce and the trade representative had been major players. "Trade and international economics have joined the foreign-policy table," the former trade representative and then Secretary of Commerce Mickey Kantor said, "Clinton is the first President to really make trade a bridge between foreign and domestic policy."[50]

It is only with this policy background that we can better understand the events like the summer storm over a trade war between the United States and China and its final breathing release, as we indicated in the previous discussion. Similarly, only by focusing on this close foreign-domestic economic connection, can we better understand how Clinton won his presidential campaign in 1996 in spite of the fact that he had broken his promise on China policy.

For the Chinese side, domestic economic construction and leadership succession were also primary concerns in policy making with regard to the United States.[51] However, there was a new phenomenon in China's internal affairs in 1996 which substantively affected its international perception and, correspondingly, its diplomatic behaviour. This new phenomenon was the rise of nationalism.

To delve into the recent emergence of Chinese nationalism is not the key task here. My major concern is with its impact on Sino-American relations. It is perhaps a little bold to generalize that China's new nationalism has a strong colour of anti-Americanism, but it is not far from the truth. An early signal appeared in the autumn of 1995, when a survey among young people conducted in September by the *China Youth Daily* indicated that 87.1% of the respondents regarded the United States as the most unfriendly country towards China. In March 1996, an American writer noted how Chinese people were involved in a "nationalist tide" when facing the Taiwan Straits tension, and even those "veteran" leaders of Chinese democratic movements now told Americans to remember how "the US barred China from getting the Olympics, the US bars China from the World Trade Organization, the US encourages Taiwan's independence." In a word, "it is the US that is keeping China from assuming its rightful place in the world."[52]

A much more radical form of Chinese nationalism was expressed in a popular book, *China Can Say No* (*Zhongguo keyi shuo bu*), which was published in Beijing in June, on the eve of the final Sino-American negotiation about intellectual property piracy, trade, and economic sanctions.[53] The book became an instant best-seller in Beijing in the summer of 1996, with 50,000 copies sold of the first print, partially due to its echoing popular nationalist sentiments and partially due to the Americans' own overheated attention. The authors recounted their own personal experiences which evolved from admiring to reviling the United States, and a book review published by a government-sponsored English-language news weekly concluded that "it may well reflect views shared by many others."[54] *The Washington Post* identified the book as an "anti-American book,"[55] since its authors had suggested "burning down Hollywood," advocated war with Taiwan, professed admiration for Iran-backed Hezbollah guerrillas in Lebanon, warned against infiltration by the CIA, and claimed the agency had promoted sexual promiscuity among Chinese students in the 1980s.

There were some other books of a similar tone, which created a "fever of nationalism" in the press. Some high-ranking officials were involved in writing and supporting the books. For example, a former Chinese Ambassador to the United States, Chai Zemin, prefaced a book entitled *Record of Confrontation between China and the United States*, to the effect that no country was allowed to impose its own will on other countries. It was exactly what the Chinese government had repeated to the face of Americans. The rise in nationalism obviously offered a "public opinion card" for Beijing in its dealing with Washington. What was especially interesting was the ban of the book *China Can Say No* by the Chinese government in the winter after Sino-American relations had improved, whereas many government-controlled media had recommended the same book in the summer. The whole story may be regarded as a unique conduct of diplomacy by an authoritarian regime, as domestic resources were mobilized in dealing with the United States.

Japan and Russia: External Factors in International Power Game

The dynamic structure of international politics in the post-Cold War era definitely had a substantive influence on Sino-American interactions in 1996. Japan and Russia, as the evidence shows, were the most prominent and active factors which directly or indirectly affected how China and the

United States interacted with one another. Now, let me briefly discuss these external factors in the Sino-American relations.

The Japan Factor

As China is rising to become a regional economic and military power in the post-Cold War Asian-Pacific area, the first country that should feel threatened is Japan rather than the United States. However, if Japan were to rise to become an aggressive political and military power along its current economic power, which country would be more seriously challenged, China or the US? There seems to be no answer so far, but the Sino-American relationship has indeed been affected by this question. In February 1996, Thomas Friedman, a columnist on foreign affairs, made his viewpoint in "whisper" that "what will keep the US and Japan together in the coming decade is China."[56]

The speculation on the possible future could be quite different for some other American scholars and policy makers. For example, Ezra Vogel, a leading scholar in both fields of China and Japan studies and a professor at Harvard University, stressed that the US should keep its troops in Japan, not for counterweighing China's influence, but for controlling the possible rise of Japanese expansionism.[57] Similarly, Joseph Nye, a former US assistant secretary of Defence and now the dean of the J. F. Kennedy School of Government at Harvard University, argued that the Chinese had the will, even though reluctantly, to allow the American military to remain in Asia, although they had always said in public that no country should have the right to put its troops outside its own borders, just because of China's concerns about the dangers of Japanese militarism.[58]

In the first half of 1996, the Clinton Administration reinforced its close relations with Japan, while it was involved in a series of disputes with China. In April, President Clinton visited Tokyo and reaffirmed the American-Japanese security alliance. After his last trip to Japan three years ago, one dominated by vicious disputes over trade, Clinton returned there to a "changed strategic landscape." The American media described the situation as "with Japan seeming a reduced economic threat, and China seeming a larger military one."[59] Therefore, Clinton's new emphasis on relations with Japan was to put the trade disputes aside and strengthen the two countries' political and security cooperation. To justify this policy, the Administration acknowledged that diplomacy was "something larger than trade."

China, of course, expressed its concern about this security cooperation between the US and Japan, which, once regarded as a vehicle to contain the former Soviet Union, might now shift its focus towards China. The Chinese Foreign Ministry spokesman stressed, "the Japan-U.S. treaty on the guarantee of security is a bilateral arrangement left over from history, and such an arrangement should not go beyond its bilateral dimension." He continued, "if the Japanese self-defense forces further build up their armaments and expand the scope of their defense, that would be bound to trigger concern and vigilance from all Asian nations. It is our hope that Japan will move with caution."[60]

Through the summer and the autumn, the development in the East Asian security situation changed somehow. The action taken on the Diaoyu Islands by the Japanese seemed to remind the United States that Japan could be an aggressive and powerful threat in this area. Furthermore, to keep a balance between Japan and China would be the best choice for the American interests. Meanwhile, major political parties announced in the Japanese general election in October that they did not "steadfastly" support "full-time presence" of American troops in Japan. A leader of the Democratic Party asked questions in this way: "Japan is an independent country. Should we have the bases of a foreign country eternally, forever?" Although the Japanese government did not hold such a position, these questions did reflect the sentiment of many Japanese voters.[61] Such development, this chapter argues, helped the United States and China improve their relationship.

The Russia Factor

The strategic triangular relationship among China, the Soviet Union, and the United States had disappeared with the end of the Cold War,[62] but Russia remained a critical and influential factor in Sino-American relations. The Americans now had not enough of the Russia card to play in counterweighing China, while China played the card successfully in the post-Cold War era, especially in 1996.

In recent years, both China and Russia had moved fast to improve relations with each other. When President Boris Yeltsin first visited China in 1992, the two countries quickly settled the last territorial disputes and signed three joint declarations concerning their relations. They exchanged extensive visits of top leaders, including that of the "three big" in China, President Jiang Zemin, Prime Minister Li Peng, and National People's Congress Chairman Qiao Shi, all in 1996, while Russian President Boris Yeltsin had trips to Beijing and Shanghai in April of the same year. On

26 April in Shanghai, the same city where the first Sino-American communiqué had been signed, China, Russia, Kazakhstan, Kirghizia, and Tadzhikistan signed an agreement on mutual trust in military affairs in the border areas.[63] Since then, Sino-Russian relations have leaped from a "constructive partnership" to a "strategic partnership." The "constructive partnership" signifies good-neighbourly relations between two countries that are neither enemies nor allies; the "strategic partnership" connotes all-round political, economic, and military cooperation. China and Russia have, not only established a mechanism for their Prime Ministers' regular meetings, but also set up a Kremlin-Zhongnanhai hotline. They have yet to restore the fraternity that existed between them in the 1950s. They are on the verge of doing so.

China could use this close relationship with Russia as a "strong card" in dealing with the United States, which in turn is a part of China's overall efforts to strengthen its position in the world in opposition to the perceived containment strategy of the West as led by the United States.[64]

How the triangle relations among China, Russia, and the United States shape world politics in the future remains unclear. So far, the Russian factor has contributed to the improvement in Sino-American relations; at least it has helped prevent the United States from adopting a strategy of containment by turning to "comprehensive engagement." A senior official of the US State Department admitted, "unlike our approach to the Soviet Union, when we had a large number of good allies, we'd have not a single ally in Asia to help us carry it out," he said of possibly containing China. "You'd cause great strains with Japan, Korea and all of Southeast Asia, let alone Australia."[65] According to President Clinton himself, the great security questions facing the United States in the 21st century is to be closely related to China and Russia. The president summarized those questions as follows:

> How will China and Russia define their greatness? Will they define their greatness in terms of their internal achievements and what kind of values and character they have, what kind of economic achievements they can have, how they can bring their culture to bear on more of their people, how they can solve their problems? How will they define their greatness in terms of their ability to force others beyond their borders to yield to their rule?[66]

In fact, such questions also face the United States in defining its own great power status. Naturally, the triangular relationship remains crucial for world politics in the next century and, particularly, for how China and the United States interact with each other.

Conclusion

The year of 1996 witnessed a crucial juncture where the relationship between China and the United States turned from potential confrontation to tentative cooperation. What played a critical role in shaping such a change was the continuing dialogue conducted between the leaders of the two countries. The experience of Sino-American relations in this year offered plenty of examples for illustrating that dialogue and negotiation could help the two giant countries avoid another "cold war," even though conflicts existed between them, ranging from military crisis to trade disputes, from human rights quarrels to nuclear proliferation, which made the situation quite similar to the world politics of the late 1940s, when the Cold War originated.[67] The "keep-in-touch" and "long-term struggle" approaches contributed much to the improvement of the relationship, which exemplified that statesmen's strategic choice could be crucial in the handling of deep-rooted conflicts, such as those between China and the United States. Even though the leaders of both countries well understood that many disputes between them had originated from the facts that China was rising to be a great power and a potential challenger to the United States in political, economic, military, cultural, and even environmental spheres, they also well knew that frequent and effective dialogue was critical.

To conduct dialogue is by no means easy. One of the difficulties is how to manage the domestic pressures on the two-level games of international negotiations.[68] Particularly, the hardline forces have been growing in recent years in both countries. In China, nationalism has risen again, and a branch of it is taking quite an extreme stand, while the White House still faces a strong Republican Congress even as Clinton, a Democrat, has won his re-election. But, some factors which have helped "engaging" rather than "containing" relations between the United States and China still exist at both the domestic and international levels. At the domestic level, the reciprocal economic interests stand prominently. At the international level, the possible threat of Japan, keeps the United States' willing to improve its relations with China, and China's growing ties with Russia strengthens China's capability to bargain with the US.

Both China and the United States now have clearer and more modest attitudes towards one another. The United States' China policy now steers a middle ground between appeasement and containment, while China follows its 16-character principle. Accordingly, the Sino-American relationship is moving between open confrontation and close cooperation. It seems that, in the future, issues like nuclear proliferation, human rights, trade disputes, and Taiwan, will remain areas of conflicts and continue appearing on the agenda of negotiations. To manage them, the 1996 experience of dialogue should be helpful for the leaders of the two countries.

Notes

1. The word "fragile" is quoted from Harry Harding, *A Fragile Relationship: The United States and China since 1972* (Washington, DC: The Brookings Institution, 1992).
2. *Wen Wei Po*, 22 March 1996.
3. This assumption is based on a theory about the hegemonic change in world politics, as elaborated by Robert Gilpin, in his *War and Change in World Politics* (Cambridge: Cambridge University Press, 1981).
4. For the confrontation between the PRC and the US in the 1950s and the 1960s and related interacting patterns, see, for example, Chen Jian, *China's Road to the Korean War: The Making of the Sino-American Confrontation* (New York: Columbia University Press, 1994); J. H. Kalicki, *The Patterns of Sino-American Crises: Political-Military Interactions in the 1950s* (Cambridge: Cambridge University Press, 1975).
5. Robert S. Ross, *Negotiating Cooperation: The United Stated and China, 1969–1989* (Stanford: Stanford University Press, 1995).
6. See, for instance, James T. H. Tang, "From Tiananmen to Blake Island: 'Re-normalizing' Sino-American Relations in the Post-Cold War Era," in *China Review 1994*, edited by Maurice Brosseau and Lo Chi Kin (Hong Kong: The Chinese University Press, 1994), pp. **6**.1–**6**.19; Judith F. Kornberg, "Comprehensive Engagement: New Frameworks for Sino-American Relations," *The Journal of East Asian Affairs*, Vol. 10, No. 1 (Winter/Spring 1996), pp. 13–44.
7. Patrick E. Tyler, "U.S. Rights Group Asserts China Lets Thousands of Orphans Die," *The New York Times*, 6 January 1996.
8. Tim Weiner, "China Detains U.S. Attaché and Seeks Recall," *The New York Times*, 17 January 1996.
9. For the early quarrel on this issue in 1996, see, for example, Seth Faison, "Copyright Pirates Prosper in China despite Promises," *The New York Times*, 20 February 1996.
10. For reviews and studies on this issue and its impact on Sino-American relations, see, for instance, Doak A. Barnett, *U.S. Arms Sale: The China-Taiwan Tangle* (Washington, DC: The Brookings Institution, 1982); William M. Bueler, *U.S. China Policy and the Problem of Taiwan* (Westport:

Greenwood Press, 1980); June Grasso, *Truman's Two-China Policy, 1948–1950* (Armonk: M. E. Sharpe, 1987); Harry Harding (Note 1); Martin L. Lasater, *Policy in Evolution: The U.S. Role in China's Reunification* (Boulder: Westview Press, 1989); Robert S. Ross (Note 5); and Hung-mao Tien (ed.), *Mainland China, Taiwan, and US Policy* (Cambridge: DG & H, 1983).

11. Reuter's report from Beijing, "Taiwan Key Issue in Future Washington Ties," *Eastern Express*, 10 February 1996.
12. John O'Neil, "U.S. Sending More Ships to Taiwan Area in Warning to China," *The New York Times*, 11 March 1996, p. 5.
13. *Eastern Express*, 18 March 1996, p. 1.
14. *Wen Wei Po*, 22 March 1996, p. 1.
15. Chas Freeman, "The End of Taiwan?" *The New York Times*, 15 February 1996.
16. Patrick E. Tyler, "China Signalling US That It Will Not Invade Taiwan," *The New York Times*, 13 March 1996.
17. *Apple Daily*, 17 March 1996; *The New York Times*, 10 July 1996, p. 3.
18. *The New York Times*, 24 March 1996, p. 15.
19. Patrick E. Tyler, "U.S. Issues Strong Warning to China about Copyrights," *The New York Times*, 16 April 1996; Richard W. Stevenson, "U.S. Cites China for Failing to Curb Piracy in Trade," *The New York Times*, 1 May 1996; David E. Sanger, "Software Pirates Growing in Number in China, U.S. Says," *The New York Times*, 8 May 1996; David E. Sanger, "No More Mr. Nice Guy?" *The New York Times*, 12 May 1996.
20. David E. Sanger, "In Trade Rift, U.S. Outlines Penalties, and So Does China," *The New York Times*, 16 May 1996, p. 1.
21. *China Daily*, 14 June 1996.
22. David E. Sanger (Note 19).
23. Seth Faison, "Down to Wire for U.S. Talks with China," *The New York Times*, 17 June 1996.
24. David E. Sanger, "China's Arms Aides Are Sought by U.S. in Smuggling Plot," *The New York Times*, 23 May 1996, p. 1.
25. *The New York Times*, 15 May 1996, p. 1.
26. Robert B. Zoellick, "Let China Join the Club," *The Washington Post*, 24 June 1996.
27. For the MFN issue in Sino-American relations, see, for example, Harry Harding (Note 1), chapter 8; James R. Lilley and Wendell L. Willkie (eds), *Beyond MFN: Trade with China and American Interests* (Washington, DC: The AEI Press, 1994).
28. *The New York Times*, 10 July 1996, p. 3.
29. *Ming Pao*, 10 July 1996, p. A1.
30. Seth Mydans, "U.S.-China Talks Continue: Tone Is Warmer despite

Differences," *The New York Times*, 25 July 1996, p. 5.

31. *The South China Morning Post*, 7 November 1996, p. 4.
32. *The Washington Post*, 18 November 1996.
33. *The New York Times*, 31 October 1996.
34. Ibid.
35. Michael Dobbs and Steve Mufson, "Christopher Cites Progress in China Talks, but Areas of Troubles Remain," *The Washington Post*, 21 November 1996.
36. "Selling Cheap in China," *The Washington Post*, 26 November 1996.
37. See, for example, Samuel P. Huntington, "The Clash of Civilizations?" *Foreign Affairs*, Vol. 72, No. 3 (Summer 1993), pp. 22–49; and Huntington, "The West: Unique, Not Universal," *Foreign Affairs*, Vol. 75, No. 6 (November/December 1996), pp. 28–46.
38. News broadcasting by the ABC (American Broadcasting Company), 11 March 1996.
39. John H. Cushman, Jr., "U.S. Strains with China: One Exception," *The New York Times*, 30 April 1996.
40. "ZhongMei guanxi xu fang zhengzhi yinsu ganrao" (Sino-American Relations Should Guard against Interference by Political Factors), *Ta Kung Pao*, 18 June 1996.
41. Steven Erlanger and David E. Sanger, "On World Stage, Many Lessons for Clinton," *The New York Times*, 29 July 1996.
42. Ibid., p. 1.
43. Ibid., p. 15.
44. *The New York Times*, 25 July 1996, p. 5.
45. An earlier draft of Christopher's speech was entitled "Building a Partnership for the 21st Century," and the revised one finally delivered was "U.S. and China: Cooperation in the 21st Century." See the news story in *The New York Times*, 22 November 1996, p. 8.
46. *The New York Times*, 22 November 1996, p. 8.
47. Ibid., 14 July 1996, p. 2.
48. Fred Hiatt, "In Search of a Plot for Foreign Policy," *The Washington Post*, 26 August 1996.
49. David E. Sanger, "Tough or Lenient? It's a Question of Risk," *The New York Times*, 9 June 1996.
50. Steven Erlanger and David E. Sanger, "On World Stage, Many Lessons for Clinton," *The New York Times*, 29 July 1996.
51. David Bachman, "Domestic Sources of Chinese Foreign Policy," in *China and the World: New Directions in Chinese Foreign Relations*, edited by Samuel S. Kim (2nd ed.; Boulder: Westview Press, 1989), pp. 31–54.
52. Thomas L. Friedman, "China's Nationalist Tide," *The New York Times*, 13 March 1996, p. 19.

53. Song Qiang, Zhang Zangzang, Qiao Bian, Tang Zhengyu and Gu Qingsheng, *Zhongguo keyi shuo bu* (China Can Say No) (Beijing: Zhongguo gongshang chubanshe, 1996).
54. Si Cheng, "Chinese Say 'No' to the United States," *Beijing Review*, 21–27 October 1996, p. 13.
55. Steven Mufson, "China Puts Forth Persistent, Caustic Anti-U.S. Themes; Diversity of Complaints Hints at Reservoir of Grievances," *The Washington Post*, 13 August 1996.
56. Thomas L. Friedman, "J-a-p-a-n and C-h-i-n-a," *The New York Times*, 28 February 1996.
57. See Fu Gaoyi (Ezra F. Vogel) "Zhongguo de juqi yu dongya anquan" (The Rise of China and Asian Security), *Er shi yi shiji* (The Twenty-First Century), No. 34 (April 1996), pp. 9–17.
58. Philip Shenon, "Gunboat Diplomacy, '96 Model," *The New York Times*, 17 March 1996, p. 1.
59. Steven Erlanger, "As Clinton Visits Changing Asia, Military Concerns Gain Urgency," *The New York Times*, 15 April 1996, p. 1.
60. Patrick E. Tyler, "China Cautions U.S. and Japan on Security Pact," *The New York Times*, 19 April 1996, p. 5.
61. Mary Jordan, "Tokyo Party Is Cool to U.S. Bases," *The Washington Post*, 4 October 1996.
62. For discussions of this triangular relation, see, for example, Gordon H. Chang, *Friends and Enemies: The United States, China, and the Soviet Union, 1948–1972* (Stanford: Stanford University Press, 1990); John W. Garver, *China's Decision for Reapproaching with United States, 1968–1971* (Boulder: Westview, 1982); and Robert S. Ross (ed.), *China, the United States, and the Soviet Union: Tripolarity and Policy Making in the Cold War* (Armonk: M. E. Sharpe, 1993).
63. An Agence France Presse report from Beijing, "Beijing alliance squeezes US," *Eastern Express*, 26 April 1996; Patrick E. Tyler, "Chinese Seek Atom Option to Fend off Asteroids," *The New York Times*, 27 April 1996.
64. China's diplomatic connections with many other countries were active. For example, President Jiang Zemin visited six countries in Africa in May and another six countries in Asia and Europe in June and early July; Prime Minister Li Peng attended the 8th congress of the Vietnamese Communist Party in June and visited France in mid-April. Meanwhile, only in the first half of the year 1996, Beijing hosted the heads of nearly 20 countries.
65. *The New York Times*, 25 February 1996.
66. *The New York Times*, 29 July 1996.
67. For that situation and the similar conflicts and disputes between the Soviet Union and the United States, see, for example, Wilson D. Miscamble, *George F. Kennan and the Making of American Foreign Policy, 1947–1950*

(Princeton: Princeton University Press, 1992); John Lewis Gaddis, *The United States and the Origins of the Cold War, 1941–1947* (New York: Columbia University Press, 1972).

68. Robert D. Putnam, "Diplomacy and Domestic Politics: The Logic of Two-Level Games," *International Organization*, Vol. 42, No. 3 (Summer 1988), pp. 427–60.

4

China and the Two Koreas: Searching for a New Balance

Brian Bridges

For the post-1949 leadership in China, the Korean peninsula has proved to be an awkward and contentious neighbouring area. Despite being closely allied to the Democratic People's Republic of Korea (North Korea) for well over four decades, China has in recent years been developing increasingly extensive contacts with the Republic of Korea (South Korea). But moving to an acceptance of "two Koreas" has not been without its difficulties for China; during the past year or so, these difficulties have become, if anything, more pronounced.

China has important ideological, security and economic interests in the Korean peninsula. As one of the few communist states still left, North Korea's survival is ideologically important to China; China came to the North's aid when it faced destruction during the Korean War, and it has continued to maintain an interest in preventing its collapse. China has also given strong support to North Korean reunification policies over the years, and there are undoubted parallels between Deng Xiaoping's "one country, two systems" formulation and North Korean proposals for two separate social and governmental systems under a "confederation" on the Korean peninsula. China's main security concern has been to maintain peace and stability on the Korean peninsula; and, particularly since China began its open-door economic policies, its desire to avoid any conflict on the peninsula which would inevitably disrupt its own economic development plans has become stronger. China is well aware that any military conflagration on the peninsula would involve the United States and, conceivably, Russia and Japan too. China has had long and close economic ties with North Korea, but over the past decade as the North Korean economy has sunk into stagnation and the South Korean economy has conversely continued to power ahead, Chinese interest in developing economic ties with the South has grown.

This chapter examines the changing nature of China's relations with the two Koreas in order to demonstrate that the 1990s have seen a significant shift in the pattern of China's interactions with these two neighbours. However, as recent developments suggest, China's dilemma over how to deal with these two powers has by no means been resolved.

Old Allies and New Friends

Since the 1950s, the Chinese and North Korean leaderships, whose ties were sealed in blood through the massive participation of Chinese "volunteers" on the side of North Korea when it faced extinction in the Korean War, have consistently referred to their close political, economic, and military relationship as being like "lips and teeth." Since the end of the fratricidal Korean War, the two Koreas have been waging a competitive struggle for prestige and legitimacy, based on economic, military and diplomatic power. Throughout the early decades, China strongly supported North Korea in this competition with the South. Under the terms of its military alliance, China provided the North with significant amounts of both economic and military supplies. Regular meetings of leaders confirmed this close bilateral relationship, even though there were some cooler periods when the North, as part of its calculated game of playing off the two contending socialist great powers, tilted closer to the Soviet Union.[1]

But, from the early 1980s, a limited number of contacts, mainly sporting, began between China and South Korea; these helped to stimulate embryonic unofficial trade contacts being developed through Hong Kong. Although the Chinese did participate in the 1986 Asian Games and the 1988 Olympics (both of which were held in Seoul) and trade began to grow steadily from the mid-1980s, the Chinese were more cautious than the Soviet Union under Mikhail Gorbachev in moving towards formal diplomatic ties with the South. Nonetheless, a series of Sino-South Korean trade and investment agreements were signed during 1991–1992, and China lifted its veto to allow both South and North Korea enter the United Nations in 1991. Eventually, in August 1992, under strong pressure from the South Koreans, China took the final step and gave full diplomatic recognition to South Korea. This marked a significant departure in Chinese policy towards the Korean peninsula.

For China, the economic motivation was paramount. As Sino-North Korean trade stagnated and the relative costs of providing goods at "friendship prices" to the North rose during the 1980s, the Chinese became increasingly attracted to the dynamic South Korean economy. China began importing South Korean electrical goods, steel and machinery and selling agricultural products, coal and textiles in return. To the Chinese, South Korea appeared to be an important source of the intermediate goods and technology necessary for modernization, but at prices which were competitive with the Japanese.[2] According to the official Chinese statistics shown in Table 1, Sino-South Korean trade was well in excess of Sino-North Korean trade by the early 1990s; South Korean economists claim that China's trade with the South overtook that with the North in the mid-1980s. Rather than continuing to give out aid and materials to sustain

Table 1: China's Trade with North and South Korea

(Unit: million US dollars)

	1989	1990	1991	1992	1993	1994	1995
Exports to N. Korea	377.4	358.2	524.8	541.1	602.3	424.5	486.2
Imports from N. Korea	184.6	124.6	85.7	155.5	297.3	199.2	63.6
Total trade with N. Korea	562.0	482.8	610.5	696.5	899.6	623.7	549.8
Exports to S. Korea	—	—	2178.7	2437.5	2860.5	4402.5	6689.2
Imports from S. Korea	—	—	1066.2	2623.2	5360.1	7318.2	10293.3
Total trade with S. Korea	—	—	3244.9	5060.7	8220.6	11720.7	16982.5

Note: As China did not recognize South Korea until 1992, official trade statistics are not available for pre-1991. South Korean figures, which are consistently higher than Chinese figures throughout the 1990s, put Sino-South Korean trade at already around the US $3 billion level in 1989 and 1990.

Sources: Guojia tongjiju (State Statistical Bureau), *Zhongguo tongji nianjian* (Statistical Yearbook of China) (Beijing: 1991, 1993, 1995, 1996 editions).

the North, the Chinese came to feel that it would be better if they instead received economic inputs from the South.

A secondary and political motivation, though nonetheless important, was that China was able to insist as part of the agreement on full diplomatic relations that South Korea would de-recognize Taiwan (whereas China was not required to take any such equivalent step with the North); this was a diplomatic blow to Taiwan which had been having some diplomatic successes earlier in 1992. In fact, having got wind of the impending China-South Korea *rapprochement*, Taiwan pre-empted it by severing relations with South Korea first, but nonetheless it had lost its last major ally in the Asian Pacific region.

For the South Koreans, the rationale was primarily political. The logic of the "northern diplomacy" adopted by President Roh Tae-woo in the late 1980s had been that by developing political and economic contacts with the socialist allies of North Korea, the North could be pushed into a more positive mode. When North Korea failed to respond, good relations with the Soviet Union and China became important in their own right.[3] The diplomatic breakthrough with China also helped to boost Roh's image domestically, at a time when he faced considerable popular disillusionment over political in-fighting and economic problems. It was these economic difficulties which provided a subsidiary reason for the move towards China. Faced with an economic slowdown from being the world's fastest growing economy in 1986–1988, South Korea was looking for new markets and new investment opportunities.

Despite reassurances from the Chinese to North Korean President Kim Il-sung that the new relationship with the South did not preclude the continuation of close relations with the North, it was clear that China had acknowledged the reality of the "two Koreas." But the Chinese still tried to separate politics from economics, i.e., develop stronger economic links with the South while maintaining close political ties with the North. However, in the past two or three years, the shift towards a more balanced relationship with the two Koreas has become more pronounced. The nuclear weapon problem in 1993–1994 and the death of Kim Il-sung in July 1994 undoubtedly helped in this process, but the North Korean food crisis and North Korea's erratic actions in 1996 have reinforced this trend.

A Korean proverb warns that the prawn (Korea) will have its back broken by the convulsions of the whales (the neighbouring great powers). Since 1945, there have been two prawns (or, perhaps more accurately, one prawn broken into two) and four whales: China, the Soviet Union (now Russia), the United States and Japan. The Korean peninsula is regarded by all these four powers as being of political and strategic importance; it lies at the heart of the East Asian theatre. This means that China's relations with the two Koreas do not exist in a vacuum, for they are influenced by and in turn impact upon the complex interrelationship of these three states with the other interested major powers.

The United States has been and continues to be a strong ally of South Korea, remains suspicious of North Korea (although occasionally, in South Korean eyes, being a little too prepared to give the North the benefit of the doubt) and looks to China to play a constructive role on the Korean peninsula. This means that even in times of Sino-American tensions, such as during 1995–1996 over the Taiwan issue, the United States feels a need to call for Chinese political support in coaxing the North into more acceptable behaviour. Japan too, which fears destabilizing actions on the peninsula and has strong economic and political links with South Korea, has tried to encourage China to be a persuader of North Korea.[4] Thus, both the United States and Japan, while working closely with South Korea over North Korean policy, have also tried to involve China less formally in their policy approaches. China, while flattered by the attention given it, has been rather reticent to position itself too close to the Americans and the Japanese over North Korea. In part, this has been because of its difficulties with these two states in other aspects of their bilateral relationships. Indeed, there have been occasions, most notably over the Japanese failure to apologize for the past, when the Chinese have seen political advantage to cosying up to South Korea as leverage against the Japanese and the Americans.

The Soviet Union used to be a strong ally of the North, but after 1991 the new Russia's political and economic links with the North all but disappeared. However, in the past year or so there have been signs that Russia, which has resented being counted out as a player on the Korean peninsula, has begun to reactivate some of its links with the North. While the situation is still far from reverting to the old Sino-Soviet competition for influence with the North, but with the added component of competition for influence in the South, Chinese officials have become more wary of a revived Russian role.

After Kim Il-sung

The Chinese leadership, some of whom fought on the North's side during the Korean War, maintained close personal relations with Kim Il-sung. On Kim's death in July 1994, Deng Xiaoping called him a "comrade-in-arms and a close friend."[5] However, it seems likely that neither Deng nor the new generation of Chinese leaders, such as Jiang Zemin, have held his son, Kim Jong-il, in the same degree of respect. No senior Chinese leader has visited Pyongyang since the elder Kim's death and neither has Kim Jong-il visited Beijing. This is in marked contrast with the continuous exchange of high-level visits between China and South Korea during the same period: visits to South Korea by Chinese Premier Li Peng in October 1994 and Jiang Zemin in November 1995, while South Korean Prime Minister Lee Hong-koo visited China in May 1995. There was no significant change to this pattern in 1996. Even though China did receive slightly more senior North Korean visitors, such as two deputy prime ministers, no senior Chinese leader went to Pyongyang. In November, Premier Li Peng met his South Korean counterpart, Lee Soo-sung, in Rome at the World Food Summit (and invited Lee to visit China in 1997), and President Jiang talked with President Kim in the margins of the Asian Pacific Economic Cooperation (APEC) summit in Manila.[6]

More than two and a half years after his father's death, Kim Jong-il has still not been installed in his father's posts of president and party secretary-general; he would appear to be in charge, but he lacks the charismatic power of his father which would enable him to give a strong steer to the ship of state. The Chinese, who have in the past criticized Taiwan for the practice of dynastic succession, nonetheless appreciate that they cannot do anything about the succession in the North[7] and, fearing above all a destabilizing power struggle there, they have been prepared to wait and adapt to the new situation.

Nuclear Manoeuvring

Kim Il-sung's death came at the height of international attempts to solve a crisis provoked by North Korea's refusal to fully open up its nuclear facilities to international inspection. From the late 1980s, the US and South Korean governments had become suspicious that North Korea might be secretly reprocessing nuclear fuel and even producing nuclear weapons. North Korea prevaricated over opening up its nuclear reactor sites to the International Atomic Energy Agency, threatened to withdraw from the Nuclear Non-proliferation Treaty and practiced brinkmanship in a long series of negotiations with the United States, before a framework agreement, which provided for international assistance to the North to build and develop nuclear power plants, was signed in October 1994.

China played a rather ambivalent role during this prolonged crisis. It saw diplomatic advantage in being courted by the South Koreans and the Americans, who believed that probably only China had any real leverage over the North Koreans, but it was reluctant to accept the arguments and tactics being suggested by these two suitors. The Chinese made it clear that they were opposed to the development of nuclear weapons anywhere on the Korean peninsula but argued that it would be unwise to back North Korea into a corner. Ideas of sanctions against the North, whether UN-backed or not, did not find favour with the Chinese.[8] Nonetheless, despite playing down the degree to which they maintained any influence in Pyongyang, especially after the death of the elder Kim, the Chinese did apply crucial pressure at the final stages of the US-North Korean negotiations to get the North to accept the 1994 framework agreement.[9] Citing financial constraints, however, China did not join the international consortium, the Korean Energy Development Organization (KEDO), subsequently set up to manage the nuclear project in the North, and it adopted a non-committal approach during 1996 to subsequent hiccups in KEDO-North Korean talks over the details of implementing the project.

North Korean Economic Crisis

Although China tried to stay out of the nuclear issue as far as possible during 1995–1996, it was less easily able to avoid involvement in the North's deepening economic crisis. In the 1990s, the economic costs of the North's heavily statist mode of development, which had been beneficial in the early years of industrial reconstruction, have become increasingly apparent. Industrial growth has been affected by the inability of the energy and mining industries to provide reliable and sufficient supplies of power and raw materials; transportational infrastructure remains inadequate; grain crop yields have fluctuated; and, foreign currency shortages and an inability to repay outstanding debts (estimated at around US$ 8 billion) have restricted the import of Western technology and plant.

Whereas other socialist economies, with China in the lead, began to incorporate market elements into their economies in the 1980s, North Korea, if anything, strengthened the role of central planning. This certainly did not help the economy sustain competitiveness.

Although the North provides no official statistics and estimates by outside observers differ, there is a general consensus that since 1990 North Korea has almost certainly been recording negative GNP growth every year.[10] The minimal degree of economic reform in North Korea has only served to increase the divergencies between the North Korean and the Chinese economic systems and philosophies.

China has always been a key economic partner of North Korea and with the collapse of the Soviet Union China's position became pre-eminent. The converse is certainly not true; trade with North Korea is now less than one-half per cent of total Chinese trade. China's exports to the North have been mainly energy (coal and petroleum products), food (mainly rice and sweetcorn), and inputs for the North Korean textile industry. The energy imports have always been significant to the North, which has no oil resources, and food supplies have become increasingly important. North Korea's exports to China have usually been minerals, cement and iron and steel.[11] After China switched its trade with the North away from "friendship prices" for key products to a cash basis at world prices, bilateral trade dropped by nearly 30% in 1994 and by around 12% in 1995, which, according to South Korean estimates,[12] has actually led to Japan, which took an increased amount of North Korean textiles, replacing China as the North's major trading partner.

However, in 1996 the Chinese appeared to be becoming increasingly concerned about the economic situation in the North. After widespread flooding in parts of the North in the summer of 1995, the North Korean government reversed its proclaimed policy of *juche*, or self-reliance, and appealed for international food aid. Although Japan and South Korea gave some rice, few other countries did, and the shortfall on North Korean grain production probably totalled between 1.5–2 million tonnes (almost one-third of the North's estimated requirements for human and livestock consumption). In May 1996, North Korean Deputy Prime Minister Hong Song-nam was dispatched urgently to Beijing to seek food aid, but he received only sympathetic words and a promise of 20,000 tonnes of grain.[13] The Chinese position was that North Korea should, if at all possible, try to obtain food aid from elsewhere.

To China, which has growing grain needs itself, significant food aid could only be spared if the North Korean situation were to be really critical. The North's continued criticism of both Japan and South Korea after the 1995 shipments and its persistent violations of the armistice restrictions in the spring and summer of 1996 did nothing to encourage international donors. Further flooding which took place in the North in July 1996 reduced the annual harvest again and raised the spectre of widespread starvation. As a result, the Chinese leadership felt forced to act, and a further 100,000 tonnes of food aid was promised to the North in July; unconfirmed reports suggest that half of this amount was donated, the other half sold to the North at well below market prices. Rumours that China also offered to provide 500,000 tonnes of food aid per year for five years have yet to be confirmed.[14] The repeated flooding has only masked what are more fundamental problems in the agricultural sector and, indeed, in the North Korean economy as a whole. China has continued to try to persuade the North Koreans that economic reform on the Chinese model is the only real answer to their economic problems. These Chinese representations undoubtedly have some resonance for the technocrats in the North Korean élite, but, with the exception of the limited steps to develop the Najin-Sombong special economic zone, near to the Chinese and Russian borders, the North has been resistant to endorsing Chinese-style economic reform, not least because of fears that opening the doors economically might bring unbearable political costs for such a closed society. Policy statements accredited to Kim Jong-il since July 1994 have been few in number and clad in the jargon of socialist self-reliance, but one statement carried in the North Korean media in July 1995, in which he attacked "openness" and "pluralism" as bringing ideological confusion, was interpreted by the Chinese as being aimed at them.[15] By early 1997, it was becoming clear that many of those officials believed to be mostly closely associated with advocating economic reform were actually being removed from their posts in the North Korean leadership. This refusal to seriously consider economic reform has undoubtedly played a role in increasing Chinese frustration with the North.

The New Economic Nexus with the South

While Sino-North Korean trade has been stagnating at best and declining at worst in the 1990s, Sino-South Korean trade has been burgeoning. As shown in Table 1, Chinese figures show that bilateral trade reached almost US$ 17 billion in 1995; the South Koreans estimate a 17% rise in trade in 1996 to nearly US$ 20 billion.[16] China is selling light-industrial goods, agricultural and fisheries goods, while it is buying mostly chemicals and heavy-industrial goods. South Korea is now the fifth largest trading partner of China, while China is the third largest trading partner of the South.[17]

South Korean investment in China has also taken off, growing by 40% per annum in 1993–1995. By 1995, China had received just over US$ 3 billion in investment from the South and had become the largest single destination for South Korean overseas investment. Much of this has been in small-sized factories and offices, but 1996 saw a significant shift to the major Korean conglomerates, such as Samsung, Daewoo and Hyundai, which are now all committed to major electronics manufacturing projects and Sunkyong which is investing in petrochemicals. In May 1996 , the Lucky Goldstar group announced a decade-long investment programme which would see the group investing US$ 10 billion in consumer electronics, telecommunications equipment, petrochemistry and financial services; by 2005, the group expects to have an annual turnover of US$ 50 billion in its China operations, which will be the group's largest overseas manufacturing base.[18] In June, the Hyundai business group agreed on a joint venture to manufacture and sell subway railcars in China and potentially overseas, and the group's chairman told President Jiang that Hyundai would be putting US$ 2.3 billion into other new manufacturing projects during the following two years.[19] In the first three-quarters of 1996, South Korean companies invested US$ 940 million, making the country the fourth-largest foreign investor in China.

The investment flow has been assisted by the presence of nearly 2 million ethnic Koreans in China, most of them concentrated in the three north-eastern provinces of Liaoning, Jilin and Heilongjiang, which now host just over half of the inward Korean investment. Recent visitors to South Korean factories in the region have reported on a handful of South Korean expatriates managing an almost exclusively ethnic Korean workforce, working with an efficiency the equal of that found back in South Korea. However, signs began to emerge during 1996 that not all these ventures were trouble-free; cases of disputes between Korean managers and their workforces were reported, and one Kia Motor Company executive was murdered, apparently after insulting his trainee workers. These kinds of cases would appear to relate to broader Chinese concerns that some South Koreans tend to treat the Yanbian prefecture in Jilin province in particular as a kind of "Korean territory." Indeed, in 1996 the Chinese government did become disturbed enough to ask South Korea to refrain from providing special assistance to the Korean community in China.[20]

Nonetheless, over the past year or so there have been signs that China and South Korea are preparing to move their economic relationship into a new phase, which involves significant industrial and technological collaboration. Symbolic of this new mood was the visit to Seoul in November 1995 by President Jiang. Taken on a tour of Samsung Electronics' most high-technology factory, Jiang was handed a digital mobile telephone, with which he placed a call to China; he then declared: "This is better than Silicon Valley."[21] But despite the rhetoric, actually a more significant step had been taken earlier during South Korean Prime Minister Lee Hong-koo's visit to China in May 1995 when an "industrial alliance" was mooted. Four industrial fields have been under active consideration: auto parts, aircraft, high-definition television (HDTV), and telephone switching systems.[22] China has dampened South Korean hopes for joint ventures in car assembly in China, because of fears of over-production, but has agreed to allow cooperation in auto parts. The HDTV project is intended to develop core technology, parts and components, and will initially mean Chinese scientists being seconded to South Korean companies and research institutes. Joint research on a time-division telephone switching system has already begun.

However, the most ambitious project, a US$ 1.3 billion deal for the joint development of a 100-seater airliner, collapsed in June 1996 because of serious disagreements between the two sides over which parts of the plane should be built where (each partner wanted the bulk of the work to be done in its own country) and the most appropriate third partner.[23] South Koreans accused China of reneging on the earlier agreements by demanding a majority stake and the right to be project leader. Despite the sobering effects of the collapse of the aircraft deal, the Chinese side remains keen, as do the South Koreans, about developing the economic synergy between the two countries.

Reconciling North-South Tensions

Despite the partial solution to the nuclear issue in the autumn of 1994, relations between the two Koreas have continued to be volatile. China has continued to express its desire for peace and stability on the peninsula, but slowly and with considerable caution China has been subtly tilting towards the South in the developing political context.

Comparison of the Chinese reaction to three incidents in 1996 and early 1997 demonstrates this gradual shift. In April 1996, China had blocked a move by South Korea to obtain a UN Security Council resolution or president's statement on a limited incursion by North Korean troops into the Demilitarized Zone which separates the two Koreas. But, the discovery in September 1996 of a North Korean submarine, carrying armed commandos, which had run aground off the coast of South Korea placed China in a much more difficult situation. Chinese officials did suggest that too harsh a criticism of the North would be unwise, but Foreign Minister Qian Qichen expressed his sympathy with the South Korean view on UN action during a discussion with his South Korean counterpart, Gong Ro-myung.[24] In the end, the Chinese gave tacit support to a statement by the president of the UN Security Council which expressed "serious concern" over the incident, criticized actions to undermine peace on the peninsula and endorsed the continuation of the existing armistice agreement. This was not as explicit in its condemnation of North Korea as the South would have liked, but, by endorsing the continuation of the armistice agreement, something which the North had been increasingly critical of during 1995–1996, it did signal a measure of Chinese dissatisfaction with the North.

But, China found itself most clearly put on the spot in having to choose between the two Koreas when in mid-February 1997 Hwang Jang-yop, a senior North Korean ideologue, sought political asylum in the South Korean embassy in Beijing. South Korea clearly expected China to act according to the norms of international law and allow him to leave for the South, through a third country if necessary, while the North laid siege to the South's embassy and demanded Hwang's return.[25] The diplomatic impasse was prolonged by Deng's death, but China, by not immediately acceding to the North Korean demands, showed once again that it was tilting towards the South.

The exposure of the North Korean submarine incident, coupled with a renewed North Korean threat to renege on part of the nuclear accord, may well also have tipped the balance within the Chinese leadership in supporting a peace initiative put forward by the Americans and the South Koreans in April 1996. During his visit to Seoul in April, US President Bill Clinton had joined with South Korean President Kim to propose peace talks involving the two Koreas, the United States and China. The initial Chinese reaction to the four-power peace talk proposal had been cautious. While repeating their desire to play a constructive role in maintaining peace and stability on the peninsula, the Chinese foreign ministry spokesman suggested that further study of the proposal was needed.[26] Privately, Chinese diplomats told the South Koreans that they should be patient in pushing forward this proposal. In July 1996, President Jiang reiterated Chinese concerns to play a constructive role in Korean peace moves. But, in mid-November the Chinese ambassador in Seoul gave the first unambiguous statement of support: "China takes a positive view of the four-way talks and plans to participate in the talks if related nations can reach an accord."[27] This Chinese support was reaffirmed when US Secretary of State Warren Christopher visited Beijing a few days later.

China had appreciated being counted as an important player by being invited to join the four-power talks, but it had not been consulted in advance on the US-South Korean initiative, and it deferred a definite answer to the invitation until the North Korean attitude had become clearer. The North Korean media had criticized the proposal, but the government had not specifically rejected the idea;[28] instead it had tried, in vain, to manoeuvre the Americans into direct talks through raising questions about the scope of the proposed talks. However, the Chinese approach was to quietly persuade the North Koreans to accept the proposal and, after the September submarine incident soured North-South relations, to coax them into making some concession to get the process started. The more positive Chinese approach to the four-power party talks in late 1996 therefore probably reflected both frustration with North Korean tactics and concerns that China's own standing would be undermined by continuing ambivalence. Of course, also within the context of a thawing in Sino-American tension in the autumn of 1996, such support for the four-power proposal went down well with the Americans. The unprecedented North Korean apology for the submarine incursion and the agreement to attend a briefing on the four-power talks proposal in late December 1996 were welcomed by the Chinese.[29]

One new factor which China was forced to consider in 1996 was signs of North Korea starting to play the "Taiwan card." In May, a North Korean delegation visited Taiwan both to seek food aid and to encourage Taiwanese companies to do business with the North. Some barter trade has developed, but Taiwanese see little commercial or political benefit from investing in the North. A direct charter flight inaugurated in April soon ceased operation because of a lack of passengers. Nonetheless, China was sufficiently concerned for Foreign Minister Qian Qichen to tell a visiting North Korean foreign ministry official in June of Chinese displeasure at the North's expanding relations with Taiwan.[30] The Chinese were therefore unhappy with the North Koreans coming to a commercial deal at the end of 1996 with the Taiwanese nuclear power company to store low-grade nuclear waste from Taiwanese power stations in the North.[31] The North Korean intention in trying to do business with Taiwan has been partly to secure much-needed foreign currency and partly, but more importantly, to try to lever China into expanding its own economic support for the North.

The South Koreans clearly want, not only to draw China into greater political support for their position, but also to undermine Chinese military support for the North. Although South Korean officials argue that the 1992 establishment of diplomatic relations between China and the South meant that the automatic military involvement clause of the 1961 China-North Korean mutual assistance treaty was rendered practically inoperative, Chinese officials do not rule out some circumstances in which they would be involved militarily on the Korean peninsula. However, the Chinese attitude has generally been to play down the significance of the China-North Korean treaty; the 35th anniversary of its signing in July 1996 passed without notable fanfare on the Chinese side. A Chinese naval flotilla did visit the North Korean port of Chongjin, the first such visit for many years, but no senior Chinese leader attended the official anniversary reception in Beijing. The South Koreans did extend an invitation to Chinese Defence Minister Chi Haotian to visit Seoul during 1997, but the Chinese have so far not responded, no doubt aware of how critical the North would be of such a step.

Tumen River Development Plan

The above discussion of China's linkages with the two Koreas has highlighted the differences in the nature of the two relationships and shown how the strong rivalry between the two Koreas is also played out in their economic and political contacts with China. However, there is one multinational scheme which has tried to bring the three countries together: the Tumen River project. The basin of the Tumen River, which borders the Russian Primorskiy (maritime territory), China's Yanbian region and North Korea, is now being advocated as the site for the multilateral development of port and other transport infrastructure and industrial facilities.[32] The original concept was to combine Japanese and South Korean capital and technology with cheap Chinese and North Korean labour to exploit and process Russian and Mongolian natural resources. A United Nations Development Programme (UNDP)-sponsored survey posited two scales of development zones: a smaller one centred on North Korea's Najin port, Hunchun in China and Posyet in Russia and a much larger one stretching from North Korea's Chongjin port to China's Yanji city to the Russian port of Vladivostok. Initially, priority had been given to the smaller triangle plan, and North Korea, indeed, took the initiative to declare the Najin-Sombong area to be a special economic zone (SEZ) in December 1991.

However, the record since then has not been very satisfactory. Voluminous feasibility studies have been produced, but even within the Najin-Sombong SEZ progress has been slow in setting up the necessary infrastructure. There are clear differences of interest and objective amongst the participants. The North Koreans view the Najin-Sambong SEZ and the broader Tumen River plan as a way of revitalizing their economy, but, at the same time, keeping contaminating "capitalist elements" strictly confined to one small area, well away from the bulk of the North Korean population. Despite extravagant North Korean claims of US$ 350 million foreign direct investment, UNDP officials think only about US$ 35 million of investment have been actually committed to the SEZ. An international investment seminar held at the Najin-Sombong SEZ in September 1996 did not excite much positive interest from overseas in terms of contractual commitments. The South Koreans can see opportunities to solve some of their emerging labour shortage problems as well as to provide another means to access the markets of north-east China, but they are suspicious of whether the North will really provide their companies with fair and feasible working conditions on site. The Chinese see it as a way of gaining access to the sea from that land-locked north-eastern part of their country but, naturally, want to see Hunchun rather than Najin at the hub of the development. So far, the Chinese have proved more successful than the North Koreans in attracting foreign investment with, according to UNDP calculations, US$ 226 million entering in Tumen-related projects.[33]

UNDP officials continue to keep faith in the project (in October 1996 they promised another US$ 3 million in support over the next three years), but they concede that the result will probably not be a single international free-trade zone but rather a meeting point for three separate zones each with its own characteristics.[34]

Towards Transformation on the Peninsula

China undoubtedly has a strong interest in the process of reunification of the Korean peninsula. The current mood in South Korea has shifted noticeably from the euphoric days of 1989, when it naively seemed possible that the Korean peninsula could follow quickly on the German model, to one of caution about reunification. Here, at least, there is some measure of tacit agreement amongst North and South Koreans. The North fears "absorption" by the South in the way that East Germany disappeared, but the South, having watched the tremendous economic, social and political costs borne by West Germany and aware of its own economic difficulties, does not want to take on the responsibilities of looking after — or paying for — North Korea yet either. The timing and manner of reunification depend now on the fate of Kim Jong-il's regime in the North. Two and a half years after his father's death, he has still not been confirmed in the top political posts; in the meantime, the growing numbers of defections and appeals for food aid suggest that the economic and social structure is breaking down.

International food relief may bring a temporary alleviation of the crisis, but the fundamental problems of the economy will remain. Unlike the Chinese, who have been able to sustain a gradualist reform programme over nearly 20 years, time is no longer on the side of the North. The South is, therefore, well on the way to achieving reunification by "absorption." Conceivably by the end of this century, Chinese policy-makers will have to learn how to deal with a reunified Korea. A reunified Korea will obviously be a powerful economic force, although the initial disruption and adjustment needs will be even greater than the transitional difficulties in Germany in 1990–1991. However, the unified economy will have over 65 million people, a complementary mix of northern mineral resources and docile labour and southern technology and capital. The Chinese, of course, hope that reunification does not come about by destabilizing violent action, but whatever form of reunified Korea emerges — and the odds are heavily stacked in favour of a southern-dominated state — China will continue not only to need Korea as a trading and investment partner but also to have to tread carefully in developing relations with the peninsula.

China's relations with the Korean peninsula have changed quite markedly since the late 1980s. But, despite the limited and even declining degree of economic interaction with the North, China still has important political and security interests associated with the North. Fully committed to its economic modernization, China needs to have stability on its borders, including the Korean peninsula. In the past the Chinese saw this as being achieved through support for their ideological ally, North Korea. But, from the late 1980s, it became clear that China had begun to see stability as being achieved through a more balanced relationship, though one primarily focused on political and ideological support for the North and economic contacts with the South. But, North Korean brinkmanship over the nuclear weapon issue and the transition from Kim Il-sung to Kim Jong-il , who has far fewer personal links with the Chinese leadership, has led to China subtly tilting towards the South. South Korean officials now feel that their relationship with China is becoming increasingly "political" in nature.

Notes

1. Chung Chin-Wee, "North Korea's Relations with China," in *The Foreign Relations of North Korea*, edited by Park Jae Kyu, Koh Byung Chul and Kwak Tae-Hwan (Seoul: Kungham University Press, 1987), pp. 169–99; Ilpyong Kim, "Sino-Korean Relations," in *The Emergence of East Asia*, edited by Jae Ho Chung and De Piao Tang (Hong Kong: Hong Kong University of Science and Technology, 1995), pp. 68–87.
2. Brian Bridges, *Japan and Korea in the 1990s* (Aldershot: Edward Elgar, 1993), p. 72.
3. Kim Hakjoon, "The Establishment of South Korean-Chinese Diplomatic

Relations: A South Korean Perspective," *Journal of Northeast Asian Studies*, Vol. 13, No. 2 (Summer 1994), pp. 31–48.

4. Christopher Hughes, "The North Korean Nuclear Crisis and Japanese Security," *Survival*, Vol. 38, No. 24 (Summer 1996), p. 88.
5. *Hongkong Standard*, 6 July 1994.
6. *Korea Herald*, 18 November 1996; *South China Morning Post*, 25 November 1996.
7. Some observers, such as the Japanese expert Yuji Nishioka, believe that the Chinese would prefer Kim Il-sung's younger brother, Kim Yong-ju, as North Korean leader rather than Kim Jong-il.
8. Quansheng Zhao, "China's Foreign Relations in the Asia-Pacific Region," in *China Review 1995*, edited by Lo Chi Kin, Suzanne Pepper and Tsui Kai Yuen (Hong Kong: The Chinese University Press, 1995), pp. **8**.9–**8**.10. James Cotton argues that Chinese abstention on UN General Assembly resolutions calling on North Korea to fully open up its facilities to international inspection also reflected an underlying fear that if international pressure, orchestrated by the United States, succeeded in the North Korean case, then greater international scrutiny of China's own human rights practices, etc. would be next. "The Unravelling of 'China' and China-Korea Relationships," *Korea & World Affairs*, Vol. 18, No. 1 (Spring 1994), pp. 79–80.
9. See statement by William Perry, the US Secretary for Defence, *Eastern Express*, 21 November 1994. See also Ilpyong Kim (Note 1), pp. 82–86.
10. *Kitachosen keizai to boeki no tenbo: 1994 nenban* (Tokyo: JETRO, 1995); *Korea Herald*, 5 June 1996; *Nihon Keizai Shimbun*, 18 June 1996.
11. Nicholas Eberstadt, "China's Trade with the DPRK, 1990–1994," *Korea & World Affairs*, Vol. 19, No. 4 (Winter 1995), pp. 665–85; Marcus Noland, *Implications of North Korean External Economic Reform* (Washington: Institute for International Economics, 1995). For more recent trends, see *Korea Herald*, 28 May 1996.
12. *Korea Herald*, 28 May 1996.
13. *South China Morning Post*, 23 May 1996.
14. Kim Young-hie, "China's Role in Korean Issue," *Korea Focus*, Vol. 4, No. 4 (July-August 1996), p. 125; Japanese Foreign Ministry officials say that they have received no confirmation of such a deal from official Chinese sources (interview, Tokyo, November 1996).
15. Kim Young-hie (Note 14), pp. 124–25. A North Korean-owned company placed a full-page advertisement in a Macau newspaper in early 1996, quoting another Kim Jong-il speech which obliquely criticized China. *Far Eastern Economic Review*, 14 March 1996.
16. *Korea Herald*, 14 January 1997. See also Hieyeon Keum, "Normalization and After — Prospects for the Sino-South Korean Relations," *Korea & World Affairs*, No. 4 (Winter 1996), pp. 578–79.

17. Ibid., 28 August 1996.
18. Ibid., 28 May 1996.
19. Ibid., 9 June 1996.
20. Kim Dae-joong, "Ethnic Koreans in China," *Korea Focus*, Vol. 4, No. 5 (September–October 1996), p. 145.
21. *Eastern Express*, 16 November 1995.
22. *Korea Times*, 29 June 1995.
23. *Foreign Report*, 31 October 1996.
24. *Korea Herald*, 30 September 1996.
25. *Korea Herald*, 15, 19 February 1997.
26. China initially responded that it "understood" the rationale for the proposal but that differences between North and South should first be resolved directly between the two parties. Kim Yong-ho, "Future of Kim Jong-Il Regime and Four-Way Talks," *Korea Focus*, Vol. 4, No. 4 (July–August 1996), p. 62.
27. *Asahi Evening News*, 18 November 1996.
28. North Korean representatives talked about "considering" the proposal. *Korea Herald*, 15 August 1996.
29. *Far Eastern Economic Review*, 9 January 1997.
30. *Korea Herald*, 21 June 1996. Taiwanese estimates of trade with North Korea reaching US$ 400 million in 1996 (*Far Eastern Economic Review*, 6 February 1997). If correct, it would not be that far below likely trade between China and the North, which has been estimated at US$ 566 million for 1996 (*Asian Wall Street Journal*, 14 February 1997) .
31. *Far Eastern Economic Review*, 6 February 1997.
32. Mark Valencia, "Economic Cooperation in Northeast Asia: The Proposed Tumen River Scheme," *Pacific Review*, Vol. 4, No. 3 (1991), pp. 263–71; Andrew Marton, Terry McGee and Donald Paterson, "Northeast Asian Economic Cooperation and the Tumen River Area Development Project," *Pacific Affairs*, Vol. 68, No. 1 (Spring 1995), pp. 9–33.
33. *Beijing Review*, 11–17 November 1996.
34. *South China Morning Post*, 29 May 1996.

5

Jiang Zemin versus Lee Teng-hui: Strained Mainland-Taiwan Relationship

Peter Nan-shong Lee

Beijing began its military exercises, including missiles tests, in the Taiwan Straits in July 1995, which reached their climax in March 1996. Being unusually close to Taiwan, not only did this show of force alarm Taipei and create anxiety among people in Taiwan, but also it alerted major countries, such as the United States (US) and Japan which have an interest in the Pacific Asia region. As manifested in this series of events and controversies, the strain across the Taiwan Straits has reflected the paradoxical mainland-Taiwan relations in their full intricacy and complexity ever since 1949.

The mainland-Taiwan relations today have been shaped by a series of events which have a long history, including the rivalry and animosity between the Chinese Communist Party (CCP) and the Chinese Nationalist Party (Kuomintang, KMT), the clashes between China and the US during the Korean War in 1950, and the exchanges of fire between mainland and Taiwan on the Quemoy and Matsu incidents during 1954 and 1958.[1] Commencing in 1972, the American policy of "one China, but not now" set aside the outstanding issue of Taiwan's status and thus created the room for the continuous improvement of the US-China relations.[2] The aggressive posture of the Union of Soviet Socialist Republics (USSR) propelled US-China normalization and the implementation of an "anti-hegemony" clause of the 1972 Shanghai Communiqué.[3] The US-China "honeymoon" continued until the establishment of fully-fledged diplomatic relations in 1979 and the 17 August 1982 Communiqué on arms sale to Taiwan. The relationship between the two nations remained stable beyond 1982 when China began its *rapprochement* with the USSR through the so-called "diplomacy of all directions."[4]

However, the US-China relations started to turn sour after the Tiananmen Square incident in 1989. Furthermore, the coming of the post-Cold War era has weakened China's position in the new international environment. In other words, the decline of China's importance became visible after the collapse of the USSR and the democratization of Russia, as the global balance of power was transferred from a system with two contending superpowers into a system of one dominating power with multiple power centres.[5] This was coupled with the shift of relative importance of military might to economic power in conducting foreign policy. Consequently, Taipei was given opportunities to strengthen its international foothold and improve its communication channels and access to relevant actors in the power game pertaining to the Taiwan issue at the international level.

This chapter concerns a series of events leading to the outburst of tension across the Taiwan Straits, which reached its climax in 1996. It is argued that the manifestation of strain between mainland and Taiwan has resulted from Beijing's endeavour to frustrate Taipei's thrust in expanding its international space and consolidating its foundation as a sovereign entity since 1993. This chapter will also highlight the strained mainland-Taiwan relations in the year of 1996, but our analysis of the relevant events will be contextualized according to the long historical evolution of the Taiwan question for the several decades since 1949, and especially since 1979. This chapter will begin by briefly dwelling on the background of Jiang Zemin's entry into the policy arena of Taiwan affairs and the assumption of his leadership role since the Tiananmen Square incident in 1989, then, our analysis will be devoted to the political and policy moves of Taiwan President Lee Teng-hui during his rise to power from 1988 to 1996. We shall discuss how the hostility between the two sides built up from July 1995 forward, reached its highest point and, finally, subsided in 1996.

Jiang Zemin's Policy Role on Taiwan Affairs

Jiang Zemin was not given unfettered power to handle Taiwan affairs when he first assumed his policy role on this question, as he was replacing the positions of Deng Xiaoping, the paramount leader, and of Yang Shangkun, the head of the Taiwan Affairs Leadership Team of the Central Committee (CC) of the Chinese Communist Party in 1989. Therefore, it is necessary to trace the evolutionary path of Beijing's policy for peaceful reunification, and to identify Jiang's leadership role on the matter.

To begin with, Beijing's policy of peaceful reunification with Taiwan can be traced back to 1979, after more than two decades of uninterrupted exchanges of artillery shells between mainland and Taiwan's offshore islands from 1958 to 1979.[6] This new peace overture to Taiwan was synchronized with the progress of normalization with Washington. In conjunction with the establishment of a fully-fledged diplomatic relationship with China, Washington went very far by giving in on all three conditions demanded by Beijing;[7] Washington in turn made explicit two conditions: first, the unofficial relationship between the US and Taiwan in commercial, cultural and other arenas would remain intact; and secondly, the US would still have "an interest in the peaceful resolution of the Taiwan issue and the Taiwan issue will be settled peacefully by the Chinese themselves."[8] These two conditions were incorporated into the Taiwan Relations Act passed by the US Congress in April 1979.[9]

Parallel to Washington's peace commitment to Taiwan, Beijing put forward the policy of peaceful reunification through a series of statements, policy papers, official speeches and less formal conversations from 1979 onward. These included the "Message to Taiwanese Compatriots" (hereafter "the 1979 Message") in the name of the Standing Committee of the National People's Congress (NPC) of 1 January 1979,[10] Ye Jianying's policy paper known as the "Nine-Point Proposal" of 24 July 1981,[11] Article 31 of the 1982 Constitution,[12] Liao Chengzhi's "personal letter" to Chiang Ching-kuo,[13] Deng Xiaoping's conversation with a Chinese American political scientist in 1983[14] and Deng's talk on "one country, two systems,"[15] among others.

There are background materials which give in-depth information about Jiang Zemin's personal position concerning the mainland-Taiwan relations, namely, his three dialogues with Professor Shen Junshan from Taiwan from 1990 to 1992. At the time, Shen had access to the policy making circle in Taiwan. He was also in position to provide an accurate account of the views of Taiwan's top policy makers because of his social background and interpersonal network and his position as "research member" of Taiwan's Mainland Affairs Council of the Executive Yuan. These three "dialogues" were scheduled in December 1990, July 1991 and January 1992, respectively.[16]

In the three "dialogues," Jiang did show his willingness to take initiatives to break the ice over the Taiwan Straits deadlock, but some preconditions which Jiang demanded appear to have been difficult for Taipei to accept. First, in Jiang's words, "one China" meant to accept the People's Republic of China (PRC), the Central Government and the rule of the one party-state of the CCP and at the same time for the Taipei to relinquish its legitimacy status claim to the regime (what has been known as the "Republic of China" since 1911).[17] Secondly, Beijing did not object to Taipei maintaining its economic and cultural space at the international level, provided that it was not in violation of the "one China" principle. However, Beijing intended to undermine any diplomatic tie with Taipei when it was in violation of the "one China" principle.[18] Thirdly, the CCP would treat the KMT or any representative authorized by the KMT on equal terms, but Beijing and Taipei could never be taken as "two [power] centres," two central governments and two Chinas. The concept of "entity" was acceptable so long as it meant "autonomy" in an administrative and judiciary sense, but not in terms of a sovereign political entity.[19]

Moreover, Jiang suggested that Beijing intended to keep the use of force as a last resort. The use of force would be a threat mainly against the separatist tendencies in Taiwan as well as against possible foreign intervention. However, in some passages of Jiang's "dialogues," he did not rule out the possibility of applying military pressure on Taiwan because of some relevant circumstances. For instances, Jiang stated that he and his comrades could not indefinitely tolerate the postponement of negotiation and also noted a long list of unreasonable conditions which were imposed by Taipei. In his own words, all these conditions "were seemingly intended to 'unify' and to 'swallow' us; there is even an explicit claim to 'trade time for space' [of survival for Taiwan]." Jiang added, "to be honest, some veteran cadres had become impatient," saying that he lately had received a letter from a group of retiring high cadres who had claimed that they could not put their heart at ease upon their retirement, because their long-held goals of socialism and national reunification had not been fulfilled ever since they had joined the party.[20]

During the "dialogues," Jiang was given opportunities to respond to a set of policy alternatives which were put forward by Shen but which were akin to the range of the consensus shared by the policy circle in Taipei. Therefore, one should be able to establish and identify those policy alternatives about which Jiang had reservations and against which he maintained opposition. In the three dialogues, Jiang registered explicit disagreement with the following policy alternatives mentioned by Shen: First, "one China" as a "blueprint" for the future to be achieved through a step-by-step transitional strategy;[21] secondly, mutual recognition as full political entities by each side across the Taiwan Straits during the process of negotiation as well as the establishment of an interim joint apparatus before reunification;[22] and thirdly, Taipei's freedom from interference in taking part in international organizations and developing international relations.[23]

It does not seem that room was provided for negotiation and compromise between Beijing and Taipei on the basis of the "dialogues." As Jiang made explicit, he himself felt more comfortable with maintaining talking terms with the old KMT ruling élites, especially those who originally had come from the mainland because of common cultural and historical experience (such as being exemplified by Shen himself). Shen made it explicit, however, that the CCP ruling élite would have to make additional effort to communicate with the emerging generation of politicians in Taiwan owing to the rapid process of localization, pluralization and democratization.[24]

From 1990 onward, the role of "spokesman" on the Taiwan issue was gradually taken over by Jiang Zemin, as he finally emerged as the sole authoritative figure in the policy making area pertaining to Taiwan. Jiang delivered a speech (containing an "eight-point proposal") (hereafter "Jiang's speech") to the "tea gathering" of Chinese Lunar New Year on 30 January 1995, which was marking the watershed when he took the helm of Taiwan policy firmly in his own hands.[25] Jiang's speech drew attention in the media in China, Hong Kong and Taiwan. Jiang was repeating his themes of the "dialogues" during 1990–1992, and exhibiting that he wanted considerable continuity in policy towards Taiwan by the CCP. While Jiang's speech offered an alternative for peace, Beijing was preparing the military, in the meantime, with the deployment of their missiles to the forward military bases of Fujian across the Taiwan Straits, placing the entire island within striking range.[26]

Jiang's appeal to Taipei was timely because he felt that the "separatist tendency" within Taiwan as well as "foreign intervention" in the Taiwan question had been aggravating. In passing, he alluded to Lee Teng-hui's policy on mainland-Taiwan relations and to the amendment by the US Congress to the Taiwan Relations Act, to be discussed later. Moreover, in Jiang's view, the return of Hong Kong and Macau to China in 1997 and 1999, respectively, created an opportune time for putting the Taiwan question squarely on the policy agenda.[27]

A close analysis of Jiang's speech, together with its "eight-point proposal," suggests that it is consistent with Beijing's established policy on mainland-Taiwan relations, with minor adjustments. First, instead of the KMT as the sole or the main party which would represent the Taiwan side, it is proposed to "incorporate" various parties, political groups and "representative figures" from both sides of the Taiwan Straits in the process of negotiation in light of the pluralization process in Taiwan.[28] Secondly, with reference to the agenda of negotiation, Jiang proposes to work towards "an agreement to terminate formally the hostility between the two shores."[29] Thirdly, Jiang recognizes the importance to the existing projects of Taiwanese investors in the mainland, suggesting to conclude a non-official agreement on the protection of investments by Taiwanese businessmen on the basis of the "Regulations for the Protection of Taiwanese Compatriots' Investment of the PRC." Besides, he reiterates the established policy of achieving the final "breakthrough" over the "three direct links," that is postal services, shipping and trade (*tong you, tong hang, tong shang*), coupled with other economic relationships. Fourthly, in a goodwill gesture with political implications, Jiang extends his welcome to Taiwanese leaders who wish to visit the mainland in an "appropriate capacity"; however, Jiang rejects the proposal that leaders of both sides should seek to meet at the occasion of international meetings, where both would be sending delegations.[30] How did Taipei respond to Jiang's speech? To answer the question, let us turn to the next section.

Lee Teng-hui's Approach to the Taiwan Issue

It took three decades from 1949 to 1979 for Beijing and Taipei to decide upon the *de facto* (rather than *de jure*) termination of hostility towards each other, but their movement towards peace has been slow, and not synchronized. In response to Beijing's shift to the peaceful approach towards reunification in 1979, the Chinese Nationalist Party determined to take its own initiative later in April 1981, and to "re-unify" the mainland through an ideological and symbolic approach, that is, under the "three principles of the people" of Dr Sun Yat-sen.[31] At the same time, Taipei maintained the policy of "no contact, no negotiation and no compromise" with Beijing.[32]

It took still another decade from the early 1980s to the early 1990s for Taipei to make some major move towards peace across the Taiwan Straits. On the eve of the KMT's major policy shift towards Beijing in 1991, Ma Ying-jeou, the KMT's spokesman on mainland affairs, summarized a three-stage transformation of the mainland-Taiwan relations: the first stage of "military confrontation" from 1949 to 1979; the second stage of "peaceful rivalry" during 1979–1987; and, the third stage of civilian exchange from 1987 onward.[33] At the third stage, the process of institutionalization of policy making on mainland affairs was accelerated in Taiwan in the midst of the growth of civilian interactions, the expansion of trade and the rapid increase of Taiwan investments in the mainland.[34]

By the early 1990s, Taipei had abandoned its goal of the "recovery of the mainland" when it announced the "Manifesto for National Reunification" (hereafter "Manifesto") on 3 March 1991. The 1991 "Manifesto" proposed a three-phase policy development to envisage the progress towards peaceful reunification between the mainland and Taiwan.[35] In order to implement the first phase of the development, Taipei announced the end of the "Mobilization Period" and therefore the conclusion of hostility against the CCP, beginning on 1 May 1991. However, Taipei's position of unilateral termination of hostility and its readiness to recognize Beijing's status of "political entity" were not reciprocated by Beijing. Being asked to comment on the ambiguous situation so created in a press conference, Lee Teng-hui said that under the circumstances, Taipei in fact "does not have any option, but has to take Beijing as a political entity with hostility, if neither does the CCP regime give up its use of force in the Taiwan Straits, nor does it cease to isolate us."[36]

Immediately after Jiang's speech with its eight-point proposal in 1995, the Mainland Affairs Council of Taiwan's Executive Yuan, under Lee's instruction, decided to respond to Jiang's speech of peaceful reunification "by stages, with different emphases and according to particular nature (political or non political)."[37] On the basis of its 1991 "Manifesto," Taipei tried to make sure that the progress of the exchange on one issue would not be affected by another. From a series of exchanges through the media, it appeared that Taipei's responses tended to be structured on two levels: the political level to be normally dictated by President Lee Teng-hui and the pragmatic level to be handled by Premier Lien Chan. The division of labour between Jiang Zemin and Li Peng on the mainland side appeared parallel to that of the Taipei side.

Immediately after Jiang's speech, Li Peng, Premier of the State Council of the PRC, scheduled a meeting on 4 February 1995 with the representatives of Taiwanese investors in Xiamen, Fujian province, to discuss not only the general issues of cross-straits relations, but also specific concerns, such as the taxation of Taiwanese merchants.[38] At this pragmatic level, Taipei's substantial response was put forth by Lien Chan, Premier of Executive Yuan, on 21 February 1995, proposing to start to strengthen the trade and economic ties across the Straits and to negotiate in order to resolve the differences between the two sides. Moreover, Lien listed some items of priority, such as the agreement on the protection of Taiwanese investors, the agreement on the protection of intellectual property, and the arbitration of disputes in the realm of trade and economic relations.[39]

Two days later on 23 February, Lien's statement was positively taken by Beijing authorities, such as the Taiwan Affairs Office of the State Council, the Association for Straits Affairs, and the Ministry of Foreign Affairs of the PRC. With optimism, Taipei officials even suggested to consider the introduction of amendments to the 1991 "Manifesto" so as to accelerate the pace of normalization between the two sides, as that round of exchange had gone well.[40]

However, with all the positive signals exchanged across the Taiwan Straits, there were also ominous indicators, e.g., Beijing's deployment of missiles to its forward position in Fujian province across the Straits. Lee's speech at the First Meeting of the National Reunification Council in early April 1995, after its reorganization, did reflect an awareness of Beijing's threat of using missiles against Taiwan, which had been reported in newspapers in Taiwan early in February. Lee stated that Taipei had announced the conclusion of the "Mobilization Period" against the CCP as well as the termination of the use of force against the mainland in 1991. However, no positive response had been forthcoming from Beijing.[41] Lee continued:

> … Mainland authorities should express goodwill by abandoning the use of force against Taiwan, Penghu [Pescadores], Quemoy and Matsu, and should no longer take any military action which cause undue worry to anyone. By doing so, [Beijing] could lay the foundation for the negotiation leading to the conclusion of hostility.[42]

In order to pursue the goal of national reunification, Lee reiterated Taipei's stand, in essence, that both Beijing and Taipei had to come to face the political reality of separate rules in Taiwan and the mainland and that both sides represented separate political entities, neither of which was subject to the jurisdiction of the other. Therefore, the goal of national reunification could only be actualized, in Lee's view, through the search for a feasible approach on the basis of the factual premise of "two separate political entities." According to Lee, both sides had yet to reach a consensus regarding the operational definition of "one China" [as a future objective] by taking a pragmatic attitude towards the issue. In addition, Lee demanded Beijing not to interfere with Taipei's efforts to join international organizations. Lee suggested that the leaders of the two sides should meet each other "naturally" at the occasion of some international gathering so as to underscore their relationship had an international dimension.[43] Above all, Lee tried, as much as possible, to identify the differences between Beijing and Taipei and to reconfirm Taipei's intention to maintain the stalemate on Straits relations for an indefinite time period, should Taipei's pre-conditions not be met.[44]

In fact, considerable tension built up in the early months of 1995 after Jiang's speech of 30 January 1995, but this tension did not surface until

Lee's controversial visit to Cornell University in June 1995. The Clinton Administration did try to disassociate itself from the US Congress' request to allow Lee Teng-hui's private visit. For example, as Taipei had been stepping up its efforts to adopt a higher diplomatic posture and expand international contacts,[45] the US Department of State had made a statement on 23 March 1994 with reference to Lee Teng-hui's visit to three Southeast Asian countries, suggesting that the Clinton Administration intended to adhere to the US established policy concerning a strict definition of "private visit" by Taipei's high officials to the USA. It had stated that, since its diplomatic recognition of the PRC in 1979, the USA had maintained an unequivocal unofficial relationship with Taiwan. Moreover, the statement had added that the USA had always been of the view that it was not compatible with US's one China policy for any high official of Taiwan to visit the USA; such visit was neither compatible with the three communiqués signed between the USA and the PRC; nor was it compatible with the unofficial relationship between the USA and Taiwan.[46]

Yet, the Clinton administration's concern was not shared by the US Congress. For examples, the Senate passed an amendment to the Taiwan Relations Act, on 2 July 1994, not to disallow Taiwan's elected officials, including its president, to visit the USA in a "private" capacity, and this was concurred by the House on 17 August 1994.[47] Furthermore, in the bill introduced on 6 April 1995 to the House Committee on International Relations to amend the Taiwan Relations Act, a prevailing view of the Congress emerged: namely, first, a less restrictive definition of "private visits" by elected officials of the Taiwanese people was introduced by adhering to its common usage and by dropping the previous definition of "private visits" which had been mainly construed, according to the "consequences criterion," in terms of "potentially serious adverse foreign policy consequences for the USA"; secondly, the discretionary power of the Secretary of State to determine the entry or proposed activities of "private visits" was challenged.[48]

By early 1995, as the pressure to relax the restriction over Taiwan's high officials to visit the USA was mounting in the US Congress, Secretary of State Warren Christopher had to inform, on 17 April 1995, Qian Qichen, the PRC's Minister of Foreign Affairs, in New York, to anticipate the Congressional move to lift the restriction on the private visit to the US of Taiwan's high officials, including Lee Teng-hui.[49] This was followed by the unanimous passage of an unbinding resolution of the House of Representatives on 2 May 1995 to support a Lee Teng-hui visit to the US in a private capacity. One week later, on 9 May 1995, the same resolution was passed in the Senate with almost unanimity (97 versus 1). Under the circumstances, it was reported that Secretary of State Christopher had to override the opposition within the Department of State after his consultation with Secretary of Defence William Perry and the Assistant for National Security by mid-May 1995. On 20 May 1995, the Department of State approved Lee Teng-hui's visit to the US in a private capacity.[50]

In fact, Lee Teng-hui's activities in Ithaca were not as eventful as in the diplomatic battle ground. With slight nostalgic flavour, Lee's speech concerned "Taiwan's experience," how it had as a developing country turned into a newly industrialized country and how it had from an authoritarian regime completed its march towards democratization. In a subtle tone, Lee pleaded for space for the international existence of Taiwan in the world community during the post-Cold War period.

Of course, there was another round of protests from the officials of the PRC, including Premier Li Peng, on 20 July 1995. This was also followed by the official protests by the Ministry of Foreign Affairs. Moreover, Foreign Minister Qian Qichen stated that, in light of the status of Lee Teng-hui, his visit to the USA was a political issue, no matter in what capacity and under what form he visited a country.[51] In view of vested interests in the normal US-China relations, such as the annual event regarding the renewal of China's most-favoured-nation (MFN) trade status, Beijing refrained from taking any drastic action of "retaliation" against Washington, except for the military exercises of some symbolic nature later on in July, August and November, reaching their climax in 1996.

Military Exercises in the Taiwan Straits

Beijing staged six war games in the Taiwan Straits from July 1995 to March 1996: three in 1995 and three in 1996. Out of the six, the three scheduled in 1996 attracted most of the attention from the public and the media on both sides of the Straits and the concerned circles at the international level. It is noteworthy that the three military exercises in 1996 were scheduled during March, the same period when the bill on Taiwan Relations Act was being actively considered by the US Congress and the president. They coincided with the campaign for the presidential election in Taiwan as well.

The available evidence suggests that Beijing started to prepare the aforementioned military exercises as early as the end of 1994. In a routine exchange of military intelligence, Washington provided Taipei with the satellite photos of the movement of "M" species of missiles from Jiangxi, their home base, to Fujian, their staging area, at the end of 1994 and early 1995.[52] The Taiwan side made public the movement of missiles to Fujian in February 1995. Premier Lien Chan did protest publicly at the same time.[53] The three war games took place on 21–26 July, 15–25 August, and 23 November 1995. The first was a missile test by the divisions of the Second Artillery Corps. The second was a live fire drill of the East Sea Fleet coordinated by the Air Force and the Second Artillery Corps. The third military exercise which lasted for half a day on 23 November at Dungshan, Fujian, was a coordinated landing exercise.[54]

The military exercises in 1996, which took place mainly before the presidential election in Taiwan on 23 March 1996, were executed in three overlapping phases. In the first phase during 8–15 March, missile tests were carried out by the Second Artillery Corps in the two splash areas which were within short distance from two shipping centres in the north and south of Taiwan, namely, Keelung and Kaoshiung. Four missiles were fired on targets. The second phase lasted for eight days from 12 March to 20 March. Located at about 100 kilometres from Quemoy and Penghu (Pescadores), the military exercise was a live ammunition drill involving the elements of the South Sea Fleet and the East Sea Fleet, coupled with the air force of the newly established Nanjing War Theatre. The third phase occurred on 18–25 March in Pingtan, close to Matsu, one of the offshore islands controlled by Taipei.[55]

Evidence suggests that Jiang Zemin was not only fully aware of these military exercises, but also in command of them. The three missile tests, which took place in July 1995, August 1995 and March 1996, were carried out by the divisions of the Second Artillery Corps which was under direct command of the Military Affairs Commission (MAC) chaired by Jiang Zemin.[56] It was confirmed that Jiang took part in the discussions and analyses and gave final approval concerning the missile tests of July and August 1995, to say the least.[57] Another piece of evidence confirms that the party centre (i.e., Jiang himself) and the MAC took the decision for the military exercises in March 1996 "with regard to the situation of the struggle against Taiwan."[58] It was further confirmed that Jiang Zemin took personal charge of several military exercises in his capacity as the leader of the Taiwan Affairs Leadership Team of the Central Committee of the CCP.[59] As far as the remaining military exercises were concerned, it appears that they were under the command of the Military Affairs Commission. For example, General Zhang Wannian, Commander of the Nanjing War Theatre and Vice-Chairman of the MAC, took charge of the concerted military exercises of the East Sea fleet on 23 November.[60]

These military exercises were allegedly intended, not only for the purpose of training, but also for the demonstration of Beijing's determination to retain the use of force as an option to achieve the reunification of Taiwan. On 18–25 March, Zhang Wannian stated that "we propose continuing our efforts for peaceful reunification, but [we will] never abandon the use of force."[61] Moreover, he stressed that Beijing would use all means available, including military means, against foreign intervention in China's reunification effort and against Taiwan's independence.[62]

These military exercises were taken as "symbols" and "propaganda," judging from the type of technology, timing and site selections. First, in terms of the level of military technology involved, expert opinions suggested that all missiles were of the vintage of 30 years ago. Therefore, this was not exactly a testing of new military technology.[63]

Secondly, the launching of these missiles coincided with politically sensitive periods. For examples, the first two missile tests were scheduled in July and August 1995 about one month after Lee Teng-hui's visit to Cornell University. The third missile test was synchronized with the period of deliberation between the US Congress and the president over the bill of amendment to the Taiwan Relations Act as well as the period of presidential campaign and election in Taiwan in March 1996.

Thirdly, contrary to Beijing's previous practice of conducting its missile tests in the hinterland, it was observed that these were among the first to be carried out not only at high seas, but also over the Taiwan Straits. Such an observation was confirmed by Minister of Defence Chiang Chung-ling.[64] Therefore, the war games did demonstrate Beijing's long-term objective to build up and deploy eventually high-technology missiles and well equipped air and naval forces across the Taiwan Straits. For the operational considerations, however, there were no obvious reasons to conduct missile war games within a close proximity of Taiwan. It was, of course, provocative that some areas of test blocked the air routes and shipping passages in the region adjacent to Taiwan.[65]

Taken together, the missile tests, live fire and war games did seem to contain the required ingredients of a real invasion of Taiwan. However, expert assessment suggested that, not only the PLA did not have the delivery capacity for a full scale landing on Taiwan, but also it had yet to establish its air and naval superiority which was a pre-requisite to a successful invasion of Taiwan.[66] The military exercises of 1995–1996 were also not in congruence with the PLA's convention to conceal its real strength in order to take advantage of the element of surprise on the battle field. This meant that Beijing did not really mean at the moment to get into a war against Taiwan.

Our interpretation can be corroborated by Jiang Zemin's briefing to the National People's Congress in March 1996. In the briefing, he explicitly identified Lee Teng-hui's visit to the USA in 1995 and the Taiwan presidential election in 1996 as the main motivations for Beijing to conduct the military exercises in the Taiwan Straits over the period. Therefore, in Jiang's view, Lee's private visit was taken as a political incident, dividing the motherland through the collaboration of Taipei with anti-China foreign forces. In Jiang's assessment, the 1995 military exercises had apparent political effects, giving Lee Teng-hui a heavy blow, warning the Americans, educating the Taiwanese and showing off military and national strength. To the domestic audience within mainland China, Jiang stated that the launching of the missiles [in 1995] demonstrated Beijing's capacity to strike the targets with accuracy, to reach any target in Taiwan and to impose a blockade of all major sea and air routes to Taiwan. According to Jiang, the military exercises in March 1996 were an integral part of the diplomatic struggle against the pro-independence force represented by Lee Teng-hui. They served as a warning against foreign interference, such as from the USA, and they influenced the direction of Taiwan's presidential election and, strategically, stopped the pro-independence movement in Taiwan.[67]

Nonetheless, there were risks of losing control. In fact, the three-phase military exercise of March 1996 caused enough tension to warrant Washington to create a special Taiwan Straits Crisis group as reported in early March 1996, and Taipei to establish an "*ad hoc* decision making team," with Lien Chan serving as convenor and KMT General Secretary Hsü Li-Teh responsible for coordination in order to cope with the crisis.[68] Through several channels, Washington sought clarification from Beijing about the military exercises scheduled in March 1996. Beijing did give assurance that these military exercises did not intend to be part of a war against Taiwan.[69]

Furthermore, these military exercises did activate, not only the mutual obligation between Washington and Taipei on the basis of the existing commitments, but also a chain of interactions in the triangular relationship between Taipei, Washington and Beijing. For examples, Winston Lord, Assistant Secretary of State for Asia Pacific affairs, stated in early November 1995 that relevant departments in Washington were studying the missile tests in the Taiwan Straits and would decide upon whether or not the sale of an advanced missile defence system would be incorporated into the review after having examined the security balance between Taiwan and the Beijing's mainland.[70] Commenting on the "White Paper on National Defence" released by New China News Agency (NCNA), Nicholas Burns, spokesman of the US Department of State, said in a routine press conference that US arms sales to Taiwan would be based upon the Taiwan Relations Act and the 17 August 1982 Communiqué. He added that the US supply of arms to Taiwan would not create instability in the region since it shall be limited to the need for self-defence only.[71]

Washington made its stand explicit with regard to the three-phase military exercises which were about to begin on 8 March 1996. Mr Anthony Lake, President Bill Clinton's National Security Advisor, said that Beijing's "firing of missiles in international waters and international air space, but closer than ever before to Taiwan, is a potentially reckless act."[72] Additionally, Mr Lake said that "it could have real consequences were such tests to go wrong, and it exacerbates tensions in the area."[73] The State Department spokesman, Nicholas Burns, urged Beijing to "refrain from further provocative action" and asked the mainland and Taiwan authorities to "settle their differences through direct and peaceful dialogue."[74]

In addition, the US government conveyed its concern over the matter through formal channels by persons such as Peter Tarnoff, Under-secretary of State, to the PRC ambassador to Washington, Li Daoyu, and the US ambassador to Beijing, James Sasser, to the Chinese Foreign Ministry.[75] Washington also sent an even stronger signal to Beijing by dispatching two aircraft carrier groups around 18 March 1996 to the regions adjacent to the Taiwan Straits to monitor the PRC's war games off Taiwan. The US Secretary of Defence, William Perry, commented on the matter, stating that "the US has a national interest in the security and stability of the western Pacific."[76] He explicitly took the mainland's military exercises as "a deplorable act of intimidation to Taiwan" and hoped that "the people of Taiwan can live their lives in peace and stability."[77]

Premier Li Peng responded by stating: "If someone threatens the use of force against China, this has been shown by past experience that it will not be having any good results."[78] However, Beijing did not schedule any more military exercises in the Taiwan Straits after 25 March 1996. One month later on 23 April, Jiang Zemin proposed to forget all that had happened in the past and to "look forward" in handling the mainland-Taiwan relations.[79] In addition, his "eight-point proposal" of 30 January 1995 would remain effective, and Beijing's basic policy of peaceful reunification would stay intact. There were expectations of the resumption of talks between the two sides upon Lee Teng-hui's inauguration on 20 May 1996 and Lien Chan's confirmation as the Premier of the Executive Yuan in June, but it does not appear that any substantial progress has been made since then.

The Competing Claims of Legitimate Rule

The 1996 presidential election in Taiwan was taken as "the first popular election of a president in Chinese history." Thus, it did have implications for the legitimacy of the Taipei regime as well as Beijing's competing claim of sovereignty over Taiwan. The controversy of the competing sovereignty claims over Taiwan became evident in the 1996 New Year Message of Lee Teng-Hui and Jiang Zemin's New Year speech to the People's Political Consultative Conference, respectively. According to Jiang Zemin, Beijing would still follow the principles of "peaceful reunification" and "one country, two systems" to handle the Taiwan question and to promote the economic and cultural exchanges across the Straits. Jiang stressed that "the Chinese people have confidence, ability and strategy to overcome any [foreign] interference and to achieve national reunification."[80]

In his New Year Message, Lee had a different emphasis, suggesting that the Taipei government endeavoured to materialize the fully-fledged democracy on the basis of popular sovereignty and the objective to forge an identity for a common destiny. He added that he had taken part in formulating the "Manifesto for National Reunification" and had been of assistance at promoting the future reunification of China under freedom, democracy and the sharing of wealth for the last seven years.[81]

On an other occasion in the same day, Lee underscored his ideal of "pragmatic diplomacy," explaining that "the ROC should quickly go out [to the international arena] and occupy a seat so that the ROC will have a secured seat when the [order of] the new century is established."[82] He added that Taipei was given an opportunity as the new international order had yet to be established and the bondage of traditional concept of sovereignty had been surpassed in the post-Cold War era. Furthermore, Lee suggested that both the sovereignty claim and international space would create favourable bargaining conditions for the negotiation over reunification.[83]

Although Beijing did not overly repeat its messages, Qian Qichen stated on 11 March 1996, about two weeks before the presidential election, that the election should not provide an excuse for the separatist rule in Taiwan.[84] Further elaboration of Qian's position was accordingly given later: even though Beijing did not oppose Taiwanese people electing their leaders, this did not mean that Taiwan should be regarded as a political entity and thus no longer treated as a local government under the constitutional framework of the PRC.[85]

To take exception to Beijing's view, Lien Chan, Premier of the ROC, in his interview with an *Asia Weekly* (Yazhou zhoukan) correspondent, expounded on Taipei's position about reunification. According to Lien, the ROC had been a sovereign entity for 85 years since 1911; and, the separate rule of China had been a reality since 1949 when the ROC government had moved to Taiwan and when the CCP had occupied mainland China. According to Lien, a recent survey in Taiwan suggested that the majority of the Taiwanese population wanted to maintain the *status quo*; it supported neither independence nor immediate reunification. While reunification remained as an ultimate objective in the future, the ROC had to continue and develop, but not to accept the Communist rule.[86]

Additionally, in Lien's view, Taipei had to conduct its "pragmatic diplomacy" which should not be distorted as an effort to manufacture "two Chinas" or "one China and one Taiwan." On the basis of the separate rule across the Straits, Lien stated that the people in Taiwan aspired for political, economic and cultural activities at the international level and wished that Taipei's endeavour to expand its international space would gain the respect and attention which it deserved. Lien pointed out that the CCP felt anxious about the chain reactions to "pragmatic diplomacy," including Taiwan's campaign for re-entry to the UN and Lee Teng-hui's visit to the USA. Therefore, the anxiety was manifested in Beijing's unilateral postponement of the negotiation on practical matters across the Straits, the military exercises and missile tests, and the personal attack against the head of state of Taiwan.[87]

Under the threat of missile tests and military exercises during 18–25

March, 1996, the presidential election took place on 23 March 1996 and was concluded with a high voting turnout, i.e., 76.4% of eligible voters had cast their vote. Higher than what had been estimated, 54% of total votes went to the ticket of Lee Teng-hui and Lien Chan.

The pro-independence ticket of P'eng Ming-min and Hsieh Chang-ting, which was supported by the Democratic Progressive Party (DPP), gained 21.13%. The two pairs of pro-reunification candidates, Lin Yang-kang and Hau Pei-ts'un, Chen Li-an and Wang Ching-feng, shared the remaining 24.88% of the vote. The pro-independence candidates suffered in the 1996 presidential election for a variety of reasons, but one important consideration was that voters tended to support Lee and Lien's ticket for they symbolized stability and security. In spite of Beijing' propaganda attack and the threat of military exercises immediately before the election, Lee and Lien still obtained a higher percentage of votes than the gain of the KMT in the last election to the National Assembly in December 1995.[88]

With the electoral mandate, Lee Teng-hui was inaugurated on 20 May 1996 as the 9th president of the ROC. Accordingly, Lee asserted that the ROC had been a sovereign state all the time. Thus, neither was it necessary, nor feasible to adopt a policy of independence. Lee added that the two sides of the Straits had been under separate rule for the last 40 years owing to historical reasons, and both sides shared aspiration for reunification in the future. Therefore, both sides should proceed and conduct negotiation and improve communication with each other in order to minimize differences and maximize the common ground. Lee underscored the point that Taiwan and the mainland were part of cultural China and belonged to the same nationality, but Taiwan differed from the mainland in terms of [political] system and life style. He blamed the difficulties of Taiwan-mainland relations on Beijing's failure to recognize the existence of the ROC in Taiwan, Penghu, Quemoy and Matsu. In Lee's view, the legitimate existence of the ROC had been further substantiated through the election on the basis of popular sovereignty.[89]

During the presidential campaign, Lee Teng-hui had taken the initiative to fend off an accusation of his unwillingness to make any improvement in Taiwan-mainland relations. Accordingly, he had campaigned on a proposal to conclude a peace agreement with Beijing on top of Taipei's unilateral announcement of the end of the "mobilization period" in 1987.[90] In his inauguration speech, he reiterated the proposal for such a peace agreement in addition to a proposed trip of peace to Beijing in light of "the need of the state and the support of the people."[91]

Beijing's response was made about one month later, on 22 June 1996; the spokesman of the Taiwan Affairs Office of the Central Committee and the Taiwan Affairs Office of the State Council answered the questions of New China News Agency in an interview, reiterating Jiang Zemin's position of 30 January 1995 that "as a first step, both sides could start to negotiate for the [formal] concluding of the hostility across the Straits under the principle of one China."[92] Here it was apparent that Beijing and Taipei did not agree on the crucial concept, "one China": the former took it to mean the PRC and the latter took it as the ROC, or alternately a reunified China on the basis of a negotiated settlement in the future. Therefore, the spokesman suggested that Beijing was waiting for deeds from Taipei as the latter had uttered its position.[93] It was obvious that Beijing could, under no circumstances, extend an invitation to Lee Teng-hui to visit the mainland in his capacity as head of the state. Consequently, neither side was ready to make concessions on these non-negotiable preconditions which had barred the progress of a peace negotiation. In fact, Beijing had never altered its sovereignty claim over Taiwan, while Taipei had renounced its legitimate claim over the mainland in 1990. This has proven to be a deadlocked position for the mainland-Taiwan relations for the time being.

Immediately after the first round of "negotiation" between Beijing and Taipei through the media on the formal ending of hostility as just noted, Lien Chan, vice-president and premier of the ROC, proposed to continue the dialogue at the pragmatic level. Lien made a brief review of mainland-Taiwan relations, focusing on the recent progress after 1990. He proposed to re-open the unofficial channel of dialogue which had been established from April 1993 between the Taiwan Straits Foundation and the Association of the Taiwan Straits. According to Lien, however, the channel had been blocked due to Lee Teng-hui's private visit to the USA and the missile tests by Beijing in 1995 and 1996. Lien took pain to assure Beijing that Taipei did not challenge the Chinese nationalism which was shared by the Chinese people across the Straits. Yet, the real obstacles to reunification between Beijing and Taipei owed mainly to Beijing's refusal to recognize the reality of the separate rule over the mainland and Taiwan. Since the CCP had failed to use force to incorporate Taiwan into the PRC during the Civil War, 1945–1949, the CCP could not achieve the same objective through the use of words. Neither had the CCP regime ever established jurisdiction over Taiwan, nor could it represent the 21 million Taiwanese people in any international organization. Conversely, it should be natural for the people in Taiwan to desire a further expansion of their international space of activities. This should not be inconsistent with the endeavour to achieve national reunification. With the assertion of the separate rule and quest for international space, Taipei aspired after the objective of national reunification and, in the meantime, both sides should pursue trade and economic exchange.[94]

While Beijing and Taipei perpetuated their stalemate by not giving in one inch at the level of political settlement, Taipei still indicated its willingness to restore the momentum of "virtuous interaction" across the Straits at the pragmatic level. Of course, Beijing had not entirely closed the door to Taipei as regard the exchanges at the pragmatic level. In light of the possibility of some kind of "breakthrough," Lien tried to explain himself to the other side as follows: First, Taipei authorities faced much constraints in dealing with Beijing because Taiwan was a democratic and pluralistic society. Secondly, the improvement of mainland-Taiwan relations should be based upon the principle of "parallel interests" and "variable sum game"; the deadlock between the two sides should be attributed to the discrepancies across the Taiwan Straits in the arenas of political system, economic system and living standards, not to foreign interference and the advocacy of independence within Taiwan. Thirdly, the expansion of exchange should start with trade and economic relations, in addition to the arenas of art, culture, education, literature and science and technology. Fourthly, the "pragmatic dialogue" according to the Koo Cheng-fu–Wang Daohan model, which had begun in 1993, should be restored in order to strengthen the institutionalization of channels of negotiation and communication and to cope with the problems which derived from the exchanges across the Straits.[95]

On top of the bilateral relations, the strains between Taipei and Beijing spread to the international arena as soon as were concluded the military exercises in the Taiwan Straits and the presidential election in Taiwan. On 28 March 1996, President Lee Teng-hui responded to Beijing's demand made two days before, by stating in an interview to the *Asian Wall Street Journal* that Taipei would not discuss its sovereignty with Beijing and would not give up its campaign for a seat in the United Nations and for diplomatic ties with other countries.[96] In fact, Taipei had first launched its campaign to rejoin the United Nations at the 48th Session in 1993; it reached a climax in 1995 when Taipei promulgated the White Paper titled, "The Republic of China and the United Nations," in September 1995.[97] It was stated in the White Paper that, on the one hand, each of the ROC in

Taiwan and the PRC in mainland China enjoyed an equal status and was not under the jurisdiction of the other in the relations across the Taiwan Straits; on the other hand, the ROC wished to reconstruct the political relations across the Straits in the future under the principles of democracy, freedom and the sharing of wealth. Before the fulfilment of the long term objective and the settlement of the relations across the Straits, the basic rights of the Taiwanese people to join the United Nations should not be denied, just as with the cases of the two Koreas and the two Germanies.[98]

After the results of the 1996 presidential election were made public, Lee Teng-hui stated he would continue to push the campaign to rejoin the United Nations before the completion of reunification of China.[99] In July 1996, the proposal for the representation of the ROC in the United Nations was put on the agenda of the 51st session of the UN on the basis of the concept of divided nation and parallel representation rather than the principle of universality of membership, as in the last three attempts since 1993.[100] From the month of March on, Beijing registered its opposition to Taipei's move concerning the UN membership, including a formal letter by China's UN Delegation to UN Secretary General Boutros Boutros-Ghali on 23 July 1996 and the declaration of Cui Tiankai, spokesman of the PRC Ministry of Foreign Affairs on 24 July 1996.[101] As expected, Taipei was not successful in pushing through its proposal, but its objective of publicizing Taipei's stand should have been fulfilled somehow. The mainland-Taiwan relations had returned to "normality" by the end of 1996 after two years of tension and controversies.

Conclusion

It has been a long way from 1949 to the present for Beijing to shift to a peaceful approach towards the reunification with Taiwan. Beijing's change of policy does not amount to its renouncing the use of force against Taiwan. Therefore, in Beijing's view, the means of force will remain as a last resort, while demanding Taipei to abandon its constitutional status as a political entity to be relegated into a special administrative region with the status of local government, and to terminate its diplomatic ties as well as membership in all international organizations of a political nature. Under the notion of a divided nation under separate rule, Taipei indicates its willingness to institutionalize the *status quo* of peace across the Taiwan Straits and sign a formal agreement on the ending of hostility between the two sides. Furthermore, Taipei proposes to Beijing that both sides should reach an agreement of mutual recognition as political entities in the transitional period of pragmatic exchange at the economic and cultural level and of political negotiation towards eventual peaceful reunification.

However, the component of force in Beijing's peace policy plants the seed of periodic outbursts as witnessed in the military exercises from 1995 to 1996. In other words, Beijing's show of force is an indication of a sense of anxiety over the possible loss of control over the direction of the development of mainland-Taiwan relations, as prompted by Lee Teng-hui's private visit to the US and the introduction of an amendment to the Taiwan Relations Act in the US Congress in 1994.

From 1995 to 1996, Beijing's demonstration of force was directed at Taipei and the Taiwanese people so as to bring pressure to bear and hopefully to extract concessions from Taipei. In the meantime, it was aimed at the American audience in order to show its seriousness about the possible retreat of Washington from the three communiqués of 1972, 1979 and 1982 when Beijing had been able to gain favourable concessions from Washington because of the anti-hegemony imperative. The end of the Cold War as well as the Tiananmen incident undermined, not only Beijing's political constituency in the US, but also the friendship and goodwill of many Americans to sustain a favourable climate for a stable US-China relationship. Needless to say, Taiwan profited considerably from the ebb in US-China relations as it started its campaign move to return to the international community in 1993.

Of course, Beijing's sense of anxiety was closely related to how Washington would act in steering the developments of US-China relations. After the 1992 presidential election, when the Republican Party began to dominate both the Senate and the House, the division between the US Congress and the US president did aggravate the tension between Washington and Beijing as manifested in Lee Teng-hui's visit and the issue of an amendment to the Taiwan Relations Act. Correspondingly, the return of US-China relations to normality was marked by the US president's veto of the congressional bill of amendment to the Taiwan Relations Act. If successfully enacted, the bill would augment arms sales to Taiwan, undercut Beijing's relative military superiority and strengthen Taipei's bargaining power in the long run.

As expected, the bill was vetoed by President Clinton on the grounds that this would not make the job of the president easier, but add complexity by recognizing, in the form of amendment, that the Taiwan Relations Act would enjoy a higher status than the 17 August 1982 Communiqué on arms sales to Taiwan.[102] Putting it in another way, President Clinton's veto took away the uncertainty and, therefore, reduced the anxiety pertaining to the amendment in the US Congress and provided assurance of the continuity and stability of US-China policy to Beijing. It was probably not the point whether Washington would reduce the level of arms sales to Taiwan. More importantly, President Clinton's veto did end the risk for Beijing to leave to the good will of a Republican-dominated US Congress to dictate the quality and quantity of arms sales to Taiwan as well as the number and level of Taiwan's high officials to visit the US.

Therefore, there was a good reason for Beijing's apparent relief after President Clinton's vetoed the bill. This was followed by the visit of Mr Anthony Lake, the President's National Security Adviser, to Beijing in early July 1996. Mr Lake, who was enthusiastically received by the PRC State Chairman Jiang Zemin, Premier Li Peng, Foreign Affairs Minister Qian Qichen and Defence Minister Chi Haotian, all within one day, thus resumed the mutual visits of the top leaders of the two nations for the first time since 1989 and brought an end to the disputes between the two sides since 1994.[103] This ended a full cycle from tension to dialogue in US-China relations between 1989 to 1996, a time span of seven years. However, the mainland-Taiwan relations have yet to recover from the low ebb, not likely in the foreseeable future.

Notes

1. John Gittings, *The World and China 1972–1992* (New York: Harper & Row Publishers, 1974), pp. 180–208; Doak A. Barnett, *Communist China and Asia: Challenge to American Policy* (New York: Vintage Books 1960), pp. 384–429; Roderick MacFacquhar (ed.), *Sino-American Relations, 1949–71* (New York: Praeger Publishers, 1972), pp. 78–181.
2. Richard Moorsteen, "US Policy Options: One China — But Not Now," in Jerome Alan Cohen, *Taiwan and American Policy* (New York: Praeger Publishers, 1971), pp. 131–55; Richard Moorsteen and Morton Abramowitz, *Remaking China Policy: US-China Relations and Governmental Decision Making* (Cambridge, Massachusetts: Harvard University Press, 1971), pp. 1–86.
3. John W. Garver, *Foreign Relations of the People's Republic of China* (Englewood Cliffs, New Jersey: Prentice Hall, 1993), pp. 70–97.
4. Ibid., pp. 98–112.

5. For a review of US-China relationship after the collapse of the USSR, see *Chinese Foreign Policy*, ibid., pp. 104–11; David Shambaugh, "Patterns of Interaction in Sino-American Relations," in *Chinese Foreign Policy: Theory and Practice*, edited by Thomas W. Robinson and David Shambaugh (Oxford: Clarendon Press, 1994).
6. "Gao Taiwan tongbao shu" (Message to Taiwanese Compatriots), *Renmin ribao* (People's Daily), 1 January 1979. Here in the "Message," the PRC announced that the PLA had stopped bombardment of Quemoy and Matsu for the first time since 1958. In fact, the bombardment had been conducted on alternate days, with a ritualistic flavour, up to 1979.
7. The three conditions are the severance of the diplomatic ties with Taipei, termination of the 1954 mutual defence treaty, and withdrawal of US military personnel from Taiwan. See "United States Statement on Diplomatic Relations Between the United States and the People's Republic of China," 15 December 1978, in Harry Harding, *A Fragile Relationship: The United States and China since 1972* (Washington, DC: The Brookings Institute, 1992), p. 380.
8. Ibid., pp. 380–81.
9. "The Taiwan Relations Act," *United States Code*, 4 January 1993, Title 22, Section 3301–16.
10. "Message to Taiwanese ..." (Note 6), *People's Daily*, 1 January 1979.
11. "Ye Jianying Xinhuashe jizhe fabiao tanhua — Jinyibu chanming guanyu Taiwan huigui zuguo shixian heping tongyi de fangzhen zhengce (Ye Jianying's Statement to the NCNA Correspondent — Further Explanation Concerning the Policy and Guideline of Taiwan's Return to the Motherland and the Actualization of Peaceful Reunification), *People's Daily*, 1 October 1981.
12. *Zhonghua renmin gongheguo xianfa* (The Constitution of the People's Republic of China, 4 December 1982); article 31 reads "The State shall establish the special administrative region when necessary; the system of the special administrative region shall be determined in the form of law by the National People's Congress according to the concrete situation."
13. "Liao Chengzhi zhi Jiang zongtong Jingguo xiansheng han" (Liao Chengzhi's Letter to President Chiang Ching-kuo), *People's Daily*, 25 July 1982.
14. "Deng Xiaoping huijian Yang Liyu jiaoshou tan Zhongguo dalu he Taiwan heping tongyi de shexiang" (Deng Xiaoping's Ideas on the Peaceful Reunification of Mainland China with Taiwan in a Conversation with Professor Yang Liyu), *People's Daily*, 30 July 1983.
15. "Deng Xiaoping shuo yong 'yiguo liangzhi' de gouxiang jiejue Taiwan wenti tiaojian keyi geng guang yixie" (Deng Xiaoping's Suggestion to Offer Generous Terms in Order to Settle Taiwan Question according to "One

Country, Two Systems"), *People's Daily*, 24 October 1984; "Deng gong ruhe tichu yiguo liangzhi" (How Did Deng Propose One Country, Two Systems?) *Ta Kung Pao*, 23 March 1995.

16. "Jiang Zemin yu Shen Junshan de sanci tanhua" (Three Dialogues between Jiang Zemin and Shen Junshen), *Jiushi niandai* (The Nineties), No. 319 (August 1996), pp. 60–111.
17. Ibid., pp. 73–74; p. 82.
18. Ibid., p. 111.
19. Ibid.
20. Ibid., p. 93.
21. Ibid., pp. 90–91.
22. Ibid., pp. 94–95.
23. Ibid., pp. 95–96.
24. Ibid., pp. 66–67; p. 75.
25. Jiang Zemin, "Wei chujin zuguo tongyi daye wancheng er jixu fendou" (Continue to Struggle to Promote the Completion of the Task of Reunification of Motherland), *Xinhua yuebao* (New China Monthly), No. 3 (1995), p. 11; an excellent piece of content analysis of Jiang's speech is also provided in Chu-cheng Ming, "Political Interactions across the Taiwan Straits," in *China Review 1996* (Hong Kong: The Chinese University Press, 1996), pp. 175–200.
26. "Feidan nanyi Fujian zhen baodao" (Taiwan Was Shocked by the Movement of Missiles Southward to Fujian), *Yazhou zhoukan* (Asia Weekly), 12 March 1995, pp. 20–21.
27. Jiang, "Continue to Struggle …" (Note 25), p. 10.
28. Ibid., pp. 10–11.
29. Ibid.
30. Ibid., p. 11.
31. "Guanzhe yi sanminzhuyi tongyi Zhongguo fangan" (Implement the Proposal of Reunification of China with the Three Principles of the People, April 1981), in *Dalu gongzuo shouce* (Handbook of Mainland Work), edited by Xingzhengyuan Dalu Gongzuo Weiyuanhui (Legislative Yuan, Mainland China Affairs Committee), p. I–5.
32. "Zhongguo Guomindang xian jieduan dalu zhengce" (The Mainland Policy of the KMT in the Current Phase), ibid., p. I–7.
33. Ma Ying-jeou, "Liangnian lai de dalu zhengce yu liangan guanxi" (The Mainland Policy and the Two-shore Relations for the Last Two Years), ibid., pp. I-57–58.
34. Ibid., pp. I-59–74.
35. "Guo tong gangling" (The Manifesto for National Reunification), in *Dalu gongzuo shouce* (Note 31), pp. I-12–14.
36. "Li Teng-hui zongtong jizhehui youguan dalu zhengce bufen" (President

Lee Teng-hui's Press Conference on Mainland Policy), 30 April 1991, p. I-17.

37. *Xianggang lianhe bao* (Hong Kong United Daily News), 10 February 1995.
38. *Ta Kung Pao*, 5 February 1995.
39. *Zhongyang ribao* (Central Daily), 22 February 1995.
40. *Zhongguo shibao* (China Times), 9 April 1995.
41. "Li Teng-hui zongtong guotonghui tanhua quanwen" (The Full Text of President Lee's Statement at the National Reunification Committee), *Lianhe Bao*, 9 April 1995.
42. Ibid.
43. Ibid.
44. Ibid.
45. The background and preparation of Lee Teng-hui's historical visit to Ithaca was reported in *Asia Weekly* (4 June 1995), pp. 22–24; (18 June 1995), pp. 20–22.
46. See "Liang'an dashiji" (The Chronology of the Relations between the Two Shores), in Li Jiaquan, *Li Teng-hui zhuzheng Taiwan yilai de liang'an guanxi* (The Mainland-Taiwan Relations since Lee Teng-hui's Rule), (Hong Kong: Xianggang wenhui chubanshe, 1996), pp. 392–93.
47. Ibid., pp. 398–403.
48. Section 1, *Public Law 96–8*, (22 USA 3301–3316).
49. *Lianhe bao*, 24 May 1995.
50. *Sing Tao Daily*, 24 May 1995.
51. *Ta Kung Pao*, 25 May 1995.
52. *Asia Weekly*, 12 March 1995, pp. 20–1.
53. *Ming Pao*, 25 February 1995; 25 February 1995.
54. *Wen Wei Po*, 19 July 1995; *Ming Pao*, 20 July 1995; *Ming Pao*, 16 August 1995; *Ming Pao*, 10 December 1995, pp. 35–36.
55. *Asia Weekly*, 17 March 1996, pp. 18–21; *Ming Pao*, 18 March 1996; *Ta Kung Pao*, 26 March 1996; *Apple Daily*, 13 November 1996.
56. *Asia Weekly*, 30 July 1995, pp. 22–25. The Second Artillery Corps has the main responsibility over strategic missiles (or intercontinental missiles) as well as surface-to-air missiles and surface-to-surface missiles of various ranges.
57. Ibid., 10 December 1995, pp. 35–36.
58. Ibid.
59. Ibid.
60. *Ta Kung Pao*, 26 March 1996.
61. Ibid.
62. Ibid.
63. *Asia Weekly*, 30 July 1995, pp. 23.
64. *Ming Pao*, 20 July 1995.

65. *Ming Pao*, 21 July 1995.
66. *Apple Daily*, 9 October and 13 November 1995; *Ming Pao*, 10 October 1995.
67. *Asia Weekly*, 31 March 1996, p. 26.
68. "The Chronology of ..." (Note 46), p. 441.
69. Xiong Guangkai, deputy chief of the General Staff and, concurrently, member of the Taiwan Affairs Leadership Team, stated on 17 May 1996 that the Taiwan Straits crisis in March 1996 would not be repeated. *Apple Daily*, 17 May 1996; Liu Huaqiu, the Director of the Office for Foreign Affairs of the State Council, stated in March 1996 that the PRC did not have a plan to invade Taiwan. *Apple Daily*, 17 March 1996.
70. "The Chronology of ..." (Note 46), p. 436.
71. Ibid.
72. *Eastern Express*, 8 March 1996.
73. Ibid.
74. Ibid.
75. Ibid.
76. *Eastern Express*, 18 March 1996.
77. Ibid.
78. Ibid.; *Apple Daily*, 18 March 1996.
79. *China Times*, 26 April 1996.
80. *Hong Kong Economic Journal*, 2 January 1996.
81. Ibid.
82. Ibid.
83. Ibid.
84. *China Times*, 13 March 1996.
85. *Ta Kung Pao*, 26 March 1996.
86. *Ming Pao*, 15 March 1996.
87. Ibid.
88. *Apple Daily*, 24 March; *Ming Pao*, 25 March 1996; *Ta Kung Pao*, 25 March 1996.
89. *China Times*, 20 May 1996.
90. Ibid., 24 February 1996.
91. Ibid., 20 May 1996.
92. *Ta Kung Pao*, 23 June 1996.
93. Ibid.
94. Lien Chan, "A Pragmatic Strategy for China's Peaceful Reunification," Sponsored statement by the Central News Agency, Republic of China, *Foreign Affairs*, Vol. 75, No. 2 (March/April 1996), pp. 124–27.
95. Ibid., pp. 6–8.
96. *Eastern Express*, 28 March 1996; *Ming Pao*, 28 March 1996.
97. For the background on the issue, see *Ming Pao*, 30 July 1995; 28 March

1996 and 22 September 1996; *Lianhe bao* 13, 20 and 22 September 1995; *Wen Wei Po*, 14, 15, 20 and 22 September 1995; *Ta Kung Pao*, 15 September 1995 and 22 July 1996.

98. *Lianhe bao*, 9 and 20 September 1995.
99. *Eastern Express*, 28 March 1996; *Ming Pao*, 28 March 1996.
100. *Apple Daily*, 25 July and 30 July 1996.
101. *Ta Kung Pao*, 25 July 1996.
102. The joint conference of the US Senate and US House of Representatives reportedly endorsed the bill on the amendment to the Taiwan Relations Act on 1 March 1996 to enable the Act to enjoy precedence over the 17 August 1982 US-China Communiqué on arms sales to Taiwan. See *Apple Daily*, 2 March 1996. The bill finally passed the US Senate on 28 March 1996 but was vetoed by President Bill Clinton on 13 April 1996. See *Ming Pao*, 30 March and 14 April 1996.
103. *Ming Pao*, 11 July 1996.

6

The Grain Issue in China: Domestic and International Perspectives

Robert F. Ash

Introduction — Putting China's Grain Issue into Context

A well-tested Chinese slogan proclaims the agricultural sector to be the "foundation of the national economy" and adds that "grain is the basis of the foundation." It is a message that seems distinctly outmoded in today's China. If food security[1] were threatened, prioritizing agriculture — and, in particular, the grain sector — would command an obvious logic.[2] But, in the mid-1990s, the Chinese economy is no longer driven by the farm sector, nor are essential food supplies in jeopardy. On the contrary, China has for many years enjoyed a comfortable cushion above the subsistence needs of its population.[3] Living standards have greatly improved for the great majority of the Chinese population in the sense, not only of raising their incomes, but also of providing them with a more nutritious and varied diet.

In such circumstances, Chinese leaders' continued advocacy of the economic imperative of agriculture appears paradoxical.[4] Fears that the hallowed principle of grain self-sufficiency might have to be abandoned seem even more surprising. In no year since 1978 have grain imports ever exceeded more than 4.5% of total domestic production.[5] In only one year (1993) in the first half of the 1990s did China's agricultural trade balance move out of surplus.[6] Meanwhile, China's foreign exchange reserves have overtaken those of Taiwan and are now second only to those of Japan.[7] In short, China has yet to fall below a 95% rate of grain self-sufficiency and even allowing for the period of peak foreign debt repayment which it has now entered, it would seem comfortably placed to pay for any adventitious purchases of foreign grain.

Evidence of a widening gap between grain demand and supply, highlighted in many projections, offer one explanation of the continuing concern about China's ability to feed itself. There is a consensus among analysts inside and outside China that rising demand for grain will outstrip

* I am grateful to an anonymous referee for valuable comments on a first draft of this chapter. My thanks too to Dr Claude Aubert (National Institute of Agricultural Research [INRA], Paris), Mr Frederick Crook (US Department of Agriculture, Washington), Dr Timothy Fox (SOAS) and Professor Y. Y. Kueh (Lingnan College, Hong Kong) for their assistance on matters of interpretation and presentation.

increases in supply during the next few decades. But, on the likely size of the associated grain deficit, as well as its policy implications, there is less agreement.

This is the context in which a major debate has unfolded, focusing on the relative merits of basic grain self-sufficiency *vis-à-vis* greater reliance on food imports. With China seeking to feed almost a quarter of the world's population on a mere 7% of its arable land, some view the further encroachment on the minimal land base caused by rapid industrialization and urbanization as a basis for advocating an increase in imports of land-intensive products. Given appropriate assumptions, it is quite easy to construct a theoretical model in which efficiency considerations, driven by the familiar principles of free trade, dictate a reduction in China's domestic cereal production, an expansion of manufactured exports and an increase in purchases of foreign grain. But, integration with world food markets, especially given China's size and level of development, might entail large risks. Not least, reliance on outside sources could have calamitous consequences, if some exogenous shock were to cut off a major source of such imports. Considerations of this kind still carry considerable weight within the Chinese leadership.

There are other factors which have encouraged the advocacy of grain self-sufficiency. One is the awareness of the impact of the great famine of 1959–1961, when some 30 million people — overwhelmingly peasants — died as a direct or indirect result of starvation. The extent to which this tragedy has penetrated the consciousness of the Chinese people should not be underestimated, and it too is reflected in the government's unwillingness to abandon control over basic food supplies.

Another factor relates to the social tolerance of the urban and rural population.[8] In cities, fear of the inflationary consequences of freeing grain prices has been a major constraint on government efforts to implement a rational retail pricing policy. In the countryside, there has been considerable social unrest as a result of behaviour which peasants have perceived as exploitative.[9] Remedial measures have been quite effective in addressing the most serious manifestations of such unrest. But, underlying problems remain, especially in the countryside and among grain farmers.[10] A survey of 100 counties revealed that in 1996, 40% of grain purchase funds were diverted to other uses — significantly more than in 1995.[11] In advance of the 1996 autumn harvest, Zhu Rongji warned against the misappropriation of such funds and explicitly forbade the issue of IOUs to farmers.[12] Meanwhile, Jiang Zemin is on record as saying that the imposition of excessive burdens on peasants has seriously damaged their relations with the party and destabilized rural areas.[13]

The grain issue in China is more than a question of mere economics. It has powerful historical resonances for both the Chinese government and the general population. The implications of a poor grain performance and of deteriorating conditions for grain farmers are viewed as much in social — even political — as in economic terms. One of the great lessons of Chinese history is that "without agriculture, there can be no stability; without grain, there is chaos."[14]

The Performance of the Grain Sector

China's grain performance since 1978 falls into three sub-periods. The years from 1978 to 1984 were a period of rapid and sustained growth, with total production rising, on average, by some 17 million tonnes a year (5% p.a.). There followed five years (1985–1989) of stagnation, the 1984 peak level of output not being re-attained until the end of the decade (1989). Thereafter, there were significant annual fluctuations in grain production, although there is a suggestion of more sustained growth having taken place since 1994 (see Table 1).

Between 1990 and 1994, growth instability was the most striking feature of the grain sector's performance. The average rate of increase between 1989–1994 (average) and 1993–1994 (average) was 1.4% p.a. — slightly ahead of population growth.[15] But, 1995 and 1996 saw the attainment of two record harvests, generating an average annual rate of expansion of 3.8%. Whether this most recent record will prove merely to have taken total production to a new plateau or represents the beginning of a new, more pronounced trend line, it is still too early to say.

The per capita estimates highlight the continuing pressure which even a low — and often declining — rate of natural increase has placed on grain availability. An unprecedented series of fine harvests took output per head from 317 to 390 kilograms between 1978 and 1984. In so doing, domestic supplies of grain rose from a level commensurate with subsistence requirements to one which promised to accommodate the demands of rapid increases in income.[16] In this sense, the achievement of 1984 was a watershed, albeit one which subsequently proved difficult to improve on. On the basis of firm estimates, 1990 is the only other year in which the 1984 level was re-attained, although preliminary figures suggest that per capita output

Table 1. Total and Average Per Capita Domestic Grain Output (Selected Years since 1978)

Year	Total output (million tonnes)	Average output per head of total population (kilograms)
1978	304.77	316.6
1984	407.31	390.3
1989	407.55	361.6
1990	446.24	390.3
1991	435.29	375.8
1992	442.66	377.8
1993	456.49	385.2
1994	445.10	371.4
1995	466.62	385.3
1996	480.00	392.5

Sources: (Production) 1978–1994: SSB, *Zhongguo nongcun tongji nianjian 1995* (Rural Statistical Yearbook of China 1995) (Beijing: Zhongguo tongji chubanshe, 1996), p. 187; 1995: *ZGTJNJ, 1996*, p. 371; 1996: preliminary SSB estimate from XHNA, 30 December 1996 in *SWB*, FE/2805, 31 December 1996. (Population) 1978–1995: SSB, *Zhongguo tongji zhaiyao 1996* (A Statistical Survey of China 1996) (Beijing: Zhongguo tongji chubanshe, 1996), p. 20; 1996: estimated from 1995 base on the basis of an assumed rate of natural increase of 1.1%.

reached a new peak in 1996.

Taken at face value, the figures in Table 1 point to a production performance which, even allowing for stagnation in the second half of the 1980s and significant variability in the early 1990s, is by no means unimpressive. It also bears stating that, from an historical perspective, China's post-1949 record is quite enviable.[17] History does not always provide a useful guide to the future, but the longer-term context is worth keeping in mind, not least against the background of the contrasting gloom which has informed many projections of China's future grain performance.

One of the most striking features of the debate about the grain issue in China is the aggregate, or national, level at which it has been conducted. In reality, the enormous diversity of China's natural and resource conditions demands that any investigation of the grain sector's recent performance and future potential should address their regional dimensions.[18]

Analysis of this aspect of the grain sector's performance under the impact of post-1978 economic reforms highlights the sharp rise in the share of national output contributed by the northern half of the country.

This is a trend which was already in evidence in the 1980s, but which has become more pronounced in the 1990s (Table 2).

Between the first and second halves of the 1980s, the northern half of the country contributed almost 57% of the average annual addition to total grain output, compared with 43% from the south. By contrast, between 1985–1989 and 1990–1994, the corresponding figures were 78% and 22%.[19] The new pattern of production reflected major changes in the contributions of some individual regions. The most striking of these affected the north-east and centre-east: in the former, rapid growth took its incremental contribution from 10% to 34%;[20] in the latter — China's former "grain basket" — output stagnation reduced its share from 42% to less than 1%.[21] The disappearance of the centre-east's surplus is an alarming phenomenon, not least because of the region's earlier pre-eminent role as a supplier of surplus *rice* — the staple diet of southern China.

Such figures only hint at changes in the identity of surplus and deficit regions in China.[22] In terms of food *security* — the provision of adequate food supplies to meet subsistence needs — China has enjoyed basic self-sufficiency throughout the post-1978 period. Indeed, on this limited basis, available evidence would point to the attainment of sizeable grain surpluses in every region by 1984.[23] But, on the basis of a more meaningful per capita criterion of 400 kilograms, a very different picture emerges. It suggests that the 1980s and 1990s have seen a steady deterioration in

Table 2. Regional Contributions to Average Annual Incremental Grain Output (1980–1984 Average/1985–1989 Average; and 1985–1989 Average/1990–1994 average)

	Average annual increase in total grain output (1980–84 av/1985–89 av) (m. tonnes)	As % of rise in total grain output	Average annual increase in total grain output (1990–94 av/1985–89 av) (m. tonnes)	As % of rise in total grain output
CHINA	+39.096	100.00	+49.738	100.00
E	+ 3.748	9.59	+16.738	33.98
N	+13.283	35.36	+14.449	29.05
NW	+ 4.587	11.73	+ 7.336	14.75
CE	+16.568	42.38	+ 0.116	0.24
S	– 1.607	–4.11	+ 4.638	9.42
SW	+ 1.977	5.06	+ 5.977	12.14

Source: Ministry of Agriculture, *Zhongguo nongye nianjian* (Chinese Agricultural Yearbook, *ZGNYNJ*) (Beijing: Nongye chubanshe), 1981–1995.

China's domestic grain balance, generating a national deficit of almost 34 million tonnes by 1994.[24]

The shift in gravity, in terms of the regional distribution of grain production, has not gone unnoticed in China. For example, one report on the growing pressure on domestic food supplies in China drew particular attention to the reversal of the traditional pattern of distribution, whereby the southern half of the country had exported surplus grain to northern regions.[25] It attributed the deteriorating position mainly to the declining arable land base, arguing that an area contraction of some 12 million hectares in 10 southeastern[26] provinces between 1984 and 1993 had resulted in a loss of almost 16 million tonnes of grain. There was a suggestion that this situation gave rise to a new policy priority, designed to halt agricultural neglect in coastal regions and to seek a "fairly high [grain] self-sufficiency rate."[27]

There is abundant evidence that by 1994 the central authorities in Beijing viewed the growing pressure on the grain sector with anxiety. This was the context in which a major initiative emerged in the guise of the "grain bag"[28] policy. As early as March of that year, Jiang Zemin described the policy as a key element in the attempt to guarantee agricultural supplies and combat price inflation.[29] As it subsequently evolved, it became an integrated package, which placed the responsibility of maintaining regional grain balance and stability on provincial governors.[30] To this end, provincial authorities were required to conserve and stabilize the grain sown area, guarantee input supplies, facilitate inter-provincial grain transfers, and stabilize grain prices.

Assessing the impact of the policy is difficult not only because of its newness, but also because of the need to separate its effects from those of other forces at work.[31] However, an examination of the performance of the grain sector since 1994 may serve to indicate its effect on the regional distribution of grain production throughout the country.

In aggregate terms, attention has already been drawn to the acceleration in the rate of growth of domestic grain output after 1994. The harvest of 1995 took total production to a new peak — one which was, moreover, bettered (by almost 3%) in 1996.[32] Table 3 seeks to highlight some of the regional dimensions of that performance.

The estimates in Table 3 point to a remarkable change in regional fortunes between 1994 and 1995. Collectively, the three regions of southern China enjoyed a rise of almost 6% in total grain output. Most spectacular was a 10.5% increase in production in the provinces of the

Table 3. Regional Grain Performance in 1994 and 1995

	Production (million tonnes)		Surplus/deficit position (million tonnes)	
	1994	1995	1994	1995
CHINA	445.11	466.62	–32.09	–14.41
NE	59.32	59.68	+17.59	+18.15
N	110.56	118.36	– 6.20	+ 0.32
NW	36.98	36.49	– 5.94	– 7.08
CE	136.75	142.71	– 1.72	+ 2.56
S	39.52	43.65	–20.78	–17.84
SW	61.98	65.73	–15.04	–10.52

Notes: Estimates of surplus/deficit based on an assumed per capita grain requirement of 400 kg.

Sources: *ZGTJNJ*, 1995, pp. 60 and 347; 1996, pp. 70 and 371.

south. By contrast, a rise of less than 4% in northern China was mainly carried by small rises in both the north and north-west. It is noteworthy that in the north-east, which in recent years had been the single most important source of increases in domestic grain supplies, total output remained largely unchanged. The net outcome of all these changes was a reversal of the previous pattern of regional output distribution, the southern half of China accounting for almost two-thirds of the national increase in total grain production between 1994 and 1995.

There is an important structural dimension to the regional changes in grain production of recent years. Between 1990 and 1993, rises in the output of wheat, maize and soya carried the major burden of national increases in grain output. However, although displaying an upward trend in the north and north-east, sharp declines in rice output throughout southern China caused a significant contraction in domestic rice supplies. In 1994 and 1995, the recovery of rice harvests in these southern provinces was responsible for a reversal of the previous declining trend, although a more general decline in wheat production now generated a fall in wheat output. Meanwhile, during 1994–1995 the output of maize rose throughout the country, while a sharp decline in soya supplies from the north-east was more than offset by major output expansions taking place elsewhere (especially in centre-east and south).

Conservation and expansion of grain sown area were not the principal source of higher output in southern China during 1995, although they certainly contributed to the enhanced performance of the south, where the grain area increased by 1.25% (1.75% in Guangdong). But, the corresponding rise in the south-west and centre-east was less than a single percentage point.[33] Rather, improved total production owed most to higher average yields, which rose by 3.5% (CE), 5.3% (SW) and a remarkable 9.25% (S). In the northern half of the country, changes in both sown area and yield were marginal.

There is a strong presumption that a major target of the "grain bag" policy has been the grain sectors of southern and eastern coastal provinces, where encroachment on agriculture by urban and industrial construction had been especially serious.[34] From this perspective, the figures for 1995 would seem to offer evidence in favour of the new policy's early success.[35] Early reports on the 1996 harvest, available at the time of writing, appear to point to further, more impressive advances in provinces throughout the country. Record levels of grain production have been reported or predicted in Jilin (NE), Hebei, Henan and Shandong (N), Inner Mongolia, Gansu, Shaanxi and Qinghai (NW), Sichuan and Tibet (SW), and Hubei and Jiangsu (CE).[36] The performance of north-western provinces has been especially noteworthy, one report suggesting that the output increases generated by Shaanxi, Gansu, Qinghai, Ningxia and Xinjiang would account for half of the national rise in production in 1996.[37]

But, whatever the longer-term significance of the 1995 and 1996 harvests,[38] it is likely that northern China will carry the burden of future growth in domestic grain production and be the main source of exports to other parts of the country. The goal of attaining self-sufficiency in central-eastern provinces by the end of the century is an ambitious one.[39] It seems likely too that the south and south-west will seem likely to remain in deficit. In this respect, it is significant that, notwithstanding improved performances in 1995, their collective deficit was almost 30 million tonnes (Table 3). Even without allowing for the effects of future population and income growth, elimination of this deficit would require a rise in total output of more than 25%. In Sichuan, which accounts for about two-thirds of the south-west's total grain production, the basic parameters of provincial grain production are unlikely to change significantly in the near future.[40] Nor should the constraints on prospects for rapid and sustained growth in Guangdong and Fujian, which together contribute more than 60% of total grain output in the south, be under-estimated.[41]

In short, it is in northern China that the best prospects for the future expansion of grain supplies lie. Individual provinces, which are expected to play a pre-eminent role in this process, have already been designated.

Henan is one, the planned increase in total production having been set at 5 million tonnes (1996–2000) — one-tenth of incremental production for the entire country within the Ninth Plan period.[42] Heilongjiang's future burden is even greater, with total output planned to rise by 7.5 million tonnes during 1996–2000 — and a further 25 million tonnes between 2000 and 2010.[43] Fulfilment of these targets means that Heilongjiang on its own will have contributed more than 20% of the planned increase in national grain production during the next 15 years. Inner Mongolia is expected to contribute a further 7% of the national increase by the year 2000.[44]

The Grain Issue in International Perspective

Much of the concern that has come to surround China's grain situation derives from the *international* dimension which is seen to attach to China's "grain problem." If China has difficulty in feeding itself, it will have to turn to outside sources in order to obtain its food supplies. A view that has attracted much attention in recent years is that of Lester Brown's, who has argued that a combination of rising demand and contracting supply within China will necessitate imports on such a scale that poor, grain-deficit countries in Africa and South Asia are squeezed out of international markets.[45] Hence, the spectre of China "starving the world."

That the world faces potentially severe problems of food security during the coming decades is not in doubt.[46] There is a measure of agreement that the most serious dimensions of the problem are likely to be felt in Sub-Saharan Africa and South Asia, where the emergence of large grain deficits is forecast.[47] Meanwhile, it is noteworthy that since the mid-1980s, global per capita grain production — and by extension, global food stocks — has been falling.[48] Given its enormous size, such observations underline the serious global implications of large-scale and increasing grain shortages in China.

The one certainty that informs projections of China's future grain balance is that continuing rises in income accruing to wider sections of the Chinese population, as well as continuing population growth,[49] will fuel further major increases in total demand for grain. Such projections are critically dependent on the underlying assumptions, the choice of which can generate a wide range of outcomes.[50] This is reflected in Table 4, which contains a random sample of estimates of future grain demand in China taken from various Chinese and Western-language sources.

Table 4. Projections of China's Future Grain Demand

Source	Predicted grain demand (million tonnes)			
	2000	2010	2020	2030
WESTERN SOURCES				
Brown[a]				641
Garnaut and Ma[b]	550–590			[772]
Garnaut and Ma[c]				
IFPRI[d]			740	
OECD[e]	520–548			
CHINESE SOURCES				
State Council[f]	500	550		640
NCJJYJCK[g]	520–560		711–783	
NCJJYJCK[h]				
JJYCYFX[i]	512	603		

Sources: a Lester Brown, *Who Will Feed China?*, p. 97. Note that Brown's estimates apparently refer to cereals, expressed in trade weight. They exclude potatoes and soyabeans, which according to the Chinese definition count as grain — and which are included as such in the other estimates shown in this table. The bracketed figure is a conversion of Brown's original figure to raw grain.

b Ross Garnaut and Guonan Ma, *Grain in China* (Canberra: Australian Government Publishing Service, 1992), p. 98.

c Ross Garnaut and Guonan Ma, "China's Grain Demand: Recent Experience and Prospects to the year 2000," in *The Third Revolution in the Chinese Countryside*, edited by Ross Garnaut, Guo Shutian and Ma Guonan, (Cambridge: Cambridge University Press, 1996), p. 59.

d Rosegrant et al., *Global Food Projections to 2020: Implications for Investment* (International Food Policy Research Institute), p. 20.

e Organisation for Economic Co-operation and Development, *The Chinese Grain and Oilseed Sectors: Major Changes Under Way* (Paris: OECD, 1995), p. 31.

f Information Office of the State Council, "The Grain Issue in China" (translated in *Beijing Review*, 11–17 November 1996; also WEB, FE/2753 (26 October 1996).

g Hu Angang, "Zhongguo changqi fazhan zhong di liangshi wenti" (The Problem of Grain in the Context of China's Long-run Development), *Nongcun jingji yanjiu cankao* (Rural Economic Research Reference, *NCJJYJCK*), No. 6 (1995), p. 13.

h Mei Fangquan, "21 shiji qianqi Zhongguo liangshi fazhan fenxi" (Analysis of the Development of Grain in China during the Early Part of the 21st Century), *NCJJYJCK*, No. 6, p. 40.

i Government Information Centre, *Jingji yuce yu fenxi* (Economic Forecast and Analysis), 3 March 1996, p. 8.

The estimates embody different degrees of optimism and pessimism about future trends in aggregate demand. A cynical view would show no surprise that the State Council's projections for 2000 should be the most conservative — and incidentally coincide with the targeted level of grain production for during the final year of the Ninth Five-year Plan (1996–2000). In fairness, however, its estimate is only a few percentage points below the lower figure cited in the OECD study. Indeed, it is interesting how little correlation there is between levels of projected demand and their national provenance. In particular, even allowing for differing definitions of "grain,"[51] the estimates for 2020 cited in authoritative Chinese sources[52] suggest that there may be some analysts in China who are quite close to Lester Brown in their assessment of future demand pressures.

Demand is only one part of the equation that will determine China's future grain balance. The other is supply. The previous section set out some of the aggregate and regional parameters of China's recent grain performance. Future prospects are more difficult to predict, supply projections again being critically dependent on the choice of underlying assumptions. The government's immediate task is to raise output to 490–500 million tonnes by 2000 and thereby fulfil the target contained in the current (Ninth) Five-year Plan (9FYP).[53] Preliminary estimates indicate that the 1996 harvest is already within 2–4 percentage points of the planned level. On this basis, fulfilment of the higher target will require an average growth during the rest of the decade of no more than 1% p.a. Even allowing for the variability that characterized China's grain performance in the earlier 1990s, the likelihood that this growth requirement will be met must be high.

But, such optimism is not unqualified. Even if output rises to 500 million tonnes by 2000, the demand projections in Table 4 indicate that China could still face a sizeable deficit. A shortfall of 50 million tonnes would, for example, imply the need for grain imports on an unprecedented scale. The degree of dependence on outside sources — almost 10% — would also be far higher than anything experienced in the past, suggesting the enforced abandonment of the hallowed principle of self-sufficiency.

As for longer-term projections, suffice to say that an average rate of output expansion of 1% p.a. would raise total grain production to 610 and 674 million tonnes by 2020 and 2030, thereby generating increasingly serious deficits which would push China to even greater reliance on imports.[54] Projections derived from the average rate of increase actually achieved between 1989–1990 (average) and 1994–1995 (average)[55] improve the picture, but still point to a deficit that could be as high as 136 million tonnes in 2020.[56]

There is no unanimity about China's future grain prospects. The sanguine official Chinese view, expressed in the State Council's "White Paper," is that future aggregate demand can be accommodated by increases in domestic supplies.[57] By contrast, Lester Brown's prediction is that the import deficit will rise to about 440 million tonnes of raw cereals by 2030.[58] Between these optimistic and pessimistic extremes, a consensus view has emerged which argues strongly that the next 20 or 30 years will see China moving inexorably towards the status of a significant net grain importer.

Brown's apocalyptic vision[59] is certainly the most dramatic expression of concern about China's likely increased reliance on international markets for its grain supplies. His argument is based on a combination of historical analogies[60] and extremely pessimistic assumptions about future growth trends in the grain sector. Not least, he predicts that, under the impact of cropland loss, increasing water scarcity, environmental stress and a weakening technological base, total production in 2030 will be 20% below the level of 1990.

Interpreted literally, Brown's thesis does not stand up to close scrutiny. The failure to take account of self-correcting mechanisms or deliberate policy intervention to address excess demand is one weakness. Brown's analysis of technological and environmental factors may well be overly pessimistic. Nor should consideration of the possible global consequences of domestic grain imbalance ignore the impressive historical achievement in raising world yields. Possible supply responses by exporting countries and regions also need to be considered.

These are some of the points which Western scholars and analysts have developed in various critiques of Brown's thesis, published in recent years.[61] The thesis has also been closely scrutinized in China.[62] If the official Chinese position remains one of insistence that future increases in demand for grain can basically be accommodated from domestic sources,[63] there is also recognition that Brown's analysis has had a salutary effect in drawing attention to major economic problems in the grain sector. The estimates in Table 4 even imply that there are some Chinese analysts prepared to acknowledge the possibility that China will confront very large import deficits in coming years. For example, projections made by a team working under Hu Angang have pointed to a grain deficit of 40 million tonnes by the year 2000, while another Chinese source has contemplated a deficit of up to 50 million tonnes (2000) and 70 million tonnes by 2020.[64]

To reject the substance of Brown's thesis is not to deny the force of some of his arguments. The problems of declines in the arable land base and grain sown area are very real.[65] So is the challenge of securing adequate water supplies for irrigation — above all, in northern China, where the burden of future growth in grain yields mainly lies. There is also evidence of poor efficiency in the use of agricultural chemicals, as well as of pollution and soil degradation.

These and other problems have been rehearsed in many Chinese analyses of the economic condition of agriculture. But, the official response to such difficulties remains one of confidence that the realization of the supposed potential that exists to improve resource use and raise productivity will be sufficient to meet future demands on the grain sector.

The most authoritative statement of this position can be found in the State Council's "White Paper" on grain, published in October 1996.[66] Here, it is argued that there still exists enormous potential to extend the arable area,[67] to enhance the scientific and technological base of grain farming and to raise yields. On the basis of projections which conservatively assume that per capita demand for grain will rise from 385 kilograms (2000) to 400 kilograms (2030), it is suggested that yields can be increased by more than 1.5 tonnes per hectare, thereby accommodating future rises in demand.[68] Some 20 million tonnes of grain can also be saved each year by reducing losses (currently running at around 10% of total output). Given that generating increases in feed grain has become the central challenge in China's grain economy, advocacy of more intense use of grassland resources to support livestock is another element which promises to ease pressures on grain farmers.[69] Effecting such changes and improvements will of course require the implementation of complementary economic policies, designed to raise investment, rationalize prices, enhance market control, improve extension services and stabilize the institutional framework of grain production. These are precisely the policies that are highlighted in the State Council document.

The strategic goal to which all these measures aspire is clearly that of grain self-sufficiency. Yet, as recently as summer 1995, suggestions were being made that a significant change in China's approach towards grain imports had taken place, signified by the adoption of a "limited self-sufficiency policy."[70] With hindsight, adoption of the "grain bag" policy may be interpreted as an attempt to counter such tendencies by reaffirming the government's continuing commitment to providing for the country's food needs. Be that as it may, even in the face of the major problems and challenges outlined above, it is clear enough that self-sufficiency remains a high priority. It is a principle which continues to be endorsed at the highest level.[71]

Concluding Remarks

Against the background of rapid economic growth and structural change in China, it is predictable that agriculture's trade contribution should have declined in recent years. But, it is also significant that in value terms, except for 1993, China's agricultural trade remained in healthy surplus between 1990 and 1995, while on the grain account alone, there was a steady improvement until 1994.[72] It is true that in 1995 a surge in grain imports generated an unprecedented deficit on the grain account of US$ 3.5 billion. But, this was easily offset by a rise in the overall agricultural trade surplus from US$ 5.4 to 16.7 billion.[73]

Such figures attest to the healthy agricultural trade context in which grain transactions — real and potential — should be viewed. By implication, they challenge the validity of Lester Brown's argument by questioning his implicit assumption that future trends in China's grain trade are synonymous with those of agricultural trade as a whole.[74] In addition, the fact that China's total foreign exchange reserves had risen to more than US$ 100 billion (end-1996) points to its enhanced ability to finance grain imports on a large and increasing scale. Such considerations might be thought to question the advisability of prioritizing self-reliance in the grain sector.

One of the most interesting apologists for this view is Hu Angang. Unlike other officials, Hu's analysis of the constraints surrounding grain production in China has led him to advocate pursuing a policy of limited self-sufficiency in the 21st century.[75] Differentiating between the short, medium and long run, he argues that China's goal should be to reduce the self-sufficiency rate from 98–95% to 90% and less. Such figures imply continuing basic self-reliance for direct grain consumption, but a higher degree of dependence for feed and industrial grain. In support of his argument, Hu explicitly cites China's healthy balance on the agricultural trade account and consequent ability "... not only [to] acquire agricultural products from the international market, but also ... to provide the international market with more agricultural products."[76]

The force of Hu's basic argument is undeniable.[77] Other economists too are on record as recognizing the economic case in favour of a substantial rise in grain imports. Fan Gang has cautioned against the advisability of raising domestic grain prices in order to stimulate long-run output growth.[78] He argues that, as domestic grain prices approach those in international markets, China should be prepared to use cheap imports in order to offset supply shortages at home. The anti-protectionist tone is clear in Fan's warning against placing undue emphasis on grain self-sufficiency and in his statement that "it would be unwise to ignore the availability of cheap grain in international markets and instead insist on investing large sums of money in order to produce small quantities of high-cost domestic grain."[79] Even more intriguing is Fan's suggestion that China might consider establishing its own grain bases in countries, such as Russia or Brazil, where favourable resource endowments would facilitate the production of low-cost cereals.

Yet, in the second half of the 1990s, the imperative of grain self-sufficiency remains a cornerstone of economic orthodoxy in China. There are, it is true, economic factors which would counsel caution in endorsing a sudden increase in grain imports.

Infrastructural constraints are one of these. For example, the annual import handling capacity of Chinese ports is between 20 and 30 million tonnes of grain, and it is unrealistic to suppose that facilities capable of unloading and discharging 100 million tonnes — let alone the scale of shipments envisaged by Lester Brown — by 2020 or 2030.[80] The railway network is another potential weak link. In 1993, 15.7 billion tonnes of freight were carried by rail in China, of which grain accounted for a mere 60 million tonnes. If significant amounts of increased grain imports had to be transported to the interior, the disruptive impact on the rail system might be considerable — with serious implications for consignments of other items and thereby for China's ability to earn foreign exchange.[81]

Ultimately, however, China's continued pursuit of grain self-sufficiency is shaped by forces which transcend mere economics. In the past, the Chinese government had resisted the temptation to raise imports in the face of declining world grain prices, preferring instead to maintain tight control over its grain trade. The inference is that adherence to the principle of self-sufficiency has been determined by broader political and strategic considerations, not by those of economic maximization.

The underlying perception is that, for a country of China's size and level of development, closer integration with world food markets carries substantial risks. The dangers stem from the ability to use grain as a "political weapon." They are exemplified in Chinese eyes by the alleged threat of export sanctions by the United States against India (in the 1960s) and the former Soviet Union (in the 1970s).[82]

This is the background against which, in 1996, Li Peng observed that "politically, the grain trade has always been used as a trump card in the international political context."[83] It also explains why — irrespective of the costs associated with excessive self-reliance in producing grain or the potential gains from alternative strategies — official policy remains apparently unwilling to abandon efforts to maximize food supplies from domestic sources.

For the time being, such strategic considerations seem likely to underline China's continuing refusal to contemplate reliance on large-scale imports of grain. Unless there is a sharp downturn in domestic grain production, or a rapid and persistent increase in demand, there is little reason to suppose that any significant departure from the imperative of grain self-sufficiency will occur in the foreseeable future.

Notes

1. "Food security" is here defined in terms of the availability of food energy (i.e. calories). This follows Dyson's observation that "the world food problem today is primarily defined in terms of dietary energy, or *undernutrition*" (emphasis in original). See Tim Dyson, *Population and Food: Global Trends and Future Prospects* (London and New York: Routledge, 1996), p. 34.
2. It is no coincidence that the original slogan was formulated in the wake of the catastrophic famine which followed the collapse of the Great Leap Forward.
3. A figure of 300 kilograms per head of total population is a reasonable proxy of grain adequacy in the sense of providing for basic food requirements, as well as contributing to seed and animal feed needs (cf. Kenneth R. Walker, *Food Grain Procurement and Consumption in China* [Cambridge: Cambridge University Press, 1984], p. 3). On this basis, analysis of the grain sector's performance since 1978 would suggest a sharp increase in the potential national grain surplus from 16 million tonnes (1978) to over 100 million tonnes in the 1990s (around 112 million tonnes in 1996) (estimates derived from data in Guojia tongji ju (State Statistical Bureau, hereafter SSB), *Zhongguo tongji nianjian* (Statistical Yearbook of China, *ZGTJNJ*) (Beijing: Tongji chubanshe), various issues. On the basis of the same criterion, the

identical data suggest that, in 1995, with the single exception of the south (Guangdong, Fujian, Guangxi and Hainan), every major region in China enjoyed a comfortable cushion over its subsistence needs.

4. As recently as June 1996, Jiang Zemin quoted Deng Xiaoping to the effect that "[i]f the economy goes wrong in the 1990s, the problems are most likely to surface in agriculture ... [I]f things go wrong in agriculture ... overall economic and social development will be affected" (British Broadcasting Corporation, *Summary of World Broadcasts: Part 3, The Far East (SWB)*, FE/2666, 17 July 1996). Jiang's remarks were contained in a speech made during an inspection tour of agricultural and rural work in Henan province.
5. The highest level of grain imports recorded by China was 20.81 million tonnes (1995), constituting 4.46% of domestic output (466.62 million tonnes). *Net* imports constituted just 4% of domestic production in this year. The relevant figures can be found in *ZGTJNJ 1996*, pp. 371 and 592.
6. Relevant data can be found in United States Department of Agriculture (USDA), *International Agriculture and Trade Reports: China* (Situation and Outlook Series) (Washington, DC: USDA, Economic Research Service), various issues. The role of grain in China's overall agricultural trade is considered in more detail below.
7. At the end of 1996, the value of China's reserves was in excess of US$ 100 billion. See *Wen Wei Po* (Hong Kong), 28 November 1996.
8. This point is developed in more detail in Robert F. Ash and Peter Nolan, *China's Agriculture: Retrospect and Prospect* (forthcoming).
9. The precipitating causes were twofold. One was the practice of giving farmers so-called "IOUs" (*baitiaozi*), instead of ready cash, for produce delivered to the state under contract; the second was the imposition of heavy "exactions" (*tanpai*) in order to finance extra-budgetary development projects, which frequently promised no direct benefits for the peasants who bore the brunt of the unauthorized levies. Contrary to some accounts, rural unrest was never endemic in China, nor did its most serious manifestations affect more than a small proportion of provinces. It was probably most widespread in 1992 and 1993. For further consideration, see *South China Morning Post* (27 June 1993), *Cheng Ming* (February 1993); *Zhongguo yanjiu* (Research on China), 1993, No. 7 (27 July 1993), p. 23. Valuable insights are also available in Masaharu Hishida, "State-Society Relations," paper presented at the 3rd Japan-US Symposium on China, Tokyo, 14–16 July 1993. The provinces most affected seem to have been Anhui, Sichuan, Guizhou, Jiangxi, Hunan, Hubei, Shanxi, Guangxi and Shaanxi.
10. For an official view, see Ministry of Agriculture, *Zhongguo nongye fazhan baogao, 1995* (Chinese Agricultural Development Report, 1995) (Beijing: Zhongguo nongye chubanshe, 1995), pp. 66–68. Also Dali L. Yang, *Calamity and Reform in China: State, Rural Society, and Institutional Change Since the*

Great Leap Famine (Stanford, CA: Stanford University Press, 1996), esp. ch. 7.

11. Xinhua News Agency (XHNA) in *SWB*, FE/2746 and 27499, 18 and 22 October 1996.
12. Ibid. Zhu was addressing a meeting in Dalian (Liaoning province), held in October 1996. Earlier, it was admitted that fund shortages to the extent of over RMB 4 billion would make it difficult to avoid issuing IOUs to farmers in Hubei (see *Jingji cankao bao* [Economic Reference Daily], 1 August 1996 in *SWB*, FE/2735, 8 October 1996; also *SWB*, FE/2746 and 2749).
13. See Jiang's speech of 4 June 1996, made during an inspection tour of Henan province, in *Renmin ribao* (People's Daily, *RMRB*), 15 July 1996. That excessive exactions continue to be levied on farmers is graphically illustrated in an account of what happened when grain was delivered to government collection points in northern Henan. Far from receiving cash for their deliveries, deductions for a wide variety of fees left some farmers *in debt* to the local government (*Jingji cankao*, 3 August 1996, cited in *SWB*, FE/2735, 5 October 1996). The report cited a list of levies, including "the Huang He [Yellow River] diversion fee, the Huang-Huai-Hai area development fee, repayment for World Bank loan, artificial rain fee, water charge, agricultural tax, ... pesticide fee, earth-moving fee and well sinking fee." One farmer who had expected to receive RMB 228 for the 150 kg. of wheat he delivered under quota was instead presented with a bill for RMB 166.2.
14. *Wunong bu wen, wuliang ze luan* — a phrase used by Chen Yun (*RMRB*, 24 September 1985, p. 2); on Deng Xiaoping (see *RMRB*, 8 December 1994).
15. Depending on the choice of base and end years, average growth rates fluctuated sharply — cf. +1.85% (1989–1994) and –0.06% (1990–1994).
16. Average per capita output of 400 kg. should permit the diversion of grain on a significant scale to animal feed and other purposes.
17. This point was made by the representative of the Food and Agricultural Organization (FAO) in China. In an interview (10 November 1996), he spoke of China's "miraculous" achievement in having quadrupled domestic grain output in China (1949–1995) and, since the early 1960s, having raised average daily calorific availability from 1500 to more than 2700 calories (*SWB*, FE/2766, 11 November 1996). Even allowing for the disingenuous choice of base years, there is no mistaking the significant long-run achievement of the grain sector in China.
18. The regional breakdown used in this chapter is as follows: *north-east [NE]*: Liaoning, Jilin, Heilongjiang; *north [N]*: Hebei, Henan, Shandong, Shanxi, Beijing, Tianjin; *north-west [NW]*: Inner Mongolia, Shaanxi, Ningxia, Gansu, Qinghai, Xinjiang; *centre-east [CE]*: Hunan, Hubei, Jiangxi, Jiangsu, Anhui, Zhejiang, Shanghai; *south [S]*: Fujian, Guangdong, Guangxi, Hainan; *south-west [SW]*: Sichuan, Guizhou, Yunnan, Tibet.

19. Estimates of per capita output underline the more rapid growth of grain output in northern China, compared with that of the south. In the 1990s, NE has consistently achieved the top ranking. But, perhaps even more spectacular has been the emergence of S as the lowest-ranking region in per capita terms. In 1995, average per capita output in S was *6% below that of 1978*.
20. A XHNA report noted that Heilongjiang, Jilin and Liaoning had increased grain production by 12 million tonnes since 1990 (*SWB*, FEW/0430, 10 April 1996).
21. The contributions of SW (12%) and S (9%) — both significantly higher than between in 1980–1984 and 1985–1989 — went some way towards redressing the balance. In particular, the shift from a negative to a positive contribution for S reflected the maintenance of high levels of rice output during 1990–1992 — a trend which was reversed in all four provinces during 1993–1994, but most spectacularly in Guangdong (where total rice output fell by 15%).
22. This aspect is explored in detail elsewhere: see Robert F. Ash, "The Search for Grain Self-Sufficiency in Mainland China" and "China's Food Security: Regional and Structural Dimensions," (both forthcoming).
23. Ibid.
24. My own estimates indicate that in 1994 the pre-eminent role of NE made possible the emergence of a small surplus (about 4 million tonnes) in the northern half of the country, compared with a huge deficit (37.5 million tonnes) in the south. As expected, CE and S are the regions whose producing status has deteriorated most sharply (ibid.). The case for using 400 kg. as a per capita criterion of "adequacy" or self-sufficiency is that it goes some way towards accommodating the aspirations for a more varied diet by an urban population — and more prosperous elements among the rural population — whose living standards have risen rapidly under the impact of the post-1978 reforms. "More varied diet" in this context reflects, in particular, the demand for more fish, meat and dairy produce — items whose production demands large quantities of grain as *feed*.
25. The report, said to be by the Chinese Academy of Sciences, was cited by Hong Kong, *Hsin Pao*, 20 March 1995 (translated in *SWB*, FE/2277, 13 April 1995).
26. The regional breakdown used in the CAS report differs from that adopted here. Thus, the "southeast," as defined by CAS, embraces Shanghai, Jiangsu, Anhui, Hubei, Hunan, Jiangxi, Zhejiang, Fujian, Guangdong and Hainan.
27. The significance of a "fairly high" rate of grain self-sufficiency would appear to be that it still allows room for a supplementary role for domestic and/or foreign imports. On this, see Chen Junsheng in *SWB*, FE/2163, 26 November 1994.
28. In Chinese, *mi daizi*.

29. Jiang was addressing a national rural work conference. See *ZGTJNJ 1995*, p. 117.
30. In a speech made on 4 June 1996, Jiang Zemin was explicit in equating the "grain bag" policy with the institution of a "governor-responsibility system" (*shengzhang fuzezhi*) (SWB, FE/2666, 17 July 1996). For a useful account of the policy, see Frederick W. Crook, "China's Agricultural Policy Development in 1995," USDA, *International Agriculture and Trade Reports: China* (Washington, DC: USDA, 1996), pp. 13–14.
31. Such forces have embraced institutional initiatives, facilitating increases in the scale of grain farming (including provision for transfers of land use rights). Experiments in Fujian, Zhejiang and Shandong have embraced the introduction of preferential policies, favouring households specializing in grain production (*SWB*, FE/2335, 21 June 1995).
32. The planned level of production in 1996 was 465 million tonnes: see Chen Jinhua (Minister in charge of the State Planning Commission), 5 March 1996, in *SWB*, FE/2599, 30 April 1996.
33. Relevant sown area data can be found in *ZGTJNJ 1996*, p. 368.
34. It seems more than mere coincidence that in his explanatory comments on the new (Ninth) Five-Year Plan (25 September 1995), Li Peng's remarks about the "grain bag" policy were set against the background of declining grain production in southern China, especially "economically developed coastal regions" (XHNA in *SWB*, FE/2428, 7 October 1995). Even more explicit was Chen Junsheng, who stated that "[t]he question of whether the economy of coastal areas develops in a healthy way depends on the balance of grain supply and demand; whether the country achieves a balance in grain supply and demand depends on the coastal areas; and whether prices on the national grain market are stable also depends mainly on these areas" (XHNA, 19 June 1995 in *SWB*, FE/2335 [21 June 1995]). For an expression of more recent concern about lagging grain output growth in coastal areas, see also Jiang Chunyun's advocacy of a higher grain self-sufficiency rate in Fujian province (*SWB*, FE/2716, 13 September 1996).
35. The pre-eminent contribution of the "grain bag" policy to the record harvest of 1996 was noted by a Ministry of Agriculture spokesman, who stated that devolving responsibility for grain growing to governors had transformed the very nature of grain production. Thus, "grain growing is not purely an economic act but, more importantly, a political task receiving the close attention of governments at all levels" (*RMRB*, 4 August 1996 in *SWB*, FE/2695, 20 August 1996).
36. See *SWB*, *Weekly Economic Report*, FEW/0447 (28 August 1996), FEW/0457 (12 October 1996), FEW/0460 (6 November 1996), FE/0461 (13 November 1996), FEW/0466 (18 December 1996), FEW/0467 (1 January 1997) and FEW/0469 (15 January 1997). In south China, reports indicate a

record output of early rice in Guangdong (FEW/0447, 24 July 1996, and FEW/0450, 28 August 1996) and a 26% increase in grain stocks in the first four months of the year (FE/2650, 28 June 1996). Reported grain production in Guangxi (15.9 million tonnes) was 5% higher than in 1996 (FEW/0469, 15 January 1997).

37. XHNA, 25 December 1996 in *SWB*, FEW/0467, 1 January 1997.
38. A Central Rural Work Conference, held in Beijing in January 1997, spoke of the plan to hold grain output "at or above" 480 million tonnes in 1997 (*SWB*, FE/2817, 15 January 1997).
39. These regions have been urged to "put a stop to the grain decrease problem and become self-sufficient in grain by the year 2000" (*SWB*, FE/2335, 21 June 1995). But, aspirations on behalf of some individual central provinces, such as Hunan and Hubei, may be greater than this statement suggests: see *SWB*, FE/2501, 5 January 1996.
40. See "Lun dangqian Sichuan di liangshi wenti" (On the Current Grain Question in Sichuan), *Liangshi wenti yanjiu* (Research on the Grain Question), No. 1 (20 February 1995), pp. 5–7.
41. The intention is that Fujian should achieve grain self-sufficiency by 2000 by raising output to 9.8 million tonnes (cf. 9.2 m.t. in 1995) (*SWB*, FEW/0434, 8 May 1996). During the same period, Guangdong plans to increase production to 19 m.t. (cf. 17.3 m.t. in 1995) (*SWB*, FEW/0418, 17 January 1996).
42. See *Liangshi wenti yanjiu*, No. 2 (20 April 1996), p. 7. Note that Henan's total grain output is said to have reached 38.5 million tonnes in 1996 — an increase of some 11% above the 1995 level (*SWB*, FEW/0457, 12 October 1996).
43. Ibid. The target for 2000 was confirmed by Li Peng during a visit to Harbin in July 1996 (*SWB*, FE/2659, 9 July 1996).
44. *SWB*, FE/2584, 12 April 1996.
45. Lester R. Brown, *Who Will Feed China? Wake-Up Call for a Small Planet* (New York and London: W.W. Norton and Co., 1995). See also two articles by Brown, "Question for 2030: Who Will Be Able to Feed China" and "When China's Scarcities Become the World's Problem," *International Herald Tribune*, 28 and 29 September 1994. Also *The Financial Times*, 2 November 1995.
46. For an excellent account of the challenges and opportunities for grain output growth in various regions of the world, see Dyson, *Population and Food* (Note 1). Dyson's cautiously optimistic conclusion about the ability of world agriculture to meet global demographic and economic demands in the next two or three decades is a useful antidote to Brown's apocalyptic vision.
47. Ibid. See also the projections in Mark W. Rosegrant, Mercedita Agcaoili-Sombilla and Nicostratou D. Perez, *Global Food Projections to 2020:*

Implications for Investment (Washington, DC: International Food Policy Research Institute, 1995), pp. 15 and 17.
48. Between the 1950s and 1984, the global average grain yield grew by 2.3% p.a., compared with less than 1% from 1984 to 1993. Dyson notes that per capita output peaked first in Africa (1967), followed by Eastern Europe and the former USSR (1978), Latin and North America (1981) and Western Europe and Asia (1984) (*Population and Food*, p. 17).
49. Even a rate of natural increase of little more than 1% p.a. adds 12 million consuming units to China's population each year. On the 1995 base, a natural growth rate of 1% p.a. will, if maintained, generate total populations of over 1.5 billion by 2020 and 1.6 billion by 2025–2030. On any reasonable assumptions, it seems inevitable that by 2020, there will be some 300 million more people to feed in China.
50. *Minimum* food needs can probably be confidently specified because the key determinants — population size and change — can be fairly accurately predicted. *Effective* demand is more difficult to forecast, since it depends on assumptions, affecting future growth and distribution of income, which are much less firmly specifiable.
51. Brown's estimates appear to embrace cereals, expressed in trade weight. As such, they exclude potatoes and soya beans, which are traditionally considered as grain in Chinese usage and which are included as such in other estimates cited in this chapter. I am grateful to Dr Claude Aubert for his help in interpreting Brown's estimates.
52. E.g., see *NCJJYJCK*, No. 6 (1995).
53. "Outlines of the 9FYP for national economic and social development and the long-term target for the year 2010," adopted on 17 March 1996 by the 4th session of the Eighth National People's Congress. The text is available, in translation in *SWB*, FE/2586, 15 April 1996.
54. Cf. a deficit of 101–173 million tonnes, on the basis of the projections in Table 4. The implied rate of dependence on imports is 17–28%.
55. I.e., 1.3% p.a. — a figure which is very close to the average rate of growth of production since 1984.
56. Projected total output in 2020 on the basis of an average growth rate of 1.3% is 647 million tonnes; the implied degree of reliance on imports is 10–21%. Interestingly, a shortfall of 136 million tonnes of grain was also predicted in a joint report of the Japanese Overseas Economic Co-operation Fund (OECF) and researchers in the Chinese Ministry of Agriculture (25 September 1995): see *SWB*, FE/2419, 27 September 1995.
57. But, it bears emphasizing that this optimistic scenario derives from conservative assumptions about future demand growth and bullish assumptions about future supply expansion. See State Council Information Office, October 1996.
58. Brown, *Who Will Feed China?* (Note 45), p. 97. I have adjusted Brown's

estimates, originally given in terms of trade grain, in order to ensure consistency in the text. The global significance of Brown's predicted import deficit for 2030 is that it is "nearly double current world grain exports" (ibid.).

59. Ironically, the "apocalyptic" implications of Brown's arguments threaten poor countries in Africa and South Asia more than China itself.
60. E.g., he points out that China apart, only three countries (Japan, Taiwan and South Korea) were densely populated, in agronomic terms, before industrialization. Over three or four decades, the grain sown area in each of these countries declined by 42–52%. His conclusion is that this "remarkable consistency … indicates how difficult, if not impossible, it will be for China to avoid a similar loss …" (ibid., p. 56). But, even accepting the force of Brown's argument, note that the pressures of urban and industrial construction are, and will remain, limited to only a relatively small part of China.
61. E.g., see Frederick W. Crook, "Could China Starve the World? Comments on Lester Brown's Article" (Washington, DC: USDA, Economic Research Service, 1994), pp. 17–19; Scott Rozelle, Huang Jikun and Mark W. Rosegrant, "Why China Will Not Starve the World" *Choices*, No. 1 (1996); and Vaclav Smil, "Feeding China," *Current History*, September 1995, pp. 280–84. Also useful is Morio Matsumoto, "The Complex Issue of China's Grain Prospects," *Japan Review of International Affairs*, Vol. 10, No. 3 (Summer 1996), pp. 239–57.
62. For an authoritative Chinese résumé of Lester Brown's argument, see Research Office of the State Council, "1995 Zhongguo liangshi wenti da taolun" (Symposium on the Chinese Grain Question in 1995), *Jingji yanjiu cankao* (Economic Research Reference, *JJYJCK*), Vol. 20, No. 820 (4 February 1996), pp. 2–6. The same source also contains a summary of some western critiques of Brown's position (pp. 21–25). See also Liu Zhiren, "Guanyu 'Bulang xuanfeng' ji woguo liangshi zhanlue xuanze de sikao" (Some Thoughts on the 'Brown Whirlwind' and Strategic Options for Grain in China"), *Nongcun jingji yanjiu cankao* (Rural Economic Research Reference, *NCJYJCK*), No. 6 (1995), pp. 6–11.
63. E.g., cf. Du Runsheng's insistence (24 March 1995) in the face of questioning about Lester Brown's gloomy prognostications that "we can certainly feed ourselves" (*SWB*, FE/2265, 30 March 1995).
64. These figures are quoted in Research Centre of the Ministry of Agriculture, "Zhongguo liangshi qianjing yu zhanlue zhuanjia zuotanhui zhuyao guandian zongshu" (General Summary of the Main Points Arising from a Conference of Experts on the Prospects and Future Strategy for Grain in China), *NCJJYJCK*, No. 6 (1995), p. 1. Hu Angang is a member of the National Conditions Group of the Chinese Academy of Sciences.
65. Official acknowledgement that official estimates of China's arable area have understated its true extent by some 30% (this is the figure cited by Li Peng in

Nongmin ribao [Farmers' Daily], 23 August 1996), suggests an important qualification. For reasons of space, it is impossible to consider this issue in any detail here. But if, as is likely, such under-reporting has not been offset by under-reporting of total production, official estimates of average grain yields must have been exaggerated. This is an important finding, if only because it is easier to secure further rises in yields from a lower base than from a higher base. Note, however, that the implied optimistic prognosis depends on the quality and location of the under-reported arable land.

66. *Beijing Review*, 11–17 November 1996, *op. cit.*
67. Reference is made to the existence of 35 million hectares of "wasteland" that is suitable for farming, of which more than 40% can be reclaimed. Reclamation of such land, supplemented by raising the multiple cropping index, is intended to offset losses caused by urbanization and industrialization, thereby stabilizing the grain sown area at about 110 million hectares (ibid.). (Note: in 1995, China's arable area was 95 m.ha.; the grain sown area, 110 m.ha. (*ZGTJNJ 1996*, pp. 355 and 368).)
68. Upgrading low and medium-yielding land has long been seen as a key means of raising average grain yields.
69. *Beijing Review*, 11–17 November 1996. See also Research Office of the State Council in *JJYJCK*, Vol. 20, No. 820 (4 February 1996), p. 8.
70. See Frederick W. Crook, *1995 China Trip Report* (Washington, DC: USDA, Foreign Agriculture Service, Economic Research Service, 1995), pp. 4 and 85–86.
71. E.g., in 1996, it was endorsed by Li Peng ("China ... will remain self-sufficient in feeding its population," 17 March) (FE/2563, 18 March 1996) and by Jiang Zemin ("the problem of feeding our country's huge population can only be solved by ourselves," 4 June) (FE/2666, 15 June 1996). See also the position of the Minister of Agriculture (Liu Jiang), cited in *JJYJCK*, Vol. 20, No. 820 (4 February 1996), p. 6.
72. The grain account moved from a deficit of US$ 1.3 billion to a surplus of 0.3 billion. Trade data are available in USDA, *International Agriculture and Trade Reports: China* (Washington, DC: USDA, 1994, 1995 and 1996).
73. The deterioration in China's grain trade in 1995 reflected surging imports and the virtual elimination of all outward grain shipments. A doubling of net cotton imports exacerbated the situation, which was only relieved by major increases in earnings from increased exports of pork, tobacco, fruit and vegetables. Ibid.
74. This point is developed in a paper by Feng Lu "Grain Versus Food: A Hidden Issue in China's Food Policy Debate" (Peking University: China Center for Economic Research, Working Paper Series, 1996). I am grateful to Dr Feng for having made his paper available to me.
75. Hu Angang, "Basing Ourselves on Domestic Production, Ensuring Basic

Self-sufficiency, Importing Appropriately and Promoting Exchanges" (as translated in *SWB*, FE/2735, 5 October 1996; for the original article, see *Liaowang* [Outlook], 26 August 1996). Hu called for the maintenance of "a fairly high degree of grain self-sufficiency rate which is … constantly declining."

76. Hu was nevertheless at pain to distance himself from Lester Brown. Thus, "[i]nternational trade based on the principle of equal exchanges, including trade in grain and agricultural products, is not an issue of who is feeding whom; therefore, we see no need to reject the use of both international resources and the international market just because Mr Brown raised the question as 'who will feed the Chinese'; neither do we … need to stop our grain imports just because he fabricated the 'theory of famine in China' … " (ibid.).
77. Also relevant is Fang Cai, "Comparative Advantage and the Internationalisation of China's Agriculture," in *The Third Revolution in the Chinese Countryside*, edited by Ross Garnaut, Guo Shutian and Ma Guonan (Cambridge: Cambridge University Press, 1996), pp. 173–84.
78. Fan Gang, "Lun jiejue woguo liangshi gongji wenti de changqi zhanlue yu duanqi duice" (On the Long-run Strategy and Short-term Policies for Solving China's Grain Supply Problems), *Zhongguo nongcun guancha* (Observing Rural China), No. 5 (1995).
79. Ibid.
80. See Research Office of the State Council in *JJYJCK*, Vol. 20, No. 820 (4 February 1996), p. 21.
81. Ibid.
82. See Agricultural Research Institute of the Chinese Academy of Agricultural Sciences, "Woguo liangshi wenti de hongguan pouxi" (A Macro Analysis of China's Grain Question), *Nongye jingji wenti* (Problems of Agricultural Economy), No. 2 (1995).
83. As translated in *SWB*, FE/2617, 21 May 1996 (citing *Ming Pao*, 10 May 1996). Li is reported as adding that the threat of American retaliation through the use of the grain trade had placed China "under heavy pressure" in recent years.

7

Reform of Large and Medium State Industrial Enterprises: Corporatization and Restructure of State Ownership

Joseph C. H. Chai and George Docwra

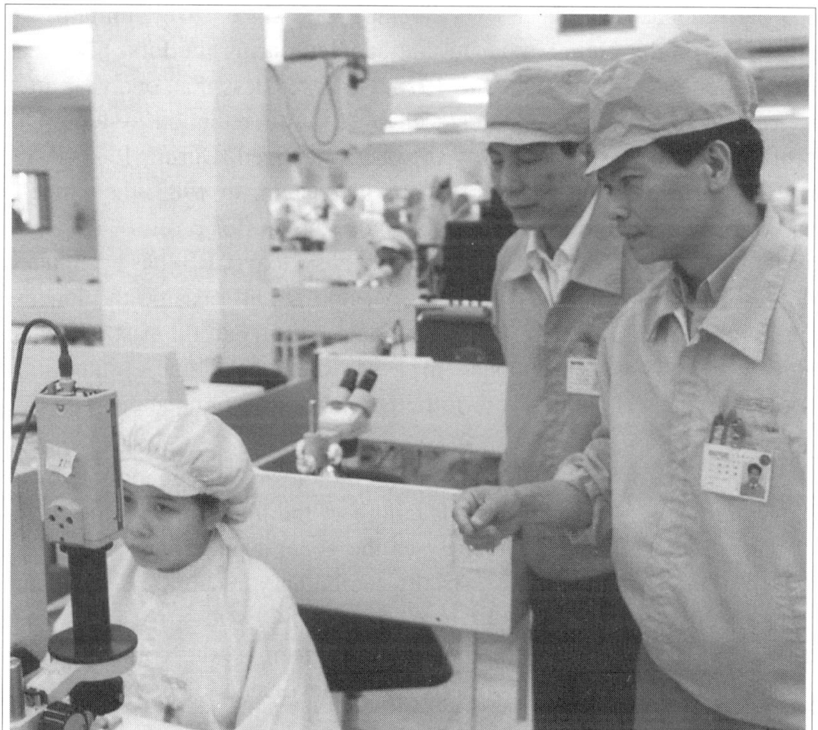

Despite the dwindling share of the state sector in the Chinese economy in recent years, large and medium state enterprises (LMSOEs) still play a dominant role in Chinese industry. According to the State Economic and Trade Commission, there were 14,400 LMSOEs in the industrial sector by the end of 1993 which amounted to a mere 4% of all industrial enterprises (with independent accounting at township level and above). Yet, they accounted for 44% of the output, 62% of the assets and 59% of the tax and profit realized of all industrial enterprises.[1]

Unlike the Eastern European countries and Russia, wholesale privatization of LMSOEs is ideologically unacceptable to China. Hence, since the inception of its transition programme, it has had to face the uphill task of finding a solution to the problem of how to instil an effective incentive system into its state-owned enterprises (SOEs), a problem the solution to which has so far been elusive to most countries in the world.

In an attempt to tackle this problem, previous reform measures centred on expanding enterprise autonomy and increasing its profit sharing (*fangquan rangli*).[2] With regard to the latter, five major types of profit sharing schemes have been experimented with since 1978.[3] Initially, an enterprise fund system similar to that adopted during the First Five-year Plan period was re-introduced in 1978. However, less than one year after its revival, this system was replaced by a profit retention system. The profit retention system also proved to be short-lived. During 1981–1983, it was replaced again by a profit contract system. In 1983, the Chinese authorities decided to place all SOEs under the tax-for-profit (*li gai shui*) system. Since 1987, a contract responsibility system (CRS) has been introduced. This system proved to be very popular and became the longest surviving incentive system in Chinese state industry in the past 17 years. However, CRS was abandoned in 1994 when the Chinese authorities decided to put yet another reform initiative, the corporatization of SOEs, on trial.[4]

The future of China's transition programme and its economic growth hinges critically on the success or failure of the latest attempt to reform Chinese SOEs. This chapter analyses the general principles of the corporatization programme, assesses its preliminary results and evaluates how effective it is likely to be in motivating SOEs to strive for greater efficiency. To set the scene for our assessment of the corporatization programme, we first review briefly the achievements of its predecessor, the CRS.

Performance of SOEs under CRS

A large variety of CRS has been practised in China since 1987. However, the most popular form was the two-guarantee-and-one-linkup system (*liang bao yi gua*).[5]

Under this system, the state and the enterprise entered into a contract, the duration of which averaged three to four years. During the contract period, the enterprise would guarantee the state the following: (a) the obligatory delivery of a certain amount of profit; (b) the completion of certain planned tasks of technical renovation of the enterprise; and (c) the link-up of the growth of its wage bill with that of enterprise efficiency indicators. The state, on the other hand, held out the promise that enterprises could retain any profit in excess of obligatory delivery. The actual amount of profit delivered was individually set for each enterprise. The retained profit could be used to boost the collective consumption of the managerial staff and workers, or to be used as bonus payments and for reinvestment within the enterprise. Thus, basically, the CRS used the rental system to solve the principal-agent problem, under which the enterprise (agent) paid a fixed sum to the state (principal) in the form of profit and tax delivered. To prevent an enterprise acting contrary to state interests, several constraints were imposed on its behaviour which included the performance of certain tasks, such as the technical renovation of the enterprises and the capping of its wage growth.

One of the main weaknesses of the CRS was that the enterprise's payments to the state were not in the nature of a uniform tax but became individualized. This individually set rate left room for bargaining between the parties to the contract and thereby softened the budget constraint imposed on the enterprise. Another weakness was that the short term nature of the contract encouraged enterprises to maximize short-run profit at the cost of long-run profit.

Since no incentive system is perfect, the ultimate test of its success lies with the performance of the enterprise concerned. However, performance assessment of an enterprise is not a straightforward matter.[6] For example, an enterprise performing well according to one criterion, say, profitability, may perform poorly in term of another criterion, say, economic efficiency. Moreover, an enterprise's performance depends, not only on its internal incentive structure, but also on its external environment, such as its market structure and the regulatory framework imposed by the government. Very often, it is difficult to isolate the influence of these two sets of factors on enterprise performance. Thus, for instance, an enterprise may perform poorly even under an effective internal incentive scheme because of the lack of competition and distortion caused by the government regulatory framework. Bearing such caveats in mind, we examine the performance of SOEs under the CRS using some of the common indicators, such as profitability, productivity and allocative efficiency, in order to form some judgement as to whether the CRS achieved its objectives or not.

In terms of profitability, it is interesting to observe that whereas the profitability gap between public and private enterprise in some Western countries, such as the United Kingdom (UK), can be as high as 1 to 4,[7] in China, this gap is much narrower. Table 1 compares pre-tax profitability between state and non-state enterprises in the industrial sector. This shows that with the exception of 1993 the pre-tax profitability of SOEs has not been significantly lower than that of the non-state enterprises. In fact, in 1989 and 1990, it was even higher than that of the non-state enterprises.

The same table also reveals that the profitability of SOEs has been

Table 1. Profitability[1] of State and Non-state Industrial Enterprises

(Percentage)

		1988	1989	1990	1991	1992	1993	1994	1995
State[2]	A	20.6	17.2	12.4	11.8	9.7	9.7	9.8	8.0
	B	10.4	7.2	3.2	2.9	2.5	3.2	2.8	1.9
Non-state									
collective	A	19.8	15.4	11.5	11.9	9.8	10.9	10.7	8.9
	B	11.3	7.7	4.1	4.5	4.5	4.9	4.0	4.1
Others									
Shareholding	A						17.4	14.1	11.3
	B						11.6	8.5	6.3
Foreign	A						13.1	10.9	9.5
	B						8.7	6.2	5.1
HK/Macau/	A						8.6	8.1	5.7
Taiwan	B						5.6	4.2	2.8
Weighted	A	24.7	16.2	11.3	12.9	10.7	13.0	11.2	8.5
average	B	16.3	9.7	5.9	7.5	7.0	8.6	6.4	4.5

Notes: A and B: Pre-tax and after-tax profitability.

1. Profit as a percentage of net capital stock which is the sum of the average net fixed capital and working capital. For the years, 1988, and 1990–1992, due to the unavailability of average figures, the year-end figures for fixed capital stock are used for profitability calculation.
2. SOEs with independent accounting system at county level and above.

Sources: *Zhongguo tongji nianjian* (Statistical Yearbook of China, *ZGTJNJ*), various issues.

declining, but this trend is also shared by non-state enterprises.This means that the declining profitability of SOEs does not necessarily reflect the declining internal efficiency of SOEs and that it may have more to do with cyclical factors which affect all industrial enterprises .

However, caution should be exercised in interpreting the profitability figures of Table 1.

To begin with, the pre-tax profitability figures of non-state enterprises are biased downward because of the under-reporting of their profits for tax evasion purpose. In particular, the profitability figures of Hong Kong/Macau/Taiwan firms are highly suspect since they are even lower than that of the SOEs. Furthermore, the profitability figures of SOEs are gross of subsidies. Thus, adjustments need to be made to take account of subsidized inputs provided to some SOEs.

In terms of after-tax profitability, however, the profitability of SOEs has been significantly lower than that of non-state enterprises. As indicated in Table 1, the after-tax profitability of SOEs on average has been only 70% of its collective counterparts and 46% of all other non-state enterprises. Moreover, the divergence in after-tax profitability between the two groups of enterprises has increased since the late 1980s.

The relative low after-tax profitability of SOEs merely reflects the unequal tax burden between the two groups of enterprises. Prior to 1994, Chinese SOEs were subject to a 55% income tax rate whereas foreign invested enterprises (FIEs) paid only 33% and those in Special Economic Zones (SEZs) 15% income tax. In addition, FIEs also enjoyed tax exemption for the first two years of their operation and tax reduction for another three years thereafter. Moreover, their indirect tax burden was only 50% of that of SOEs.[8] Similarly, collective enterprises also enjoyed several tax concessions, and their profit tax rate was only 35%.[9]

The tax reform of 1994 aimed at the equalization of the tax burden among the different types of enterprises. But so far, the effect appears to be limited. As revealed in Table 1, the after-tax profitability between the two groups of enterprises narrowed in 1994 but widened again in 1995.

Turning to the much-publicized SOEs' financial performance, there is little doubt that the losses sustained by SOEs have been sizeable and increasing (see Table 2). However, in interpreting these data the following factors are noted: First, some of the losses incurred by SOEs are a consequence of government policy. For instance, some sale prices of SOEs' products had been set below cost by the government for many years. More

Table 2. Share of Industrial SOEs' Loss in Their Net Output

Year	Loss	Net output	Share
	(billion RMB)		(%)
1990	34.9	356.9	9.8
1991	36.7	401.9	9.1
1992	36.9	519.3	7.1
1993	45.3	728.1	6.2
1994	48.3	790.3	6.1
1995	54.1	830.7	6.5

Sources: Broadman (see Note 4), p. 12; *ZGTJNJ*, various issues.

recently, in 1995, the government lifted the prices of energy and rail freight rates which had the effect of converting invisible subsidies into a visible loss.[10] Secondly, some of the SOEs' losses were due to the change in accounting methods. Thus, for example, about 77% of the profit reduction of SOEs in 1993 can be traced back to the adoption of the new accounting rule in that year.[11] Thirdly, some of the SOEs' losses are a statistical artefact. SOEs performing well financially were transformed either into joint-venture enterprises or share-holding companies which were listed as non-state enterprises, whereas those making a loss were still listed as SOEs.

Finally, though the absolute amount of their losses has increased, measured relative to the value of their net output, they have declined. As shown in Table 2 the proportion of SOEs' loss to the value of their net output was reduced from around 10% in 1990 to about 6.5% in 1995.

When the loss of SOEs is adjusted to take into account the explicit and implicit subsidies provided to the SOEs, the improved financial performance of the SOEs during the period (1990–1993) remains untarnished. Data on subsidies provided to industrial SOEs are scarce. Table 3 shows subsidies provided to all industrial enterprises. It reveals that, while explicit fiscal subsidies provided to SOEs have declined, implicit and quasi fiscal subsidies have increased. As a result, the total subsidies provided to the SOEs have been increasing. For the years where both sets of subsidies figures are available, Table 3 shows that the combined loss and subsidies of SOEs grew at an annual average rate of 4.8% during 1990–1993. During the same period, the growth rates of SOEs' nominal output and services ranged from 4.7 to 49.4% in the following sectors:[12]

Table 3. Loss and Subsidies of SOEs

(Unit: billion RMB)

Year	Explicit	Implicit	Quasi	Loss	Total
1990	57.8	46.0	66.3	93.3	263.4
1991	51.0	48.4	NA	93.1	NA
1992	44.5	55.2	NA	75.7	NA
1993	41.1	69.0	117.7	75.0	302.8
1994	36.6	NA	NA	65.7	NA
1995	32.8	NA	NA	88.3	NA

Notes: NA: not available. Implicit subsidies consist primarily of interest rate subsidies for fund allocated by PBOC and SPCs to the SOEs. Quasi subsidies are mainly low cost loans provided by PBOC to the financial system to finance the short term working capital need of the SOEs.

Sources: *ZGTJNJ*, 1996, p. 227; Broadman (see Note 4), pp. 12 and 15; *SCMPIW*, 29 June 1996.

Industry	20.2%
Construction	36.2%
Transport	4.7–8.8%
Retail trade	12.5%
Bank (deposit)	49.4%

Since the growth of SOEs' combined loss and subsidies has been much lower than the growth of their output, their share in SOEs' output must have declined.

The increased internal efficiency of SOEs under CRS is also confirmed by their total factor productivity (TFP) estimate. During 1988–1992, the growth of TFP of SOEs has been estimated at 2.5% a year.[13]

Despite the improvement of internal efficiency, there is little doubt that the allocative efficiency of SOEs remains very low. The growth of TFP in SOEs has been only one-third to one-half of the corresponding rate for non-state enterprises. SOEs loss and debt have continued to soar and the government has had to increase subsidies to bail out loss-making SOEs. It is estimated that SOEs' loss has amounted to between 2.4 and 5.3%[14] and total subsidies to 5–6% of Chinese gross domestic product (GDP).[15] Though the share of loss plus subsidies in SOEs' output has been declining, it has nevertheless remained at 20% of their net output in 1993. There is also strong evidence of misallocation of investment resources and labour. Though the capital/output ratio of SOEs is twice that of the non-state enterprises, SOEs receive two-thirds of the state industrial investment.[16]

Similarly, although 20% of the work force of SOEs is regarded as redundant, workers still keep on receiving pay cheques with the result that they are employed at the point where the wage rate is significantly higher than their marginal productivity.

SOEs also contribute directly to the growing environmental degradation of China.[17] The magnitude of SOEs' losses and debts has made it difficult for them to adopt cleaner and environment-friendly technology. For fear of aggravating the losses, the fines for breaking anti-pollution laws have been kept to a minimum and have accounted for less than 0.1% of the value of China's annual industrial output.[18]

Of late, SOEs have also become a drag on China's final transition to a fully-fledged market economy. The postponement of structural reforms in its SOEs has enabled China to lower its visible short-run transition cost. In contrast to its Eastern European and Russian counterparts, Chinese SOEs have been spared the impact of supply shocks since, not only have their markets been sheltered from foreign competition, but they have also continued to receive subsidies and soft bank loans from the state. Hence, a large dip in SOE output and employment during the transition period has been prevented.[19] More recently, however, the invisible transition cost associated with the postponement of the structural reform in the state sector has become increasingly visible in terms of the restraints which the relatively poor SOE economic performance has imposed on the progress of the overall reform process.

Thus, for example, the much awaited commercialization of China's four big specialized banks announced in 1994 has made little progress because of the lack of SOE reform. Specialized banks have not been able to free themselves from policy-loan issuing functions. In 1996, for instance, in order to arrest the decline in SOE exports and sales as well as to lower their interest burden, the People's Bank of China (PBOC) issued a 10-point plan requiring banks to lend to ailing LMSOEs and, in particular, to 300 priority enterprises singled out by the government for transformation into mega-SOEs.[20] Specialized banks have continued to be loaded with large non-performing loans to SOEs. As of 1996, it has been estimated that banks are owed about US$ 620 billion which amounts to about 30% of their total lending and 25% of the Chinese GDP.[21] The liberalization of interest rates has also been stalled because of government fears that the freeing of the interest rate policy may cause SOEs to default on their debts to banks and trigger eventual bankruptcy.

Slow progress in the reform of LMSOEs also retards the development of China's capital market. The issue, pricing and transfer of securities continue to be subject to heavy government regulation because of government fears that the incomplete reform of SOEs may cause them to over-borrow, which would result in the misallocation of financial resources and aggravate inflation. The planned phase-out of the stock quota system which limits the number of new shares issued has had to be stalled several times because of the limited progress of SOEs' reform.

To summarize: while the internal efficiency of SOEs has improved under the CRS, their gross allocative inefficiency remains. Of late, the incompleteness of the reform of SOEs has become a stumbling block for China's final move to a market economy. Thus, the scene is set for another wave of enterprise reform in the mid-1990s.

The Modern-Enterprise-System Reform

The new reform initiative introduced in the mid-1990s consists of two components.[22] One is the transformation of most LMSOEs into a modern enterprise system through corporatization, the restructuring of their debts and the divestiture of their community service obligations. Another component is the restructure of the state ownership.

The main objective of the first component of the new reform plan is to preserve the state ownership of LMSOEs and modernize their internal governance and incentive structure so as to make them compatible with the goal of the establishment of a socialist market economy, as adopted by the 3rd plenary session of the 14th Central Committee in November 1993. As outlined in the 15-Year-Development Plan, the establishment of a modern enterprise system is expected to be accomplished during the 9th Five-year Plan period (1996–2000) and that of a socialist market economy by the year 2010.[23]

To achieve the first objective, 100 LMSOEs were selected by the State Council at the end of 1994 for experimentation with the full conversion into the modern enterprise system. In addition, 2000 local SOEs were also earmarked by the local governments to undergo a similar experiment.[24]

The main features of a modern enterprise system as envisaged in the reform blueprint are as follows: First, SOEs will be incorporated as either limited liability companies or share holding companies according to the Company Law introduced in 1994.

Secondly, state ownership in the company can either be sole, majority

Chart 1. Control of SOEs under New Enterprise System

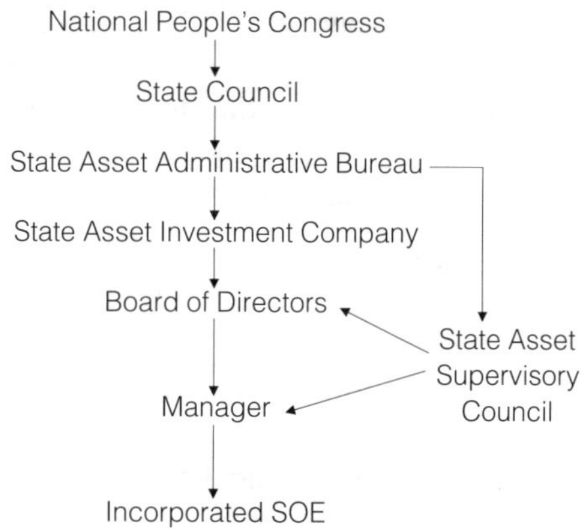

and minority depending on the significance and competitiveness of the industry. Though the delineation of which industries fall into each of these three categories of state ownership has yet to be finalized, there are indications[25] that strategic industries, such as defence, rare material mining and production as well as currency minting, will remain under total state ownership. For natural monopolies and basic industries, such as electricity, petroleum extracting and refining, and certain technology-intensive processing industries (shipbuilding, automobile, electronics), as well as important service industries, such as airlines, ocean liners, airports, harbours, telecommunication, banking and insurance, majority state ownership will be required. Finally, for competitive industries, such as textile and light industries, only minority state-ownership control is required initially and, later, a complete withdrawal of state ownership from these industries may be permissible.

Thirdly, incorporated SOEs are financially independent. They have their own financial resources and are free to manage their own affairs without detailed control by the state.

Fourthly, the state exercises its ownership rights and control through the following channels: For SOEs under central control, the incorporated SOEs will be administrated by the managing institutions of state-owned assets (MISOA) which consists of (a) the State Asset Administrative Bureau (SAAB); (b) the State Asset Investment Company (SAIC); and (c) the State Asset Supervisory Council (SASC) (see Chart 1). SAAB is responsible for general policy formulation with regard to the overall administration of the state ownership interest, and SAIC is responsible for the implementation of these policies through direct or indirect participation in incorporated SOEs' board of directors. SASC is in charge of monitoring the performance of the incorporated SOEs, in particular, with respect to the valuation of state assets and their preservation as well as growth. For SOEs under local control, there is an analogous three-tier controlling and monitoring hierarchy: municipal SAAB, SAIC and SASC.[26]

Fifthly, the performance monitoring arrangement for incorporated SOEs is lacking in detail. However, there are indications that such arrangement will focus mainly on the setting up of financial targets aimed at the preservation and growth of state assets within the enterprises. Further, in the last two years or so, specific incentive structures have been developed to motivate managers and workers to achieve financial targets. For workers, for example, their wage increase is linked to the increase in the value of the state asset value in their enterprises.[27] For managers, the following rewards and punishments have been introduced:

(i) Managers upon fulfilment of the financial target receive in addition to their normal salary a "risk" salary which may amount to 100% of the normal salary.
(ii) A manager who fails to meet the target, not only receives no "risk" salary, but also suffers a cut in his/her normal salary.
(iii) A manager who fulfils the target two years consecutively is rewarded with a "risk" salary twice the value of his/her normal salary.
(iv) Those unable to fulfil the target for two consecutive years will be dismissed and barred from taking up a managerial position in another company.

To enable incorporated SOEs to function as viable commercial enterprises, measures have been introduced to reduce their debt burden. These include:[28]

(i) A moratorium on their interest and principal repayments.
(ii) Provisions for a debt-equity swap under which debts which SOEs owe to the PBOC for their borrowing to finance their basic construction investment are allowed to be converted into state equity.
(iii) Arrangement for a tax-equity swap under which a proportion of income as well as other tax payment are refunded to SOEs as a state equity contribution.

Similarly, to help SOEs to get rid of surplus labour, surplus workers of SOEs are allowed to register with local labour bureaux and receive unemployment benefits.[29]

SOEs are also allowed to keep part of their after-tax profits and dividends on state shares to establish job replacement services and a workers' retraining centre to help the re-employment of the dismissed workers.[30]

Traditionally, each SOE had operated like a small society providing social services to their employees which included housing, education, hospitalization, social security, food services, fuel and retail outlets.[31] As part of the reform process, incorporated SOEs located in the major cities are allowed to divest themselves of the responsibility for such services to the city administration. However, social service obligations will still be met by incorporated SOEs located in the remote areas; but, this supply will be separated from the enterprise's commercial activities. Moreover, it is anticipated that these services will be run on a cost-based principle, with the exception of some essential services which will still be funded by the government.

Aside from policies aimed at transforming SOEs into a modern enterprise system, the government has also introduced measures to consolidate its ownership in conjunction with the 18 cities' Comprehensive Economic Reform programme.[32] Under these measures, small loss-making SOEs will be declared bankrupt, and low-profit making SOEs will be sold or leased, contracted out or merged with other enterprises. There will also be a withdrawal of state ownership from competitive industries to strategic and natural monopoly industries. In addition, some 300 LMSOEs have been selected to be groomed into mega-enterprises so that they can withstand foreign competition after China's entry into the World Trade Organization. These enterprises have been given preferential treatment in the form of tax concession, subsidized loans and depreciation allowance retention. Finally, there is also an attempt to form numerous conglomerates (100 have been earmarked) so that they can compete in the international market with multi-national corporations from other countries.

Assessment and Preliminary Results

In the West, SOEs are organized either as (a) a department of the state under the direct control of a government ministry, or (b) a commercial company with the state as sole or majority shareholder, or (c) a public corporation.[33] Most SOEs in continental Europe are based on model (b), whereas most SOEs in the UK until recently were based on model (c).

China's traditional SOEs were based on model (a). The new reform initiatives, in essence, are an attempt to transplant the Western public enterprise model (b) into China's state sector. Model (b), a publicly controlled commercial company, is supposed to achieve the best of two worlds. On the one hand, SOEs will be run on a commercial basis in a competitive environment, and their managers will be freed from the government supervision of day-to-day operations. On the other hand, the government as an owner will continue to control the broad policies of the enterprises through its sole or majority shareholding.

However, like many ideal systems, the system is difficult to implement. Publicly controlled companies face the same kind of principal-agent problem as their private counterparts, namely, the monitoring of their management performance. While, in the case of a private company, the monitoring is performed by private shareholders, in a publicly controlled company, this is performed by the government. In China, this function is supposed to be performed by the various MISOAs set up by the government. But, the details of how these MISOAs are to be formed and to fulfil their specific functions and how they are supposed to monitor the incorporated SOEs are still left very unclear. From a theoretical perspective, the public monitoring system, in contrast to its private counterparts, suffers from three potential sources of inefficiencies, according to Vickers and Yarrow.[34] First, the objective of the controller, the government department, is often not clear-cut, and political objectives tend to displace economic objectives. Secondly, government authorities tend to prefer political inter vention in managerial decisions over an "arm's length" relation with the management. Finally, the government control mechanisms tend to be highly bureaucratic, inefficient and excessive.

In addition to the above, publicly controlled companies also suffer from a limited market for corporate control and takeover. For a private company, since shares are marketable, managerial behaviour is constrained by threat of corporate takeover. In publicly controlled companies, however, ordinary shares are limited. In China, according to the reform blueprint, most SOEs are to be incorporated into limited liability companies. Only a few SOEs will be converted into shareholding companies, and only a limited number of them will be allowed to list their shares on the stock markets.[35]

Lastly, the efficiency of the monitoring system of the publicly controlled company is also weakened by the fact that its managers are likely to be subject to less threat of bankruptcy than their private counterparts.

The performance of a modern enterprise depends, not only on its effective internal governance and incentive system, but also on its external incentive system and environment.[36] With regard to the latter, the degree of product market competition and the effectiveness of regulation for firms with market power are most important.[37] China's new reform blueprint seems to over-concentrate on the issues of firms' internal governance and incentive structure to the neglect of its external environment, as it contains few details on competition policy and regulatory regimes. Worse still, part of the state ownership restructuring programme appears to contradict the goal of enterprise reform. For example, the formation of 100 conglomerates and the special treatment granted to the 300 mega-SOEs are likely to reduce the extent of competition facing SOEs.

Incorporated SOEs with market power need an effective regulatory framework since maximizing internal efficiency does not necessarily imply the maximization of allocative efficiency. For example, a monopoly may maximize profits but at the cost of allocative efficiency as it incurs deadweight loss. China's new enterprise reform blueprint tends to focus heavily on internal efficiency in general and on financial efficiency in particular to the neglect of allocative efficiency. Hence, there has been very little mention of the regulatory framework to be adopted (if at all) for firms with market power.

The only regulatory framework mentioned in the reform blueprint concerns the financial targets set by the government for SOEs to exhort them to preserve and increase the value of the state assets so as to prevent state asset stripping. However, this kind of financial targets implies that the net investment of the firm should be positive or its gross investment should exceed its depreciation. This would encourage incorporated SOEs to overinvest or to undertake investment even if its rate of return is less than the discount rate. This would lead to a reduction of the value of the state assets.

With regard to the state ownership restructuring programme, the withdrawal of state ownership to strategic industries and industries with limited possibility of competition and the dispossession of the state of inefficient and loss-making small SOEs should enhance the allocative and X-efficiency of the Chinese economy significantly. Similarly, the admission of private shareholding within a predominantly publicly controlled company should also strengthen the effectiveness of the public monitoring mechanism of these enterprises. However, the restructuring programme also implies further down-sizing of the state sector. During 1978–1993, as a result of government policy of promoting non-state enterprises and using them to "surround" SOEs, the share of SOEs in GDP had dropped from 56 to 43%,[38] and their share in national industrial output had declined from 79 to 34% during the same period.[39] In the next five years, the share of SOEs in national output is expected to be drastically reduced for two reasons. One is the planned withdrawal of state ownership from competitive industries as these industries account for 80% of China's industrial output.[40] Another reason is the planned dilution of state ownership within the state majority controlled shareholding companies by allowing other institutional and individual investors to hold shares in these companies. Thus, the state ownership restructuring programme is undoubtedly a partial privatization of the LMSOEs.

Another factor which is likely to accelerate the decline of the state sector is the continued existence of the growth gap between the state and non-state industrial enterprises. During 1979–1993, the annual average growth rate of the latter had been three times that of the former.[41] In the light of the above discussion, the efficiency and, hence, growth of publicly controlled industry are expected to continue to lag behind those of the non-public sector. Thus, it may be difficult for China to keep the commitment of maintaining a high degree of public ownership in the industrial sector.

The initial results of the modern enterprise reform during the past two years has not been so encouraging. The pilot scheme of converting 100 selected LMSOEs into fully corporatized SOEs by 1996 has been postponed for another year. Out of the 100 enterprises, 13.5% have been converted into limited liability or shareholding companies, while 46.2% have been converted into enterprise groups (conglomerates) within which the parent companies assuming the MISOAs' function and the subsidiary companies being converted into limited liability or shareholding companies.[42]

The incorporated SOEs have limited internal asset as even those assets formed in the past through their own retained profits and bank loans are regarded as state asset.[43] Incorporated SOEs are still far from being free of the government department intervention in their management decisions since government departments still control the appointment of the managers of the incorporated SOEs. In fact, in most cases, the directorship of the board and the position of manager of the enterprise are held by the same person for the sake of avoiding disputes.[44]

Though the name of the SOEs' supervisory bureau has been changed to MISOA, the attitude and behaviour of its officers towards the incorporated SOEs remain unchanged. Most are reluctant to part with their control power and tend to interfere with the incorporated SOEs' day-to-day operations.[45] There have also been complaints that the management autonomy gained by the SOEs under the experiment of Transforming the Management Mechanism initiated in 1992 has been lost to the state holding companies which were established by the government to manage incorporated SOEs.[46] These state holding companies also create an additional layer of bureaucracy over the operating companies and, hence, reduce efficiency, accountability and transparency in the control system of the incorporated SOEs.[47]

Limited success has been achieved in the restructuring of SOEs' debt.The debt-current asset ratio of industrial SOEs had shot up from 50 to 96% between 1980 and 1993.[48] By the end of June, however, it has reportedly fallen to 59%.[49] Several factors have contributed to the reduction of this ratio. Among them are the implementation of the various debt- and tax-equity swap schemes, the raising of SOEs' rate of depreciation, and the writing off of some of their bad debts by the state banks which are estimated at about US$ 20 billion in 1996. The two downward adjustments of interest rates in 1996 also helped.

Success in the shedding of SOEs' surplus labour has been limited. Though the number of bankruptcies has soared from 816 in 1995 to 1,692 during the first half of 1996, most have involved small SOEs.

The divestiture of SOEs of their community service provision obligations has also hit some snags because of the shortage of funding. "Non productive" social service expenditures still loom large in SOEs' total expenditures.

Finally, both the growth and financial performance of SOEs continue to leave much to be desired. During the first eight months of 1996, the rate of growth of value-added of the state solely and majority owned enterprises has continued to lag behind the rate of collective and private enterprises by a ratio of 1 to 5.8 and 1 to 2.8, respectively.[50] Both the losses and debts of SOEs have continued to soar. In the first quarter of 1996, net loss was recorded for the first time for the state sector since 1978.[51] In early 1996, total debts of SOEs reached US$ 620 billion, and interest payments on outstanding debts accounted for an average of 74% of the operating revenues of SOEs.[52]

Summary and Conclusion

Wholesale privatization of LMSOEs is ideologically unacceptable to China. Hence, since 1978, China has been faced with the difficult task of how to instil an effective incentive system into its SOEs. Several alternatives have been put on trial. These have included the CRS adopted during 1987–1994 and the modern enterprise system introduced in 1994.

The CRS instilled tighter financial discipline into the SOEs, and as a result, contributed to a significant improvement of their internal efficiency. Nevertheless, the CRS did little to improve the allocative efficiency of SOEs. SOEs' losses and debts continued to soar and the government had to increase subsidies and force the state banking system to lend money and bail out the loss-making SOEs. Gross misallocation of investment resources and labour were also highly visible. Further, SOEs also contributed to a worsening of environmental degradation and, of late, became increasingly a restraint on the pace of China's overall reform programme.

The new SOEs' reform initiatives introduced in 1994 have centred on the corporatization and restructuring of SOEs. The corporatization programme aims to transplant the Western public enterprise model into China so as to enhance its internal efficiency. The restructuring programme aims to reduce SOEs' debt burden, shed their surplus labour, divest themselves of their community services provision obligations and withdraw state ownership from the competitive industries.

An examination of the new reform strategies and their preliminary results reveal that the fundamental issues of accountability and control of SOEs have remained unresolved. The property rights of incorporated SOEs remain ambiguous, and it is not clear how the newly established MISOAs are going to perform their monitoring functions. In view of the fact that the basic weakness of the public monitoring system remains unresolved and that managers of publicly controlled companies are subject to less pressure from corporate control, from takeover bids as well as from the threat of bankruptcy, the efficiency gap between corporatized SOEs and non-state enterprises is likely to remain.

The new SOEs' reform programme focuses mainly on each firm's internal governance and incentive structure and pays little attention to the competitive environment and the regulatory regime. Some components of the restructuring programme also appear to be inconsistent with the aims of corporatization.

Incorporated SOEs with market power need to be regulated in order to reconcile internal efficiency with economic efficiency. However, the new SOEs' reform blueprint is vague on the matter of an appropriate regulatory regime. The only financial target mentioned is the preservation and growth of state assets. This target regulates SOEs' investment behaviour rather than their pricing behaviour, and it is likely to encourage them to over invest.

In view of the above, corporatization is no panacea for the fundamental weakness of China' state sector, and new institutional innovations in this sector are expected in the near future. Much hope has been placed upon the share holding system reform. The share holding system enables private investors to hold shares and become members of the board of directors in a state majority controlled share holding company. As private investors may exert a strong influence over managerial decision because of their strong profit incentives,[53] the share holding system will undoubtedly strengthen the public monitoring system and cut down its agency cost. But, the full development of a share holding system hinges on the development of a well-functioning stock market the establishment of which cannot be expected in the near future. Hence, the role of the share holding system in the near future of Chinese enterprise reform should not be exaggerated.

Notes

1. Qin Xiao, "Restructuring Large State-owned Enterprises: Internal Mechanisms for Allocating Resources as a Substitute for the Market," in *Policy Options for Reform of Chinese State-owned Enterprises*, edited by H. G. Broadman (Washington, DC: World Bank, 1996), p. 180.
2. For a good discussion of China's state enterprise reform between 1978 and 1994, see Chi-Wen Jevons Lee, "The Reform of the State-owned Enterprises," *China Review 1996*, edited by Maurice Brosseau, Suzanne Pepper and Tsang Shu-ki (Hong Kong: The Chinese University Press, 1996), chapter 10 and Joseph C. H. Chai, *China: Transition to a Market Economy* (Oxford: Clarendon Press, forthcoming), chapters 4 and 5.
3. See Chai (Note 2), chapter 5.
4. H. G. Broadman, *Meeting the Challenges of Chinese Enterprise Reform* (Washington, DC: World Bank, 1995), p. 23.
5. See *Qiye chengbao zhinan* (A Guide to Enterprise Contract System) (Beijing: Science Publishing House, 1988), pp. 153–55.
6. J. Vickers and G. Yarrow, *Privatization: An Economic Analysis* (Cambridge, Mass.: MIT Press, 1989), pp. 142–43.

7. M. Iskander, "Improving State-owned Enterprise Performance: Recent International Experience," in Broadman (ed.) (Note 1), p. 27.
8. Yang Peixin, "Guoyou qiye buneng zai weisuo xiaqu le" (State-owned Enterprises Should Not Be Allowed to Shrink Further), *Gaige neican* (Internal Reference on Reform), No. 14 (1995), p. 4.
9. See Broadman (Note 4), note 45.
10. *Gaige neican*, No. 15 (1996), p. 16.
11. Ibid., No. 4/5 (1995), p. 48.
12. *Zhongguo tongji nianjian 1996* (Statistical Yearbook of China, 1996).
13. G. H. Jefferson and T. G. Rawski, " Enterprise Reform in Chinese Industry," *The Journal of Economic Perspectives*, Vol. 8, No. 2 (1994), p. 56.
14. See Iskander (Note 7), p. 23.
15. N. C. Hope, "Opening Remarks," in Broadman (ed.) (Note 1), p. 14
16. *SCMPIW*, 29 June 1996 and Cao Yushu, "Guanyu zhuanbian jingji zengzhang fangshi de ruogan kanfa" (Certain Observations on Changing Economic Growth Strategy), *Jingji yanjiu cankao* (Economic Research Reference), No. 124 (1996), pp. 13–14.
17. J. C. H. Chai, "Consumption and Living Standard in China," in *The Chinese Economy under Deng Xiaoping*, edited by R. F. Ash and Y. Y. Kueh (Oxford: Clarendon Press 1996), pp. 255–56.
18. *China Daily*, 16 March 1994.
19. Chai (Note 2), chapter 11.
20. *SCMPIW*, 10 August 1996.
21. *SCMPIW*, 29 June 1996.
22. Dong Ying, "Dui jinhou shiwu nian woguo guoyou qiye gaige juti mubiao he cuoshi de sikao" (Thought on Specific Objectives and Measures of Our Country's State-owned Enterprises Reform in the Next 15 Years), *Jingji yanjiu cankao*, No. 105 (1996), pp. 2–9 and Yu Dong and Yuan Xilu, "1995 nian guoqi gaige huigu he 1996 zhanwang" (Review of 1995 SOEs' Reform and Its Prospects for 1996), *Jingji yanjiu cankao*, No. 3 (1996), pp. 2–13.
23. Dong (Note 22), p. 13.
24. *Gaige neican*, No. 4/5 (1995), p. 35.
25. See Dong (Note 22), p. 7 and Yu and Yuan 1996 (Note 19), pp. 9–10.
26. Broadman (Note 4), p. 23.
27. *Jingji zhengce fagui cankao* (Reference Materials on Economic Policy Laws and Regulations), No. 14 (1996), p. 11.
28. Yu and Yuan (Note 22), p. 3.
29. Ibid., p. 8.
30. Dong (Note 22), p. 6.
31. Hu Xiaoyi, "Reducing State-owned Enterprises' Social Burdens and Establishing a Social Insurance System," in Broadman (ed.) (Note 1), pp. 125–48.
32. See Dong (Note 22), p. 8.

33. Vickers and Yarrow (Note 6), p. 125.
34. Ibid., p. 34.
35. *Gaige neican*, No. 4/5 (1995), p. 39.
36. Iskander (Note 7), pp. 36–38.
37. Vicker, and Yarrow (Note 6), p. 44.
38. Chen Xiaohong, "Guoyou qiye de xianzhuang he zhuyao wenti" (Current Situation and Main Problems of SOEs), *Jingji yanjiu cankao*, No. 58 (1996), p. 16.
39. Zhang Ming, "Guoyou qiye zhuanhuan jingying jizhi de nandian yu duice" (Problems and Solutions to Transforming the Management System of the State-owned Enterprise), *Jingji yanjiu cankao*, No. 127 (1996), p. 49.
40. *Gaige neican*, No. 17 (1996), p. 30.
41. Fang Xiandong, "Jiuwu shiqi woguo suoyou zhi jiegou biandong qushi" (Trends of Our Country's Ownership Structural Change during the Ninth-Five-year Plan Period), *Gaige neican*, No. 8 (1995), p. 29.
42. Fan Bi, "1995 nian jingji tizhi gaige huigu" (Review of 1995 Economic Reform), *Jingji yanjiu cankao*, No. 54 (1996), p. 17.
43. *Jingji yanjiu cankao*, No. 3 (1996), p. 33.
44. Jia Heting, "On Corporatisation of Enterprises and Corporate Governance," in Broadman (ed.) (Note 1), p. 114.
45. Zhang (Note 39), p. 32 and Jia (Note 44), p. 112–42.
46. *Gaige neican*, No. 16 (1995), p. 23.
47. Iskander (Note 7), p. 49.
48. Wu Xiaoling, "Debt Restructuring of State-owned Enterprises and Role of Banks," in Broadman (ed.) (Note 1), p. 189.
49. *SCMPIW*, 31 August 1996.
50. *SCMPIW*, 14 September 1996.
51. Ibid., 29 June 1996.
52. Ibid., 18 May 1996 and 13 July 1996.
53. See Qian Yingyi, "Enterprise Reform in China: Agency Problems and Political Control," *Economics of Transition*, Vol. 4, No. 2 (1996), pp. 427–47.

8

Is the Battle Against Inflation Over?

Hiroyuki Imai

Introduction

In 1996, a three-year long double-digit inflation period ended in China. At its height in 1994, the annual rate of inflation measured by the retail price index (RPI) reached 21.7%. The 1996 annual rate settled at 6.1%, and the year-on-year rate in December 1996 dropped to 4.2%. As these rates are significantly below the mean growth rate of the retail price index (7.7%) in the economic reform period (1979–1996), one may conclude that the austerity programme which began in the spring of 1993 achieved its goal of macroeconomic stabilization. This outcome looks even more impressive if one considers the side effects of the current retrenchment. Unlike the last two disinflation periods, 1981 and 1989–1990, the extent of gross domestic product (GDP) growth deceleration has been quite modest, and the Chinese economy has avoided a recession. The GDP growth rate in 1996 was 9.7% as against 5.2, 4.1, and 3.8% in 1981, 1989, and 1990 (Table 1). In December 1996, an official Chinese newspaper declared justifiably that the Chinese economy had pulled off a "soft landing" and regained macroeconomic equilibrium.[1] As one has witnessed the end of the last inflation cycle, which began with the investment surge in 1992, this is an appropriate moment to review China's recent inflation experience and assess the factors defining future price trends.

The objective of this chapter is to evaluate the 1992–1995 inflation in the broad perspective of the Chinese reform-period economy. To this end, this author discusses the sources, patterns, and dynamics of China's inflation since 1979 in the next section, then reviews the 1992–1996 inflation cycle and considers the price outlook in section three. A summary of the main findings concludes the study.

Structure of Inflation in the Reform Period

Statistical Regularities: Three Main Elements

The economic reforms have changed the nature of inflation in China. Under the pre-reform planned economy, the long-run rate of inflation had stayed low although repressed inflation had persisted. As the prices were liberalized and direct control over economic activities was relaxed successively under economic reforms after 1979, the long-run rate of inflation shifted upward to the 6 to 10% range from around 1% in the pre-reform period.[2]

Part of the rise in the trend rate of inflation in the reform period, particularly in the earlier years, was a by-product of the price policies adopted. The government chose to adjust the relative price structure without resorting to reductions in nominal prices of the goods and services whose relative prices had to fall. In order to facilitate the realignment of prices, the government in essence allowed a moderate rise in the rate of inflation by easing monetary policy. Also, the unwinding of repressed inflation showed up as successive rises in the price index after low regulated prices were allowed to climb to the market-clearing levels. By the end of the 1980s, many egregious price distortions had been corrected and China's consumption goods market had largely regained equilibrium.[3] These new price policies therefore may have had a significant impact on the rise of retail prices during the 1980s when the bulk of price liberalization took place. Nevertheless, the fact that the rate of inflation rose further during the second half of the 1980s and then stayed high through the 1990s suggests that the main driving force of China's inflation in the reform period lies elsewhere.

Table 1 tabulates the annual growth rates of some macroeconomic variables associated with inflation in the reform period. Since 1979, the Chinese economy has achieved GDP growth rates of more than 7% in all but three years, 1981 and 1989–1990, which can be regarded as two periods of recession. There have been two long economic booms, one from 1982 to 1988 and the current boom since 1991. The most distinct feature of the behaviour of the rate of inflation, measured by the RPI, is cyclical patterns rather than the relatively high levels. The RPI and real GDP series have generally moved together over cycles, and two double-digit inflationary spells (1988–1989 and 1993–1995) have appeared in the last decade. Because a period of high (low) inflation have largely coincided with a boom (recession), we observe a short-run output-inflation trade-off in the reform period.

Considering the statistical series further, there appears to be three main elements that have governed the price movement in the reform period. The first one is investment expansion. Among the series listed in Table 1, year-to-year variation is by far the highest in fixed investment. The standard deviations of the growth rates of total (1981–1995) and state (1979–1992) fixed investment are 11.3 and 13.4%, respectively. Not only unstable in the short run, fixed investment has exhibited high growth. Total fixed investment expanded by 14.9% in the 1982–1996 period, and state fixed investment by 9.8% in the 1979–1992 period. These growth rates are

Table 1 Macroeconomic Data

Year	RPI	Real GDP	Industrial output	Agricultural output	Fixed investment			Personal consumption	Nominal wage	Labour productivity
					Total	State	Total/GDP			
			Growth rate, %				Share, %		Growth rate, %	
1979	2.0	7.6	8.2	6.1	—	2.9	—	8.1	18.9	5.3
1980	6.0	7.8	13.6	–1.5	—	2.8	—	10.8	20.8	4.4
1981	2.4	5.2	1.9	7.0	—	–12.1	19.8	8.3	6.8	2.0
1982	1.9	9.1	5.6	11.5	26.2	24.8	23.2	6.7	5.0	5.2
1983	1.5	10.9	10.4	8.3	13.3	9.8	24.1	8.4	11.5	8.2
1984	2.8	15.2	14.5	12.9	23.2	19.7	25.6	12.5	20.6	11.0
1985	8.8	13.5	18.6	1.8	30.3	33.2	28.4	14.8	23.3	9.7
1986	6.0	8.8	10.2	3.3	11.0	10.1	29.6	5.8	14.4	5.9
1987	7.3	11.6	13.7	4.7	14.7	10.5	30.4	7.4	15.4	8.4
1988	18.5	11.3	14.5	2.5	11.0	8.1	30.1	8.5	23.9	8.1
1989	17.8	4.1	3.8	3.1	–14.0	–14.2	24.5	0.8	8.7	2.2
1990	2.1	3.8	3.2	7.3	2.4	9.6	24.0	3.7	4.6	1.3
1991	2.9	9.2	13.9	2.4	16.7	17.1	25.5	9.7	10.8	6.2
1992	5.4	14.1	21.2	4.7	23.7	26.0	29.5	13.0	21.6	12.2
1993	13.2	13.5	19.9	4.7	25.3	14.7	36.0	10.5	—	12.0
1994	21.7	12.6	18.4	4.0	23.9	13.8	36.6	—	—	10.4
1995	14.8	10.5	14.1	5.0	10.9	7.0	34.4	—	—	8.9
1996	6.1[a]	9.7[a]	12.3[a]	5.1[a]	11.8[a]	—	34.9[a]	—	—	—
					1979–1992, %					
Mean	6.0	9.4	10.8	5.2	14.8[b]	9.8	—	8.4	14.5	6.4
SD	5.6	3.6	5.8	3.9	11.2[b]	13.4	—	3.7	6.9	3.3

Notes: RPI is the retail price index. Mean is the geometric-mean growth rate. SD is the standard deviation of the growth rate. Industrial output and agricultural output are, respectively, the output of the secondary and primary sectors in GDP at constant prices. Total fixed investment/GDP is based on the nominal series. Personal consumption at constant prices is from the NMP accounts. [a] preliminary estimates by the State Statistical Bureau, *RMRB*, 23 January 1997. [b] 1982–1996.

Sources: RPI: *ZGTJNJ 1996*, p. 255. Real GDP, industrial output, and agricultural output: *ZGTJNJ 1996*, p. 42 and *Zhongguo tongji zhaiyao 1996* (A Statistical Survey of China 1996), p. 8. Fixed investment: *ZGTJNJ 1996*, pp. 139 and 272, 1994 edition, pp. 139, 144, 243, 1993 edition, p. 145, and 1988 edition, p. 559; *Zhongguo tongji zhaiyao 1996*, pp. 6–9. Personal consumption: *ZGTJNJ 1994*, p. 41. Nominal wage: *ZGTJNJ 1993*, pp. 602 and 611, 1991 edition, p. 582, and 1986 edition, p. 443; *Zhongguo shichang nianjian 1993* (China Market Statistics 1993), p. 182. Labour productivity: *ZGTJNJ 1996*, p. 88 and 1993 edition, p. 97.

higher than those of GDP (10.5 and 9.4%, respectively). Another notable aspect of fixed investment is that its turning points coincide generally with those of the economic cycles. The two recessions, 1981 and 1989–1990, were matched by sharp decelerations in fixed investment, and subsequent economic recoveries were accompanied by marked accelerations of investment.

State fixed investment, most of which is the capital formation of state enterprises, makes up about 60% of total fixed investment. And, total investment's share of GDP has been increasing, reflecting its high growth rate, fluctuating between around 25 and 35% in the past decade. In contrast with fixed investment, personal consumption, the largest demand component of GDP, has a relatively low variability (a standard deviation of the growth rate, 1979–1992, of 3.7%) and growth rate (8.4%). These characteristics suggest that fixed investment has been the main propellant of China's output cycles during the reform period and, because of this role, it should have had a strong bearing on the rate of inflation.

The second element that affects prices is the relatively tight supply capacity of consumption goods, one of the reasons of which has been Chinese policy makers' long-standing neglect of the consumption goods sector in allocating state resources. Although the steady increase of employment and the fast rise of real incomes enabled households to expand spending, personal consumption appears to have been constrained by the productive capacity of the consumption goods sectors throughout the reform period. The slow growth of agricultural output kept high the demand pressures in the consumption goods market, because spending on food still made up about half of household cash expenditures in recent years.[4] To the extent that the consumption goods market is supply-constrained, high growth of nominal wages should lead to higher prices.

Whether agricultural output affects personal consumption by restricting market supply can be assessed through the correlation of the two variables. Short-run correlation between agricultural output and personal consumption, if confirmed, would underline that the consumption goods market is supply-constrained. Although the correlation coefficient of the growth rates of personal consumption and agricultural output in the same year is almost zero (1979–1993, –0.065), that of the current year's personal consumption and the previous year's agricultural output is sizable (1980–1993, 0.482), presumably on account of the timing of harvests. Harvest fluctuations in China often stem from random variations in climatic conditions. The correlation implies that such disturbances in supply conditions are transmitted to personal consumption and consumption goods prices. A corollary is that the tight and varying supply leaves the consumption goods market susceptible to demand pressures when household money incomes grow abruptly and augment the demand for agricultural products.

The third element that affects prices is rapid growth of nominal wages. Table 1 indicates that the nominal wage grew annually by 14.5% and that the variability of the growth rate has been high, with a standard deviation of 6.9% (nominal wage in Table 1 is earned cash income per worker) in the 1979–1992 period. The growth rate of the nominal wage was more than twice as high as that of labour productivity (real GDP per worker) at 6.4%, indicating clearly that wage increases resulted in significant rises in production costs. Despite the difference in growth rates, nominal wages and labour productivity in Table 1 appear to have moved along with GDP. It is reasonable to consider that the procyclical movement of labour productivity affected wage levels rather than the other way around.

In identifying the basic mechanism of China's inflation in the reform period, I have introduced three building blocks: strong aggregate demand led by fixed investment, tight supply conditions in the consumption goods market, and the growth of wage costs. It is this author's view that they together constitute the driving force of China's inflation which has been the combination of the demand and cost inflation. Let us consider separately the demand and cost sides of China's inflation.

Demand Inflation: Consumption Goods Market Pressures Resulting from Investment Expansion

The official Chinese sources have repeatedly acknowledged the three demand-side factors contributing to inflation during economic booms: expansion of fixed investment, increases in household incomes, and fast growth of the money supply.[5] These three factors have appeared together in every period of high inflation during the reform period. Under China's current, partially-reformed economic system, fixed investment moves more autonomously than household incomes and the money supply and can sway the level of household incomes. One may therefore regard the surge in fixed investment as the main source of demand inflation. Rapid expansion of fixed investment in the reform period can be thought of as one of the consequences of the gradualist reform policy applied to the state sector, in which investment decision-making has been decentralized without imposing strict financial accountability on enterprises.[6] Because state enterprises generally bear little risk when embarking on investment projects, expanded enterprise autonomy under economic reforms has led to strong growth of fixed investment.

Since investment growth necessitates higher labour input in the investment sector, it leads to larger total wage bills through increased employment. Given the gestation period of investment projects and the tight supply conditions of agricultural products, the immediate effect of investment expansion on the consumption goods market would be an increase in demand pressures stemming from rises in household money incomes. As fixed investment grows rapidly along the cyclical path, pressures in the consumption goods market appear in the form of high and varying rates of inflation. This is a reason for fixed investment, GDP, and the rate of inflation increasing at the same time during booms. The growth of the money supply also parallels investment in this process because the state banking system, lacking managerial independence, finances fixed investment passively with loans. Under these circumstances, fixed investment, household incomes, and money supply move together, as observed during past inflationary spells, indicating that a strong demand inflation is at work.

Cost Inflation: Wage Drift

As the growth of fixed investment accelerated during the reform period, a series of policies adopted over a decade from 1977 in the field of labour compensation appears to have provided reinforcement mechanisms for demand inflation from the cost side. Central among the policies was the wage reform in state enterprises implemented in two stages after 1977. The wage reform contributed greatly to the fast growth of cash income per worker in the reform period by raising the labour compensation of state-sector workers.[7]

In the first stage of the wage reform (1977–1984), the government restored piece rates and bonus payments and implemented several rounds of upward adjustments of the wage scales. Furthermore, state enterprises that fulfilled plan targets were in 1979 allowed to establish reserves from profits to be applied to bonus payments, workers' welfare expenditures, and fixed investment. In 1983, the Substitution of Tax for Profits Programme was introduced to replace the reserve fund system. Under this programme, enterprises could keep after-tax profits, half of which could be applied to bonuses and workers' welfare spending. In the second stage of the reform (1984–1986), state enterprises adopted a wage system that linked the total wage bill, bonuses, and benefits to indexes of performance, such as increases in labour productivity, remitted profits and taxes, and retained earnings. The ceilings on bonuses were phased out in this period.

These new measures under the wage reform provided state enterprises with greater discretion in determining labour compensation and allowed these enterprises to expand wage and bonus payments rapidly. As mandatory wage plans and uniform wage scales had been replaced by a complex set of indirect regulations, enterprise managers had, on the one hand, found much room to negotiate with the authorities for favourable treatment, or to circumvent regulations.[8] On the other hand, the greater power granted to managers by the authorities exposed them to expectations and pressures from workers. The new regulatory environment had unwittingly strengthened the power of workers relative to that of the state in setting labour compensation.

Kornai and Walder consider the new power relations and nominal wage drift as inevitable consequences of the reformed socialist system. While the wage reform has relaxed centralized control, "wage discipline imposed by private ownership, market competition, and unemployment" has been slow to develop in the economy.[9] Enterprises are still able to find "cover for losses from any increase in wage costs" from the state (soft budget constraint).[10] Because the hiring and dismissal of workers is still subject to various formal and informal restrictions, cooperation from workers on payrolls is indispensable for enterprise managers to organize production smoothly. This leaves managers more dependent on workers than in the pre-reform period, and consequently managers are held responsible for continuously increasing employees' incomes and benefits.[11]

Is the growth of nominal wage per worker in Table I consistent with the wage trend in state enterprises? Woo et al. (1994) reports findings from a survey of 300 large and medium-sized state industrial enterprises.[12] Total labour compensation increased from 31.8% of value added in 1984 to 48.8% in 1988. The share of taxes and remitted profits declined from 31.5% to 13.7% in the same period as a consequence. A study by Li and his associates indicates a similar rise of labour compensation in a broader category. The labour share of China's GNP based on their reconstructed factor-cost data grew from 43.2% in 1978 to 55.3% in 1990.[13] This leads one to suspect that the benefit of the dramatic distributional change in favour of labour during the reform period went beyond state-sector workers to workers in non-state enterprises and the agricultural work force.

The wage reform in the state sector has been part of a comprehensive policy on labour compensation. The wage conventions in collective enterprises followed the changes in the state sector. Policies directed toward incomes of the non-agricultural work force also had some links to those towards incomes of the agricultural work force, because the government acted to keep urban-rural income gaps from widening. Besides decollectivizing agriculture in the early 1980s, the government implemented periodic rises of the purchase price of agricultural products, to augment the incomes of peasants. Consequently, an intended modest realignment of the wage system and distributional policies in the early years of the reform period appears to have set off continued strong drives for high incomes from a wide spectrum of the work force. The growth of wages in the reform period, in addition to raising the labour share of output, has continually generated inflationary pressures by pushing production costs upward.

The growth rate of the nominal wage per worker has not only stayed high but has also fluctuated widely, following the procyclical movement of the growth rate of labour productivity, in the reform period. The parallel movement of the two variables appears to have reflected the wage-setting convention in the state sector. Total wage bills, bonuses, and benefits in state enterprises are linked with some performance criteria, one of which is the increase in labour productivity in the reform period. Other performance criteria commonly used, such as increases in remitted profits and taxes and retained earnings, have also tended to move procyclically along with labour productivity. Therefore, whichever criterion is adopted, the new mode of wage determination generally leads to the parallel movement of nominal wages and labour productivity.

The conspicuous procyclical movement of labour productivity, which is transmitted to wage growth fluctuations, appears to be associated with the presence of surplus workers in the industrial sector, those in state enterprises being most evident.[14] To maintain high employment in urban areas, the government has until recently encouraged enterprises to increase their work force over time. Surplus labour kept on payrolls allows the industrial sector as a whole to expand output with a less than proportional increase in workers. The new mode of wage determination has brought about cost inflation by awarding sharp wage hikes during a boom, because an increase in labour productivity is common when output grows rapidly.

Inflation Dynamics

To assess the underlying numerical relationships in China's wage setting during the reform period, the author has estimated a wage function. Because of the simultaneity problem, the wage function and the price equation are estimated together by three-stage least squares (3SLS).[15] The dependent variable of the wage function is the growth rate of the nominal wage ($\Delta W\%$). The explanatory variables are the growth rate of labour productivity ($\Delta V\%$) and the rate of inflation, based on the consumption goods price index ($\Delta P\%$). The data for $W\%$ and $\Delta V\%$ are from Table 1, and $P\%$ is the growth rate of the consumption goods price index.[16] Labour compensation for state-sector workers is, as mentioned above, linked to performance criteria, such as the increase in labour productivity, and it also includes partial compensation for the rise in the cost of living.[17] One therefore anticipates positive relationships between the nominal wage growth rate and the labour productivity growth rate and the current-year rate of inflation.

$$\Delta W\% = \underset{(13.090)}{1.563}\Delta V\% + \underset{(4.585)}{0.526}\Delta P\%.$$

$$R^2 = 0.998 \quad DW = 2.777 \quad \text{Period: 1981–1992.}$$

(The figures in parentheses are *t* statistics; the period cannot be updated beyond 1992 because one of the official data series used was discontinued.)

The coefficient of labour productivity (1.633) and the current year rate of inflation (0.527) are positive and significant at the 1% level. These imply the presence of the reinforcing mechanisms through wage determination. It can be inferred that the government's intention has been to keep the growth of nominal wages close to that of labour productivity. The estimated coefficient of the labour productivity growth rate, which is substantially higher than unity, attests to the strong bargaining position of workers in the new institutional environment. With a higher-than-unity coefficient, when output fluctuates owing to demand shocks, the subsequent procyclical fluctuation of labour productivity turns into an even wider movement of nominal wages, amplifying the initial impact on prices from demand shocks. The positive coefficient of the current-year rate of inflation implies the presence of another reinforcing mechanism. Starting from a stable wage level, any new inflationary pressure sets off an upward adjustment of the wage level.

Combining the demand-side factors and the mode of wage determination, one can construct the dynamics of China's inflationary spells during the reform period. The process begins with investment expansion, which generates new employment and brings about increases in aggregate output. Labour productivity rises as surplus labour within enterprises is used more effectively. Employment still increases, nevertheless, because the labour productivity growth is unlikely to offset fully the additional labour requirements for investment expansion. Productivity gains and the cost-of-living adjustment bring about sizable nominal wage hikes through the prevailing mode of wage determination. Household money income grows, thanks to the rise in both wages and employment. In the face of slow supply increases, particularly of agricultural products, augmented household income exerts demand pressures in the consumption goods market. Prices rise as a result of these pressures, allowing some producers to meet increased wage bills. While the expansion of fixed investment serves as a demand shock that raises output, its positive initial impact on prices (demand inflation) is amplified as the shock triggers cost increases through wage hikes (cost inflation).

The rate of inflation reaches high levels as this process continues, and this prompts the government to implement contractionary policies, the main content of which is tight money policy. Accordingly, the state banking system restrains loans for fixed investment and for working capital, part of which finances wage payments. Then, the dynamics reverses itself and the economy enters a disinflation phase.

This basic mechanism, governed by the combination of demand and cost inflation during an investment-led boom, is modified by a number of exogenous factors. Depending on these factors, the rate of inflation observed varies. These exogenous factors include short-term variations of agricultural output, of household saving-consumption choice, and of external economic variables, such as the trade balance and the volume of direct foreign investment. For instance, the high growth of agricultural output associated with agricultural decollectivization offset the inflationary impact of rapid investment expansion in the first half of the 1980s. Panic buying of consumption goods around the summer of 1988 resulted in a sharp upsurge of the rate of inflation that year. To the extent that the volume of consumer goods imports has been allowed to vary, inflationary pressures in the domestic market have been smoothed. Significant increases in consumer goods imports in 1985 and 1995 may have softened inflationary pressures then.

The 1992–1996 Inflation Cycle

Review and Evaluation

Having considered the structure of inflation in the reform period, let us review the inflation cycle from 1992 to 1996 (See Tables 1 and 2). Because the rate of inflation began to accelerate continuously from early 1992 and then decelerated from late 1994, the inflation and disinflation periods are, respectively, 1992–1994 and 1995–1996 in this cycle. Using the year-on-year growth rate of the RPI in December, which represents the incremental inflationary pressures of each year more accurately than the annual RPI growth rate, one can confirm that the above five-percent rate of inflation lasted for four years from 1992. I therefore name the four-year period the "1992–1995 inflationary spell."

The Chinese economy was in the early stage of a boom when Deng Xiaoping proposed the acceleration of economic growth in early 1992.[18] An expansionary policy was adopted, and a powerful investment boom followed immediately; total fixed investment grew by 23.7% in 1992 and by 25.3% in 1993. This brought the fixed investment share of GDP to a very high level by 1993 (36.0%), and the GDP growth rate reached 14.1% in 1992 and 13.5% in 1993, compared to 9.2% in 1991. The investment-led economic boom resulted in accelerating inflation and a deteriorating trade balance. The prices of construction materials began to rise in the summer of 1992, and the consumer goods prices, led by food prices, followed by the year's end.[19] Increases in grain prices were particularly pronounced, because the abolition of grain rationing in major cities coincided with this period.[20] Grain retail prices rose by 27.7% in 1993, and the growth of retail price index accelerated to 13.2% that year from 5.4% in 1992.[21] The increase of savings deposits slowed, and currency in circulation expanded abruptly as households hoarded cash or switched to other types of investment in the spring of 1993.[22] The trade balance moved from a surplus in 1992 ($4.4 billion) to a deficit in 1993 (-$12.2 billion), reflecting mainly the surge in imports of producers' goods.[23]

Reacting to these signals of macroeconomic imbalance, the government initiated a contractionary policy programme, which included restraint on bank lending, state sector spending, and interest rate hikes, in the spring of 1993. The main proponent and arbiter of the programme was Zhu Rongji, one of the deputy prime ministers. New restrictions on the growth of state bank loans were imposed in late spring and tightened successively

Table 2 Price Indexes: 1991–1996

Year	RPI				Resident CPI		Fixed investment price index	Average nominal wage: staff & workers	Currency in circulation	Trade balance
	RPI	RPI (Dec.)	Food	Grain	CPI	Services				
	Growth rate, %								Increment, billion RMB	billion US$
1991	2.9	4.0	3.3	8.6	3.4	8.7	—	9.3	53.3	8.1
1992	5.4	6.7	7.7	24.3	6.4	13.4	15.3	15.9	115.8	4.4
1993	13.2	17.6	14.3	27.7	14.7	27.9	26.6	24.3	152.9	−12.2
1994	21.7	23.3	35.2	48.7	24.1	25.7	10.4	34.6	142.4	5.4
1995	14.8	8.3	24.7	34.4	17.1	20.2	5.9	21.2	59.7	16.7
1996	6.1[a]	4.2[b]	7.6[a]	6.5[a]	8.3[a]	16.0[a]	5.7[c]	—	91.7[c]	12.2[c]

Note: RPI (Dec.) is the year-on-year growth rate in December.

Sources: [a] *RMRB*, 16 January 1997.

[b] *RMRB*, 21 January 1997.

[c] *RMRB*, 23 January 1997. RPI (Dec.): World Bank, *The Chinese Economy* (Washington, DC: World Bank), 1996, p. 104; *RMRB*, 21 January 1997. Food, grain, CPI, and services: *ZGTJNJ 1996*, pp. 256–58, 1995 edition, pp. 234–36, and 1994 edition, pp. 232 and 240. Fixed investment price index: *ZGTJNJ 1996*, p. 272 and 1994 edition, p. 243. Average nominal wage of staff and workers: *ZGTJNJ 1996*, p. 117. Currency in circulation: *ZGTJNJ 1996*, p. 614 and 1994 edition, p. 544. Trade balance: *ZGTJNJ 1996*, p. 580.

to lessen the growth of fixed investment and wage payments.[24] The central bank raised the deposit and lending rates in May and July of 1993.[25] The *Renminbi* exchange rate was devalued from RMB 5.8 to 8.7 (official rate per US$) in January 1994.[26]

The trade balance moved to a surplus ($5.4 billion) as exports expanded following the sizable currency devaluation.[27] Although price hikes in producers' goods decelerated markedly in the second half of 1993, the impact of contractionary policy on fixed investment, wage payments, and retail prices was slow to appear. The rapid growth of net exports and direct foreign investment in 1994 seems to have blunted the effect of the restrictive monetary policy as foreign exchange receipts were converted into domestic money.[28] The growth rate of total fixed investment fell only marginally (to 23.9%), and high GDP growth continued (12.6%) in 1994. The average wage of staff and workers increased by 34.6% that year after a 24.3% rise in 1993. Grain retail prices rose sharply in 1994 (48.7%), because the rises in purchasing prices implemented that year were passed along to retail prices and because the summer and autumn harvests decreased from previous-year levels. The year-on-year monthly rate of inflation (RPI) peaked in October 1994 (25.2%) before starting its descent.[29] The annual rate of inflation (RPI) peaked in 1994 (21.7%), overshooting by far the optimistic official target for that year (10%).[30]

The restrictive monetary policy, after progressive tightening, began to overpower the strong investment demand and drive for high wages by the end of 1994. Most enterprises faced serious fund shortages by then. The growth rate of total fixed investment dropped to 10.9% in 1995. As aggregate demand weakened, inflationary pressures subsided markedly. The growth of currency in circulation more than halved that year (from RMB 142.4 billion in 1994 to 59.7 billion in 1995). Also, good harvests and increases in grain imports moderated food price hikes.[31] The GDP growth rate fell to 10.5% in 1995, and the 15% annual rate of inflation target (RPI) was fulfilled (actual record, 14.8%). The drop in the rate of inflation was more pronounced in the year-on-year growth rate of the RPI in December (1994, 23.2%; 1995, 8.3%).

Having passed the critical phase, the central bank eased its monetary policy orientation to a moderately tight one to avoid a recession. State commercial banks were allowed to adjust their lending policy accordingly by spring, and interest rates were lowered in May and August 1996.[32] Thanks to a well-timed monetary easing, continued inflow of direct foreign investment, and the resilience in non-state business sectors, fixed investment maintained relatively high growth through 1996 (total fixed investment, 12.5%), unlike the past disinflation periods. The GDP growth rate slowed moderately to 9.7% that year.

Although grain retail prices rose after the hikes in state purchasing prices in the summer, good summer and autumn harvests, reflecting clement weather abated demand pressures, and the rise in food prices decelerated further in 1996.[33] Having gone through a series of price hikes, domestic grain prices had risen roughly to world-price levels in 1996.[34] For industrial consumer goods, whose output can expand relatively easily, few goods were left with strong demand pressures in 1996.[35] Consumer items that experienced double-digit price hikes in 1996 were limited to services, housing, and some non-staple food, such as eggs and vegetables.[36] Because the retail price index omits the service prices and housing costs, the growth rate of the resident consumer price index (CPI, 8.3%) stayed significantly higher than that of the RPI (6.1%) for the year.[37] The year-on-year rate of inflation (RPI) in December 1996 dropped to 4.2%, a level comparable to that in the period immediately before inflation acceleration began in early 1992 (December 1991, 4.0%). Having acknowledged the macroeconomic situation to be the best in the preceding few years, Dai Xianglong, the central bank governor, stated in December 1996 that the moderately tight monetary policy would continue for the time being in consideration of the nature of China's inflation.[38]

The chronological review of the 1992–1996 inflation-disinflation cycle seems to indicate that the inflation dynamics of the reform period, introduced in the previous section, was in force. During the reform period, as can be seen from Table 1, the association between investment expansion and high inflation was most conspicuous in the 1992–1995 inflationary spell. This inflationary spell followed a powerful investment-led economic boom from early 1992. How much then was the 1992–1995 spell investment-led?

In order to assess the numerical relationship between fixed investment and the prices behind the inflation dynamics, the author has constructed a nine-equation block-recursive macroeconomic model, estimated three structural equations with the data in the reform period, and run dynamic simulations.[39] The model replicates the price movement driven by the demand and cost inflation. The estimated wage and price equations, reported above, form part of the model and were used for simulation.[40] The simulations were designed to demonstrate how the prices of consumption goods would respond when fixed investment grew abruptly in a stable environment.[41] The numerical relationship between the growth rate of fixed investment and the rate of inflation computed from simulation results is 0.874. This implies that a one percentage point increase in fixed investment growth in a given year brings about approximately a 0.9% increase in the rate of inflation of that year.[42]

The mean annual rate of inflation (RPI) and the mean annual growth rate of total fixed investment during the 1992–1995 period were, respectively, 13.6 and 20.8% (Table 1). The mean growth rates of these two variables during the 1982–1996 period were, respectively, 8.5 and 14.8%. Taking the differences between these two periods, the upward deviations in the 1992–1995 period from the trend growth rates in the reform period were 5.1% for the rate of inflation and 6.0% for fixed investment growth. The theoretical upward deviation of the rate of inflation originating from investment surge would be 5.2% if the coefficient above for the growth rate of fixed investment (0.874) were used. This value is very close to the actual value (5.1%). The 1992–1995 data thus appear to be consistent with the numerical relationship between fixed investment growth and the rate of inflation computed from simulation results. This suggests that the surge in fixed investment that triggered demand and cost inflation indeed explains almost fully the 1992–1995 inflationary spell. Needless to say, there were various exogenous factors which significantly affected the prices in the 1992–1995 period. It appears, nonetheless, that these factors largely cancel out each other if one considers the entire four-year span.

Outlook

Skilful demand management engineered by Zhu Rongji had, by the end of 1996, conquered the sharp inflation which followed Deng's 1992 growth acceleration policy. Despite the unique combination of circumstances that modified its magnitude and duration, the 1992–1995 inflation fell within the general patterns of the reform-period inflationary spells. A large part of China's inflationary pressures in the reform period stems from two behavioural peculiarities of the public sector in systemic transition: fast growth of fixed investment and wage payments. Under the current institutional environment, fixed investment and nominal wages are bound to grow by themselves leading to demand and cost inflation. It is the weak spending constraint of the public sector, the appendage of the old planned system, that brings about high inflation. Nevertheless, the nature of inflation may alter dramatically over time as economic reforms proceed.

Institutional and structural changes brought about by reforms will either modify the behavioural characteristics of China's public sector or reduce the sector to an insignificant part in the economy by the time the systemic transition is completed.

Although the 1992–1996 cycle has just ended, the past patterns suggest that a period of price stability will be broken before long by another inflationary spell. The government, responding to the favourable macroeconomic conditions, will almost certainly ease monetary policy further by expanding the loan quotas of state commercial banks and by offering new rounds of interest rate reductions in the months to come. This would, sooner or later, usher in a renewed investment-led boom and inflation acceleration though its scale may not be as grand as the 1992–1994 one. The 1992–1996 inflation cycle, therefore, may not be the last during the reform period.

Unlike sketching a picture for a short time frame, identifying the factors defining the long-run outlook is a more complex task. Although each new measure may have a limited effect, the overall economic reform package should deliver a sizeable cumulative impact over a significantly long period. To what extent, then, will the ongoing reforms prompt economic agents in the public sector to modify their behaviour and, by so doing, reduce inflationary pressures in the economy? Despite little tangible impact registered hitherto, the reform measures directed at state enterprises and labour markets in the past few years should serve to harden gradually the budget constraints of state enterprises.[43]

Since the Communist Party's 3rd plenum in November 1993, the government has amplified its efforts at restraining the growth of subsidies, and state commercial banks have begun to apply stricter standards in granting loans to state enterprises. In major industrial centres, as the government has actively encouraged the restructuring of enterprises with poor performance, numbers of workers have been laid off and bankruptcy cases have increased from the extremely low figures of the past years.[44] To mitigate the negative consequences of labour dislocations and to increase labour mobility, governments, central and local, and enterprises have funded social security, pension, and unemployment insurance programmes.[45] During the period when these institutional reforms have been implemented, township and village enterprises and private businesses have continued their rapid expansion and exposed a growing segment of state enterprises to keen competition in product and factor markets. These developments, by imposing market discipline and introducing incentives, should ultimately restrain state enterprises' fixed investment and check their wage hikes.

Complementing these positive developments are the reforms in banking and foreign trade. On the one hand, the government in 1994 began to fully finance budgetary deficits with bond issues by terminating new borrowing from the central bank in order to increase the central bank's authority in monetary policy.[46] The new Central Bank Act passed in March 1995 also confirmed the bank's key role in maintaining stable prices.[47] The government, on the other, has been reorganizing the banking sector; one of the measures employed has been sanctioning the entry of cooperative and private banks to promote competition. Because state commercial banks are the main creditors of state enterprises to be restructured, it appears inevitable for the government to recapitalize these banks to make up for loan losses in the future.[48] Such recapitalization will almost certainly mark the end of the state commercial banks' role as the source of easy credit for state enterprises.

In the field of foreign trade, a series of liberalization measures in recent years have lowered import barriers significantly and domestic prices have moved closer to world prices. The number of state enterprises authorized to conduct foreign trade directly has grown as foreign trade administration was decentralized. The government reduced tariffs by large margins in April and abolished restrictions on currency convertibility for current-account transactions in December 1996.[49] Intermittent exchange-rate devaluations in the past appear to have ended with the sizeable one-time devaluation of January 1994.[50] As the successive marketization of the economy curbs the public sector's spending and augments the effectiveness of stabilization policy tools, the magnitude of cyclical swings in the rate of inflation may decrease in the future. The diminishing impact of institutional factors also implies that the economy's fundamentals will dictate largely the nature and patterns of China's inflation in a longer time horizon.

It appears that China's economic fundamentals are not highly inflationary. With plenty of low-skill labour mainly in rural areas, the Chinese economy can be regarded as a labour-surplus economy.[51] A significant segment of the national economy has already been integrated into the world markets through trade and capital flows. The economy not only has easy access to advanced technology abroad, it also has displayed high learning capability. The domestic savings rate has been high, and the economy has therefore been experiencing rapid capital accumulation in human as well as physical capital stock.[52] Despite the erosion of the revenue base, budgetary deficits have been kept at modest sizes.[53] The main source of money supply growth has been expansion of commercial loans by the state banking system.

In view of China's resource endowment, the strong nominal wage drift observed in urban areas is an anomaly supported by the availability of easy credit. The nominal wage growth will not be able to deviate greatly from labour productivity growth in the industrial sector if state banks' lending policy is restrictive and the labour markets function well. The high savings rate and well-demonstrated comparative advantage in labour-intensive manufactures should enable the Chinese economy to maintain the *Renminbi* exchange rate (against US$) around the current level for an extended period if periodic investment surges are checked. Such a stable exchange rate policy, in which the exchange rate anchors the domestic prices of tradables to world prices, has been adopted by a number of high-performing Asian economies and has proven effective in controlling inflation. Considering vigorous liberalization efforts in trade and currency convertibility since the 1994 exchange rate devaluation, it appears that the Chinese government has indeed adopted the stable exchange rate policy.[54]

With a stable exchange rate, the trend rate of inflation measured by the RPI or the resident consumer price index will settle in the long run at a level a few percentage points higher than the rate of inflation in the US. Note that the larger positive difference in the long-run labour productivity growth rate between the tradable good and non-tradable good sectors in China relative to that in the US would raise the long-run rate of inflation in China above the US level, according to the standard two-goods model.[55] Using the CPI growth rate in the past decade as the long-run rate of inflation in the US (1986–1995, on average, 3.5%), one has to conclude that China's long-run rate of inflation will stay above the five-percent level in the decades to come.[56] Nevertheless, the double-digit trend rate of inflation (RPI growth rate, 1986–1996, 10.3%) is unlikely to continue if one's time horizon is long enough. China may therefore win the battle against inflation in the next decade.

Concluding Summary

By the end of 1996, without driving the economy into a recession, the three-year long austerity programme which began in 1993 had overcome the inflationary spell. While the GDP growth decelerated moderately to 9.7% in 1996, the year-on-year rate of inflation dropped from the peak of 25.2% in October 1994 to 4.2% in December 1996. In order to consider the 1992–1996 inflation cycle in a broader perspective, I have identified three main elements behind China's inflation in the reform period since 1979: strong aggregate demand led by fixed investment, a tight supply of agricultural products which constrains the consumption goods market, and the growth of wage costs. With these forces, the inflation dynamics in the reform period began with an investment surge leading to a boom. As household incomes grew, inflationary pressures rose in the consumption goods market, given slow supply responses. This demand inflation was followed by cost inflation through nominal wage hikes. Wage settlements in the urban sectors had been linked generally with labour productivity growth and cost-of-living increases. The wage growth accelerated, reflecting cyclically high boom-time labour productivity and the cost-of-living adjustment.

A chronological review of the 1992–1996 cycle indicates that the last inflationary spell falls within this general pattern. Dynamic simulation of a macroeconomic model, which replicates the inflation dynamics, yields a numerical relationship in the reform period; each additional percentage point of fixed investment growth leads to about a 0.9% increase in the rate of inflation that year. This rule of thumb is also confirmed in the 1992–1995 period, suggesting that the last inflationary spell is almost fully attributable to the investment-led economic boom from early 1992 that triggered demand and cost inflation.

A large part of China's inflationary pressures in the reform period originates in the high growth of fixed investment and wage payments in state enterprises. High spending has been associated with institutional characteristics: the weak financial accountability of state enterprises and the availability of easy credit from state banks. As ongoing reforms, particularly those directed at state enterprises, banking, and labour markets, gather steam, the behaviour of state sector agents should change and, at the end, economic fundamentals rather than institutional factors will define the nature and patterns of inflation. In view of the abundance of labour, the high national savings rate, and the high degree of integration of the domestic economy with the world markets, underlying inflationary pressures may be modest when the systemic transition is largely completed. The 1992–1995 inflationary spell may not be the last one during the transition period, but it appears unlikely that the high rate of inflation of the past decade will continue through the coming decade.

Notes

1. A *Renmin ribao* (People's Daily, *RMRB*) commentator's article, "Liaobuqi de ruanzhuolu" (Soft-landing, An Extraordinary Achievement), *RMRB*, 6 December 1996.
2. The mean annual growth rates of the retail price index in the 1979–1985 and 1986–1996 periods were, respectively, 6.3 and 10.3%. *Zhongguo tongji nianjian 1996* (Statistical Yearbook of China 1996, *ZGTJNJ*), p. 255. The mean growth rate between 1955 and 1978 was 0.6%, *ZGTJNJ 1993*, p. 238. The 1955–1978 rate may be higher marginally if the increase in repressed inflation is taken into account. According to an estimate by the author, the repressed inflation-adjusted rate of inflation based on the consumption goods price index, the largest sub-category of the retail price index, for the 1955–1978 period was 1.1%, only 0.1% higher than the unadjusted rate. Because the rise of repressed inflation (shortages) was modest over the period, the low annual growth rate of the retail price index implied that the long-run rate of inflation was indeed low in the pre-reform period. Hiroyuki Imai, "Inflationary Pressure in China's Consumption Goods Market: Estimation and Analysis," *The Developing Economies*, Vol. 32, No. 2 (June 1994), p. 148.
3. One may conclude that chronic repressed inflation which began in the latter half of the 1950s ended in the late 1980s. According to an official account, at the macroeconomic level, aggregate supply and demand were basically in equilibrium in 1990. Also, the retail market that year was reportedly characterized by an ample supply of merchandise, a conspicuous fall in price rise rates, and an increase in merchandise stock held by the state commercial sector. *Zhongguo jingji nianjian* (Almanac of the Chinese Economy)(Beijing: Jingji guanli chubanshe, 1991), pp. II-1, 44, and 45.
4. Food made up 54.9% of consumption goods sales in 1993, *ZGTJNJ 1994*, p. 498. Also, a substantial proportion of non-food consumption goods use materials of agricultural origin, and therefore their supply depends indirectly on harvest outcomes.
5. Tian Jiyun acknowledged "the problems of inordinate price increases" in 1985, and reported that the Party and the government had begun strengthening "overall control over the scope of capital investment and consumer funds" to eliminate "destabilizing factors from the national economy." Tian Jiyun, "On Present Economic Situations and the Restructuring of the Economy," *Beijing Review*. Vol. 29, Nos. 6–7 (10 February 1986), pp. IX–X.

   Commenting on the rising rate of inflation in 1988, Liu Guoguang stated: "From 1984 to 1987, the money supply grew at a far greater rate than actual economic growth, leading to devaluation and price hikes" and "at the same time, there has been a large expansion in demand for investment and consumption, stemming from the impulse to pursue high-speed growth." Liu

Guoguang, "China Faces the Problem of Inflation," *Beijing Review*, Vol. 31, No. 41 (10 October 1988), p. 14.

Li Peng attributes the high rate of inflation in 1994 to "objective reasons and to mistakes of governments at all levels." Along with (i) poorly planned and managed rises in official prices and price liberalization of grain, cotton, crude oil and others and (ii) the short supply of agricultural products partially associated with crop damage on account of natural calamities, Li points out demand-side factors: "There had been a rapid growth of investment in fixed assets and consumption funds, and too much currency had been put into circulation for several years running. The government took no emergency measures to stop these practices ..., in order to prevent a sharp decrease in economic growth, but thereby the difficulty in curbing price rises increased." Li Peng, "Report on the Work of the Government," *Beijing Review*, Vol. 38, No. 13 (27 March 1995), p. III.

6. Barry Naughton, *Growing Out of the Plan* (Cambridge: Cambridge University Press, 1995), pp. 322–33.
7. The details of wage reform measures in this paragraph are from Hu Teh-Wei, and Li Elizabeth Hon-Ming, "The Labor Market," in *China's Economic Reform*, edited by Walter Galenson (South San Francisco: The 1990 Institute, 1993), pp. 147–76.
8. For example, enterprises whose profits fall short of targets or which run a temporary deficit can still pay out substantial bonuses if managers can convince the supervisory authorities that the losses are due to objective factors. Objective factors can be anything beyond the direct control of the enterprise manager. See Andrew Walder, "Wage Reform and the Web of Factory Interests," *The China Quarterly*, No. 109 (March 1987), p. 35.
9. Janos Kornai, *The Socialist System* (Oxford: Clarendon Press, 1992), p. 533.
10. Ibid., p. 532.
11. Andrew Walder "Factory and Manager in an Era of Reform," *The China Quarterly*, No. 118 (June 1989), p. 244.
12. Woo Wing Thye, Hai Wen, Jin Yibiao, and Fan Gang, "How Successful Has Chinese Enterprise Reform Been? Pitfalls in Opposite Biases and Focus," *Journal of Comparative Economics*, Vol. 18, No. 3 (June 1994), p. 433.
13. Li Jingwen, Dale Jorgenson, Zheng Youjing and Masahiro Kuroda *Shengchanlu yu ZhongMeiRi jingji zengzhang yanjiu* (Productivity and Economic Growth in China, USA and Japan)(Beijing: Zhongguo shehui kexue chubanshe, 1993), p. 64.
14. According to Gu, excess workers in the urban state sector numbered about 30 million, out of a total of 109 million, in a recent period. He mentioned that in some state enterprises as many as half of the workers were redundant. Gu Shengzu. "Guoyou qiye gaige yu fuyu laogongli anzhi" (State Enterprise Reform and the Placement of Surplus Work Force), *RMRB*, 23 March 1995.

Another report also cites 30 million as the approximate number of surplus workers in the state and urban collective enterprises as of 1996. Zhang Fan and Wu Pibin, "Ruhe kandai dangqian de shiye wenti" (How Should We Look at the Current Unemployment Problem?), *RMRB*, 4 January 1997.

15. Assuming that consumption is supply-constrained, the price equation is represented by the household consumption goods demand function. The estimated equation is:

$$\Delta Q = 0.712\Delta[G/P]$$
$$(10.661)$$
$$R^2 = 0.992 \quad DW = 1.653.$$

Q, G, P, and Δ, are, respectively, consumption goods output in 1978 prices, nominal household incomes, the consumption goods price index, and the increment. Upon estimating the equation, the above equation was rearranged to place P on the left side as the dependent variable. P and W are the endogenous variables of the two simultaneous equations; the other equation is the wage function presented in the text.

16. The consumption goods price index, the largest sub-category of the retail price index, comprises the retail prices of consumption goods after excluding agricultural producers' goods from the retail price index. The growth rate of the consumption goods price index is very similar to that of the retail price index.

17. State sector workers are paid cost-of-living allowances and subsidies in order to offset partially the negative impact of price rises on real incomes. According to a household survey in July 1988 cited by Hu and Li (Note 7, p. 166), these allowances and subsidies made up 18% of the total household wages of staff and workers. Also, enterprises wishing to protect workers' interests may award high wages in reaction to a rise in the rate of inflation, in addition to increasing cost-of-living allowances.

    Note that the growth rate of nominal labour compensation is likely to move with that of labour productivity in non-state sectors as well as the state sector. For example, the compensation schemes of many collective enterprises follow closely those in state enterprises. The nominal farm incomes of a peasant generally move along with harvest fluctuations.

18. Deng Xiaoping, "Gist of Speeches Made in Wuchang, Shenzhen, Zhuhai, and Shanghai (from 18 January to 21 February 1992)," *Beijing Review*, Vol. 37, Nos. 6–7 (7 February 1994), pp. 9–20.

19. The market prices of steel, cement, lumber, and non-ferrous metals began to rise rapidly in June 1992. *Nihon Keizai Shimbun* (Japan Economic Journal), 31 July 1992.

20. Twenty per cent of counties and cities had abolished grain rationing by early December 1992, and this ratio had reached 90% by early July 1993. *RMRB*,

10 December 1992 and 8 July 1993. Shanghai and Tianjin phased out grain coupons in April 1993 (*RMRB*, 3 April 1993). Preceding the abolition of rationing, grain retail prices were raised to narrow the negative gaps between the state purchasing prices and retail prices. Therefore, rapid increases in grain retail prices began in 1992.

21. *ZGTJNJ 1994*, p. 232.
22. Barry Naughton, "China's Macroeconomy in Transition," *The China Quarterly*, No. 144 (December 1995), p. 1098.
23. *ZGTJNJ 1996*, p. 580.
24. Strong restrictions on bank lending began around May 1993, *Nihon Keizai Shimbun*, 20 June, 1993 and *Financial Times*, 24 May 1993.
25. *RMRB*, 15 May and 11 July 1993. The interest rate hikes in May had been the first since February 1989.
26. "Then there was yuan," *The Economist*, 8 January 1994.
27. *ZGTJNJ 1996*, p. 580.
28. As foreign exchange received was converted into domestic currency, the official foreign exchange reserves more than doubled in 1994 (1993, US$ 22.4 billion; 1994, US$ 52.9 billion), World Bank, *The Chinese Economy* (Washington, DC: World Bank, 1996), p. 79.
29. *China Daily*, 5 December 1994.
30. Chen Jinhua, "Report on the Implementation of the 1993 Plan for National Economic and Social Development and the Draft of 1994 Plan for National Economic and Social Development," *Beijing Review*, Vol. 37, No. 15 (11 April, 1994), p. 24.
31. Grain imports grew from 9.2 million tons in 1994 to 20.8 million tonnes in 1994 *ZGTJNJ 1996*, p. 592.
32. *RMRB*, 1 May and 23 August 1997; *Asian Wall Street Journal*, 9 May 1996; *South China Morning Post*, 26 June 1996.
33. The State Council decided to raise the grain purchasing and retail prices, respectively, by 30 and 40% starting in summer 1996, *RMRB*, 2 August 1996. The Beijing municipal government, accordingly, raised the prices of flour, rice, and related processed food at state-owned shops by between 10.7 and 80% on July 1, *South China Morning Post*, 2 July 1996.
34. According to Zhu Rongji's remark, the state purchasing prices of grain in 1996 were higher than the c.i.f. prices of imported grain, *RMRB*, 10 January 1997.
35. Reportedly, supply and demand are either balanced or supply exceeds demand in 95% of industrial consumer goods items as of late 1996, *RMRB*, 6 December 1996.
36. The prices of housing, eggs, and vegetables rose, respectively, 11.4, 16.5, and 19.7%. *RMRB*, 16 January 1997.
37. The gap between the growth rates of the RPI and CPI widened from 1.0% in

1992 to 2.2% in 1996 because of the fast rises in services and housing expenses in this period. A significant part of the price hikes in these categories reflected government policies to make sharp upward adjustments in apartment rents and publicly-provided services which had been left at very low levels for decades.

38. In Dai's view, inflation originates from a long-standing economic problem yet to be resolved: the low efficiency, excess spending, and soft budget constraints of economic sectors that oblige the central bank to issue more new money. "Interview with Dai Xianglong," *RMRB*, 12 December 1996.
39. The details of the procedure and results are reported in Hiroyuki Imai, "Output-Inflation Tradeoff in China," scheduled for *The Developing Economies*, Vol. 35, No. 2 (June 1997).
40. The third behavioural equation estimated is the labour productivity equation, in which the growth rate of labour productivity depends positively on the growth rate of fixed investment. An assumption here is that the presence of surplus workers enables the investment goods industry to expand output (fixed investment) flexibly with a less than proportional growth in workers.
41. According to the model's specification, a rise in fixed investment leads to higher labour productivity and employment in the investment goods industry. High productivity further brings about wage hikes through the wage function. Because nominal household income grows as a result of increases in employment and nominal wages, consumption goods prices must rise to the market-clearing levels. Consumption goods prices, nominal wages, and nominal household income move together in this process on account of simultaneity. The initial impact on prices is magnified as the wages adjust successively to new price levels. Simulations solve recursively the values of eight endogenous variables (which include the consumption goods price, the nominal wage rate, labour productivity, nominal household income, consumption goods output) as the exogenously set fixed investment is inserted each year.
42. According to the simulation results, a one-percentage point increase in fixed investment growth in a given year also brings about approximately a 0.9% increase in the nominal wage growth rate of that year. The numerical coefficient here is 0.912.
43. The low profitability of state enterprises and increases in layoffs there do not appear to have restrained much the growth of fixed investment and the wage settlements so far. During the January–September period in 1996, out of 68,800 state industrial enterprises, 31,400 ran deficits (*RMRB*, 12 December 1996). Yet, a commentator of *Renmin ribao* pointed out that state enterprises' fixed investment had been characterized by the pursuit of completeness in designing plants, poor planning, and duplication of projects among competing firms. Large investment spending has simply resulted in excess capacities in many products. "Ba gaohao guoyou qiye fangzai gengjia tuchu de diwei"

(The Vital Task of Managing State Enterprises Well), *RMRB*, 7 December 1996.

A World Bank study cites a government survey on wages at state enterprises in 1995. During the January–September period of 1995, the year-on-year growth rates of nominal wages at profit-making and loss-making state enterprises were almost the same, 22.6 and 21.3%, respectively. The study comments, "Such large wage increases in loss-making enterprises would have been impossible without some support from the government or financial sector," World Bank (Note 28), pp. 17–18.

44. From around 1994, state enterprises began to furlough a portion of their employees for an extended period with reduced wages. The number of these workers in virtual layoff was reported at about 3 million in mid-1995 (*RMRB*, 15 June 1995). Those workers were not classified as unemployed in China's labour statistics. The urban-registered unemployment was 5.20 million and the urban unemployment rate was 2.9% at the end of 1995. *ZGTJNJ 1996*, p. 114.

    In the first half of 1996, 215 state enterprises were merged with other enterprises following bankruptcies. The number of bankruptcies from 1987 to 1994 were 940 enterprises, *Nihon Keizai Shimbun*, 5 December 1995 and 19 August 1996. The government recently announced it would spend RMB 30 billion in 1997 to facilitate restructuring of state enterprises in deficit through mergers and bankruptcies in 110 pilot cities, *RMRB*, 31 January 1997.
45. Zong Yan, "Retrospective on 1996 Economic Reform," *Beijing Review*, Vol. 40, No. 1 (6 January 1997), pp. 22–23.
46. Li Ning, "From State Treasury to Real Bank," *Beijing Review*, Vol. 37, No. 18 (2 May 1994), p. 12.
47. *RMRB*, 22 March 1995.
48. According to Dai Xianglong, a survey conducted in 1995 revealed that 20% of bank loans were either overdue or bad, and 8% of bank loans were of the poorest quality: 6% were overdue by three years or more and 2% were held by enterprises that were practically bankrupt.
49. On 1 April 1996, the Chinese government lowered tariffs on 4,994 commodities and abolished non-tariff barriers on 176 commodities. The average tariff rate dropped from 36 to 23%, *RMRB*, 29 December 1995 and *Nihon Keizai Shimbun*, 2 April 1996. The government has announced that it would accept the obligations under Article Eight of the IMF Agreement, *RMRB*, 29 November and 3 December 1996.
50. The *Renminbi* exchange rate against the US$ depreciated at an average annual rate of 8.3% from 1979 to the end of 1993, International Monetary Fund, *International Financial Statistics, 1996 Yearbook* (Washington, DC: International Monetary Fund, 1996), pp. 278–79.
51. *Nihon Keizai Shimbun* reported recently (21 October 1996) an estimate made

by the Ministry of Labour published at a government conference on the agricultural labour force. The labour surplus in rural areas was approximately 120 million at the end of 1995, 20 million higher than five years before. This number may rise to 140 million by year 2000. The number of employed in rural areas was 450.42 million at the end of 1995, *ZGTJNJ 1996*, p. 87. For economic growth patterns of a labour-surplus economy, see Arthur Lewis, "Economic Development with Unlimited Supplies of Labour," *Manchester School*, Vol. 22 (May 1954), pp. 139–91.

52. The gross domestic saving rate has been quite high (1994, 44%) and increasing over the reform period (1980, 35%), World Bank, *From Plan to Market, World Development Report 1996* (New York: Oxford University Press, 1996), p. 212.
53. While the government revenue to GDP ratio halved from 25.0% in 1994 to 12.4% in 1994, the budgetary deficits to GDP ratio stayed in a narrow range, between –0.5 (1985) and –2.3% (1992). World Bank (Note 52), p. 94.
54. The *Renminbi* exchange rate against the US$ has been largely stable for three years since the devaluation in January 1994. On 7 February 1997, the rate stood at RMB 8.294, 4.9% higher than the level immediately after the devaluation, *South China Morning Post*, 10 February 1997.
55. The logic behind this idea is that fast productivity growth in the tradable good sector brings about high nominal wage growth and, consequently, non-tradable good prices rise rapidly reflecting increasing labour costs in China. Under the pegged exchange rate regime, the prices of tradables in the two economies move together. With the price index comprising both tradable and non-tradable prices, China's price index would rise faster than that of the US. See Kenneth Rogoff, "The Purchasing Power Parity Doctrine Puzzle," *Journal of Economic Literature*, Vol. 34, No. 2 (June 1996), pp. 647–68.
56. The US CPI growth rate declined in the 1990s (1991–1995, on average, 3.1%). *International Financial Statistics, 1996 Yearbook* (Note 50), p. 789.

9

Foreign Economic Relations

K. C. Fung and Lawrence J. Lau

Introduction

China's presence in the world economy continues to grow and deepen. The foreign trade sector plays an important and multifaceted role in China's economic development.[1] At the same time, China's expanded role in the world economy is beneficial to all its trading partners. Regions that trade with China benefit from cheaper and more varieties of imported consumer goods, raw materials and intermediate products. China also provides a large and growing export market. While the entry of any major trading nation in the global trading system can create a process of adjustment, the outcome is fundamentally a win-win situation. It is a simple but powerful lesson from economics that freer international trade and investments benefit all parties concerned.

In 1995, China's merchandise exports to the world amounted to US$ 148.77 billion, an increase of 22.9% over the year before. Merchandise imports in 1995 were US$ 132.08 billion, an increase of 14.2% (Table 1). In 1995, there was a modest drop in the growth rate of exports, but the growth rate of imports accelerated. Compared to 1991, both the value of exports and the value of imports have more than doubled. In 1995, its share of world exports rose slightly from 2.9% to 3.0%. China ranked as the eleventh largest global exporter in 1995.

Table 1. China's Foreign Merchandise Trade

Year	Exports	Imports
1991	71.91	63.79
1992	84.94	80.59
1993	91.74	103.96
1994	121.01	115.62
1995	148.77	132.08
1996	151.07	138.84

Notes: Figures are in US$ billion. Exports are measured on a f.o.b. basis, imports are recorded on a c.i.f. basis.

Sources: General Administration of Customs of the People's Republic of China, *China's Customs Statistics*, various years.

* Comments from two anonymous referees and an editor are appreciated. Financial support from the Asia/Pacific Research Center, Stanford University, and University of California Pacific Rim Research Grant, is gratefully acknowledged.

In 1996, China's merchandise exports to the world were US$ 151.07 billion, while merchandise imports were US$ 138.84 billion. These data represent a dramatic slowdown in the growth rates of China's foreign trade. In 1996, exports rose by 1.5% only, while imports grew by 5.1%.

Foreign Trade by Major World Regions

Using China's official statistics, Tables 2 and 3 highlight merchandise exports and imports to and from major world regions: Asia, Africa, Europe, Latin America, North America and Oceania.[2]

From Table 2, we see that China's most important export region in 1996 was Asia, which absorbed more than 61% of exports. North America (which included the United States and Canada) took in more than 18% of exports and Europe took in more than 15%. Together, these three world regions took more than 94% of China's exports. From 1993 to 1996, the shares of the major regions were relatively stable, with no abrupt changes.[3] A somewhat surprising finding is that Africa was a slightly larger export market for China than Oceania, which includes Australia and New Zealand. Preliminary figures for January to November 1996 show that the

Table 2. Merchandise Exports to Major World Regions

Exports to:	1993	1994	1995	1996
Asia	52.62 (57.35%)	73.45 (60.70%)	92.00 (61.84%)	91.25 (60.40%)
North America	18.16 (19.80%)	22.86 (18.89%)	26.24 (17.64%)	28.30 (18.73%)
Europe	16.43 (17.91%)	18.77 (15.51%)	22.98 (15.44%)	23.87 (15.80%)
Latin America	1.78 (1.94%)	2.45 (2.03%)	3.15 (2.12%)	3.12 (2.07%)
Oceania	1.23 (1.34%)	1.72 (1.42%)	1.90 (1.28%)	1.96 (1.30%)
Africa	1.53 (1.66%)	1.75 (1.45%)	2.49 (1.68%)	2.57 (1.70%)

Notes: Figures are in US$ billion. Percentages in parentheses are shares of China's total merchandise exports to the world. Exports are recorded on a f.o.b. basis.

Sources: General Administration of Customs of the People's Republic of China, *China's Custom Statistics Yearbook 1994; China's Customs Statistics Monthly*, December 1995 and December 1996.

shares of China's exports going to different regions of the world remain similar to those in 1995.

Table 3 highlights merchandise imports by China from various world regions. Again, Asia dominated as being by far the largest supplier of imports. Asia accounted for more than 60% of China's imports in 1996, while the next largest supplier was Europe, which had a share of more than 19%. North America was third, with a share of more than 13%. These three regions supplied more than 93% of China's imports. As in the case of exports, these shares were only subjected to minor changes over the years 1993–1996. The relative importance of these various regions remained quite stable.

China's Merchandise Exports and Imports by Major Trading Partners

Tables 4 and 6 document China's merchandise exports to and imports from its major trading partners, using China's official statistics.

According to Table 4, the major export markets for China in 1996 were (in order of importance): Hong Kong (21.78%), Japan (20.44%), the

Table 3. Merchandise Imports from Major World Regions

Imports from:	1993	1994	1995	1996
Asia	62.60	68.77	78.05	83.44
	(60.22%)	(59.48%)	(59.09%)	(60.10%)
North America	12.07	15.74	18.80	18.73
	(11.61%)	(13.61%)	(14.23%)	(13.49%)
Europe	23.97	25.02	27.81	27.66
	(23.06%)	(21.64%)	(21.05%)	(19.92%)
Latin America	1.93	2.25	2.97	3.61
	(1.86%)	(1.94%)	(2.25%)	(2.60%)
Oceania	2.36	2.92	3.02	3.94
	(2.27%)	(2.52%)	(2.29%)	(2.83%)
Africa	1.00	0.89	1.43	1.46
	(0.97%)	(0.77%)	(1.08%)	(1.05%)

Notes: Figures are in US$ billion Percentages in parentheses are shares of China's total merchandise imports from the world. Imports are recorded on a c.i.f. basis.

Sources: General Administration of Customs of the People's Republic of China, *China's Customs Statistics Yearbook 1994*; *China's Customs Statistics Monthly*, December 1995 and December 1996.

United States(17.66%) and the European Union (13.13%).[4] Together these markets took 73.01% of China's exports in 1996. Since 1994, Japan had overtaken the United States as the second largest export market for China. Within ASEAN (Association of Southeast Asian Nations), Singapore was the largest export market. China exported a total of US$ 3.75 billion to Singapore in 1995. Within the EU (European Union), Germany was the

Table 4. Merchandise Exports to Major Trading Partners

Exports to:	1993	1994	1995	1996
Hong Kong	22.05 (24.03%)	32.36 (26.74%)	35.98 (24.19%)	32.91 (21.78%)
Taiwan	1.46 (1.59%)	2.24 (1.85%)	3.10 (2.08%)	2.80 (1.85%)
Japan	15.78 (17.20%)	21.58 (17.83%)	28.46 (19.13%)	30.87 (20.44%)
USA	16.96 (18.49%)	21.46 (17.74%)	24.71 (16.61%)	26.69 (17.66%)
EU	12.24 (13.34%)	15.39 (12.72%)	19.09 (12.83%)	19.83 (13.13%)
Germany	3.97 (4.32%)	4.76 (3.93%)	5.67 (3.81%)	5.84 (3.87%)
France	1.29 (1.41%)	1.42 (1.18%)	1.84 (1.24%)	1.91 (1.26%)
Netherlands, The	1.61 (1.75%)	2.27 (1.87%)	3.23 (2.17%)	3.54 (2.34%)
Italy	1.30 (1.42%)	1.59 (1.31%)	2.07 (1.39%)	1.84 (1.22%)
United Kingdom	1.93 (2.10%)	2.41 (1.99%)	2.79 (1.88%)	3.20 (2.12%)
ASEAN	4.68 (5.10%)	6.38 (5.27%)	9.04 (6.07%)	9.70 (6.42%)
Singapore	2.25 (2.45%)	2.56 (2.11%)	3.50 (2.35%)	3.75 (2.48%)

Notes: Figures are in US$ billion. Figures in parentheses are percentages of China's total merchandise exports to the world. Exports are reported on a f.o.b. basis. ASEAN (Association of Southeast Asian Nations) includes Brunei, Indonesia, Malaysia, Philippines, Singapore and Thailand. EU (European Union) includes Belgium, Denmark, United Kingdom, Germany, France, Ireland, Italy, Luxembourg, The Netherlands, Greece, Portugal, Spain, Austria, Finland and Sweden. For the years 1993 and 1994, Germany refers to the Federal Republic of Germany; EU consists of imports and exports of EEC plus China's trade with Austria, Finland and Sweden.

Sources: General Administration of Customs of the People's Republic of China, *China's Customs Statistics Yearbook 1994*; *China's Customs Statistics Monthly*, December 1995 and December 1996.

largest export market, with China exporting a total of US$ 5.84 billion in 1995. The second largest EU market was the Netherlands, with an export value of US$ 3.54 billion in 1996.

Table 4 gives a comparative impression of China's various export markets based on officially recorded figures. However, a considerable amount of China's exports go through Hong Kong. For example, in 1995, 55.30% of China's officially recorded exports went through Hong Kong to be re-exported elsewhere.[5] Despite China's improved efforts since 1993 to classify exports by final destinations, it is still very likely that a considerable amount of China's indirect exports via Hong Kong were miscounted as exports to Hong Kong. This explains why, according to Chinese official statistics, a small economy like Hong Kong was the largest export market for China.

In Table 5, we attempt to provide more accurate estimates of China's export figures. We do this by assuming that China's re-exports through Hong Kong represent China's indirect exports to its various trading partners. The re-exports are first discounted by a re-export margin of 25%.[6] They are then added to the direct exports, i.e., China's officially recorded exports. For the case of China's exports to Hong Kong, we use figures of estimated Hong Kong's retained imports, as provided by the Hong Kong government.[7] Table 5 presents our estimates of China's exports to various trading partners. However, due to insufficient re-export data, we are not able to estimate China's adjusted exports to the EU and ASEAN, even though we provide estimates of China's adjusted exports to most of the important members of EU and ASEAN. In addition, due to insufficient re-export data for 1996, we only provide adjusted estimates up to 1995.

Our adjusted estimates provide a more accurate picture of the relative importance of China's various export markets. First and foremost, Hong Kong was no longer the largest export market for China. Hong Kong's share of China's exports in 1995 dropped from 24.19% in Table 4 to 2.64% after our adjustments. As an export market for China (rather than re-export market), Hong Kong was smaller than The Netherlands, the United Kingdom and Singapore. The export values and export shares of all other trading partners rose after adjustments. The 1995 share of the United States jumped from 16.61% to 31.45%, making it China's leading export market. As mentioned before, because of data constraint, we are not able to compute the total Chinese exports for the entire EU and for the whole of ASEAN. For the EU countries for which we do have data (Germany,

Table 5. Adjusted Estimates of Merchandise Exports to Major Trading Partners

Exports to:	1993	1994	1995
Hong Kong	4.89 (5.33%)	5.65 (4.67%)	3.93 (2.64%)
Taiwan	2.35 (2.56%)	3.29 (2.72%)	4.37 (2.94%)
Japan	19.47 (21.22%)	26.26 (21.70%)	34.58 (23.24%)
USA	34.37 (37.47%)	41.73 (34.49%)	46.79 (31.45%)
Germany	7.96 (8.68%)	8.83 (7.30%)	10.11 (6.80%)
France	2.54 (2.77%)	2.76 (2.28%)	3.55 (2.38%)
Netherlands, The	2.80 (3.05%)	3.61 (2.98%)	4.86 (3.27%)
Italy	2.28 (2.49%)	2.67 (2.21%)	3.30 (2.22%)
United Kingdom	4.30 (4.68%)	5.05 (4.17%)	5.86 (3.94%)
Singapore	3.14 (3.42%)	3.77 (3.11%)	5.14 (3.46%)

Notes: Figures are in US$ billion. Figures for Hong Kong are estimated retained imports from China; figures for all other major trading partners are the sums of China's officially recorded exports and re-exports via Hong Kong adjusted by 25% re-export margins. Exchange rates of various years are taken from *Annual Review of Hong Kong External Trade 1995*. Figures in parentheses are percentages of the total exports.

Sources: *Hong Kong External Trade*, December 1994 and December 1995 (Hong Kong: Census and Statistics Department; *Annual Review of Hong Kong External Trade 1995* (Census and Statistics Department); *Hong Kong Monthly Digest of Statistics* (Census and Statistics Department, February 1996); *China's Customs Statistics Yearbook 1994*; General Administration of Customs of the People's Republic of China, *China's Customs Statistics Monthly*, December 1995.

France, The Netherlands, Italy and United Kingdom), they combined to give a share of 18.61% in 1995.

In Table 6, we use official data to show the relative significance of China's various import providers.

One can argue that Table 6 suffers from the same pitfalls as Table 4, as China may also have failed to distinguish between importing from Hong Kong and importing from other countries via Hong Kong. For our purposes, Table 6 is by and large all right. Most countries including China are much more careful in tracing the origins of their imports. This is particularly the case since 1993. Furthermore, if we check China's import figures from Hong Kong and from the United States (as given in Table 6), we find that they match fairly closely to estimates derived from United States government figures and Hong Kong government figures. For example, in 1995, if we adjust the United States government's figure for exports from the United States to China by the extent of re-exports of US

Table 6. Merchandise Imports from Major Trading Partners

Imports from:	1993	1994	1995	1996
Hong Kong	10.45 (10.05%)	9.44 (8.17%)	8.59 (6.50%)	7.83 (5.64%)
Taiwan	12.93 (12.44%)	14.09 (12.18%)	14.78 (11.19%)	16.18 (11.66%)
Japan	23.29 (22.40%)	26.33 (22.77%)	29.00 (21.96%)	29.18 (21.02%)
USA	10.69 (10.28%)	13.89 (12.02%)	16.12 (12.20%)	16.16 (11.64%)
EU	15.72 (15.12%0	18.58 (16.07%)	21.25 (16.09%)	19.87 (14.31%)
Germany	6.04 (5.81%)	7.14 (6.17%)	8.04 (6.09%)	7.32 (5.28%)
France	1.64 (1.58%0	1.94 (1.68%)	2.65 (2.01%)	2.24 (1.61%)
Netherlands, The	0.71 (0.69%)	0.71 (0.61%)	0.82 (0.62%)	0.92 (0.66%)
Italy	2.74 (2.63%)	3.07 (2.65%)	3.12 (2.36%)	3.25 (2.34%)
United Kingdom	1.66 (1.60%)	1.77 (1.53%)	1.97 (1.49%)	1.88 (1.35%)
ASEAN	6.01 (5.78%)	6.84 (5.92%)	9.40 (7.12%)	10.70 (7.70%)
Singapore	2.65 (2.55%)	2.49 (2.16%)	3.40 (2.57%)	3.60 (2.59%)

Notes: Figures are in US$billion. Figures in parentheses are percentages of China's total imports from the world. Imports are recorded on a c.i.f. basis. ASEAN includes Brunei, Indonesia, Malaysia, Philippines, Singapore and Thailand. For the year 1996, ASEAN also includes Vietnam. EU includes Belgium, Denmark, United Kingdom, Germany, France, Ireland, Italy, Luxembourg, The Netherlands, Greece, Portugal, Spain, Austria, Finland and Sweden. For the years 1993 and 1994, Germany refers to Federal Republic of Germany; imports from EU are calculated by adding imports from EEC to imports from Austria, Finland and Sweden.

Sources: General Administration of Customs of the People's Republic of China, *China's Customs Statistics Yearbook 1994*; *China's Customs Statistics Monthly*, December 1996.

goods via Hong Kong, the total direct and indirect US exports to China will be US$ 16.7 billion. From the above table, China's official data indicate that imports from the United States in 1995 were US$ 16.12 billion. Similarly if we take Hong Kong's domestic exports to China, its 1995 figure was US$ 8.22 billion, as compared with China's figure of US$ 8.59 billion. Thus, Table 6 can be taken to present a reasonably good picture of the relative significance of China's major suppliers of imports.

In 1995, Japan was the number one provider of China's imports, with a share of 21.02%. EU came in second, with a share of 14.31%. Taiwan and the United States were respectively third and fourth, with shares of 11.66% and 11.64%. It is surprising that the amount of exports from the United States were somewhat lower than those from Taiwan. In fact, in 1993 and 1994, Taiwan also exported more than the United States to China. In 1996, ASEAN accounted for 7.70% of China's imports, a share that was higher than that of Hong Kong's (5.64%). Within ASEAN, the largest exporter to China was Singapore, with a value of US$ 3.60 billion in 1996. Within EU, Germany was the largest exporter, with 1996 exports totalling US$ 7.32 billion. This was followed by Italy, with an export value of US$ 3.25 billion. Third within EU was France, which exported US$ 2.24 billion in 1996.

Foreign Direct Investment

Table 7 highlights major sources of utilized foreign direct investments for the years 1993–1995.[8]

According to Table 7, Hong Kong continued to be the largest direct foreign investor in China. In 1995, Hong Kong's share of foreign direct investment in China was 53.47%. While it is very likely that a large amount of such investments actually came from sources other than Hong Kong (including capital originally from China due to round-tripping), it is also reasonable to assume that even if one discounts the magnitude of Hong Kong investments in China, Hong Kong would still likely remain the number one supplier.

The next set of foreign investors all contributed about the same amount of foreign direct investments to China. In 1995, the second largest supplier was Taiwan, with a share of 8.43%. Close behind were Japan and the United States, which had respective shares of 8.28% and 8.22% in 1995. A mild surprise in Table 7 is the finding that, in 1995, ASEAN had

Table 7. Utilized Foreign Direct Investment Flows into China

	1993	1994	1995
Hong Kong	17.27 (62.78%)	19.67 (58.24%)	20.06 (53.47%)
Taiwan	3.14 (11.41%)	3.39 (10.04%)	3.16 (8.43%)
Japan	1.32 (4.81%)	2.08 (6.15%)	3.11 (8.28%)
USA	2.06 (7.50%)	2.49 (7.38%)	3.08 (8.22%)
EU	0.67 (2.44%)	1.54 (4.55%)	2.14 (5.69%)
ASEAN	1.00 (3.65%)	1.87 (5.55%)	2.62 (6.97%)

Notes: Figures are in US$ billion. Figures in brackets are percentages of total foreign direct investment in China.

Sources: *Almanac of China's Foreign Economic Relations and Trade* (Beijing: China Economics Publishing House, Economic Information and Agency), various years.

more direct foreign investment in China than the EU. As expected, among ASEAN countries, Singapore had the highest level, with a total of US$ 1.85 billion in 1995. The magnitude of Singapore's 1995 foreign direct investment in China was higher than that of any EU member country. Within EU, the United Kingdom had the largest foreign direct investment, with a 1995 value of US$ 0.91 billion. Next was Germany, with a value of US$ 0.39 billion.

Foreign direct investments include investments in the form of Sino-foreign equity joint ventures, Sino-foreign cooperative joint ventures, wholly foreign-owned enterprises and joint development. In addition, there are also foreign investments that are related to processing and compensation trade. These foreign investments, recorded as "other foreign investments" in official Chinese statistics, are technically not direct investments. In an investment related to processing, a foreign firm subcontracts a part of the production process to a Chinese entity. In 1995, Hong Kong had the largest amount of these "other foreign investments," with a utilized investment value of US$ 0.12 billion (a share of 43.74% of the total "other foreign investments"). The next largest was Japan, which had US$ 104 million of utilized "other foreign investments" (a share of 36.47%). Taiwan reportedly had only US$ 3.61 million of such investments.

Economic Relations between China and Its Trade and Investment Partners

Economic Relations with Hong Kong and Taiwan[9]

The most significant event that will affect the economic relationship within Greater China (China, Hong Kong and Taiwan) is no doubt the impending reversion of Hong Kong to Chinese sovereignty on 1 July 1997. Relevant laws governing the new Hong Kong Special Administrative Region (HKSAR) can be found in the Basic Law of the Hong Kong Special Administrative Region of the People's Republic of China, adopted by the 7th National People's Congress on 4 April 1990. The Basic law gives a high degree of autonomy to the HKSAR. Under the Law, Hong Kong will maintain the status of a free port and pursue a free trade policy. It will remain a separate customs territory. The HKSAR may act on its own to maintain, develop and conclude agreements with other states, regions and relevant international organizations in fields such as trade, money and finance.[10] Under the Basic Law, one consequence is that even after China joins the World Trade Organization (WTO), Hong Kong can and will still remain a separate member.

There is no question that both Hong Kong and Taiwan are extremely important to the economic development of China. In 1995, Hong Kong and Taiwan were the first and second largest foreign investors in China. Together, Hong Kong and Taiwan contributed US$ 23.22 billion (or 61.9%) of foreign direct investments to China in 1995.[11] These foreign direct investments bring to China new managerial know-how, new forms of firm organization, newer techniques of production and additional sources of capital.

In 1995, foreign direct investments from Hong Kong increased by 1.98% to US$ 20.06 billion. As pointed out earlier, Hong Kong is also the major centre of re-exports of goods coming out of China and going into China. In 1995, 55.30% of exports went through Hong Kong and got re-exported elsewhere, while 37.58% of imports were re-exported to China via Hong Kong.

Taiwan still officially maintains a "no direct trade" policy with China. A substantial portion of trade between China and Taiwan is in the form of re-exports via Hong Kong. In addition to Hong Kong, there is also indirect trade between Taiwan and China via Japan, Singapore, Guam and other third parties. China–Taiwan trade is also carried out in the form of trans-shipment via Hong Kong. Trans-shipment occurs when goods are consigned directly from the exporting country (say Taiwan) to a buyer in the importing country (say China). The goods go through Hong Kong and are often transferred to another vessel for further transport, but unlike re-exports, the goods do not go through Hong Kong customs. Consequently, we do not have trans-shipment data in value terms. Official trans-shipment data are only given by weight. Table 8 highlights re-exports and trans-shipment between China and Taiwan via Hong Kong.

Available data in Table 8 indicate that both re-exports and trans-shipment continue to increase between China and Taiwan. From Table 5 and Table 6, China's total exports and imports have also been increasing.[12] However, in 1995, foreign direct investments from Taiwan slowed (see Table 7) to US$ 3.16 billion, a drop of 6.78%. Military exercises over the Taiwan Straits in March of 1996 could further slow the flows of foreign direct investments from Taiwan for 1996 and 1997. But in the longer run, given the complementary nature of the two economies, further economic integrations led by the private sectors will seem likely.

China–United States Economic Relations

Based on our estimates in Table 5, the United States was likely the largest export market for China in 1995.[13] For the same year, it was also the third largest supplier of China's imports and fourth largest foreign direct investor. Economic relations between the United States and China continued to expand. In 1995, exports to the US increased by 12.13% over the year

Table 8. Re-export and Trans-shipments between Taiwan and China via HongKong

	Re-exports		Trans-shipment	
	Taiwan to China	China to Taiwan	Taiwan to China	China to Taiwan
1993	7.65	1.11	NA	329,548
1994	8.60	1.30	NA	442,000
1995	9.96	1.59	NA	NA

Notes: Figures are in US$ billion for re-exports; trans-shipments are measured in tonnes. Exchange rates used are annual averages given in *Annual Review of Hong Kong External Trade* (Hong Kong: Census and Statistics Department, 1995). The exchange rates are HK$ 1 = US$ 7.736 for 1993, HK$1 = US$ 7.728 for 1994 and HK$ 1 = US$ 7.736 for 1995.

Sources: *Annual Review of Hong Kong External Trade* (Hong Kong: Census and Statistics Department, 1995) and *Hong Kong Shipping Statistics*, various years.

before, while imports from the US rose by 16.05%. Foreign direct investments by the United States in 1995 went up even more, by 23.69% to US$ 3.08 billion.[14]

In 1996, the Clinton Administration again renewed China's MFN (most-favoured-nation) status. This allowed the United States and China to continue to trade under a normal trading framework. The Clinton Administration had previously de-linked issues of human rights from the MFN renewal debate, even though some members of the US Congress continued to argue for denial of a normal trading status based on China's alleged human right violations. In general, it is expected that MFN renewal will likely continue.

While MFN renewal seems to have returned to the right track, there are two other trade issues looming between the two large Pacific economies. The first is the large and growing bilateral trade deficits.[15] It is well recognized by professional economists that bilateral trade imbalances are not correlated with measures of openness, nonetheless, policy-makers in the United States consistently argue that the US deficits with China represent a lack of market access.

Using US official statistics, in June 1996, China surpassed Japan for the first time as the country with the largest trade surplus with the United States. However, there are significant accounting and measurement problems in obtaining a true picture of China's external balance with the United States. The main problem of measuring the China–United States bilateral trade imbalance is again the large amount of US re-exports that go through Hong Kong. By definition, re-exports occur in Hong Kong when goods are first shipped to Hong Kong, change legal possession and, then, get re-exported to China. Since the goods change hands in Hong Kong, it is very difficult, if not impossible, for the US Customs to trace how much of the US exports will end up in China.[16] Furthermore, the extent of re-exports is large. In 1995, official US government data showed that US exports to China were US$ 11.7 billion.[17] Re-exports of US goods from the US to China via Hong Kong amounted to US$ 5.0 billion, or 42.74% of official US exports.[18] The point is that, in bilateral trade with China, even the US trade statistics are inaccurate.

Another important aspect of the China–United States trade imbalance issue is the neglect of the role of service trade. It is well known that the United States is a net exporter of services. In considering external relations between countries, there is no particular reason why one should focus only on the trade balance in goods and ignore the trade balance in services.

Finally, an alternative way to look at trade relations between the United States and China is to consider Hong Kong and China together as one entity. If Hong Kong and China are treated as one, then re-exports will only be internal trade among regions of the same economic entity. Another advantage in looking at a combined China–Hong Kong entity is that it takes into account "deficit-shifting." Due to the massive movement of factories from Hong Kong to China, a large amount of Chinese exports are sent from plants owned by Hong Kong firms. This causes exports from China to increase and exports from Hong Kong to decrease. Thus, parts of the deficits are shifted from Hong Kong to China. Furthermore, the same "deficit-shifting" argument applies to Taiwan. Instead of just looking at the China–United States trade balance, it may be more meaningful to focus on trade balance between Greater China and the United States. In the next table, we present estimates of the impact of these three considerations on the China–United States trade balance.

The first column of Table 9 shows the US government's figures for the China–United States trade balance. The second column shows our estimates of the US–China trade balance after adjusting for re-exports and re-export markups.[19] It can be seen that, after adjustments, China's 1995 trade surplus dropped from US$ 33.8 billion to US$ 24.0 billion. The third column adds in the net service export position of the United States with respect to China. With the addition of the service account, the 1995 bilateral balance dropped further to US$ 23.3 billion. The last column of Table 8 shows the balance between the United States on the one hand and China, Hong Kong and Taiwan (Greater China) on the other. Obviously, with three economic entities counted as one, the deficits become higher. But, the growth of the deficits over the years is slower than the increase of the US–China balance alone. This relative stability provides some evidence for the "deficit-shifting" hypothesis. Overall, we note that the US deficits with China are significantly lower than the official US figures.

Another area of significant trade friction between China and the United States is textile trade. China is the third largest supplier of textiles and apparel to the United States. In September 1996, the United States imposed quotas on 13 categories of textile goods and raised import duties of some other textile goods. The United States alleged that despite the 1994 Sino-US Textile Agreement, Chinese firms continue to circumvent US import quotas by trans-shipping textile goods through third parties. The increase in textile trade restrictions amounted to an estimated US$ 19 million in punitive charges. The 1994 Sino-US Textile Agreement

Table 9. Estimated Trade Balances between China and the United States and Greater China and the United States

	Official estimate of US–China trade balance	Our estimate of US–China trade balance after adjusting for re-exports and re-export markups	Our estimate of US–China balance in goods and services after adjusting for re-exports and re-export markups	Official estimate of total US–Greater China trade balance
1993	–22.8	–15.5	–15.0	–31.4
1994	–29.5	–21.1	–20.4	–37.4
1995	–33.8	–24.0	–23.3	–39.6

Notes: Figures are in US$ billion. For the 1995 estimate of adjusted US–China balance in goods and services, we assume that the net service exports of the United States are the same as those in 1994. A negative sign indicates deficits by the United States. Estimates are taken from Table 7, Table 8 and Table 9 of K. C. Fung and Lawrence J. Lau, "The China–United States Bilateral Trade Balance: How Big Is It Really?" (Occasional Paper, Asia/Pacific Research Center, Institute for International Studies, Stanford University, April 1996).

Sources: *US Foreign Trade Highlights* (US Department of Commerce), various years; *Exports, Imports, and Balance of Goods by Selected Countries and Geographic Areas — 1995* (US Bureau of the Census, 1996); *Survey of Current Business* (US Department of Commerce, 1995); *Hong Kong External Trade* (Hong Kong: Census and Statistics Department), various years.

expired in December 1996.[20] That agreement allows less than 1% annual growth in import volume of Chinese textiles and apparel to the United States. Partly because of increased competition from Mexico and partly because of more stringent and time-consuming checking of the country of origin of textile goods from China by US Customs, in the first nine months of 1996, imports of Chinese apparels fell 13% from the year before.[21] In response to the US penalties, China threatened to ban imports of certain US textiles, farm goods, fruits and alcoholic beverages. On 8 December 1996, China delayed by one month its deadline to implement these bans. After some hard bargaining, the fifth Sino-US Textile Agreement was reached in February 1997.[22]

The textile trade friction involving China and the United States is an example of the increased use of the rule of origin by importing countries to reduce imports.[23] Except for some selective textile items, the United States has lost its comparative advantage in the textile and clothing sector for quite some time. It is often difficult to ease out an important declining industry, and import restrictions are used instead. While there may or may not be attempts to evade textile quotas on a large scale by China, the point is that from an economic efficiency standpoint, these textile quotas and other trade restrictions should not have been there in the first place. Using the rule of origin to reduce imports is just another way to enforce inefficient restrictions on trade.

China–Japan Economic Relations[24]

According to our estimates of adjusted Chinese exports figures, China exported US$ 34.58 billion worth of goods to Japan in 1995, up by 31.68% compared to 1994. Japan was likely the second largest export market for China, behind the United States (see Table 5). China imported US$ 29.18 billion from Japan in 1995, an increase of 0.62%. Japan was the largest supplier of China's imports in 1996. Utilized Japanese foreign direct investment in China amounted to US$ 3.11 billion, up by 49.5%. Japan in 1995 was the third largest foreign direct investor, behind Hong Kong and Taiwan. By the end of 1995, the cumulative number of direct investment projects by Japan in China totalled 13,257. In 1995, China also imported 533 items of technology and equipment from Japan, making Japan the second largest provider of imported technology items, behind only the United States.[25]

Japan has been by far China's largest source of concessional financing and aid since China started its reforms in 1978.[26] Japan's development assistance to China mainly has come in the form of concessional loans administered by Japan's Overseas Economic Cooperation Fund (OECF). These are low-interest loans, with a 30-year repayment period and a 10-year grace period. Since 1979, Japan has announced four yen loan packages to China. Most loans have been used to support infrastructure projects, including transportation, electric power and telecommunications.[27] For the year 1995, the amount of the loan was ¥ 141.429 billion, at an interest rate of 2.3%. The fourth yen loan package was to cover the years 1996–1998, as publicly announced in December 1994. These new concessional loans would amount to a total of US$ 6.1 billion. Whether it is trade, investments or loans, it is clear from the above figures that despite historical hostilities, the economic relationship with Japan is very important to China.

If there is an area that is likely to be a source of friction between the two countries, it is trade in textiles. Textile raw materials and products have consistently been China's most important export commodity to

Japan.[28] China's official data show that in 1995 its exports to Japan in this area amounted to US$ 7.38 billion, a whopping 26% of total official exports to Japan. Japan indicated that it was very concerned by the increase in imports of shirts, sweaters and towels from China. In February 1995, the Japanese government actually initiated investigations of China's exports of cotton cloth and cotton yarn. Even though no major action was taken, Japan would officially monitor imports of these items.

China–EU Economic Relations

Based on our estimates of adjusted export figures in Table 5, the EU was likely the third largest export market for China in 1995, behind the United States and Japan. In the same year, the EU was also the second largest provider of imports and the sixth largest foreign direct investor in China. Foreign direct investments from the EU rose by 38.96% to US$ 2.14 billion in 1995. But in 1996, exports from the EU to China actually decreased by 6.49% to US$ 19.83 billion.[29]

Despite the slowdown of EU exports in 1996, the general pattern over time is that both trade and direct investment linkages between China and the EU have been expanding. But, as is normal with any major trading partner, China and the EU also have had some difficulties in their economic relationships. One major area of trade friction between China and the EU has been the frequent use of anti-dumping duties by the EU. The EU imposed temporary anti-dumping duties of 22.6% on 30 unbleached cotton fabrics on 20 November 1996. Final decisions will be made in May 1997. China has vowed that it will fight the decision. The EU is an important market for China's unbleached cotton fabrics, with an export volume reaching US$ 96 million in 1995. Furthermore, on 17 September 1996, the EU imposed 94.1% anti-dumping duties on imports of shoes. The EU is also carrying out anti-dumping investigations of bags imported from China.[30]

There is a widespread consensus among professional economists that the use of anti-dumping duties against imports is just another way for domestic producers to harass foreign exporters. More specifically, there are two major complaints against existing anti-dumping laws. First, governments of importing countries are given too much leeway in deciding whether dumping exists and how large the dumping margins are. Secondly, in cases where dumping is judged to have occurred, the criteria on whether anti-dumping duties should be levied rest primarily on whether import-competing producers have been injured. The welfare of the consumers is not taken into consideration at all. The results are typically higher prices for consumers.[31] It is important to remember that consumers are not always individual final consumers — in some cases, they can be other domestic producers.[32]

Traditionally, the EU has been one of the biggest users of anti-dumping duties in the world (along with the United States, Canada, and Australia). As global economies continue to liberalize and as tariffs continue to come down, more and more countries (including Japan and Mexico) are resorting to the use of anti-dumping duties. The EU's imposition on China's textile and other products represents a way for the EU domestic firms to seek protection rather than to adjust to increased international competition.

China–ASEAN Economic Relations

Using estimates of our adjusted exports, ASEAN was likely the fourth largest export market for China in 1995. In the same year, it was the fifth largest provider of imports and also the fifth largest foreign direct investor. Foreign direct investment increased by 40.11% over 1994, while exports to China rose by 37.43%. Among ASEAN members, Singapore was China's most important trading partner. Estimated Chinese exports to Singapore were valued at US$ 5.14 billion, in 1995 while imports were US$ 3.60 billion in 1996 (see Table 5 and Table 6). Singapore's utilized direct foreign investments were US$ 1.85 billion in 1995, making it the sixth largest direct foreign investor.[33] Singapore's 1995 direct investments were up 56.93% compared with 1994.

Some of the biggest investment projects in China have involved ASEAN countries. For example, Singapore has been involved for more than two years in the construction of the China–Singapore Suzhou Industrial Park. Its ambitious plan is to transform 70 square kilometres of farmland into an industrial township. One of the aims is to transfer Singapore's management know-how.[34] Some of the biggest foreign investors in China were also from ASEAN member nations. For instance, Charoen Pokhand, a Thai conglomerate, has been involved in 130 joint venture companies in China since 1979. It recently invested in a US$ 118 million motorcycle plant in Pudong.[35] Both the systematic trade and direct investment figures, as well as isolated company and project reports, suggest that China's economic relations with ASEAN and, in particular with Singapore, have been very significant, and in all likelihood they will continue to expand rapidly.

Other International Issues concerning China

China and the WTO

Since March 1986, China has tried unsuccessfully to (re)enter the WTO (and its predecessor organization, GATT). As of March 1997, it is uncertain whether China can become a member of the WTO in the near future. The United States continues to argue that China's WTO offer is not "commercially meaningful" enough.[36] Reports indicate that the United States would like to see special and additional provisions in safeguards, dumping and balance of payments to be applied to China, provisions that appear to go beyond normal WTO requirements.[37] Furthermore, the United States also wants to look at specific conditions of market access one sector at a time to determine what the concessions for China should be. Generally, the United States has indicated that it wants China to further open up its markets, including its financial service sector and make its trade rules and regulations more transparent.

China has so far insisted on three basic positions with respect to the WTO: first, the WTO would be incomplete without the participation of China. Secondly, China is a developing, not a developed country.[38] Thirdly, it is necessary to have a transition period while it gradually meets the relevant requirements of the WTO. The second and the third positions are related since a developing country status would allow China a longer transition period to bring tariffs in line with other WTO members. China also argues that it has already met the basic requirements for WTO membership. It started to cut tariffs on 4,900 products on 1 April 1996. China also announced at the Asian-Pacific Economic Cooperation forum in November 1996 that it would further slash tariffs by 15% by the year 2000 from the current average tariff of 23%.[39]

However, as late as 11 December 1996, the dialogue to speed up the process of China's entry to the WTO at the Singapore Ministerial Meeting of the WTO apparently produced little results.[40] But, Chinese entry is as much a political issue as an economic issue, and a breakthrough compromise agreement between the leaders of the two countries is always possible.

Chinese entry into the WTO would be beneficial to both China and its trading partners in the long run. From China's standpoint, being a WTO member will provide better protection from the various capricious and inefficient trade barriers imposed by different importing countries. Trade disputes involving China will more likely be settled by the dispute settlement panels of the WTO, rather than by mutual threats of trade wars. Moreover, membership in WTO represents a strong pre-commitment to a competitive open economy which in turn promotes overall economic efficiency. It should be remembered that membership in WTO is far from universally supported in China. From the point of view of narrow self-interests of domestic Chinese enterprises and industries, it may well be better if China stays out indefinitely. There is also another school of thought that suggests that China should join the WTO only after "invisible" non-tariff barriers to trade have been put in place, as Japanese enterprises and industries allegedly did before they fully acceded to GATT.[41] From China's trading partners' standpoint, they can expect, in addition to lower tariffs, increased transparency and non-discrimination and, in time, a China that fully subscribes to accepted international norm.

Yet, WTO by itself still cannot resolve all trade disputes. For example, it still allows too much discretion in the application of anti-dumping duties by individual countries. Nonetheless, China's entry into the WTO will reduce the influence of international power politics on international trade. Instead, trade and economic relations will be governed by international laws, rules and regulations.

Status of Currency and Foreign Reserves

On 1 December 1996, China made its currency convertible for the settlement of current accounts. Thus, for purposes related to exports and imports of goods and services, foreign exchange may be freely bought and sold on the market. For the purpose of settling capital accounts, the RMB remains not convertible. Chinese official foreign reserves reached US$ 105 billion by the end of 1996. The People's Bank of China (the central bank) held a significant portion of its reserves in US Treasury securities. China spent US$ 11 billion on US Treasury securities during the first half of 1996, compared with only US$ 703 million in 1995.[42]

The People's Bank of China is not an entirely independent entity. It operates under the State Council. In particular, its proposals on exchange rate policies have to be approved by the State Council. In February 1996, the People's Bank of China signed a bilateral repurchase (repo) agreement with the Hong Kong Monetary Authority. This agreement was the first Chinese agreement with another monetary authority. Governor Dai Xianglong of the People's Bank also reaffirmed that the People's Bank will act to support the Hong Kong-US dollar peg in the event of a currency crisis.

Conclusion

In 1996, there is a sharp decline in the growth of China's foreign trade activities. The slowdown of exports is a fairly widespread phenomenon in East Asia and is not confined to China. This slowdown is related in part to the slow demand for imports from OECD countries, particularly Europe and Japan. However, because of high domestic inflation in 1994 and 1995, and the slight appreciation of the RMB against the US dollar (and hence against the other currencies as well) Chinese exports have lost some competitiveness relative to other developing countries. The premature exhaustion of funds for the tariff and tax rebate programme for exports also had an impact. The slowdown of China's import growth is related to the continued tight domestic credit policy. However, 1996 was also not a normal year because some imports of equipment by foreign direct investors and joint ventures into China were accelerated from 1996 into 1995 because of the expected expiration of tariff exemption. As a result, 1995 imports were somewhat higher than normal, and 1996 imports were somewhat lower than normal. The slowdown in 1996 is therefore expected to be transitory. It is anticipated that in 1997 the growth of both exports and imports will return to its historical trend.

China is expected to make significant progress on her application for membership in the World Trade Organization in 1997. However, even though the positions of China and the OECD countries, principally the United States, have become closer, it is still too early to tell whether China will be able to enter WTO in 1997 or 1998. But there is reason to be cautiously optimistic. The renewal of "most-favoured-nation" status for China by the United States does not appear to be a serious problem this year.

Besides the WTO and the MFN issues, China has reasonably good trade and investment relationships with all its trading partners. From

China' standpoint, there are still three related concerns. First, almost all major trading partners impose trade restrictions against China's exports of textiles and garments. Secondly, countries importing Chinese goods are increasingly resorting to anti-dumping duties to reduce the growth of Chinese exports. Thirdly, some countries such as the US are using rule-of-origin as a way to reduce import of Chinese goods. These concerns will likely continue.

Notes

1. In Lawrence J. Lau, "The Chinese Economy in the Twenty-First Century" (Working Paper, The Asia/Pacific Research Center, Stanford University, 1994), it was pointed out that China's economic development will likely be led by domestic demands. Given China's size, there are simply no foreign markets that are large enough for China's growth to be primarily export-led. The foreign sector continues to play an important role. It provides managerial know-how, increases competition, transfers technology and often leads in legal and institutional reforms. This view of the multifaceted role of China's foreign sector is also consistent with empirical results in K. C. Fung, "Trade and Investment Flows: Mainland China, Hong Kong and Taiwan" (Hong Kong: City University of Hong Kong Press, 1997, forthcoming).
2. The regions in Asia include: Hong Kong, Macau, Taiwan, Brunei, Indonesia, Malaysia, Philippines, Singapore, Thailand, Afghanistan, Bahrain, Bangladesh, Bhutan, Burma, Democratic Kampuchea, Cyprus, Korea DRP, India, Iran, Iraq, Israel, Japan, Jordan, Kuwait, Laos DRP, Lebanon, Maldives, Mongolia, Nepal, Oman, Pakistan, Palestine, Qatar, Saudi Arabia, Korea Rep., Sri Lanka, Syrian Arab Rep., Turkey, United Arab Emirates, Republic of Yemen, Vietnam, and China; the regions in Africa include Algeria, Angola, Benin, Botswana, Burundi, Cameroon, Canary Is., Cape Verde, Central Africa, Ceuta, Chad, Comoros, Congo, Djibouti, Egypt, Eq. Guinea, Ethiopia, Gabon, Gambia, Ghana, Guinea, Guinea-Bissau, Cte d'Ivoire, Kenya, Liberia, Libyan Arab Jm., Madagascar, Malawi, Mali, Mauritania, Mauritius, Morocco, Mozambique, Namibia, Niger, Nigeria, Reunion, Rwanda, Sao Tome & Principe, Senegal, Seychelles, Sierra Leone, Somalia, S. Africa, Western Sahara, Sudan, Tanzania, Togo, Tunisia, Uganda, Burkina Faso, Zaire, Zambia, Zimbabwe, Lesotho, Melilla, Swaziland and Eritrea; regions in Europe include Belgium, Denmark, United Kingdom, Germany, France, Ireland, Italy, Luxembourg, The Netherlands, Greece, Portugal, Spain, Austria, Finland, Sweden, Iceland, Liechtenstein, Norway, Switzerland, Estonia, Latvia, Lithuania, Georgia, Armenia, Azerbaijin, Belorussia,

Kazakhstan Kirghizia, Moldavia, Russia, Tadzhikistan, Turkmenistan, Ukraine, Uzbekstan, Albania, Andorra, Bulgaria, Gibraltar, Hungary, Malta, Monaco, Poland, Romania, San Marino, Yugoslavia, Slovenia, Croatia, Czech Republic, Slovakia, Macedonia Rep., and Bosnia & Hercegovina; regions in Latin America include Antigua & Barbuda, Argentina, Aruba, Bahamas, Barbados, Belize, Bolivia, Bonare, Brazil, Cayman Is., Chile, Columbia, Costa Rica, Cuba, Curacao, Dominican Republic, Ecuador, French Guyana, Grenada, Guadeloupe, Guatemala, Guyana, Haiti, Honduras, Jamaica, Martinique, Montserrat, Nicaragua, Panama, Paraguay, Peru, Puerto Rico, Saba, Saint Lucia, Saint Martin, Saint Vincent & Grenadines, El Salvador, Suriname, Trinidad & Tobago, Turks & Caicos Is., Uruguay, Venezuela, British Virgin Is., and St. Kitts-Nevis; regions in North America include Canada, Mexico, United States, Greenland and Bermuda; Oceania includes Australia, Cook Is., Fiji, Gambier Is., Marquesas Is., Nauru, New Caledonia, Vanuatu, New Zealand, Norfolk Is., Papua New Guinea, Society Is., Solomon Is., Tonga, Tuamoto Is., Tubai Is., Samoa, Kiribti, Tuvalu, Micronesia FS, Marshall Is. R., and Palau.

3. We start our comparison with the year 1993 because, in 1993, China started to seriously trace the country of origin and the country of destination of its imports and exports. Before 1993, China had lumped its exports to Hong Kong, whether they were for re-export elsewhere or for consumption in Hong Kong, as exports to Hong Kong. Consequently, before 1993, China's trade with Hong Kong was greatly exaggerated. For details, see K. C. Fung and Lawrence J. Lau, "The China-United States Bilateral Trade Balance: How Big Is It Really?" (Occasional Paper, Asia/Pacific Research Center, Stanford University, April 1996).
4. It is fairly well known that a significant portion of China's exports to Hong Kong are re-exported through Hong Kong. Even though China has reformed its system of collecting export and import data since 1993, it is still likely the case that the role of the Hong Kong market is exaggerated. See the next table for our adjustments to these export values and export shares.
5. This is calculated by dividing the 1995 China's re-exports via Hong Kong by China's 1995 total exports to the world. The re-export figure is from *Hong Kong External Trade* (Hong Kong: Census and Statistics Department, December 1995). China's total export figure is from *China's Customs Statistics Monthly* (General Administration of Customs of the People's Republic of China, December 1995).
6. In 1994, the re-export margin of Chinese goods via Hong Kong was estimated to be 24.9%. See *Hong Kong Monthly Digest of Statistics*, February 1996.
7. Retained imports by Hong Kong from China are given for the years 1993 and 1994 in *Hong Kong Monthly Digest of Statistics*, February 1996. For the year 1995, we took the figure for China's re-exports via Hong Kong, discounted it

by the re-export margin of 25%, then subtracted it from 1995 Hong Kong total imports from China to obtain the 1995 Hong Kong's retained imports from China.

8. For a study of Hong Kong's and Taiwan's investments in China, see Fung (Note 1).
9. For detailed discussions of some economic relationships among China, Hong Kong and Taiwan, see Lawrence J. Lau, "The Role of Government in Economic Development: Some Observations from the Experience of China, Hong Kong and Taiwan," in *The Role of Government in East Asian Economic Development: A Comparative Institutional Analysis*, edited by M. Aoki, H-K Kim, and M. Okuno-Fujiwara (Oxford University Press, 1996); and K. C. Fung and Francis Ng, "Trade in Greater China," in *Proceedings of International Conference on Greater China: Problems, Prospects and Policies*, (Hong Kong: Hong Kong University Press, 1997). Early discussions of the economic relationship between Hong Kong and China was in Sung Yun-wing, *The China-Hong Kong Connection* (Hong Kong: Cambridge University Press, 1991) and C. Kao, "A Study of the Economic Interactions among Taiwan, Hong Kong and Mainland China," (in Chinese), mimeo (Taipei: Chung Hua Institution for Economic Research, 1993). For a detailed examination of Taiwan's economic development and a study of the sources of economic growth of Hong Kong and Taiwan, see respectively, Lawrence J. Lau, *Models of Development: A Comparative Study of Economic Growth in South Korea and Taiwan* (enlarged and expanded ed.; San Francisco: ICS Press, 1990) and Jong-Il Kim and Lawrence J. Lau, "The Sources of Economic Growth of the East Asian Newly Industrialized Countries," *Journal of the Japanese and International Economies*, (1994).
10. These provisions can be found in Articles 114, 115, 116 and 151 of the Basic Law.
11. It has to be remembered that foreign direct investments supposedly originating from Hong Kong also include an unknown but significant amount of recycled Chinese capital.
12. The adjusted exports from China to Taiwan given in Table 5 already include re-exports via Hong Kong. Similarly, the import figures in Table 6 should also have taken re-exports into account.
13. See Table 5 and discussions following the table.
14. See Table 5, Table 6 and Table 7.
15. For details, see K. C. Fung and Lawrence J. Lau (Note 4) and K. C. Fung, "Accounting for Chinese Trade: Some National and Regional Considerations" (NBER Working Paper #5595, 1996). Further discussions on this topic can be found in *People's Daily*, May 1996.
16. It is important to note that, by definition, re-exports mean that little or no change will be made to the US goods in Hong Kong. By the time these goods

arrive at China's Customs, they will still be US goods, *not* goods "made in Hong Kong."

17. See *Exports, Imports, and Balance of Goods by Selected Countries and Geographic Areas — 1995* (US Bureau of Census, 1996).
18. See *Hong Kong External Trade* (Hong Kong: Census and Statistics Department, December 1995).
19. We treat US official exports to China as direct exports. We then take Hong Kong re-exports of US goods discounted by the re-export margin of 14% as indirect US exports to China. The sum of these direct and indirect exports are estimates of our adjusted US exports to China. We treat US official imports from China as including both China's direct and indirect exports (with the re-export markup) to the US. We discount China's indirect exports to the US by the re-export margin of 25%, add them to China's direct exports to get estimates of US adjusted imports from China. For details, see K. C. Fung and Lawrence J. Lau (Note 4).
20. See "US and China to Resume Textile Talks," *The Asian Wall Street Journal*, 2 December 1996.
21. Ibid.
22. See "China Delays Ban on US Goods," *Hong Kong Standard*, 9 December 1996.
23. For a discussion of the rule of origin as a trade barrier, see Anne Krueger, "Customs Union versus Free Trade Area" (Working Paper, Department of Economics, Stanford University, 1995).
24. For a discussion and comparative analysis of Japanese and US trade and investment in China, see K. C. Fung and Hitomi Iizaka, "US-Japan Rivalry and China" (University of California-Santa Cruz Working Paper #323, July 1995).
25. See "The Economic and Trade Relations Between China and Japan in 1995," in *Almanac of China's Foreign Economic Relations and Trade* (Beijing: China Economics Publishing House, Economic Information Agency, 1996/97).
26. This contrasts sharply with policies with the United States, which provide virtually no bilateral financial assistance to China.
27. See Peter C. Evans, "Japan and the United States Diverge on Assistance to China" (Japan Economic Institute Report No. 19A, May 1995) and Nicholas Lardy, *China in the World Economy* (Washington, DC: Institute for International Economics, 1994).
28. China's export of textile to Japan from 1989 to 1994 are given in K. C. Fung and H. Iizaka (Note 27). Figures for 1995 (see Note 25).
29. See Table 6 and Table 7.
30. See "Textile Firms Seek Action on EU Duties," *Hong Kong Standard*, 9 December 1996.

31. See for example, Michael J. Finger, *Antidumping: How It Works and Who Gets Hurt* (Ann Arbor, Michigan: University of Michigan Press); K. C. Fung and Michael J. Finger, "Will GATT Enforcement Control Antidumping?" *Journal of Economic Integration*, Vol. 9, No. 2 (June 1994), pp. 192–213; Robert Staiger and Frank Wolak, "The Trade Effects of Antidumping Investigations: Theory and Evidence," in *Analytical and Negotiating Issues in the Global Trading System*, edited by Robert Stern (Ann Arbor, Michigan: University of Michigan Press, 1993), etc.
32. For some discussions of the US flat panel display case which hurts domestic US personal computer industries, see Michael J. Finger and K. C. Fung, "Can Competition Policies Control '301'?" *Aussenwirtschaft*, No. 49 (1994), pp. 379–416.
33. As a foreign direct investor, Singapore was behind Hong Kong, Taiwan, Japan, the United States and the EU.
34. See "Transplanting Singapore into China Proves Tricky," *The Asian Wall Street Journal*, 25 September 1996.
35. See "Follow the Leader: Charoen Pokhand Introduces Thai Firms to China," *Far Eastern Economic Review*, 26 September 1996.
36. Note 20.
37. See "'Unreasonable' US Demands Jeopardise WTO Entry Talks," *Hong Kong Standard*, 26 August 1996.
38. The US insists that the volume of China's exports and the size of China's economy make China a developed economy.
39. See "Beijing Unlikely to Give Up Stance as Developing Nation," *Hong Kong Standard*, 9 December 1996.
40. See "China WTO Accession Falters," *South China Morning Post*, 11 December 1996.
41. For an empirical study of how the Japanese *keiretsu* may have acted as an "invisible" trade barrier, see K. C. Fung, "Characteristics of Japanese Industrial Groups and their Potential Impact on US-Japanese Trade," in *Empirical Studies of Commercial Policy*, edited by R. Baldwin, NBER Conference Volume (Chicago: University of Chicago Press, 1991), pp. 137–64.
42. See "China Goes on US$ 11 b. Buying Spree," *South China Morning Post*, 3 October 1996.

10

Towards the Full Convertibility of the *Renminbi*?

Tsang Shu-ki

A New Stage in Convertibility or an Anti-climax?

In 1996, there were two important pieces of foreign exchange regulations implemented in China. On 1 April, the "Regulations on Foreign Exchange Management of the People's Republic of China (PRC),"[1] formulated by the State Council, came into effect. They replaced the "Provisional Regulations for Exchange Control of the PRC," adopted since 18 December 1980,[2] and provided a more coherent policy framework. Then, the "Regulations on Forex Sale, Purchase and Payment" were promulgated by the People's Bank of China (PBOC) — China's central bank — on 20 June.[3]

With these regulations in place, the PBOC announced in July 1996 the intention of achieving current account convertibility for the *Renminbi*, the Chinese currency, by the end of the year.[4] On 27 November 1996, Dai Xianglong, the governor of the PBOC, wrote to the International Monetary Fund (IMF) officially stating that the transitional arrangements under the second clause of Article XIV of the Articles of Agreement no longer applied to the country as a member of the IMF. China would from then on accept the obligations of Article VIII.[5] Such an acceptance meant that Beijing would no longer impose any restriction on the payments and transfers in current account transactions, in terms of discriminatory monetary policies or in the form of multiple exchange rates. It was reportedly hailed as a "milestone" by the IMF.[6]

For the foreign funded enterprises (FFEs) investing in China, a bonus was that they were admitted into the bank-based foreign exchange market instituted in the 1994 reforms, instead of being confined to the swap centres. The permission took effect on 1 July 1996. One notable point is that the swap centres were retained for their use. In other words, as far as foreign exchange purchases and sales were concerned, the FFEs now have two channels compared with one for domestic enterprises.[7]

These moves were the interim conclusion of a series of measures taken by the government since late 1993. I have written several pieces on them.[8] The foreign exchange reform was the most progressive, in both conception and practice, among the various macroeconomic reforms of 1994 (which included also fiscal, banking and trade reforms). It has also been the most successful so far, helped by a huge capital inflow and other institutional

* The author wishes to thank Edgardo Barandiaran, Y. Y. Kueh and an anonymous referee for useful inputs without any implications of responsibilities on their part.

factors that have kept the exchange rate of the *Renminbi* surprisingly firm, despite very high domestic inflation rates in 1994–1995.

The formal achievement of current account convertibility for the *Renminbi* came earlier than expected.[9] In a way, though, it also turned out to be a kind of anti-climax, as the relations between trade restrictions and foreign exchange restrictions in the current account became clear. At the same time, in the course of 1996, the Chinese authorities took measures to rationalize capital account controls. Although nominally the degree of restrictions remains the same, it actually means that market participants now find it more difficult to exploit loopholes, even if they want to do so. Hence, not everyone regards the progress on the front of foreign exchange in 1996 as really so exciting. Such an interpretation is not intended to belittle the achievements of the Chinese reforms in foreign exchange, which have indeed been huge, but to offer a more sober view of the progress so far, three years after the mis-named "big bang."[10]

Many economists of the gradualist persuasion, including myself, would even welcome such a cautious development. China should not rush towards full convertibility for its currency, without laying the necessary domestic foundations, which remains a formidable task.

The Meaning of Current Account Convertibility

I have commented that before the 1994 reform there existed two hurdles for an importer in China: trade approval and foreign exchange rationing. The 1994 reform theoretically removed the latter restriction and left only one hurdle for most trade transactions.[11] But, in reality, the foreign exchange control regime is closely related to the trade control system. It means little for a country to "achieve" current account convertibility if significant trade restrictions in the form of licensing, quotas, canalization, and registration requirements still persist, or very high tariffs are imposed on imports. Nsouli has aptly used the term "Article VIII convertibility" to label the situation where a country practices "current account convertibility" in foreign exchange but maintains trade restrictions, in contrast to the state of "total current account convertibility." "Article VIII" of course refers to the Articles of Agreement of the IMF binding its members on foreign exchange but not trade behaviour.[12]

To be fair, China has been making important efforts to reduce both the non-tariff trade barriers and the tariff rates. As far as import tariffs are concerned, the average tariff rate in China was cut from 35.6% to 23% in 1996, as President Jiang Zemin promised at the Asia Pacific Economic Cooperation (APEC) Leaders' Conference in Osaka in November 1995. Again, at the APEC Leaders' Conference in Manila in November 1996, Jiang announced that China would reduce the average rate to the level of 15% by the year 2000. This compares with the 4–5% and 13–15% for the developed and developing countries, respectively, reached at the Uruguay Round of the General Agreement on Tariffs and Trade (GATT). Already the plan was reportedly regarded as "insufficient" by European diplomats.[13] As we know, one contentious issue in China's application to join the World Trade Organization (WTO) is whether she should be treated as a developed or a developing country.

In any case, with regard to current account transactions, there are still some items which require "verification of truthfulness" by the State Administration for Exchange Control (SAEC).[14] They are specified in Articles 13 and 15 of the "Regulations on Forex Sale, Purchase and Payment." These concern advance payments exceeding 15% of the total contractual value or US$ 100,000 in absolute amount (Article 13[4] and Article 15[1]), forex payments for implicit commissions exceeding 2% and explicit commissions exceeding 5% of the total contractual value, respectively, or above US$ 10,000 in absolute amount (Article 13[6] and Article 15[2]), "external payments under entrepôt trade characterized by payment in advance of reimbursement" (Article 15[3]), interest payments for external debts (Article 15[4]), and cash withdrawal exceeding an equivalent amount of US$ 10,000 (Article 15[5]).[15]

FFEs and Control on the Capital Account

At the same time, while Chinese domestic enterprises have had to sell all their current account receipts since 1994, FFEs are also required under the new post-1996 system to open a settlement account with designated banks where they may only keep a stipulated ceiling of such receipts. According to Chen Yuan, a vice governor of the PBOC, the maximum was to be set administratively in the light of "the actual investment made by the FFEs and their need for circulation in the current accounts." This differs from the pre-1994 situation where FFEs could keep all their receipts. The justification is that "idle balances" beyond the genuine current account needs of FFEs can help the country to maintain macro control and stabilize the exchange rate. Chen, however, promised that "the ceilings will be set rather loosely to ensure the need of the FFEs in businesses under current accounts."[16]

In the course of 1996, as China moved towards "current account convertibility," measures were also implemented on capital account transactions to rationalize control. Chapter three of the "Regulations on Forex Sale, Purchase and Payment," promulgated by the PBOC on 20 June, stipulates that "entities in China" (including both domestic and foreign-funded enterprises) must open accounts for "capital items" with designated banks.

Moreover, these "capital items" are divided into three separate categories: (1) foreign exchange related to direct investment; (2) foreign exchange involved in overseas borrowing and repayment; and (3) other capital account transactions. Foreign-funded enterprises have to open separate accounts on these different transactions so that the authorities can monitor them closely.[17]

The Surprising Stability of the *Renminbi*

In any case, defying pessimistic forecasts which focussed on macro instability and high inflation, the *Renminbi* has shown remarkable strength in the post-1994 system. On 4 April 1994, the first trading day of the China Foreign Exchange Trade System (CFETS) in Shanghai, the Chinese currency was sold at RMB 8.6967/US$ 1. The exchange rate later strengthened and ended 1994 at 8.4462 and 1995 at 8.3174. In the course of 1996, favourable supply and demand conditions continued to underpin the *Renminbi* (see Table 1). The currency was quoted at 8.2982 at the end of the year. The rates offered by financial and other institutions in Hong Kong were very close to these prices, indicating that they were accepted as reasonable by the offshore free market.

The stability of the *Renminbi* in the new system is a testimony to the success of the reform. However, it is also surprising, particularly given the very high inflation rates until only the second half of 1996. There are various explanations.[18] The most important one has been the very impressive rise in China's foreign exchange reserves, which went up from US$ 21.199 billion at the end of 1993 to US$ 51.62 billion a year later. The rise continued in the subsequent two years, albeit at slower rates, to reach US$ 105 billion by the end of 1996 (see Table 2).

Table 1 Monthly Movement of the *Renminbi* in 1996

(Unit: RMB/100 US$)

Month	Quotation at the end of month	Average quotation in the month
January	8.3147	8.3186
February	8.3207	8.3132
March	8.3339	8.3289
April	8.3306	8.3315
May	8.3263	8.3288
June	8.3221	8.3225
July	8.3109	8.3160
August	8.3063	8.3081
September	8.3017	8.3043
October	8.3007	8.2999
November	8.3007	8.2988
December	8.2982	8.2992

Table 2 China's Gold and Foreign Exchange Reserves

Year	(1) Gold reserves (10,000 ounces)	(2) Foreign exchange reserves (US$ billion)	Growth of (2) (%)
1986	1267	2.072	–21.6
1987	1267	2.923	41.1
1988	1267	3.372	15.4
1989	1267	5.550	64.6
1990	1267	11.093	99.9
1991	1267	21.712	95.7
1992	1267	19.443	–10.5
1993	1267	21.199	9.0
1994	1267	51.620	143.5
1995	1267	73.597	42.6
1996	1267	105.000	42.7

Sources: The People's Bank of China, *China Financial Outlook '96*, Tables 3–13; *Wen Wei Po*, 21 January 1997.

The surge in reserves was the result of a combination of factors. The imposition of the foreign exchange settlement system (and the abolition of the foreign exchange retention scheme) in 1994 had helped to centralize resources in the hands of the PBOC. At the same time, the steady arrival of funds from the very high post-1992 level of foreign capital absorption had been a powerful boosting factor in producing net capital inflows.

In the three years of 1994–1996, actually utilized foreign direct investment (FDI) totalled US$ 113.853 billion, compared with the amount of

US$ 32.263 billion for utilized foreign borrowing.[19] At the end of 1996, the outstanding balance of China's foreign debt reached US$ 116.28 billion,[20] which represented an increase of US$ 32.705 billion over the balance of US$ 83.575 at the end of 1993. From these figures, one may be tempted to conclude that FDI has been a more important factor than external borrowing in the post-1994 rise of China's international reserves. Nevertheless, there are two uncertainties. First, it is not clear how much of the US$ 113.853 billion of utilized FDI in 1994–1996 actually arrived in the form of money. There were reports that significant portions of many foreign investments came in the form of imports of material and machines, which would not show up as monetary reserves. Secondly, there was the question of how much foreign money was used to service the post-1994 FDIs in the form of profit repatriation, which however should have been small because of the short history of these investments.

Another important reason was of course that China had only aimed at current account convertibility. Capital account transactions were not further liberalized, indeed controls on them were "tightened," as pointed out above. This may have helped in checking informal or illegal capital outflow, and in preserving reserves.

Surprise of an opposite nature may also arise: that the *Renminbi* could have stabilized against the US dollar for so long despite the huge capital inflows. Given more understanding about the operation of the bank-based foreign exchange market launched since April 1994, we can now make the observation that the strength of the *Renminbi* has also been underpinned by a number of institutional peculiarities. The existence of "bilateral monopolies" in the Chinese interbank market has been a key factor. According to one source,[21] the share of the Bank of China (BOC) in the total sale of foreign exchange in the market was about 70% to 80%, while the central bank, the PBOC, also bought up to 70% to 80% of the foreign exchange offered. In other words, the transactions between the BOC and the PBOC could easily dictate the movement of the exchange rate.

Behind such a market structure is the imposition of the foreign exchange settlement system in 1994, with the concurrent limit by the PBOC for designated banks to keep working balances in foreign exchange. This has resulted in a persistent situation of excess supply in the interbank market. There could have been two types of responses: (1) the mopping up of the excess by the PBOC; or (2) further relaxation of foreign exchange control. It appears that the PBOC has opted for the first response. Hence, its dominance in the interbank market.

Full Convertibility Sequencing: Where Does the *Renminbi* Stand?

The liberalization of China's foreign exchange system has in general followed the sequence advised by a number of economists in the field of international monetary economics: achieving current account convertibility first before attempting capital account convertibility. This is by no means a non-controversial issue. In practice, different countries have adopted different sequences: South Korea had opened the capital account without much trade liberalization in the mid-1960s, with rather serious inflationary consequences that had lingered.[22] In the so called "Southern Cone experiment" of Latin America in the late 1970s, Argentina and Uruguay had opened the capital account first, while Chile had opened the current account first, but both sides had faced a common fate in the early 1980s: deep economic recession and some reversal of liberalization.[23]

Theoretically, the debate has still not been settled. In the words of Sebastian Edwards:

> Some authors have argued that, to the extent that the opening of the capital account will generate destabilizing capital flows, the exchange rate will be highly volatile ... for this reason the capital account should be opened only after the trade reform has been completed, and the new structure of production is "consolidated". Other authors, however, have argued that the best way to avoid undesired real exchange rate movements is by having a freely floating exchange rate with full convertibility. This exchange rate system ... should be implemented before the trade reform. Consequently, the capital account should be liberalized first.[24]

Edwards himself, in any case, is in favour of opening the current account first. Using a three-sector-two-good model, he reasons that the opening of both accounts will generate *opposite* effects on production and income distribution. Resource movements in and out of particular sectors will involve real costs. There is therefore a need to *synchronize* current and capital account liberalization to minimize those costs. If, as Frenkel[25] and Kahn and Zahler[26] have suggested, the speed of adjustment of the capital account is faster than that of the current account, the current account should be opened first.

Note that Edwards' findings do not imply that a country with total inconvertibility of its currency should "achieve" current account convertibility first, without doing anything on the capital account. Such a discrete opening sequence is not a "synchronized" move as it will still lead to resource movements in opposite directions. The issue at hand is how one should synchronize the reform of a slow-moving sector with that of a fast-moving sector. There is no doubt that the former should start first and the latter should come in later, but at what point? and how? Edwards has not offered any clear answer.

Ronald McKinnon, on the other hand, argues more strongly that financial liberalization which allows the free flow of foreign capital should come "only at the tail-end of an otherwise successful programme of liberalization."[27] His worry concerns the possibility of over-enthusiastic foreign capital that may disrupt a liberalization attempt that looks "successful." Citing the examples of South Korea, the Southern cone, and Pakistan and India, McKinnon reasons that the sudden rise in profitability may entice myopic movements of funds which throw up the wrong signals. In particular, the real exchange rate would turn "against exporters and firms competing with imports and make it unduly hard for them to adjust to the removal of protection."

From this perspective, the Chinese monetary authority has been doing a relatively successful job of keeping the right degree of "convertibility" and avoiding the undue effects of capital flows on its largely trade-oriented liberalization programme. An opening of the capital account in the aftermath of the "Deng whirlwind" of 1992 could have produced results similar to South Korea's in the mid-1960s, and aggravated China's inflationary problems.[28] With hindsight, it is quite amazing that the real appreciation of the *Renminbi* in 1994–1996 has not produced a trade deficit in China.[29]

In another analysis,[30] McKinnon concludes that financial liberalization to the external world should come at the end of the liberalization programme. In his view, historical evidence points to the fact that countries which succeeded in stabilizing their price levels and real exchange rates, while maintaining positive yields on bank deposits in an open capital market, showed a higher productivity of physical capital than those whose financial systems remained repressed. But, to reach this "noninflationary financial equilibrium," fiscal, monetary and foreign exchange policies need to be sequenced in an "optimal" manner.

McKinnon's recommendations for the liberalizing developing country or economy in transition are quite "classical": eliminate fiscal deficits and bring down inflation first. Then, the domestic capital and money markets can be liberalized to ensure a positive return to depositors, but, at the same time, the budget of the borrowing enterprises must be hardened (with help from positive real interest rates). After the successful liberalization of domestic trade and finance, foreign exchange liberalization can proceed; but, transacting on the current account is best liberalized much faster than capital movements:

> Before allowing enterprises (or households) to borrow from, or deposit in, international capital markets, the national capital market should be fully liberalized, which in turn depends on the stabilization of the domestic price level and the elimination of substantial reserve taxes on domestic banks.... As long as domestic banks remain restricted and heavily taxed, it is pointless — indeed destructive — to allow foreign banks ... to operate freely in domestic financial markets. Even more destabilizing is to allow "hard" foreign currencies to circulate in parallel with the still "soft" domestic one.

Only when domestic borrowing and lending take place freely at equilibrium (unrestricted) rates of interest and the domestic rate of inflation is curbed so that the ongoing depreciation in the exchange rate is unnecessary, are the arbitrage conditions right for capital account convertibility. Otherwise, there may be unwarranted capital flight or an unwarranted buildup of foreign indebtedness or both. "Free foreign exchange convertibility on capital account is usually the last stage in the optimal order of economic liberalization."

From these perspectives, one may say that China has hardly reached the benign stage where she could open the capital account while maintaining a "noninflationary financial equilibrium." Indeed, the fiscal deficit in China has not been eliminated, and the budget of most financial institutions and enterprises (in particular, state enterprises) has not been really hardened. Positive yields on deposits and positive real lending rates have emerged, thanks to the rapidly falling inflation rates since 1996. But nobody is sure how long they would last as they have not stemmed from successful institutional reforms. The "financial mess" within the lending institutions and between banks and enterprises still needs to be cleaned up.

Of course, one can criticize McKinnon's "optimal sequencing" as being too theoretical to be of much practical and policy relevance. After all, China has not followed the first half of his sequencing: Chinese enterprises have borrowed heavily before the fiscal deficit is eliminated, or before the national capital market is "fully liberalized," against his advice. His scheme looks like a "first best" abstract reasoning, rather than a "second best" analysis that caters for the impossibility of completing any one step without starting another, as well as the existence of formidable constraints on the policy maker's choices.

Nevertheless, his expressed worry about the possible dire consequences of opening the capital account without putting the domestic economy and financial system in proper order is still worthy of serious attention.

One Country, Two Currencies?

Irrespective of the actual speed of realization, as the *Renminbi* moves further towards the state of full convertibility, given the progress in China's domestic economic reforms, a question will arise concerning the fate of the currency of Hong Kong — the Hong Kong dollar. Hong Kong becomes a special administrative region (SAR) under Chinese sovereignty in 1997; but, from the early 1980s onwards, its economic linkages with mainland China have been rapidly strengthening through apparently phenomenal trade and capital flows. Are two separate currencies (the *Renminbi* and the HK dollar) really necessary when the *Renminbi* becomes fully convertible, some time in the future? Moreover, some cynics have already openly predicted that, because of political as well as economic considerations, the HK dollar would be "swallowed" by the *Renminbi* in the post-1997 era, even before the *Renminbi* turns fully convertible. One reason sometimes cited is that China is after Hong Kong's huge foreign exchange reserves, as if China's own ballooning reserves were not enough.

The official position on this issue is clear. As stipulated in the Basic Law, the Hong Kong SAR will continue to issue its own currency and decide its own monetary policies. Monetary relations between the mainland and the SAR have been characterized by Joseph Yam, chief executive of the Hong Kong Monetary Authority (the territory's central bank), as "one country, two currencies, two monetary systems and two monetary authorities which are mutually independent."[31] Chen Yuan, a vice governor of the PBOC, has openly endorsed such a view. Chen emphasizes that "(t)he Hong Kong dollar and the *Renminbi* will circulate as legal tender in Hong Kong and the mainland, respectively. The HK dollar will be treated as a foreign currency in the mainland. Likewise, the *Renminbi* will be treated as a foreign currency in Hong Kong."[32]

Is this official line credible? In another paper,[33] we have analysed the economic rationale for the coexistence of the HK dollar and the *Renminbi* after 1997. As the other side of the same coin, such an analysis amounts to addressing critically the rationale of monetary unification, the alternative to the coexistence of the two currencies.

The benefits of a unification of currencies are basically related to (a) the transaction costs of the currencies and (b) the risk posed by exchange rate variations. In the case of China and Hong Kong, unification would reduce the transaction costs and the risk of exchange rate variations only between the HK dollar and the *Renminbi but not* between the *Renminbi* (or for argument's sake a new unifying currency) and other currencies.

The economic linkages between the mainland and Hong Kong have no doubt been strengthening rapidly, but their true scale and significance should not be exaggerated.[34] As I have analysed elsewhere, the huge trade flows between Hong Kong and China have been dominated by trade in intermediate goods arising from Hong Kong's utilization of the mainland as an outward processing zone. Netting out such activities, Hong Kong's dependence on the United States as a market for *final goods* has not fallen much since the 1980s.[35] While Hong Kong accounts for over 60% of foreign direct investments in China, China's cumulative stock of direct investments in Hong Kong by 1994 made up only 18% of total foreign direct investments and ranked third, after the United Kingdom and Japan. In the year of 1994, China's direct investments in Hong Kong were estimated to constitute a meagre 4.5% of Hong Kong's capital formation.[36]

In other words, the "integration" between Hong Kong and mainland China has not been that advanced. It has certainly not come to a stage that the two economies constitute an "optimum currency area."[37] Nor should such a stage be targeted in the post-1997 era. Among the criteria for monetary union, fiscal integration and a high degree of factor mobility are often regarded as the most important.[38] According to the framework of "one country, two systems," however, fiscal integration between Hong Kong and mainland China is not supposed to take place as there will be no fiscal transfers to smooth out asymmetrical shocks to the two economies. Moreover, labour mobility across the border is to be strictly controlled. Hong Kong cannot export its unemployment to the mainland, nor vice versa.[39]

From the perspective of optimality, the unification of two currencies of different qualities produces a net social benefit only if the "inferior currency" is eliminated. This is why, in a multi-currency environment such as the European Union, the "best currency" (the German mark) is always seen as the model for the unified currency (the Euro). In the case of China and Hong Kong, it is extremely unlikely that the *Renminbi* would be regarded as an "inferior" currency to be eliminated. Because of the political reality, a system of one currency could only mean the demise of the HK dollar. This will hardly be beneficial to Hong Kong,[40] and its benefit to China is also in serious doubt.

Moreover, the net benefit is unlikely to become significant over time, particularly if the *Renminbi*, in its further progress towards full convertibility, is increasingly seen as a stable currency by international traders and investors. As is well known, the benefit of unifying two stable currencies is very low. All in all, the arrangement of "one country, two currencies" is perfectly consistent with the framework of "one country, two systems." There is no good economic argument for unifying the HK dollar and the *Renminbi* after 1997.

Notes

1. See *Economic Reporter*, 12 February 1996, pp. 49–51.
2. For the text of the 1980 regulations, see Li Fen et al., *China's Exchange Control and Banking Practice* (China Financial Publishing House, 1991), pp. 161–72.
3. See *China Economic News*, 2 September 1996, pp. 6–10; and 9 September 1996, pp. 7–8.
4. "China Announces Convertibility of RMB under Current Account within 1996," *China Economic News*, 15 July 1996, pp. 3–4.
5. See "A Decisive Step Toward RMB's Convertibility," *China Economic News*, 16 December 1996, pp. 1–2.
6. *Economic Reporter*, Hong Kong, 2 December 1996, p. 19.
7. "Bank Forex Settlement for FFEs"; "Banker on Significance of Eased Forex Control," *China Economic News*, 15 July 1996, pp. 1–2 and pp. 6–7.
8. See Tsang Shu-ki, "Towards Full Convertibility? China's Foreign Exchange Reforms," *China Information*, Vol. IX, No. 1 (Summer 1994), pp. 1–41; "Financial Restructuring," in *China Review 1995*, edited by Lo Chi Kin, Suzanne Pepper and Tsui Kai Yuen (Hong Kong: The Chinese University Press, 1995), chapter 21; and "The Economy," in *China Review 1996*, edited by Maurice Brosseau, Suzanne Pepper and Tsang Shu-ki (Hong Kong: The Chinese University Press, 1996), chapter 8.
9. In 1993, officials and economists were talking about ten years as the time frame for current account convertibility. The span was shortened to six years in early March 1994, then down to four or three years as the largely unexpected progress became obvious. See the first two papers in Note 8.

10. In any case, the 1994 reform was never intended to be a "big bang" despite popular misconceptions. See Tsang Shu-ki, "Financial Restructuring" (Note 8).
11. See the papers cited in Note 8.
12. Saleh M. Nsouli, "Current Account Convertibility: Anachronism or Transition?," in *Currency Convertibility in the Middle East and North Africa*, edited by Manuel Guitán and Saleh M. Nsouli (International Monetary Fund, 1996).
13. *Ming Pao*, Hong Kong, 26 November 1996.
14. The SAEC was renamed the State Administration for Foreign Exchange (SAFE) towards the end of 1996.
15. See Note 3 and Chan Pak-cheong, "Dalu zuijin jinrong biange ji Taishang yinying zhi dao" (Recent Financial Reforms on the Mainland and Appropriate Reactions by Taiwan Merchants), *Liangan jingmao* (Cross-Strait Economics and Trade), 10 August 1996, pp. 3–6. Chan's summary of the relevant regulations, whilst useful, is not 100% accurate.
16. "Banker on Significance of Eased Forex Control," *China Economic News*, 15 July 1996, p. 6.
17. See Chan Pak-cheong (Note 15) and Wang Tai-yun, "Dalu waihui guanli de zuixin guiding" (The Latest Regulations on Foreign Exchange Management on the Mainland), *Liangan Jingmao*, 10 January 1997, pp. 4–7.
18. Tsang Shu-ki, "Financial Restructuring," (Note 8).
19. *China Statistical Yearbook 1996*, Tables 16–13; *China's Latest Economic Statistics*, February 1997, p. 15.
20. "China: Foreign Debt Increases by 9% in 1996," *Business Briefing*, BBC Monitoring Service, 5 February 1997.
21. Lin Guijun, "Dui woguo yinhangjian waihui shichang yunxing de fenxi" (An Analysis of the Operation of the Interbank Foreign Exchange Market of Our Country), *Guoji maoyi wenti* (Problems of International Trade), No. 3 (1996), pp. 43–50.
22. See, for example, Ronald McKinnon, "Comment 2" on Sebastian Edwards's paper in *Economic Liberalization in Developing Countries*, edited by Armeane M. Choksi and Demetris Papageorgiou (Oxford: Basil Blackwell, 1986).
23. Sebastian Edwards, "The Order of Liberalization of the Current and Capital Accounts of the Balance of Payments," in Choksi and Papageorgiou (eds) (Note 22).
24. Ibid.
25. Jacob Frenkel, "The Order of Economic Liberalization: Discussion," in *Economic Policy in a World of Change*, edited by K. Brunner and A. H. Meltzer (Amsterdam: North-Holland, 1982).
26. Moshin Kahn and Roberto Zahler, "The Macroeconomic Effects of Changes

in Barriers to Trade and Capital Flows: A Simulation Analysis," *IMF Staff Papers*, 1983.

27. See his comment on Sebastian Edwards (Note 22).
28. Note that the inflow of foreign capital in China since 1992 has already been phenomenal, without much liberalization in the capital account.
29. The trade surplus was US$ 5.35 billion, US$ 16.69 billion and US$ 12.24 billion in 1994, 1995 and 1996, respectively. One complication is that of processing trade, i.e. trade in intermediate goods reached 50% of total trade in 1996. Processing could drive a wedge between China's trade balance and foreign exchange balance. A classic example is that of Guangdong in 1993. A trade surplus of US$ 7.13 billion contrasted with a deficit of US$ 3.4 billion in the province's foreign exchange balance. For every US$ 100 of export in 1993, Guangdong received only US$ 26 in hard currency. See Cheng Yuk-shing and Tsang Shu-ki, "The Economic Link-up of Guangdong and Hong Kong: Structural and Developmental Problems," paper presented at the *International Conference on China and the Asia Pacific Economy*, organized by the Department of Economics, University of Queensland, Brisbane, Australia, 14–16 July 1996.
30. *The Order of Economic Liberalization* (Baltsmore: John Hopkins University Press, 1991).
31. Joseph Yam, "Hong Kong's Monetary Scene: Myths and Realities," speech at the Bank of England Seminar on *Hong Kong Monetary Arrangements through 1997*, London, 10 September 1996.
32. Chen Yuan, "Monetary Relations between China and Hong Kong," speech at the Bank of England Seminar on *Hong Kong Monetary Arrangements through 1997*, London, 10 September 1996.
33. Edgardo Barandiaran and Tsang Shu-ki, "One Country, Two Currencies: Monetary Relations between Hong Kong and China," in *Hong Kong under Chinese Rule: The Economic and Political Implication of Reversion*, edited by Warren I. Cohen and Li Zhao (Cambridge: Cambridge University Press, 1997, forthcoming).
34. This point is borne out by two quantitative studies. See Shu-ki Tsang and Yue Ma, "Simulating the Effects of Foreign Capital in an Open Macroeconometric Model of China," *Economic Modelling*, 1997, forthcoming; and Yue Ma, Shu-ki Tsang and Shu-hung Tang, "The Impact of the China Factor on the pre-1997 Hong Kong Economy: A Macroeconometric Analysis," paper presented at the Conference on Economic Developments in China, organized by the British Economic Association of Chinese Scholars, London School of Economics, London, 17–18 December 1996.
35. Tsang Shu-ki, "The Political Economy of Greater China," *Asia Pacific Business Review*, Vol. 2, No. 3 (Spring 1996), pp. 23–43.
36. See Industry Department, Hong Kong Government, *1994 Survey of External*

Investments in Hong Kong; and Census and Statistics Department, Hong Kong Government, *External Investments in Hong Kong's Non-manufacturing Sectors*. For an analysis of the significance of China's investments in Hong Kong, see Yue Ma, Shu-ki Tsang and Shu-hung Tang, "The Impact of the China Factor on the pre-1997 Hong Kong Economy" (Note 34).

37. The theory of optimum currency areas was pioneered by Mundell and extended by McKinnon and others. The classic article is R. A. Mundell, "Theory of Optimum Currency Areas," *American Economic Review*, Vol. 51, No. 4 (September 1961), pp. 657–65. The push towards monetary union in Europe has prompted a new generation of models and analysis. For an update, see George S. Tavlas, "The 'New' Theory of Optimum Currency Areas," *The World Economy*, Vol. 16, No. 6 (November 1993), pp. 663–85.
38. See George S. Tavlas (Note 37).
39. I have emphasized these aspects of the economic relations between Hong Kong and China and argued that the Hong Kong economy should maintain a degree of "coherence" in the post-1997 era. Because of the constraints of the "one country, two systems" framework, Hong Kong should not be "Manhattanized" or "totally de-industrialized," to become just another, albeit very important, city economy in China. See Tsang Shu-ki, "The Economy," in *The Other Hong Kong Report 1994*, edited by Donald McMillan and Man Si-wai, (Hong Kong: The Chinese University Press, 1994), pp. 125–48; and Tsang Shu-ki, "Economy" (in Chinese), in *Hong Kong in Focus 1997*, M. K. Lee et al. (Hong Kong: The Commercial Press, 1997), chapter 4.
40. The linked exchange rate system under which the Hong Kong dollar is pegged with the US dollar has been relatively robust since its inception in October 1983. Problems persist, but they can be solved with various moves that fall short of any fundamental overhaul. There is little reason to seek protection through unification with the *Renminbi* in the foreseeable future. See Tsang Shu-ki, *A Study of the Linked Exchange Rate System and Policy Options for Hong Kong*, a report commissioned by the Hong Kong Policy Research Institute, October 1996. An abridged version of the report appears as "Linked Rate System: Through 1997 and into the 21st Century," in *The Other Hong Kong Report 1996*, edited by Nyaw Mee-kau and Li Si-ming (Hong Kong: The Chinese University Press, 1996), chapter 11.

11

Fiscal and Banking Reform: The 1994 Fiscal Reform Revisited

Barry Naughton

Financial reform will assume special prominence in China during the final years of the 1990s. This prominence is partly due to the fact that many other aspects of economic reform have already been successfully completed. Reforms began by dismantling planning and opening up markets for goods, with the result that the economy "grew out of the plan." In the 1990s, labour markets have also developed vigorously. Migration and labour mobility have increased substantially, and unemployment has also increased. With a much larger and more complex economy, and the success of the initial phases of reform, reform of the financial and ownership system have now moved to the top of the agenda. But in these areas, China faces enormous challenges, and the ultimate outcome of reforms is still uncertain.

Since 1994, China has created an institutional framework that can potentially govern a modernized and much more efficient financial system. Important fiscal reforms were introduced at the beginning of 1994. Ongoing changes in the banking system envisage the conversion of state banks to independent commercial banks, and the segregation of noncommercial functions into new institutions. However, the new financial framework that has been erected remains to a certain extent an empty façade. That is, institutional relationships and procedures have been defined, but they do not yet actually govern the operations of the system, nor do they determine the real flow of resources. The challenge facing the Chinese system is to convert the rules of operation from a prescription for a reformed system into a description of the actual system. Having established the forms, it is necessary to infuse them with content.

The stakes are high. Real reform in this area is essential in order to guide China's economy onto a full market basis. Substantial improvements in economic efficiency depend on the ability to carry through meaningful financial reform. Moreover, without successful reform, there is a significant danger of financial crisis. Financial reform of all kinds, but especially fiscal reform, will play a major role in determining the ultimate relationship between the government and the economy, and between central and local governments. This chapter will consider some of these issues in the context first of fiscal reform and, subsequently, of banking sector reform.

Fiscal Reform

The 1994 fiscal reform was an ambitious project with three main objectives. The most immediate and urgent objective was to halt the erosion of budgetary revenues and, especially, the erosion of central government revenues. Budgetary revenues as a share of gross domestic product (GDP) had declined annually since 1978, and the main reason that Chinese central government leaders were willing to embark on major fiscal reforms was the protracted fiscal crisis which they were facing. Secondly, reform was intended to establish a new fiscal relationship between the central and local governments. The existing system of fiscal contracting, under which provincial governments essentially bargained with the central government to determine net tax payments, was deemed no longer viable.[1] The objective of the reform was to create a system under which revenues would be assigned to different levels of government according to clear and transparent principles. Thirdly, reform aimed to establish a more efficient taxation system. This implies a broader, more inclusive, tax base along with lower, more uniform tax rates. In other words, the tax system should contribute to a "level playing field," with predictable rules and a moderate tax rate.

The three objectives are not completely separate. They are tied together by the changes they envisage in the roles of state-owned enterprises and local governments. Under the pre-reform economic system, most budgetary revenues had come from state-owned enterprises (SOE) in the industrial sector. In turn, most industrial SOEs were under the tutelage of local governments, for whom they produced revenue. As a result of economic reform, SOEs lost their protected position, and their ability to provide surpluses to the government budget steadily eroded. But at the same time, the government had been unable to tap into potential revenue sources in the rapidly growing sectors of the economy. Private businesses, township and village enterprises, and foreign trade and investment all remained lightly taxed. It had already become impossible to rely on the SOEs as government "cash cows." Halting fiscal decline meant spreading the tax burden more equitably across the economy. Thus, the goal of a more efficient taxation system was compatible with the objective of halting fiscal erosion.

At the same time, local governments had and have great discretionary powers in the Chinese system. They use this discretionary power not only to intervene in local economies (in ways that are sometimes good and sometimes bad), but also to deflect budgetary revenues away from central government coffers and towards their own priority uses. Thus, reducing the discretionary control of local governments over budgetary revenues is also key to shoring up the central government's financial position. The three objectives of fiscal reform are therefore compatible, and the reforms are internally consistent.

Writing in this publication two years ago, Christine Wong gave the 1994 reform high marks for comprehensiveness and transparency and for simplification of the revenue system, while pointing out a number of problems that might undermine effective implementation.[2] Two years later, Wong's misgivings about implementation have been confirmed. Through 1996, not one of the three objectives of fiscal reform has been unambiguously achieved. Some progress has been registered in potentially arresting fiscal decline and creating a level playing field, because the new system has been put in place and gradually strengthened, and it continues to be a sound framework upon which to build. Less progress is evident in putting the relationship between central and local governments on a sound footing. The following sections briefly review the content of the 1994 reform, and review accomplishments with respect to each of the three objectives.

The 1994 Fiscal Reform

The fiscal reform has been described in detail elsewhere,[3] and is not to be described fully here. There were three crucial elements: new taxes, a tax assignment and sharing system, and a new central government taxation agency. The most important of the new taxes was the value-added tax (VAT) levied on most manufactured goods at the uniform rate of 17%. Very small private enterprises without regular bookkeeping systems were to pay a tax of 6% of gross sales in lieu of VAT. In addition, a 33% profit tax was introduced, with uniform rates for state, collective and private enterprises. The system of personal income taxes was unified and made slightly more rigorous. A "consumption tax" (actually a luxury or excise tax) was introduced for cigarettes, alcohol and a few other luxuries. A number of minor local taxes were introduced (or more accurately, regularized). In return, the previous system of industrial and commercial taxes was abolished, and the SOE profit contract system was eliminated.

These new taxes were assigned to various levels of government. The central government had complete claim on the consumption tax, customs duties, and most direct and indirect taxes on central government-controlled sectors (i.e., railroads, financial institutions, and some large centrally controlled enterprises). Provincial governments now collected and controlled direct taxes on local enterprises (i.e., profit taxes), as well as a number of relatively modest taxes, including real estate and property taxes, and pollution and resource fees. The key provision was the designation of most VAT revenues as "shared income," which would be collected by the central government tax agency, but with 75% of the take going to the central government and 25% to the local government. The VAT and consumption (luxury) taxes became the main source of central government revenue, accounting for three-quarters of the total.[4] Because of their key role in the new system (especially for the central government), they are often referred to in the Chinese literature as "the two taxes."

In order to collect "the two taxes," a new central government taxation authority was created. Under the previous system, most tax revenues had been collected by local government tax bureaus, and localities had then transferred funds to the central government. Under the new system, the central government first collected the bulk of revenues — including all VAT revenues — and then shared them with the provinces. Clearly, under such a system, local governments had little incentive to collect the "two taxes." As a result, it was imperative that a central government tax agency be created and given substantial authority.

Assessment: Halting Fiscal Erosion

The tax reform has not reversed the process of fiscal erosion. Before fiscal reform, budgetary revenues as a share of GDP had declined steadily from 35% in 1978 to 14% in 1993. In 1994, the first year of fiscal reform implementation, revenues slid to 12% of GDP, and then to 11.3% of GDP in 1995. The budget for 1996 called only for a modest increase in nominal revenues, which would have implied further erosion of the revenue share. In fact, according to preliminary figures, budgetary revenues increased 18% in 1996, slightly faster than nominal GDP, which grew 17.4%. As Figure 1 shows, this implies that the revenue to GDP ratio will have stabilized, inching up to 11.4% of GDP in 1996.[5] This is still an extremely low ratio in comparison with other countries, even other developing countries. In a sample of 22 developing countries in the late 1980s, government expenditures were 32% of GDP on average, compared with about 14% currently in China (expenditures exceed revenues by the size of the budget deficit, about 2% of GDP in China). Other East Asian newly industrialized economies have relatively low revenue-to-GDP ratios as well (17.8% for Hong Kong; 21.2% for Taiwan; 18.5% for Korea), but none is as low as China.[6]

Figure 1. Budgetary Revenues (Share of GDP)

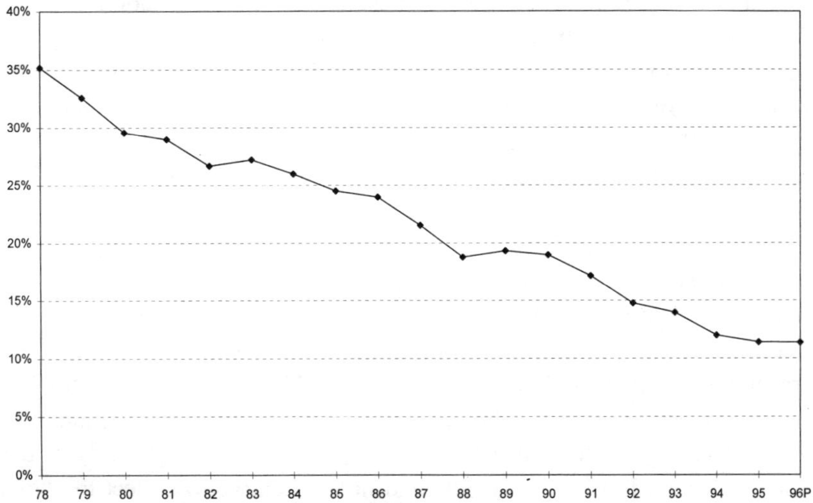

Although budgetary revenues did not increase as a share of GDP in 1996, stabilization of revenues represents a more impressive achievement than what might initially appear. This is true because of the dismal performance of SOEs in 1996. Through 1995, SOE profits, primarily from industrial SOEs, continued to be an important source of budgetary revenues. SOE profit taxes still accounted for 12% of total net revenues.[7] Hammered by a tight credit policy and increasing competition from township and village enterprises (TVEs), private firms, and foreign-invested enterprises (FIE), SOEs had a very bad year: profits of state independent accounting industrial enterprises declined 55% in the first eleven months.[8] The fact that budgetary revenues grew at the same pace as GDP, and more rapidly than budgeted, despite the dismal performance of SOEs, shows that the tax reform was achieving its goal of broadening the tax base.

This achievement would be an important reversal of established trends in the reform era. Generally speaking, China's taxation authorities before 1996 have been unable to tap into revenues in the most rapidly growing sectors of the economy. For example, in 1995, individual income tax collected was only 0.2% of GDP; and income tax on collectively owned enterprises was also only 0.2% of GDP (compared to 1.3% of GDP for SOE income tax). Precise figures on the amount of income tax paid by foreign-invested enterprises do not seem to be available, but one source notes that FIEs pay an average income tax rate of only 5% in the special economic zones, only 9% in other open coastal zones, and 15% in inland areas, all substantially less than the statutory 33% rate that applies to SOEs.[9] Unable to collect direct taxes on corporate or individual income, the budget has become increasingly dependent on indirect taxes (taxes on sales or commodity turnover). Indirect taxes accounted for more than three-quarters of total revenues by 1995. Even with respect to indirect taxation, the burden on the state sector had traditionally been heavier: SOEs accounted for 73% of total budgetary revenues in 1995, while collective firms accounted for 16% and the private sector for 6%. This is despite the fact that SOEs account for only 34% of industrial output, and industry is the most heavily taxed sector.[10] If fiscal authorities are unable to tap into the rapidly growing sectors of the economy, the budget will inevitably shrink as a share of GDP and become dependent on a narrow range of possible revenue sources. It is this dilemma that appears to have been partially addressed in 1996. The stabilization of revenues could not have occurred without a substantial broadening of the tax base with respect to 1995.

Thus, while the aggregate trends do not at first appear strikingly different, 1996 nonetheless appears to reflect substantially changed circumstances from the previous years. Indeed, it is not hard to see why budgetary revenues declined as a share of GDP in 1994–1995, immediately following the adoption of the new system. Many tax collection procedures for the VAT were unfamiliar, and appropriate record-keeping and necessary paperwork and accounting personnel were not always available. The fiscal reform actually reduced the incentive of local tax bureaus to collect VAT and other taxes, since localities were now to receive only a small portion of incremental taxes collected. It is essential that the central tax agency takes responsibility for tax collection and behaves as an agent of the central government. But, central tax offices were only gradually created during the course of 1994, and most were simply the original local agencies with an additional nameplate on the door. Finally, localities made an extra effort collecting taxes in 1993, in order to insure that their base figures for subsequent tax sharing (discussed below) be relatively high — accordingly, there was some inevitable drop-off in revenue effort in the following year. Thus, it is not surprising that revenues dropped in 1994.

The continued erosion of revenues in 1995 must then be explained by the wide range of concessions that were made in order to ensure the smooth adoption of reform. During the run-up to the reform, Vice-Premier Zhu Rongji, who was in charge of the design and implementation of the reform, toured the provinces lining up support and allaying fears. As part of this intensely political process, Zhu was forced to make a number of explicit and implicit concessions.[11] Concessions to foreign-invested enterprises were the most explicit and public. Since most FIEs were operating under some form of concessionary taxation or special agreement, in order to retain the confidence of foreign investors, China was forced to promise that taxes on existing FIEs would not be raised. A series of regulations were publicly promulgated. In fact, similar concessions were made to many domestic SOEs, although no public regulations were issued. Existing tax concessions were thus grandfathered into the reformed system. Worse, as the financial position of SOEs began to deteriorate in 1995, there was a strong tendency to continue SOE tax breaks and tolerate growth in unpaid back taxes. Thus, from January to October 1995, VAT and consumption tax arrears increased from RMB10 billion to 23 billion, a sum equal to 0.4% of GDP.[12]

Detailed evidence for 1996 is not yet available to enable us to state confidently exactly how the tax base was broadened in that year. There are, however, strong indications that much of the progress was achieved in the foreign trade sector. Until 1996, the foreign trade sector was extremely lightly taxed. Indeed, despite China's dramatic entry into the world economy, trade taxes actually *declined* from 0.8% of GDP in 1978 to only 0.5% in 1995![13] The explanation is that a large proportion of China's imports enter the country duty-free (either because they are imported for export production or because duties are exempted for government approved investment projects), that the actual duty collection rate is only one-sixth of the nominal tariff rate.[14] During 1996, China began to reverse the trends towards lower trade taxes by increasing coverage of import taxes, and by cutting back on tax rebates given to exporters (discussed below). A precise accounting for these tax increases is not yet possible, but their combined effect would have been large enough to cover much of the increase in budgetary income.[15]

Although the 1996 stabilization of tax revenue represents an important achievement, it is only the beginning of a prolonged process of establishing fiscal health in China. In the first place, if it turns out that stabilization was due only to changing policy towards the export sector, that would imply that serious problems of unequal treatment and pervasive tax evasion in the domestic sector remain unaddressed. Furthermore, the budgetary share in China has sunk so low that it must recover at least a few percentage points of GDP before anything like fiscal stability can be declared. Indeed, there is some evidence that the continuing reductions in budgetary resources up to this point are beginning to have a significant impact on China's social development. Much of the reduction in budgetary expenditures has been accommodated by reducing government investment and military outlays, and by reducing the subsidy burden. Reductions have been far less drastic in the broad category of ordinary civilian outlays (i.e., all outlays except those for fixed investment, or for military or subsidy purposes). Throughout the 1980s, civilian current expenditures hovered around 10% of GDP, which included administrative expenses, as well as outlays for health, education, and welfare. However, since the early 1990s, civilian current expenditures have begun to slip below the level previously sustained and, by 1995, amounted to only 8.4% of GDP. Similar trends are apparent for specific sub-categories of expenditure as well. Government recurrent health expenditures were maintained at around 0.5% of GDP through the mid-1980s; subsequently, they had declined to 0.3% of GDP in 1993. Total government health expenditures (excluding outlays for the insurance programme that covers government employees) were still 0.8% of GDP in 1986, but only 0.5% in 1993. Current educational expenditures were still slightly over 2% of GDP in 1985, but had declined to 1.7% in 1994. Moreover, there is some preliminary evidence that these reductions in relative government expenditures are showing up in measurable indicators of the health of the population. China's impressive achievements in terms of infant mortality rates and life expectancies have not been significantly improved upon in the decade since 1985, despite substantial growth in household income.[16]

Assessment: Restructuring Central-Local Relations

The 1994 reform certainly succeeded in reclassifying revenues and boosting the centre's share of revenue collection. Excluding borrowing, central government collections tripled between 1993 and 1994, jumping from 95.75 billion to just over 290 billion, while local collections dropped from 339 billion to 231 billion (Table 1).[17] The central share of non-debt income jumped from 22% to 56%.[18] Figure 2 shows that in aggregate terms, central-local fiscal relations have now entered their third period since the reform era began. During the first period, from 1979 through 1984, central government expenditures were more than 50% of total expenditures, but central government revenues were much less than this, initially less than 20% of total revenues. Thus, the central government was largely dependent on remittances from local governments. Between 1985 and 1993, during the second fiscal period, the central and local governments were in rough overall balance. The share of revenue collected by the central government was equivalent to the central government share of expenditures. During this period, the central government redistributed revenues from surplus to deficit provinces, but was not on balance dependent on local revenues. However, the central share of both revenues and expenditures was declining slowly throughout this period. The third period began with the fiscal reform in 1994. Central government revenue collections jumped, and local governments now became dependent on remittances from the central government, primarily in the form of VAT collected by the centre and subsequently shared with local governments. Thus, in terms of the means of collection and process of sharing revenues, the 1994 tax reform created a fundamentally new relationship between central and local governments.

However, the share of central government expenditures in total non-debt related expenditures did not increase significantly in 1994. Indeed, it

Table 1. Central and Local Shares of Budgetary Revenues and Expenditures

(Billion RMB; Percent of Total)

	Revenues			Expenditures		
	Centre	Local	Central share	Centre	Local	Central share
1979	12.25	94.55	11.5%	65.508	62.671	51.1%
1980	13.06	91.16	12.5%	66.681	56.202	54.3%
1981	15.164	86.472	14.9%	62.565	51.276	55.0%
1982	17.458	86.549	16.8%	65.181	57.817	53.0%
1983	29.265	87.694	25.0%	75.96	64.992	53.9%
1984	44.717	97.739	31.4%	89.333	80.77	52.5%
1985	61.8	115.85	34.8%	79.525	120.9	39.7%
1986	77.84	134.36	36.7%	83.636	136.86	37.9%
1987	73.58	146.31	33.5%	84.563	141.66	37.4%
1988	77.47	158.25	32.9%	84.504	164.62	33.9%
1989	82.25	184.24	30.9%	88.877	193.5	31.5%
1990	99.24	194.47	33.8%	100.447	207.912	32.6%
1991	93.83	221.12	29.8%	109.081	229.58	32.2%
1992	97.95	25.39	28.1%	117.044	257.18	31.3%
1993	95.751	339.144	22.0%	131.206	333.024	28.3%
1994	290.65	231.16	55.7%	175.443	403.819	30.3%
1995	325.662	298.558	52.2%	199.539	482.833	29.2%
1996						

Does not include borrowing or SOE losses.

Source: *Statistical Yearbook of China 1996*, p. 235.

Figure 2. Central Share of Revenues and Expenditures (excluding borrowing)

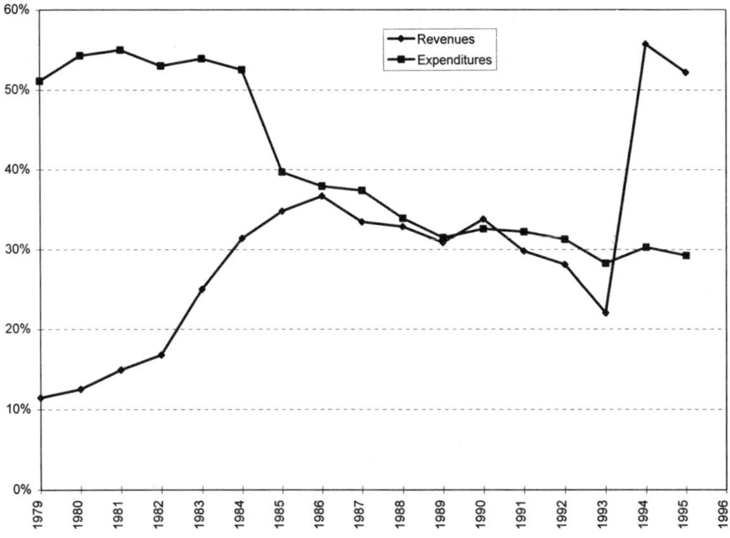

was not intended that increased central control of revenues would translate immediately into an increased central share of expenditure. During the first three years of the reform system (i.e., 1994–1996), division of ultimate control over financial resources between central and local governments was actually determined not by the assignment of taxes, but rather by two commitments made by the central government. The first commitment was that no province would receive less than its (nominal) 1993 revenues in the subsequent three years. The second commitment was that of the *increase* in central government and shared (VAT) revenues in any given province after 1993, the central government would rebate 30% to that province. As a result, the central government now rebates about half of its total collections to the provinces. It was these commitments — along with a few other minor side payments and adjustments — that determined the actual division of resources in the years 1994 through 1996. In fact, however, neither of these commitments was worth very much. The first commitment was given in nominal terms, so its value has been severely eroded by cumulative inflation in excess of 40% since the implementation of the new fiscal system. The second commitment was, at the very least, substantially weakened in late 1995, as central government officials discovered that their financial position was not improving as much as hoped. There were reports that the provision would be eliminated, but it is unclear what the actual outcome has been.[19]

Such agreements have in any case been swamped by trends in the collection of revenue by central and local level governments. In the budgets for both 1995 and 1996, it was projected that central and local level revenue collections would grow at about the same pace, around 12% per year. In fact, during both years, local tax collections grew much more rapidly (at 29% and 25%, respectively) than did central tax collections (12% both years). The differential does not appear to be due to any inherent differences in the "buoyancy" of these taxes (that is, the rate at which tax collections should increase for any given increase in GDP), but rather reflects the difference in the effective incentives to collect the taxes. Local governments are much more effective at getting their taxes actually collected than is the central government.The 1997 budget again predicts that central and local collections will go at approximately the same rate, despite the experience of the past two years.[20]

As a result of these changes, there is now no clear or straightforward basis by which central government payments to provinces can be calculated. It would appear that, as in the old system, they are essentially based on *ad hoc* bargaining. The difference is that now, at least in theory, since the central government collects the bulk of revenues in the first place, it ought to be in a stronger bargaining position *vis-à-vis* the provinces. But whether central government's bargaining power has in fact been significantly enhanced depends on a number of factors. One is whether the central government really has command of an effective tax collection agency. For the initial year of 1994, it is clear that this was *not* the case: when first established, the offices of the central tax agency continued to function more as offshoots of the provincial governments to which they had traditionally been subordinate. But, the experience of 1995 and 1996 seems to indicate that the central government still does not have effective control over the tax bureaucracy. The crucial power to define revenue collection categories and assign collected revenues still seems to belong to provincial governments in most instances.

A particular case of the difficulty of coordinating local and central government interests, and one of the causes of the continuing squeeze on central government revenues, has been the fate of the VAT rebate programme for exports. Many countries rebate VAT for exports and, then, collect a VAT-substitute tax on imports. This enhances export competitiveness, and is allowed by the rules of the World Trade Organization. If trade is balanced, exports equal imports, and there is little net effect on government revenues. Along with the 1994 fiscal reform, China adopted a complete VAT rebate for exports by domestic firms.[21] Since taxes on imports are central government revenue, the central government was also made responsible for paying the VAT rebates. In practice, claims for export-related VAT rebates exploded, in part because China's exports grew extremely rapidly, and in part because of widespread fraud and phony invoicing. By the end of 1994, the programme had accumulated arrears of RMB 29 billion; by late 1995, arrears had reached 60 billion, or about nine months worth of rebates.[22] Indeed, given low VAT compliance, there were clearly cases of exports in which the government was rebating more VAT on an export product than it had ever collected. Under the circumstances, there was no choice but to reduce the drawback rate, notwithstanding the adverse impact on China's exports. The actual rebate rate was reduced in two stages from the full 17% to 9% by early 1996. Indeed, scaling back the rebate was one of the main causes of the recovery of revenues during 1996. In any case, though, the episode provides additional evidence that actual taxation is to a large extent determined by local government interests, even when the type of tax (import duties) are nominally a central government monopoly.

The most fundamental problem underlying the difficulties in working out a rule-based division of central and local finances is the continuing inability to specify the principles upon which it should be based. A number of commentators have noted that tax sharing systems ought to be based on assignment of expenditure responsibility in the first place.[23] This has not been done in the Chinese reform. In fact, less frequently noted is that the recentralizing impulse of the reform actually contradicts the *de facto* division of expenditure responsibilities that has evolved in China over the years. It was noted above that the decline in budgetary expenditures over the years has been accommodated by shedding investment, subsidy and military expenditures, while protecting civilian current outlays. However, it is precisely in the area of civilian current outlays that local governments have predominant responsibilities. The bulk of education, health, and administrative outlays (more than 80%) are assumed by governments below the central level. These responsibilities are already severely constrained by financial shortfalls, as described above. Realistically, the central government cannot hope to implement a more centralized budgetary system unless it is also prepared to assume responsibility for a much greater share of these outlays. Thus far, the central government has not been willing or able to propose a realistic programme to assume these responsibilities.[24]

In a related fashion, the tax system still does not allow local governments to determine the tax *rates* which they apply even to local taxes. Local governments do not have taxing autonomy, even in areas which have been assigned to local government jurisdiction. This limitation has a number of important implications. First, it is virtually impossible for provinces to resolve issues relating to sub-provincial finance and the distribution of revenues among sub-provincial governments. Yet, the situation there replicates the old relationship between national and provincial governments that fiscal reform was designed to eliminate. For example, in Shandong, 56% of provincial fiscal revenues are collected at the county level or below, but they are then shared upward with the provincial government in accordance with remittance targets and sharing ratios inherited from the former system. The provincial government redistributes revenues from the more prosperous coastal counties to the poorer western counties, but the redistribution is *ad hoc* and influenced by multiple bargaining considerations. There is a need to proceed with further reform of sub-provincial fiscal relations, but while a number of partial "experiments" are underway, no promising experiment is close to widespread implementation.[25]

Furthermore, the high degree of nominal centralization does not lead to real centralized control of resources. Instead, because the central government is unable to effectively monitor compliance, it leads to a proliferation of hard to see and hard to control local revenue sources. The actual degree of decentralization of the system is much greater than the nominal centralization. Indeed, since the central government has been unable to commit to a realistic rule-based system, local governments have no choice but to continue to protect their own interests through whatever stratagems and evasions they can devise. Both sides would be better off if there was a clear rule-based system to adhere to, but neither has been able to commit to such an approach unilaterally.[26] Indeed, local governments seem to be increasingly skilled at setting aside funds outside the budgetary system. According to official data, extra-budgetary funds controlled by governments and government agencies (excluding enterprises) have increased from around 3% of GDP in the mid-1980s to 4% of GDP in 1993 and 1994.[27] Most of these funds ought to be included in budgetary accounts under a rule-based and transparent system. Indeed, the 1997 budget report declares that extra-budgetary construction funds for power plant and railway construction will be incorporated in the budget from now on. This is the logical place to begin, since these are the most regularized and "tax-like" of all the extra-budgetary funds. But, it is only a beginning in the long-term process of making extra-budgetary funds more regular and transparent.[28]

Assessment: Creating a Level Playing Field

From the preceding discussion, it will be clear that the objective of creating a more predictable and impartial tax system has not been unambiguously achieved. The system continues to be rife with special concessions and arrangements, tax breaks and hidden subsidies. Moreover, the arrangements that tie enterprise income tax to the level of government with jurisdiction over the enterprise creates ongoing (and in some ways intensified) distortions. Local governments try to protect "their" enterprises, and they battle for jurisdiction over profitable enterprises. Both these problems remain despite the fact that comprehensive reforms should alter local government incentives in this respect.[28]

Nevertheless, there are signs of progress. In the first place, the simple assertion of uniform tax rates for all producers regardless of ownership system has an important positive effect on the operation of the system. In this sense, the new fiscal system is at least partially responsible for the explosion of private activity in the years since 1993. The actual tax burden on private activity has almost certainly increased somewhat, but this has been more than compensated for by the declaration of legitimacy for private enterprise implicit in the assessment of equal tax rates. Even if, in practice, many SOEs may achieve short-run competitive advantage from tax remissions or hidden subsidies, this is far less harmful to the economy than a system under which discrimination is built into the tax and legal code.

Conclusion: The Fiscal Reform of 1994 in Retrospect

Inevitably, we are left with a paradoxical assessment of the 1994 reform. In a fundamental sense, the reform has achieved none of its immediate objectives. It has been unable to halt the erosion in government revenues, has not provided a firm rule-based system to regulate central and local government relations, and is far from guaranteeing a level playing field for economic activity. Yet, in spite of these limitations, the fiscal reform still retains promise: it may still turn out to be a successful reform.

In the first place, the underlying principles of the fiscal reform are so far superior to those that underlay the previous fiscal systems that simply to enunciate the principles represents a significant step forward. This fiscal system has the potential to serve as the basis for a modern revenue system in a market economy: the previous system could never have served the same function. Secondly, in a number of respects, the ultimate outcome of the fiscal reforms will depend on gradual changes in the balance of power between central and local government agencies. In particular, the central government's attempt to reclaim the power to tax is something that can only be established incrementally through assertion and repeated exercise of that power. In particular, it depends on the gradual strengthening of the central tax authority and steady improvement of its efficiency.

It is worth stressing the importance of this change. By the end of the 1970s, the Chinese system had evolved into one in which all government functions were concentrated into a single hierarchy. That is, although the provincial governments were formally subordinate to the central government, the central government had no independent administrative agencies that could operate in the provinces. Banks, courts, and tax agencies were all subordinate first to the provincial government, and only through the provincial government could the theoretical sovereignty of the central government be exercised. With only a single instrument, the centre's ability to achieve multiple objectives in different regions was severely compromised. The central tax agency is the first agency of the central government empowered to operate independently in the provinces. As such, its gradual strengthening has the potential to contribute to a fundamental restructuring of political power in China. As noted above, however, that restructuring is unlikely to be successful without a more thorough rethinking of central and local expenditure responsibilities than has heretofore taken place.

Finally, the new fiscal system provides a basis for a gradual tightening of the rules with regard to tax collection, and for a consistent emphasis on making procedures uniform. Indeed, one can see throughout the Chinese system an emphasis on consistent application of existing rules. Both the 1996 and 1997 reports of the Finance Minister, Liu Zhongli, are full of exhortations to tighten fiscal discipline and make practice uniform. As part of the adoption of the 1994 fiscal reform, localities were explicitly allowed to continue tax exemptions for two years. The fact that permission for tax breaks expired in 1996 obviously does not mean that procedures will thereby become uniform, but it does provide a basis for a renewed insistence on fiscal discipline. Technological improvements, particularly the integration of computer processing of tax returns and VAT receipts, can significantly improve the tax take, and are currently being stressed by Chinese tax officials.[30] In a related area, that of trade taxes and the treatment of foreign invested enterprises, a parallel effort is underway to reduce tax exemptions on imports, and gradually unite the treatment of domestic and foreign-invested enterprises. In the international arena, one of the objectives is to unify treatment in order to guarantee that FIEs receive "national treatment" (that is, tax and regulatory treatment no worse than that accorded to domestic enterprises), which is one of the requirements of membership in the World Trade Organization. More broadly, it appears that there is growing recognition that only a consistent emphasis on uniform treatment can arrest the tendency to a proliferation of special deals and concessions. Once special treatment is accorded to one agent, it spreads rapidly to many other actors. Only an insistence on arm's length treatment can moderate this tendency. Fortunately, the existing fiscal system at least provides a basis for an insistence on this kind of treatment.

In this sense, then, the verdict on the 1994 fiscal reform is still out. Will the reform provide a solid framework, or turn out to be an empty façade? The answer is still not certain and will depend on incremental progress in implementation over the next few years. The Chinese system appears to be capable of such progress, but whether it actually occurs will depend upon a number of factors outside the purview of this article, including the succession of political power in the post-Deng Xiaoping era.

The Banking System

In some important respects, the situation with respect to the banking systems is parallel to that of the fiscal system. Substantial institutional reforms have been made since 1985. A series of laws passed in 1995 made those institutional changes explicit and gave them legal sanction. Nonetheless, they do not yet govern the way the system actually operates.

Among the laws adopted during 1995 were the Law on the People's Bank of China (the central bank) in March and the Commercial Banking Law in May. In August 1996, a new regulation was adopted that made it illegal for a government official to order a bank to make a loan against its will. These should be considered along with the establishment of the State Development Bank (formally set up in March 1995) which, along with two other "policy banks," is intended to take over the burden of government-directed lending from the state-run specialized banks. The purpose of these charters is to allow the state commercial banks to genuinely shift their operations to a purely commercial basis and shed their quasi-governmental functions.

These formal changes are intended to achieve a kind of culmination of a gradual evolutionary process in the banking sector. The process has been a movement from a traditional socialist "monobank" system to a diversified financial system. By the mid-1990s, the Chinese financial system continued to be dominated by the state-owned specialized banks (the Agriculture Bank, Industrial and Commercial Bank, Bank of China, and Construction Bank). However, those banks now account for about 60% of the total financial assets, down from more than 95% in 1978. State policy banks — of which the largest is now the Agricultural Development Bank — account for another 5% or so of total assets, as do various newly established commercial banks, the largest of which is the Bank of Communications. The most important non-bank financial institutions are the Rural and Urban Credit Cooperatives, both of which have grown rapidly in recent years and have obtained substantially more autonomy than in previous years. They currently hold about 8% of total financial assets. Other non-bank financial institutions — including Trust and Investment Companies, Finance Companies and Insurance Companies — hold another 4% or so of financial assets. The remainder — some 16% of total financial assets — are held by the central bank, the People's Bank of China.[31]

Yet, there are important limitations on this process of diversification. Foreign banks still play an insignificant role in the domestic currency market, although some tiny cracks have been opened in the previous monopoly. A few foreign bank branches were allowed to begin domestic currency lending in December 1996, but their operations are limited to FIEs, and their sources of domestic currency strictly controlled.[32] Most important, nearly all significant financial institutions have some kind of close link to existing government-owned banks or other government institutions. A few experimental "private" banks have been allowed, but these are run by trusted individuals who can be counted on to follow informal government guidance. Rural and urban credit cooperatives are important sources of funds to the vibrant small-scale sector in both the countryside and in cities, but these cooperatives often have close links to local government officials.[33] Many of the Trust and Investment Companies (TIC) have been established by state banks: 181 of 394 authorized TICs in September 1995 were associated with the specialized banks. Many of the others are subordinate to local governments. The TICs provide convenient outlets for bank money to avoid regulatory strictures and seek out higher returns than are available through regulated lending. Thus, while the financial system has become diversified, it has not really become competitive.

The limitations on the growth of competition in the banking system can be traced to government fears about the impact of a rapid increase in competition. Currently, the financial system is hampered by the extensive use the government makes of the banking system to fund its own projects, and to support SOEs. SOEs are increasingly in debt to the banking system. In 1978, the debt burden of industrial SOEs was only 11% of book value, and by 1988 it had grown to 45%. By 1994, the aggregate bank debt of the state industrial sector had grown to 73% of aggregate book value (depreciated fixed capital plus all inventories). Indeed, SOEs finance 99.8% of their inventory accumulation through bank credit.[34] Moreover, the debt load has grown inexorably since the beginning of the reform era. This ratio is now much higher than in most other transitional economies. In essence, as government fiscal difficulties have curtailed the government's direct interference in industry, government officials at the central and local levels have increasingly turned to the banking system for financing. This has resulted in sustained pressure on the banking system to provide funds, pressure which recent legal changes are designed to reduce.

The dependence of the industrial sector on the banking system is not necessarily a bad thing. In Korea and Japan, for example, industrial firms are also highly dependent upon bank credit. The problem in China is that the dependence is the highest among SOEs that appear to be among the weakest performers. As a result, estimates of the bad debt of the banking system have been creeping steadily upward. According to Dai Xianglong, the governor of the People's Bank of China, 20% of outstanding bank loans are delinquent: 8% of outstanding loans are more than three years behind repayment schedule, and another 12% are behind schedule, but less than three years.[35] Two things are striking about this figure: First, it is quite large; and secondly, it is such an obvious underestimate of the total volume of problem loans. The bulk of state bank lending is for working capital, made up of short-term loans that are continuously being renewed (rather than long-term loans with a fixed repayment schedule). SOEs unable to repay short-term loans will in many cases simply keep increasing total indebtedness in order to make interest payments. Such problem cases are clearly not included in Dai's accounting of delinquent loans. We must conclude that there is a very substantial problem with non-performing loans. The magnitude of the problem can also be seen in the fact that the Ministry of Finance currently limits bank provisions against bad loans to no more than 1% of total loans outstanding. This sum is woefully inadequate and clearly exposes the banking system to substantial risk. Perhaps recognizing the need for the banking system to build reserves and strengthen capital adequacy, the profit tax on banks will be reduced in 1997 from 55% to the 33% standard for other Chinese corporations.[36]

As a result of these considerations, China's new framework for its financial sector is still a long way from realization. Policy-makers are afraid that rapid liberalization of the financial sector will result in a flight of funds from banks. Unable to retrieve funds from SOEs that are close to insolvency, banks could face a financial crisis. Thus, policy-makers are constrained both in introducing competition into the financial system, and in the pace with which they push the restructuring (and perhaps bankruptcy) of production enterprises within the state sector. Furthermore, such considerations also retard the liberalization of the foreign trade system, which the outside world is urging on China as part of its application for WTO membership.

Conclusion

Fiscal and banking reforms are both parallel and interrelated. They are parallel in that in both cases, institutional frameworks have been established that have not yet begun to function in the manner in which they are intended to function. We are thus entering a critical period in which these new institutional setups will undergo testing. Whether they can serve as the basis for a new period of deeper marketization and improved efficiency in the Chinese economy remains to be seen. The challenges are severe, and there is no grounds for complacency. However, based on the past record of reform in the Chinese economy, the vitality of the economy, and the high rate of saving and investment, it is reasonable to expect that these challenges will ultimately be overcome.

The interrelationship between fiscal and banking reform comes from the impact of the government on the financial sector. Starved for budgetary revenues, government officials pressure the banking system to finance their needs. Today, the government is trying to empower the banking system to refuse the exactions of government officials at all levels and operate on commercial principles. But at the same time, the central government is attempting to claw control of budgetary revenues away from local officials without also undertaking a parallel increase in central government expenditure responsibilities. This amounts to a kind of squeeze on local government finances that is unlikely to prevail in its current form. Local officials simply have too many options, and too much local knowledge, to allow themselves to be starved for resources in this fashion.

Instead, we can imagine two different emerging scenarios. Under the negative scenario, both fiscal and financial reforms would eventually fail. This failure would come about because of the government's failure to increase budgetary revenues. The central tax agency would not become established as a true central government agency, and local tax officials would have little incentive to increase budgetary revenues. In such a case, local officials would continue to divert resources into extra-budgetary funds, and would be forced to maintain their control over local financial institutions. The result would be the miscarriage of financial reforms, and an intensification of patterns of irregular finance and personal corruption in the Chinese economy. Under the positive scenario, government finances would begin to recover in 1997. Led by an increase in revenues collected by the central tax agency, the government would be able to direct more resources to the critical health, education, and administration components of the budget. Effective transfers to local governments would increase, and steps would begin to be taken to incorporate extra-budgetary funds into local government budgets. Under these circumstances, the effective autonomy of financial institutions would increase, and their real independence begin to be established. As competition increased in financial markets, banks and non-bank financial institutions would start to have strong incentives to clean up bad debts and put themselves on a firmer financial footing. Individual financial institutions might well face some short-term crisis situations, but the system as a whole would gradually become more rule-bound and transparent. Under this scenario, the dramatic growth that has characterized the Chinese economy in the past few years would become well established and accompanied by major increases in productive efficiency and well-being.

The distinction between the negative and positive scenarios is no doubt somewhat overdrawn. Nevertheless, the outcome of current reforms in the fiscal and financial areas will lead in one direction or the other. Important beginnings have been made in both areas. In contrast to earlier Chinese reforms, these beginnings have involved the comprehensive design and transplantation of institutional frameworks. The beginnings are promising. But, we have not yet seen sufficient positive results from these reforms to be confident that they will ultimately prevail.

Notes

1. For a comprehensive description of the fiscal system on the eve of the 1994 reform, see Christine P. W. Wong, Christopher Heady and Wing T. Woo, *Fiscal Management and Economic Reform in the People's Republic of China* (Hong Kong: Oxford University Press for the Asian Development Bank, 1995).
2. Christine Wong, "Fiscal Reform in 1994," in *China Review 1995*, edited by Lo Chi Kin, Suzanne Pepper and Tsui Kai Yuen (Hong Kong: The Chinese University Press, 1995), pp. **20**.6–7.
3. For descriptions of the 1994 tax reform, see Yunnan shuiwuju (Yunnan Tax Bureau), "Shenhua shuizhi gaige wei jingji fazhan fuwu" (Deepen Reform of the Tax System to Serve Economic Development), *Jingji luntan*, No. 1 (Economic Forum) (1994), pp. 28–35; Tsang Shu-ki and Cheng Yuk-shing, "China's Tax Reforms of 1994: Breakthrough or Compromise?" *Asian Survey*, Vol. 34, No. 9 (September 1994), pp. 769–88; Christine Wong (Note 2).
4. Li Huizhong, "Dui wanshan fenshui zhi wenti de jidian kanfa" (Several Views on Perfecting the Tax-sharing System), *Zhongguo caizheng* (China Finance) (formerly *Caizheng*), No. 11 (1996), p. 26.
5. Liu Zhongli (1997), "Report on the Implementation of the Central and Local Budgets for 1996 and on the Draft Central and Local Budgets for 1997," Unofficial English translation of Minister Liu's speech at the 5th session of the 8th National People's Congress on 2 March 1997, issued by the Ministry of Finance in Beijing. Guojia tongji ju (State Statistical Bureau), "Clear Success in Macroeconomic Control; Necessity for Structural Optimization: The 1996 Economic Situation and Outlook for 1997," *Renmin ribao* (haiwaiban) (People's Daily, overseas edition), 23 January 1997, pp. 1, 2; see also "Tax Collection," *China Daily*, 28 December 1996. The numbers in Figure 1 have been computed from adjusted Chinese data. Price subsidies and SOE losses have been included as revenues and expenditures in all years, and debt income has been excluded for all years. These adjustments accord with standard international practice; in fact, except for the treatment of SOE losses, all these adjustments to the data are now made in the standard Chinese sources, and retroactive data in these sources have been revised beginning in 1996. See State Statistical Bureau, *Zhongguo tongji nianjian 1996*, pp. 217, 223.
6. Comparative data are cited by Bert Hofman, "Fiscal Decline and Quasi-fiscal

Response: China's Fiscal Policy and Fiscal System 1978–1994," forthcoming in *Different Approaches to Market Reforms: A Comparison Between China and the CEECs* (Paris: OECD); and by Li Fangwang, "Woguo caizheng shouru guimo de guoji bijiao" (International Comparisons with China's Fiscal Revenue), *Caizheng yanjiu* (Finance Revenue), No. 9 (1996), pp. 16–20. It should be said that Chinese data exclude certain sums that would be considered fiscal in most countries. Most obviously, pensions and health benefits paid by SOEs are excluded from fiscal data, although they are indistinguishable from government social security programmes. These exceed 2% of GDP. In addition, although it is appropriate to exclude investment funded directly by SOE retained funds from budgetary outlays, a significant amount of fixed investment is funded by government extra-budgetary funds, and these ought to be consolidated with budgetary accounts. A plausible estimate is that these amount to 3–4% of GDP. Thus, a more realistic comparison is that Chinese budgetary expenditures equal 18–20% of GDP, compared to 32% average for a group of developing countries.

7. *Statistical Yearbook of China 1996*, pp. 226, 228. If subsidies to loss-making SOEs are included, then SOE profits account for 17% of gross revenues, with about five percentage points of this going back to loss-makers in the state sector.
8. State Statistical Bureau, "Clear Success in Macroeconomic Control...." *Renmin ribao*, 23 January 1997.
9. Li Fangwang (Note 6), p. 18; *Statistical Yearbook of China 1996*, p. 228; Wang Zheng et al., "Tungyi neiwaiji qiye suodeshui de nandian yu duice" (Difficulties and Appropriate Countermeasures in Unifying the Income Tax Rate on Domestic and Foreign-invested Enterprises), *Caizheng yanjiu*, No. 9 (1996), p. 27.
10. Liu Xinyi, "Lun shuishou jiegou yu gaige" (On the Structure of Tax Revenue and the Reform of the Tax System), *Caizheng yanjiu*, No. 8 (1996), pp. 19–26; *Statistical Yearbook of China 1996*, p. 228. As one economist from the Ministry of Finance put it, "The government cannot get its income from the fast-growing economic groups and must tap revenues from the slow-growing ones. This inevitably will exhaust its financial resources and force it to resort to predatory measures. This in turn not only hampers long-term economic growth, but also eventually affects future revenues." Jiang Xiaowei, "Hongguan yunxingzhong de caizheng zhengce" (The Role of Fiscal Policy in the Macroeconomy), *Jingji yanjiu*, No. 10 (1996), p. 22. SOEs accounted for 34% of current price industrial output in 1995, or 37% if all joint stock industrial enterprises are lumped in with traditionial SOEs. *Statistical Yearbook of China 1996*, pp. 401, 406.
11. Jae Ho Chung, "Central-Provincial Relations," in *China Review 1995* (Note 2), pp. **3**.12–18.

12. "Zhongguo qunian gongshang shuishou wancheng lianghao" (Last Year's Tax Collection Was Well Completed), *Zhongguo jingji xinwen* (Chinese Economic News), 1 January 1996, p. 15.
13. *Statistical Yearbook of China 1996*, pp. 228–42.
14. Barry Naughton, "China's Emergence and Prospects as a Trading Nation," *Brookings Papers on Economic Activity*, No. 2 (1996), pp. 273–344.
15. Xiao Lu, "Customs Collects $10 Billion in Revenue," *China Daily*, 14 January 1997, claims that customs duties reached RMB 85 billion in 1996, but also states that this was a 21.75% increase over 1995. According to *Statistical Yearbook of China 1996*, p. 228, tariff revenues were only RMB 29.2 billion in 1995, implying that this would be a 191% increase, or nearly a tripling of tariff take.
16. Note that the reduction in budgetary outlays for health came in addition to the dismantling of the rural health care delivery system, which was never included in budgetary accounts. In 1981, when the rural collectives still existed, 71% of the Chinese population had some kind of rudimentary health insurance; in 1993, only 21% had health insurance coverage. See World Bank, *Health Finance in the 1990s* (Washington, DC: World Bank Working Paper, 1996), p. 9. In theory, budgetary outlays should have increased in order to compensate for the collapse of the collective health care system.
17. Data for this and the subsequent paragraphs are taken from State Statistical Bureau, *Statistical Yearbook of China 1996* (Beijing: Zhongguo tongji chubanshe, 1996), p. 235; and Liu Zhongli (1997) (Note 5), and Liu Zhongli, "Report on Implementation of the 1995 Budget, and Preparations for the 1996 Budget," 4th session of the 8th National People's Congress, 5 March 1996. In the local-central comparisons, subsidies to loss-making enterprises have not been included.
18. The central government share of total revenues is of course greater than this, because only the central government has the authority to borrow. In all years, central government revenues are augmented by substantial domestic and foreign borrowing, and central government expenditures include substantial interest and debt repayment. These factors are not included in the figures discussed in this paragraph.
19. "Zhongguo qunian ..." (Note 12).
20. Liu Zhongli (1996) (Note 17).
21. Foreign-invested firms were not eligible to participate (until 1996), because most of their exports were produced with imported components and materials in any case. See Barry Naughton, "China's Emergence and Prospects ..." (Note 4).
22. Zheng Jingpin, "Growth Will Continue but at Lower Rates," in *1996 nian Zhongguo jingji xingshi fenxi yu yuce (lanpi shu)* (Analysis and Projection of Economic Conditions in 1996 [Bluebook]), edited by Liu Guoguang (Beijing:

Zhongguo shehui kexue, 1995), pp. 159–65; Wang Yaping, "Analysis of Foreign Trade Trends in 1996 and Appropriate Policies," *Guoji maoyi wenti* (Problems of International Trade), No. 4 (1996), pp. 21–25, 32.

23. Christine Wong (Note 2), p. **20**.10. See also Roy Bahl and Christine Wallich, "Intergovernmental Fiscal Relations in the Russian Federation," in *Decentralization of the Socialist State: Intergovernmental Finance in Transition Economies*, edited by Richard Bird, Robert Ebel and Christine Wallich (Washington, DC: World Bank, 1995).
24. Indeed, as if in recognition of the failure of the fiscal system to provide a sound framework for central-local relations, the government established in 1996 an interim system of interregional transfers to foster development in less-advanced provinces. Such a programme is doubtless well-intentioned, but it is impossible to take it seriously as a fiscal reform. The objective of fiscal reform is to create a transparent, rule-based system that distributes revenues according to an agreed-upon set of objectives. Fostering regional equity is an important objective, and it deserves inclusion in the design of an efficient fiscal system. However, nothing the Chinese government has done so far in the fiscal arena has the potential to seriously affect developing regional disparities.
25. Shandong sheng caizhengju xuexi xiaozu (Shandong Province Finance Bureau Study Group), "Xianxing caishui tizhi yunxingzhong Shandongsheng caizheng jingji mianlin de kunnan wenti yu duice" (The Difficulties, Issues and Responses Currently Being Faced by Shandong's Fiscal Economy under the Current Tax System), *Caizheng yanjiu*, No. 8 (1996), pp. 33–37, 32.
26. See Jun Ma, "Modeling Central-Local Fiscal Relations in China," *China Economic Review*, Vol. 6, No. 1 (Spring 1995), pp. 105–36.
27. Calculated from *Statistical Yearbook of China 1995*, pp. 222–23, and *Statistical Abstract 1996*, p. 41.
28. Liu Zhongli (1997) (Note 5), p. 10.
29. For discussion, see Li Huizhong (Note 4), p. 24; Wang Zheng et al. (Note 9), p. 28.
30. Wang Xiaoguang, "Shuizhi gaige zai wanshanzhong tuijin" (Perfect the Operation of the New Tax System), *Liaowang* (Outlook), No. 1 (1996), p. 5.
31. World Bank, *The Chinese Economy: Fighting Inflation, Deepening Reforms*, (Washington, DC: World Bank Country Study, 1996), p. 26.
32. Matthew Miller, "China Opening Renminbi Door to Foreign Banks," *Asia Times*, 13 December 1996, pp. 1–2. In addition, the privileges were extended initially only to banks operating in the Pudong special zone, so the newly privileged banks had to move their headquarters from downtown Shanghai to the Lujiazui financial district in Pudong.
33. Indeed, one explanation for the rapid growth of urban credit cooperatives in the past few years is that local governments are said to have been given more

freedom to expand urban credit cooperatives as compensation for the effective recentralization of provincial branches of the state banks.

34. *Statistical Yearbook of China 1995*, pp. 388–91.
35. Quoted in Seth Faison, "Inflation Curbed But not Growth, China Asserts," *The New York Times*, 16 July 1996, pp. C1, C7.
36. Liu Zhongli (1997) (Note 5), p. 11. However, the excise tax on interest income is being increased from 5% to 8% at the same time, reducing the impact of this measure.

12

"Cultural China": Irritation and Expectations at the End of an Era

Helmut Martin

Which major elements have been the basic constituents of modern Chinese literature during its re-emergence in the last two decades? What are the cultural characteristics of these decades of rapid social reforms in China, Hong Kong and Taiwan? Are there important common factors in the development of literature, film, painting and the arts as well as in mass culture? Then, how can China's insistence on the preservation of political and ideological unity be reconciled with the outburst of regional cultural activities in all their complexity and variety which include cultural realities in the regional centres of Singapore and Kuala Lumpur? These are some of the questions we want to address in this survey from very different angles. The world of "Cultural China" seems to be one of the major links for social development and cultural exchange between China, Hong Kong and Taiwan. The term itself[1] was originally coined in 1990 as an uncertain attempt to declare "the periphery as the centre," to conceptualize economic and cultural creativity in the area and its growing impact on China itself. Today, "Cultural China" is shaped much more by China's own creative contribution, but also by Beijing's enforcement of a redefined cohesive nationalism and its repercussions on the mentioned communities. Beijing's insistence on preserving and promoting unity and the rapid development of southern China has meanwhile produced among Asian scholars the more socio-political notion of "Greater China" as a dominant element in the Asia-Pacific region.

If we look back on the path Chinese literature has taken during the two decades between the death of Mao Zedong in 1976 and the year 1996, we find things in a state of constant flux. There is sometimes even volatility, a rapid succession of short-lived literary fashions and writers leaving the literary stage as suddenly as they have appeared. We find most of them struggling with an identity conflict; since the early 1990s, there has been widespread cynicism among younger authors. Such disillusion appears to function as an anchor in a situation where values are crumbling, where the individual is confronted with the ruins of the past and wonders where the future lies.

Revisiting the literary scene of the early 1980s, the impression of hectic reorientation and sudden change is reinforced. Whilst there is sufficient justification for differentiating two phases of literature since the beginning of the reforms in China — a literature of the 1980s and a literature of the 1990s — other critics are suggesting that the shock of the 1989 massacre was not the watershed it had been made out to be. They prefer to believe that, strictly speaking, the protest and the uneasiness which were being expressed two or three years earlier in the debates about the essence of China's new culture must be seen as the real dividing line between the 1980s and the 1990s.[2]

China's Perspectives

"Prehistory": Narrative Tradition, Late Qing Culture and the Literature of the May Fourth

It was only after abandoning the Maoist concept of society and tacitly giving up the ambition of global realization, even in the Third World, that China again started to adopt a less regimented approach to its own cultural developments before 1949. Scholars began to rediscover and reconstruct the country's history and, more specifically, social and cultural history.

For literary historians attempting to define the creative periods of the 20th century, it is the literature of May Fourth after 1919, i.e., the literature of the 1920s and 1930s, or the Republican period, that marked the rise of modernism in China. The 1980s and 1990s brought a similar intellectual and cultural reawakening after several decades of war and the long succession of devastating Maoist campaigns. The experimental literature produced during the Republican period has been presented to the West[3] through a colourful mosaic of translations, and a wide range of research projects have highlighted the basic developments, interpreting them both from a more global, cultural, and a narrower, literary, perspective.

The movement of May Fourth 1919 was intellectually iconoclastic, it set out to do nothing less than break the shackles of traditional culture. The young intellectuals, many of whom had studied at universities in the United States, Europe and Japan, saw themselves as China's true spiritual innovators. However, in retrospect it appears that important foundations had already been laid for modern China as far back as the Late Qing period, the two decades between 1890 and 1910. Like many Late Qing novels, Liu E's *Travels of Lao Can* (*Lao Can youji*),[4] for example, may be read as the fictitious autobiography of an alienated intellectual. Social criticism by the fashionable new authors of the foundering Manchu empire, most of them living in Shanghai, often evolved into a cynicism of despair, confronted as they were with the decay of their country. It is a similar kind of disillusion that some contemporary Chinese writers are expressing in their works today.

Popular literature of the transitional period,[5] the so-called "Mandarin Duck and Butterfly" school, actually reached many more readers than the innovative writers of the May Fourth Movement and their immediate predecessors, the reformers of the Late Qing, were willing to admit.

The pre-modern classic vernacular literature of the 17th century, to go back even a step further, has been introduced to us in the West through standard translations and a great deal of research in minute detail. Thus, we are able to trace the lines of development much more clearly and are now hopefully somewhat less vulnerable to the misleading forms of *chinoiserie* that had dominated the early contacts between China and the West.[6]

Authors of the literature of the 1980s were at first unable to see their works as a link in the long chain of China's literary tradition because most earlier literary texts of their predecessors had been inaccessible for many decades. Only almost at the end of the century are writers becoming aware of this tradition — in the context of China's overall quest for a cultural identity.

Culture of the 1980s and 1990s and the Periphery

How can we characterize these two periods of "literary reawakening" of the 1980s and 1990s against such a background? How do the irritating "cynical" post-modern 1990s differ from the "naive innovative" cultural attitudes of the 1980s?

After the constraints of Mao Zedong's People's Republic of China (PRC), where writers were dis-accustomed from taking an interest in any problems not related to China, intellectuals are now extending their sights to a "Greater China," with all its peripheral cultures, for which the term "Cultural China," or *wenhua Zhongguo*, has been increasingly used. Not only has the situation in the PRC changed rapidly in recent years, leading to an ever-widening gap between the coastal cities and rural towns and villages. We also have to take into consideration Hong Kong which, faced with the return to China in 1997 and therefore beset with a multitude of political and economic anxieties, has, with renewed urgency, raised the question of its own regional cultural identity. But above all, we look at Taiwan, which since 1987 has eagerly taken advantage of the new liberties to define its own identity and to shape development. In the longer term, strong majority forces on Taiwan hope to safeguard regional independence and to clarify relationships with China — both with traditional culture and the realities of a "demanding" motherland, which again seems to be suffering the labour pains of imminent changes. The influence and the cultural self-confidence of the élites of Chinese origin in Southeast Asia, especially in Singapore and Malaysia, are playing an increasingly visible role. There are both additional ethnic group audiences and markets very much in line with Pierre Bourdieu's concept of the cultural field.

At the same time, a small but influential group of Chinese intellectuals in the United States, and to a lesser extent in Europe, is having an increasing impact on China. Personalities who have lived abroad for many years are being welcomed with open arms by China's students and the intelligentsia in general. The huge, chaotic and uncontrollable network of cultural communication, which embraces the whole gamut of opinion voiced by Chinese intellectuals in exile, is colouring and in some instances shaping the picture of China in the 1990s.

As a reference field of the new media, literature appears to have taken on new functions — and to have forfeited some of the influence it once had, if we are to believe poet Yang Lian and playwright-painter Gao Xingjian,[7] addressing their readers from Paris. Alternative and dissident artists are creating forms of expression in their paintings and other works which are very much like those presented by writers. The New Chinese Film, which in many respects has its roots in literature, and its regional variants in Taiwan and Hong Kong, during the 1990s have become rather more influential than the literature of the 1980s, both nationally and internationally. During the last decade, furthermore, the Chinese public has been inundated with mass culture products. A popular culture has evolved, from film to television, from journals to the products of innumerable publishing houses, which tend to dominate the new realities of cultural consumption.

Here, only few developments can be mentioned by way of example, given the fundamental upheavals that are occurring in China. We may consider the naiveness, the limitations of the literature of the 1980s, may refer to the élitist literature, painting and art of the absurd, of post-modernism and of the *avant-garde* in China. Literary texts and paintings by the *avant-garde* stand in sharp contrast to the products of the all-embracing mass culture. The audiences opt for a very different perception of the role of literature and art. The sneers of the new brand of cynicism, paralleled by a new and somewhat spurious mood of *fin de siècle*, are phenomena which make sense neither to the *nouveau riches* among top Chinese cadres and functionaries nor to many literary scholars and China pundits in the West. While most readers find Wang Shuo and his vagabond literature simply irritating, his writings have been a revelation for China's youth for several years.

Alongside the diverse forms of mass literature on the big screen and on television, I would like to refer to a tendency towards critical self-portrayal and self-examination that has emerged. A new generation of Chinese literary and media critics, both at home and abroad, is commentating on important new developments in the field of Chinese art. For the first time, these Chinese critics are defining their own position with merciless accuracy and an impressive awareness of global trends and developments.

The Limited Experiments of the 1980s

After three years of agonizing transition between 1976 and 1979, the 1980s produced a hopeful mood of a new beginning in literature such as China had not seen since the May Fourth Movement of the 1920s. The field of literature became a playground for many impatient would-be actors wishing to pave the way, on this symbolic level, for the anticipated reforms. Most of the authors who now rushed to put pen to paper or who finally found their way back to literary creation after years of repression, had lost touch with tradition, they had to begin from scratch, from a "zero hour" situation. And, it was also precisely for this reason that the conventions of Maoist socialist-realism and its Soviet Russian role models continued to have a — rarely noticed — subconscious impact on China's "new era literature" (*xin shiqi wenxue*).

Several dozen anthologies, especially of prose and poetry, which documented this literary re-awakening became available in translation in the West almost instantaneously.[8] More than a hundred book translations were produced from this period, and specialized periodicals provided an overview of developments. I should now like to look back at some of the key features of this experimental literature and comment retrospectively on some important authors of the 1980s, many of whom have since become silent.

It would not be inaccurate to characterize the literature of the 1980s as eruptive efforts "to come to terms with the past" (*Vergangenheitsbewältigung* in German, *fansi* in Chinese) and, at the same time, as a rather clumsy retraining in the literary *métier*. Some writers like Zhang Jie, author of the novel *Heavy Wings* (*Chenzhong de chibang*, 1981),[9] or Jiang Zilong in his stories about a reform manager-cadre, produced some rather unsophisticated stories and novels which, as before, were interpreted and presented by the party as propaganda in support of reform policy. A whole series of reportage documentaries brought back vivid memories of the horrors suffered by individual Chinese, especially women. An example is Yu Luojin's autobiography which was the target of excessive official and bureaucracy-inspired semi-official criticism. Journalists like Liu Binyan used reportage literature to hit out at social injustice; these critics felt pressed to spell out the moral of their stories to be sure that even the least sophisticated of their readers could understand. Uncompromising critics of the regime's political blunders like Wang Ruowang, who had challenged Deng Xiaoping personally, even in this euphoric phase of reform were made to pay for their outspoken essays and reportages. They were subjected to all kinds of harassment, even harsh prison sentences.

Restless talents like prose author and dramatist Zhang Xinxin in her book *Chinese Lives* (*Beijing ren*, 1985)[10] presented their readers with portraits of real people which contrasted sharply with the embellished picture of society as depicted in party propaganda. Attempts "to come to terms with the past" always remained linked to the themes of the Cultural Revolution, as Feng Jicai demonstrated in his somewhat superficial and glowing stories, and especially in an ambitious reportage literature project which, in the end, he was unable to complete and publish as envisaged, because of the changed political atmosphere. Dai Houying (murdered in 1996), herself originally a misguided radical leftist and later a fervent advocate of "humanism," gave a remorseful account — written from Shanghai — of the fate suffered by the intellectuals at China's universities and the seduction of an entire generation of young people by Maoist radicals close to the ageing chairman Mao Zedong (Dai's novel *Stones of the Wall, Ren a ren*, 1980).[11]

Writers who had spent 20 years in the camps, rehabilitated "rightist elements" like Cong Weixi made some hesitant attempts to create prison literature.[12] But, they camouflaged their message in verbose and ideological passages and, in the end, pledged their unshaken gratitude to the party which had allegedly extricated itself by pointing to the successful efforts at reforming its organization. Writer Zhang Xianliang probably attracted the most attention because he drew shattering literary portraits of the psychological destruction and sexual repression of the detainees and former "rightists"; he impressed his audience as a shaken witness of the irreparable damage that had been inflicted on them.

Many victims of the mass campaigns like Lu Yanzhou, Bai Hua or Gu Hua published rather simplistic retrospections and lachrymose, "safe" accusations of a very general nature. Only few writers, the erudite Zong Pu and Yang Jiang being notable exceptions, managed to provide a deeper insight into the existential trauma they had suffered. Yang, a dramatist, famous in the cosmopolitan Shanghai of the 1940s, and acknowledged as a highly skilled translator, described, with inimitable understatement, absurd scenes in the rural camps involving China's most brilliant intellectuals (*Six Reports from Cadre School, Ganxiao liuji*, 1981).[13] Poets like Bei Dao and narrator-novelists like Acheng spoke out in their early works on behalf of China's protesting youth who in their hearts had abandoned Chinese Communism. Major transformations were also apparent in the development of Wang Anyi as a dedicated chronicler of Shanghai and portrayer of the youth of her day.[14] She was a typical representative of China's new women's literature, differentiating and adapting her style in a rapid succession of experimental steps.

The 1980s also produced a number of authors who attempted to square the circle, writers who tried to combine politics and literature. Servile fixation on high-placed politicians, their moods and socio-political inclinations eventually proved to be the undoing of the creative impulses of Shen Rong and others who for a time had artfully "sailed" with the political wind. Wang Meng, as minister of Culture acceptable to the regime only until 1989, made his imprint with remarkable essays which did much to further the cause of the group of young aspiring writers. Ironically, Wang's noncommittal stance (e.g., when he likened himself to a "butterfly" that cannot be pinned down by the term "modernist," "*avant-garde*," or anything else) was also the reason why his stories and novels, which tended to paper over many complexities of the situation in China, had only a limited impact at home. An example is his novel *Rare Talent Stupidity* (*Huodong bianrenxing*, 1987).[15] Rather ordinary or even mediocre talents like the former teacher, Liu Xinwu, also excelled with their essays in which they criticized with an admirable sense of justice the social outrages that had been created by the destructive mass campaigns. The genre of the cultural-political essay, so dear to Chinese literary tastes, reestablished itself prominently with several collections of such texts by critic Liu Zaifu, former director of the Institute of Literature of China's Academy of Social Sciences. Written in the United States and modelled partly on the essays of Lu Xun, Liu's string of short pieces[16] combine an honest revelation of the predicament of Chinese intellectuals in exile with a sober re-examination of the fundamental problems affecting Chinese society in the 20th century.

Chinese critics and authors have occasionally complained that some

Western sinologists have preferred to regard modern Chinese literature basically as a commentary on the country's social and political development in the early reform years. But, there were reasons for this attitude. Recognizing the limitations of China's literary experiment of these years which was launched without much knowledge of the Chinese situation in a global context and thus without much understanding of the outside world, it followed that important literary works with a global impact could not be written at the time. The only possible goal that could be achieved was to provide the now well-publicized, depressing literary commentary on social injustices in China, a description of the often unsuccessful attempts by harassed and marginalized individuals to survive the chaos of a society thrown into turmoil by the campaigns.

"New Wave" and "*Avant-garde*" in the 1990s

From about 1984, writers and intellectuals began to re-enter the debate of the 1920s asking how far the Chinese Confucian culture and tradition had been at the root of China's failed modernization attempts. Many authors like Acheng, Han Shaogong, Zheng Wanlong, and Zheng Yi then established the literature of "Searching for the Roots" (*xungen*) in an attempt to revitalize Chinese culture. They looked beyond traditional and modern mainstream culture, searching in rural China and among non-Han local cultures of the "minorities" for an untouched elemental culture outside the recognized norms of civilization. Of course, this approach could easily be misinterpreted as a literature of escape from urgent social problems and thus be dismissed as a "diversion" into a blind alley of just another romanticizing Chinese "self-strengthening" attempt. The emerging *avant garde* literature, on such premises, may be seen as a peculiar artistic reaction against the chaos of present-day China.

It was at this point that the New Chinese Film successfully took off and irritating, colourful new styles of painting emerged, which have been, somewhat condescendingly, acknowledged abroad when on exhibition.[17] Rock music by stars like Cui Jian[18] and others also evolved into a subculture element of identification for a youth with few illusions and became, for some years, a further powerful expression of protest.

Since the mid-1980s the "*avant-garde*" was first referred to tentatively as "New Wave Literature" (*xinchao*). It was now that Chinese publishers were forced to become financially responsible or autonomous for the first time ever and that Western popular literature in translation was given an ecstatic welcome by China's reading public. In addition, the market was flooded with reprints of love stories and popular novels and *wuxia* cloak and dagger romances from Taiwan and Hong Kong as the second main direction in modern Chinese entertainment literature. At the same time, when the intellectuals began to discuss the character of Chinese culture, a new dimension was added in 1987 by the debate on the hybrid pseudo-reportage genre of the television series *Ode of the River* (*Heshang*, 1988).[19] The series brought colourful images of China's cultural crisis as a topic of discussion to an unbelievably large audience of some 600 million viewers.

Readers lost much of their initial interest in the literature of "coming to terms with the past," and the authors of more demanding and sophisticated literature suddenly found themselves out in the cold. Many of them left the cause, stopped writing or adapted; key impulses now increasingly came from a younger generation of writers born in the 1960s. This "New Wave" literature has been broken down into the narrative prose of the Lost Generation, the movement of "Searching for the Roots," and finally the "*avant-garde*" literature (*xianfeng*). Stories by Liu Suola and Chen Jiangong were seen as reflecting the mood and the thoughts of this Lost Generation. They had a precursor in *Waves* (*Bodong*),[20] an early novel by poet Bei Dao in which young survivors of the generation formed (or de-formed) by the Cultural Revolution have a fateful encounter of hesitating, sceptical affection. "Roots Literature" covers a wide range of works from Acheng's *Three Kings* (*Qiwang*, *Shuwang*, *Haiziwang*, 1985) to the plays and prose of Gao Xingjian,[21] the novelist, playwright, painter and calligrapher who remains in exile in Paris. His root-searching novel *Mountain of Souls* (*Lingshan*, 1990) caused a great stir in 1995–1996 when it appeared abroad in French translation.[22] Names that stand for the *avant-garde* movement are, e.g., the talented Ma Yuan who, meanwhile, Rimbaud-like, has given up writing to go into business, Can Xue who has delved into every absurd atrocity, and to some extent "anarchist" Wang Shuo who quickly became a wealthy media star directing his own company. His writings are a market place of post-modernist defiance and cynical truths; he has eliminated any remaining illusions of a shining future.

The works of Chinese *avant-garde* literature have so far, in contrast to the descriptive realism of the 1990s, been included in only a few anthologies and are accessible through just a handful of translations. Li Rui has depicted wild scenes from the changing rural society which will never have a place in state-prescribed text books. Mo Yan's novels present baroque heroes who would be at home in the furious battle scenes of the 17th century *Simplicissimus*, but his novels in fact are directly inspired by Marquez, Borges and the magic realism of other Latin American models.[23]

This period of "cultural reorientation," to use the term coined by the critic Henry Zhao (Zhao Yiheng), was essentially subversive, the tenor of the texts being clearly anti-culture, e.g., *The Muddy Street* (*Huangni jie*) by Can Xue or *You Have No Choice*, a story by Liu Suola. These authors were rebelling against the existing norms as reflected, e.g., in Wang Anyi's *The Century on the Hill* or in many stories by Han Shaogong, and the existing value system was mercilessly ridiculed, e.g., in Ye Zhaoyan's *The Dusk of May* and *The Story of the Date Tree* or in Duo Duo's *The Last Song*. Authors were feeling their way back to "eternal values" outside the narrow confines of mainstream culture like Acheng in his story *The King of Chess* (*Qiwang*) or Mo Yan in his novel *Red Sorghum* (*Hong gaoliang*).[24] Among the earliest works of the *avant-garde* was the narrative prose of such writers as Su Tong, e.g., *The Escape of 1934* (*Yijiu sansi de taowang*). Stories like *Fate* by Shi Tiesheng and *The Lost Boat* by Ge Fei tell of the tragedy of the individual who cannot survive in such a society. Esoteric and bizarre messages come across in stories like *The Letter from the Postman* by Sun Ganlu or *The White Bird* by He Liwei.

An important *avant-garde* writer after 1987 is Yu Hua with his *One Kind of Reality* (*Xianshi yizhong*) in which he presents a ludicrous example of brutality in a Chinese family. A murder of revenge at the end of the story is again reminiscent of a scene in Grimmelshausen's novel *Simplicissimus*: a small dog causes a fatal fit of hysterical laughter by licking the feet of the victim.[25]

For the young egotists among the Chinese writers born in the 1960s, the Cultural Revolution and its repercussions had, for the first time, lost significance. The evolving *avant-garde* literature could no longer be viewed as a simple variant of the "service trade" commodity, as R. Wagner has called the politically correct products of Chinese socialist realism, as well as the only partly successful prose experiments of the 1980s. For the first time there was no one correct interpretation left. A new élite had taken the floor, an élite which was moulding and living the new anti-culture, for which the time was now right. Not surprisingly, these authors were both curious and enthusiastic about their own cultural history, which had been withheld from them, back to the May Fourth Movement of the 1920s and beyond. Their works, moreover, were clearly influenced in many ways by

Western literature, especially by the "magic realism" of Latin America. Several novels and stories were modelled on Salinger's *Catcher in the Rye*, Marquez' *Hundred Years of Solitude* and the novels of Borges'.

Women Writers of the 1990s

Many women writers continued to make their imprint on the literature of the 1990s. Two of the most prominent are Fang Fang and Chi Li from Wuhan whose writings reflect their attempts at a new realism. Fang Fang exposes the lives of transport workers and urban intellectuals in *Grandfather in Father's Heart* (*Zufu zai fuqin xin zhong*, 1992). Chi Li in stories like *The Flow of Clear Water* (*Lüshui changliu*, 1993) portrays the relationship of couples in ill-matched marriages and in the satire *What Do You Think You Are* (*Ni yiwei ni shi shei*, 1995) depicts the trials and tribulations of everyday life. Zhang Xin from Guangzhou has made her impact with texts like *Absolutely No Coincidence* (*Jue fei ouran*, 1995) and *It's Love, So What?* (*Ai you ruhe*, 1995) about women's struggle for acceptance in China's cities.

Avant-garde writers among women authors include Chen Ran from Guangxi, and Lin Bai from Beijing. Lin gained recognition with her novel of childhood reminiscences *Moss* (*Qingtai*, 1995), and Chen with stories like *Sunshine between the Lips* (*Zuichun li de yangguang*, 1992) in which she explores remaining ways towards love and mutual understanding. Since 1994 authors from Beijing have created "novels of new experience" (*xin tiyan xiaoshuo*) initiated by Bi Shumin[26] and others with unusual stories, some of them treating topics like getting rich and encountering death.

"Anarchist" Wang Shuo and the Post-modern Disillusion of the 1990s

A feature of the narrative style of the writers born in the 1960s which distinguishes them quite clearly from the subtle idealistic "protesters" of Bei Dao's generation, is a pervasive cynicism, a negation of practically all values, a negation of society, even a negation of the sense, a deeper meaning, of their own existence. Wang Shuo soon took centre stage with stories like *Leader of the Gang* (*Wanzhu*, 1987), *Hot and Cold, Measure for Measure* (*Yiban shi huoyan, yiban shi haishui, 1988*),[27] *Living Dangerously* (*Wan de jiushi xintiao*, 1988), and *Don't Take Me Seriously*

(*Qianwan bie ba wo dang ren*, 1989). In them, Wang developed and became a virtuoso in the art of juxtaposing two different worlds of expression, the fossilized language of the declining system and its ideology and the urban slang of China's disillusioned youth. Last but not least, he and his generation took unprecedented sexual liberties in their presentation which the authors of the 1980s would have scarcely dared practice and, least of all, write about.

Wang criticizes the pitiful ineffectivity of Chinese intellectuals. He has only contempt for their hollow ramblings about a "new cultural revolution" and prefers instead to live without ideals and without master strategies for the future. He dismisses the somber attempts of Zhang Chengzhi, for example, in *History of the Soul*[28] and in his other narrative prose, to establish a system of new values.

It was not until Wang's "life-style" began to be accepted by a wider public through television adaptations and the repeated screening of his stories (four films in one year alone) that the literary watchdogs among cadres and propagandists felt the need to intervene. Most semi-official literary critics had initially dismissed Wang as nothing but a harmless writer of popular literature.

Wang throws his readers straight into the *liumang* culture of the riff-raff and out-of-work adolescents. It is indeed a very peculiar world. The *liumang* fears no one; in some ways, we are reminded of the heroes of both the traditional vernacular *xiaoshuo* novel and of modern *wuxia* adventure romances.

Wang himself had served a gaol sentence for his involvement in youth gang warfare, scraped along as a salesman and after his military service in the marines lived off a succession of women — the secretary of a party youth organization, a stewardess, and a dancer. The anti-heroes of his love stories are *liumang*, *pizi* anarchists, and inveterate *wanzhu* gambler types.

In the screen version of *Hot and Cold, Measure for Measure*, the protagonist is an escapee from the camps, quite the opposite of the egocentric and often theatrical figures of Zhang Xianliang or Dai Houying. Masquerading as a policeman, he makes a living out of blackmailing and procuring prostitutes for visitors from Hong Kong. In *Don't Take Me Seriously*, a group of young *liumang* people is fighting for survival in chaotic circumstances. Shaken up by Bo Yang's diatribe against *The Ugly Chinese* (*Choulou de Zhongguoren*), Wang uses this political satire to "avenge" the defeat suffered at an international sporting event in Sapporo. A member of a kung fu martial arts team is selected who naturally ends up as world champion in this discipline — satirically celebrated in an absurd competition of Chinese self-effacement.

The humorous story *I Am Your Dad* (*Wo shi ni baba*, 1991) shows the absurdity of the attempts by different generations to live together in harmony. The father, a divorcé who works in a bookstore, fails miserably in his attempt to bridge or to ignore the generation gap. His son, in exasperation, demands a return to the observation of boundaries between the generations.

In short, Wang Shuo has depicted the disillusioned urban youth as alienated elements among the intellectuals, very much as historian Yu Ying-shi has analysed. Wang demands that everyone should have the right to his or her own world and disparages Chinese "modernism" for assuming new forms as if they were new clothes, without adjusting the underlying structures. In his own erratic way, buffoon Wang ridicules the aberrations of such worn-out clichés as a China striving for "total westernization." Small wonder that Wang Shuo has become both role model and artistic endorsement for the rootless *bopi* school of painters.

Not least because of his huge commercial success, following his decision to become a cultural private entrepreneur (*wenhua getihu*) and to operate from his Sea Horse Movie and Video Production Centre in Beijing, Wang has had numerous imitators, several of them women writers. But the *blasé* cynicism in the works of Hong Ying,[29] for example, is much less harsh, and her fashionable depiction of extreme situations seems somewhat contrived. In the story *Club of Carnations* (*Kangnaixin julebu*, 1994) Hong portrays a group of young girls with lesbian inclinations hunting down men who have committed serious offenses against women.

The uproar caused by the phenomenon of the "cultural anarchists" continued right up to the middle of the 1990s. Younger, rather self-righteous critics joined in a concerted attack on all those writers and critics, including the senior figure, Wang Meng, who tolerated the Wang Shuo phenomenon and who accepted such cheap entertainment literature on a par with the serious art for which they themselves were striving. During 1996 and early 1997, Wang Shuo became a scapegoat in the struggle of the party against "moral decay."

Cynical Realism in Painting?

The events of 1989 also pushed a large group of artists and sculptors throughout the country in a direction that has been, simplistically, termed "cynical realism." The existence of these people who very much represent China's contemporary anti-culture, living together in colonies on the outskirts of Beijing, one day tolerated, the next day dispersed by the police, is much like a high-wire act. Others have meanwhile accepted positions in the official art establishment, in academies and universities; but, what they paint in private is slowly gaining official acceptance. Small exhibitions are occasionally held, and some of their works are showing up on the international art market directly or via Hong Kong, provoking angry commentaries on Beijing television.[30]

Post-modern experiments are characteristic of the style in this transitional phase: We find, for example, the often rather puerile pop art (Mao collages — no one appears to have had the courage to prepare a collage of Deng Xiaoping!), garish caricatures of sexual escapades and canvases in poster colours (Wei Guangqing, b. 1963), rows of identical grinning faces and children with the features of old men and women (Yue Minjun, b. 1962; Guo Jin, b. 1964). Here too, therefore, the "anarchic" attitude, adopted from writers like Wang Shuo, has taken hold — but the Chinese public has so far shown little enthusiasm for these Western-orientated forms of aesthetic transition.

Regained Self-assurance: China's New Cultural Critics

The two decades of the 1980s and 1990s finally saw the emergence of new literary and cultural critics, who again appeared able to cope with their task as intellectuals. They displayed the same self-assurance that we have been witnessing since the early 1990s in several South- and East-Asian countries.[31]

Some of these critics are active from within China, for example, some years ago, Ji Hongzhen and, now, Chen Xiaoming.[32] Others are literary historians, for example Chen Pingyuan from Beijing University. With already unaccustomed, silent contempt for any further constructions of orthodoxy, Chen Pingyuan has attempted to elaborate new methods of looking at modern narrative literature on the lines of a genre history of early modern narrative literature: methodically sound, brilliant in the display of details and open to new solutions.[33] Many of these critics, and I would like to select Henry Zhao by way of example here, have joined in the international literary debate from outside China. The reflections of these intellectuals on recent developments in China are presented in such a way[34] that Western literary critics and literary historians have begun to take notice and to listen for the first time again after many decades. China's new critics are guiding scholars, translators, publishers and readers cautiously (and in spite of remaining pressures) to important new works and developments, they are reassuming — with an understandable degree of pride — the role of native interpreters, a role which since the 1950s had to be relinquished in much the same way as the interpretation of China's history and the study of contemporary political developments had become impossible, because of the party's radical claims to exhaustive interpretation.[35]

Henry Zhao, as a representative of this new generation of critics, studied abroad (at UC Berkeley) and, like the Republican author Lao She or Taiwan's Ma Sen, spent many years at the School of Oriental and African Studies in London. Zhao comments on contemporary cultural developments, both in English and in Chinese. As a critic close to the poet Bei Dao's emigrant journal *Today* (*Jintian*), which is published separately in Chinese and, in compressed form, in English, Zhao has strengthened the position of the mentioned young PRC literary scholars and critics by the compilation of various anthologies. Here I would specifically like to mention his collection of *avant-garde* literature *The Lost Boat* (1993), which, as the editor emphasizes, was compiled strictly from a literary viewpoint. I might refer to his selection *UnderSky UnderGround* (1994); also to his outstanding volume of essays *The Need for Solitude* (*Biyao de gudu*, 1995) which is devoted only on the surface to a formal analysis of narrative discourse, and in reality treats "inevitable loneliness" as an essential condition for the leading literati of the *avant-garde* — and possibly also for most other contemporary Chinese intellectuals.

Zhao documents the absurd texts of the "new literary start" produced out of nowhere by the writers of the 1990s. His perception of recent Chinese developments, departing clearly from the Maoist cultural "desert" of abandoned traditions, fits anew into the overall scheme of Chinese cultural evolution down through the centuries. He sees the present phase of transition above all as a creative element in a cultural reorientation that is taking place in ruptures. The emergence of an anti-culture — the iconoclastic elements in it — are for him more or less just metaphors, as they existed within the new literature of the May Fourth Movement after 1919. In reality, the foundations have now been laid for a new contemporary culture of China.

Zhao, therefore, is essentially optimistic about China's cultural future. He remains critical of the anti-traditionalists who are ever ready to forecast the downfall of China's culture and who also fail to detect any reason to artificially prolong the existence of a crumbling Chinese culture, interpreting the clumsy attempts at modern Chinese literature only as further evidence of this demise. Critic Zhao likewise takes the traditionalists among his Chinese contemporaries to task who claim that the May Fourth Movement of 1919 broke too radically with the past, and who, consequently, also dismiss as over hasty all recent attempts to modernize and to actually create new forms of literature.

Zhao instead argues, against the two above positions, that the new literature of the *avant-garde* has "risen" indirectly out of the ashes of Mao realism, following a decade of unsteady preliminary experimenting. The *avant-garde* writings reveal a new sensitivity and a fundamental autonomy, because Western elements have served only as a stimulus and have not been merely imitated. Zhao registers neither pseudo-modernism nor pseudo-post-modernism but rather points out autochthonous forms of a new Chinese art.

It remains to be seen, however, whether Henry Zhao is just trying to provoke a new self-awareness, whether he is simply encouraging Chinese writers, or whether he is actually commentating on facts. Whatever the case, critic Zhao Yiheng advises patience. He sees such reorientation phases in the Chinese context as complex, somewhat mysterious processes, and he appeals to all those who have raised the alarm about China's cultural crisis:

> More than one hundred years have passed, with still no immediate prospect of success. Yet history tells us that the reorientation of Chinese culture always took much longer than one century. If that is the case, my pessimistic friends should perhaps be less worried.[36]

Zhao Yiheng takes his time, proudly accusing Western critics of failing to recognize the new developments; he insists that Chinese literature is indeed again of such quality as to be able to compete globally. And, he concludes with a warning that the West in its cultural lethargy might be missing something significant.

Clearly, critics like Henry Zhao are keen to leave the West behind, to return to China and eventually to play their part in fulfilling the tasks of their generation from the inside. Other younger comparatists and literary scholars originating from the PRC like, for example, Kang Liu, Lu Tonglin, Lydia H. Liu and Tang Xiaobing,[37] have chosen to play their part from American universities as their platforms. They organize conferences and present original alternative views of interpreting Chinese literature from their specific "comparatistic" perspective — in amicable but somewhat tense rivalry with the influential group of US Chinese scholars who are linked more closely to Taiwan. A group of PRC-born critics and comparatists has made it its aim, I feel, to win back the right to interpret "Cultural China" with what they hope will be eventually unchallenged authority in the West, a privilege which over recent decades had slipped into other hands.

Beyond such new Chinese literary criticism, we are also seeing new developments in film criticism following closely the recent international success of the Chinese cinema; one of the tendencies has been to inquire into the reasons why so many prominent recent films have their roots and origins in contemporary Chinese literature. China's art critics on the other hand have so far made little impact.

Literature and the Authorities: Some Developments during 1996 and the 5th Writers' Congress

Tensions between the authorities and writers are a perennial theme of cultural life in authoritarian societies of leftist as well as rightist provenance. It is the literary historian's job to record the effects of repression on the creative efforts of the country's intellectuals and writers. There is much to be learnt from such a record, and in the case of China even more so if parallels are drawn with the Soviet or Russian situation: The Leninist, Stalinist, Late Soviet, *Perestrojka* (1985–1991), and Post-*Perestrojka* (1991–1996) developments have their parallels in early Maoist, Cultural Revolution, Early Reform and Post-1989 perspectives.[38] The years 1976 to 1989 have been recorded in He Yuhuai's analysis *Cycles of Repression and Relaxation: Politico-Literary Events in China* (1992), the following years e.g. in *Biographies of Famous Cultural Personalities from China Mainland — Creators of a Civil Society* (*Dalu dangdai mingren pingzhuan*, 1995).[39] The year 1996 and early 1997 faced Chinese intellectuals in the cultural field with tensions in their relations with the authorities, the degree of which became an issue of debate[40] among Chinese critics outside the PRC.

Strictly speaking, the struggle is only about creating the *pre-conditions* of literature. And as we all know, liberation from repression, when the freedom of the press is guaranteed for the creative intellectual, as seems to have been the case in Taiwan since 1987, does not in itself guarantee that literary art works will be produced.

Political aggressiveness, as evidenced by the military exercises against Taiwan during March 1996, and a hardening of China's attitudes towards the USA and Western Europe have been accompanied by new cultural pressures. Deng Xiaoping's policy since 1992 to avoid conflicts in the ideological field (*bu zhenglun*) became the target of attacks by some veteran left-wingers (*zuo wang*), a manoeuvre evidently backed by Party chief Jiang Zemin, Premier Li Peng and the ideological hardliner Ding Guan'gen, Deng's bridge partner and head of the Propaganda Department. Even so, the party centre saw the need to compromise and removed from office leading literary cadres who had been installed in 1989. These included vice-party secretary of the Chinese Writers Association Malaqinfu, who had estranged the core group of PRC writers from the Association, their professional representative organization.

Outsiders like Zhai Taifeng from the Beijing city trade union were brought in. As party secretary of the Writers Association, Zhai tried to mend fences with authors like Zhang Xianliang and especially Jia Pingwa, who had earlier been attacked for his popular, and temporarily banned, novel *Rotten City* (*Feidu*, 1993) about a local PRC writer. The novel's erotic scenes had caused a local sensation which in turn had made the book a national bestseller.[41] Jia, who consequently had been prevented by the party from accepting invitations from abroad, was in a way "re-accepted." He showed his gratitude to the leadership by publishing a new novel *Doors of the Earth* (*Tumen*, 1996) in which he portrayed the many positive changes in China and the conflicts of the peasantry confronted with urbanization.

After the 6th plenum of the Central Committee, Zhai Taifeng, together with party secretary of the All-China Federation of Literature and Art Gao Zhanxiang and other party collaborators, organized the 5th Writers' Congress on 16–20 December, 1996, parallel with the 6th Congress of the Federation of Literature and the Arts (*wenlian*).[42] The Writers' Congress was the first meeting of its kind since December 1984[43] because of the upheavals and uncertainties before and after the watershed of 1989. The December 1996 event opened with attacks on the preceding 4th congress, which had been conducted under the guidance of Hu Yaobang. The 1984 Congress was cited as one of the direct reasons for all the "liberal excesses" (*ziyouhua*) of 1987 and particularly the "storm in Beijing" of 1989.

During the congress in 1979, Deng Xiaoping had opted in his address for a cautious relaxation in the cultural field. Jiang Zemin in his conservative programmatic talk in 1996, attempted to strengthen his authority in ideological questions and propagated a new orthodox nationalism directed against the "infiltration of (Western) colonial culture."

The 1996 Writers' Congress proved uneventful, using Ba Jin, now at the age of 92, once again as a mere figure-head; the organizers reserved all influence within the Association for the party committees; the chairpersons, elected from among the writers on the central and provincial level, were assigned no active role whatsoever. Dramatist Cao Yu, designated to remain the head of the Federation, died suddenly a few days before the event; former acting minister of culture Zhou Weizhi, a composer, was moved in as the second figure-head in this farce, alongside Ba Jin. Prominent exile writers and journalists like Liu Binyan, Liu Zaifu and Ge Yang were ousted from the Association as also were other critics, e.g. the outspoken translator Yang Xianyi and the scholar Wu Zuguang. Shanghai writer Bai Hua had already been removed earlier through intrigues during spring 1996, ahead of the "elections" of the local branch of the Association.

In the run-up to the Congress, Zhai and his vice-party secretaries visited and wooed a dozen veteran leftist writers, including Lin Mohan, Zang Kejia, Yao Xueyin and the dethroned Malaqinfu, as well as a few liberal authors like Bing Xin, Ba Jin, Ai Qing, Chen Huangmei and Shao Yanxiang. At the same time, a new kind of campaign was launched against Wang Meng, the versatile former minister of culture, who barely succeeded in defending his position as one of the deputy chairmen and who now appears to have become a symbol of the cultural liberalization so detested by these hardliner cadres. After earlier attacks which had triggered a lawsuit before petering out, Wang Meng was again attacked in 1996 and early 1997 because he had in the past welcomed Wang Shuo and his nonchalant *pizi* texts as refreshing literary innovations of the 1990s. Mo Yan too drew renewed criticism for his novel *Full Breasts and Fat Asses* (*Fengru feitun*, 1995) about superficial consumerism, and, in 1996, was forced to halt distribution of the book. The sex scenes in the novel were used as a pretext to attack him politically. Everybody in the PRC got the message: Disillusionment and cynicism of the kind propagated by Wang Shuo, which had swept the country via his books in tens of millions of copies, were now to be ostracized; politically unreliable cultural figures like Mo Yan and Wang Meng were no longer to be left alone. Wang Shuo, the voice of a disillusioned generation, because he had had the audacity to stand in the way of the government efforts to raise the nation's level of "spiritual civilization," was now in serious trouble: During the summer of

1996 the Propaganda Department ordered a halt to new printings of Wang's collected works; he was accused of having ridiculed China's noble values. Two movie projects were scrapped, TV scripts failed to pass the censors, and his screen play *Dad* was banned. Wang was accused of "promoting the worship of money, hedonism and extreme individualism."

Beside the criticisms of Mo Yan and the two Wangs,[44] which by implication included writers like Can Xue and the whole *avant-garde*, new attacks were directed against Li Zehou and Liu Zaifu's dialogue *A Farewell to Revolution* (*Gaobie geming*, 1996).[45] Ironically, the book itself is an attack on radicalism by the historian of Chinese philosophy Li and the literary scholar Liu from their exile in the USA and a plea for gradual reforms in a future China which had already drawn some negative commentary from a very different direction — namely the younger generation of PRC intellectuals living abroad.

Again, several cases of open censorship have become known. Politically controversial novels like Deng Xian's *Setting Sun* (*Luori*, 1996) were banned, regarded as too lenient on the Kuomintang (KMT). A reportage — *At the Grassroots* (*Zai diceng*, 1996) by the journalist and writer Lu Yaogang,[46] which described the depressed situation of state-owned industry in the three north-eastern provinces and the plight of the many unemployed — was also suppressed, and the issue of the implicated Writers Association's literary journal destroyed. A host of TV productions have been censured or withdrawn, among them a series about the corrupt world of officialdom during the Late Qing period, *Bureaucracy Exposed* (*Guanchang xianxing ji*).

We should not forget, however, that outrage at international criticism of China's political system and the various forms of cultural repression did not produce reactions from the government alone. Both young intellectuals and the general public reacted with a new kind of political and cultural nationalism, reminiscent of earlier calls for a kind of neo-authoritarianism. From such nationalist positions, many young scholars, writers and journalists launched counter-attacks on all criticism of China — from inside the country and from abroad. Suggestions that this kind of hollow nationalism and patriotism had once before proved a trap for Chinese intellectuals, ultimately ordered to act "as cogs in the state machine," as Gao Xingjian put it, were ignored.

Dissident Harry Wu (Wu Hongda), for example, was vilified as a phony careerist for his exposure of the Chinese Gulag in the international media. The bestseller *China Can Say No! — Options for Politics and Emotions in the Post-Cold War Period* (*Zhongguo keyi shuo bu*, 1996)[47] by a group of malcontent young journalists, after publication tacitly approved by the Jiang leadership, and similar book-length all-round attacks on China's "enemies" have been analysed in the West with too much emphasis on the political angle: only the attacks on the superpower America and an economically and politically threatening Japanese empire were registered and emphasized, the desire for a new strategic alliance with Russia noticed. But, these books may also be read as a rather revealing commentary on and protest from the cultural field — in a situation where the lack of international recognition, e.g. a "reticence" to consider a Chinese author for the Nobel Prize in literature, is castigated. Seen from a psycho-analytical angle, national reactions to irritating rapid changes, disturbance or crisis and more personal, even sexual emotions of perplexity and inadequacy seem to have been unacceptably mixed and compensated rather as we saw in early Republican literature, e.g. in Yu Dafu's story *Sinking* (*Chenlun*, 1921).

What seems absent in China is a sober analysis of real accomplishments in the cultural field since 1980 and the definition of an official cultural policy which seeks international recognition for such accomplishments. Many Chinese critics in 1996 appear to have felt frustrated. In this climate of new irritations, any hopes of a debate, any improvement in the cultural field from the political side, any hope of a reasonable representation of the contemporary Chinese cultural scene had to be temporarily abandoned.

The reshaping of the Writers' Association was largely ignored abroad. Following the party's 6th plenum of the 14th Central Committee and Jiang Zemin's emphasis on the "Decision on Some Important Questions to Strengthen the Building of Spiritual Culture," the manipulation of the Association provoked ironic commentaries even among cadres, as it proved incapable of opening up new roads: A reversion to yesterday's solutions and double morality have widened the gap between media language and reality; too many futile attempts have been made to revive old recipes of Maoist-socialist campaigning. It is conceivable, therefore, that all the verbiage of the Writers' Congress, all the propaganda efforts of late 1996, were forgotten the moment they had been uttered.

Chinese Films Outperform Literary Works in the International Arena

The policy of "guiding" intellectuals has been applied to the genre of film even more vigorously than to the literary field. In spite of all the restrictions, however, China's New Film has attracted a much broader audience than the many translated works of modern literature. Literary works have nevertheless continued to be a powerful source of inspiration for most film directors. What are the most important coordinates that have shaped the evolution of the new Chinese film? Let us look at the main features of the prehistory and, in addition, at some of the decisive elements of contemporary development and the literature–film connection.

In 1995, Asia too celebrated a hundred years of cinema: On 11 August 1896 the first film was shown in Shanghai. Theatre and literature have always played a key role in the development of the Chinese cinema: As early as 1905, a Beijing opera based on the classical novel *The Three Kingdoms* (*Sanguo yanyi*) was filmed. During the 1930s and 1940s, a leftist-orientated cinema was established by artists and political activists whose social films made the new art form an important instrument of leftist propaganda. At the same time, the Communist movement made clever use of mobile cinema operators in rural areas. By this time, several works of the new literature such as, for example, Mao Dun's story *Silkworms in Spring* (*Chunchan*, 1932), were being screened. The wave of KMT terror in the mid-1930s forced leftist-orientated film studios to close, and actors and producers went underground or fled to Hong Kong.

After Japan's capitulation, the film industry gradually recovered. Changchun in the northeast became the cradle of the revolutionary films which put Mao's guidelines into practice and determined the face of the cinema and film production for the next three decades. Folk traditions and models from the Beijing opera continued to provide inspiration. The year 1956, for example, saw the production of two films based on popular fiction, Ba Jin's *Family* (*Jia*, 1933) and Lu Xun's *New Year's Sacrifice* (*Zhufu*, 1924), and a film version of the Beijing opera *Fifteen Strings of Cash* (*Shiwu guan*). Director Xie Jin and others eventually created the revolutionary Beijing opera as a film event under the guidance of Mao's wife and former Shanghai film starlet Jiang Qing — after originally planned productions had been stopped by force in 1966 with the start of the Cultural Revolution.

The reform years of the early 1980s produced hero-worshipping films featuring Sun Yat-sen, Mao Zedong, Liu Shaoqi and the mythical hero of the Great Leap Forward, Lei Feng. During the Beijing Spring, several literary works which attempted to "come to terms with the past" were screened. These included, for example, *Sun and Man* (*Taiyang he ren*) which was based on Bai Hua's film script Bitter Love (*Kulian*, 1979) and *A*

Town Called Hibiscus (*Furong zhen*, 1986) by Gu Hua. The so-called Fourth Generation of PRC film-makers, which included such names as Xie Fei, now succeeded increasingly in liberating themselves from direct political regimentation. They screened the works of younger authors who had grown up in the Cultural Revolution and who had been sent to the countryside as Red Guards, works like Zheng Yi's *Old Well* (*Laojing*, 1987); other subjects that were treated included an earlier story by Shen Congwen, *The Girl from Hunan* (*Xiangnü Xiao Xiao*, 1986).

The Fifth Generation is represented by names like Chen Kaige and Zhang Yimou. In his autobiography *Children of the Dragon* (*Shaonian Kaige*, Japanese 1989, Chinese 1991),[48] Chen gives a vivid and honest portrayal of his youth during the Cultural Revolution. The works of these film makers reflect the process of self-inquiry, the breaking free of political tutelage and the involved problems of overcoming the ubiquitous propagandistic lies. In 1985, Chen's *Yellow Earth* (*Huang tudi*) brought the Chinese film its international breakthrough. This is a film in which past and future are skilfully interwoven, with heavy use of symbolism. Chen Kaige based another film on Acheng's well-known novella about primary education in far-away Yunnan, *King of Children* (*Haizi wang*, 1987). And, in the same year, Zhang Yimou's *Red Sorghum* (*Hong gaoliang*) based on Mo Yan's novel presented an utopically exuberant picture of China's elemental life forces and vital energies. In 1991 Zhang produced *Raise the Red Lantern* (*Dahong denglong gaogao gua*), a screen version of the modernist Su Tong's story *Wives and Concubines* (*Qiqie chengqun*). In 1992, he enjoyed box-office success with *The Story of Qiuju* (*Qiuju da guansi*), a strikingly naturalistic production about a peasant woman who, like a modern Chinese Michael Kohlhaas, sets out to fight for her rights in a kafkaesque society. Chen Kaige's *Farewell to My Concubine* (*Bawang bieji*, 1993) centres on scenes from theatrical life but can be seen likewise as a filmed history of modern China, rather as writers such as Gu Hua and Lu Wenfu had attempted in *A Town Called Hibiscus* (*Furong zhen*, English 1983) and *The Gourmet* (*Meishijia*, story 1983), respectively.

Post-modern "Black Film Art" of the Sixth Generation

The new film *avant-garde*[49] is made up of directors who, having completed their professional training, were banned from film-making and who had no alternative but to work illegally. In 1995, they teamed up under the well-known producer Tian Zhuangzhuang in order to be able to jointly fund their production plans. So far, their works have been decried as "black film art" and not shown publicly in their entirety in China. They reflect the same chaotic life-style as the works of many post-modern authors including Can Xue, Ma Jian and Wang Shuo.

The *avant-garde* expresses the disillusionment of post-socialist China. At the centre of their films are the towns and cities of the 1990s, described as painfully true time documents. In *Red Beads* (*Xuanlian*, 1993), He Jianjun describes the brain-washing and other operations carried out in a psychiatric clinic to force people to toe the line. *The Postman* (*Youchai*, 1995) portrays the same loss of identity and the erosion of values in a different way: For many years, a postman has been opening the letters with which he is entrusted every day. Through these protagonists, we are introduced to figures on the edge of society, homosexuals, prostitutes, and suicide candidates. Zhang Yuan portrays the same marginal groups in a similar state of hopelessness. *The Square* (*Guangchang*, 1994) is a postmodern montage of documentation and fiction about Beijing's Tiananmen. Another talented film-maker in this group is Wang Xiaoshuai who in *Wintertime, Springtime* (*Dongchun de rizi*, 1993) reflects on the futility of life for China's intellectuals. He portrays the inability of a married couple, both of them artists, to adjust. In the film *The Big Game* (*Da youxi*, 1994), an artist stages his own sensational suicide in an attempt to achieve the recognition that he has been denied in life.

The film-makers of the Fifth Generation have by now firmly established their place in the international film scene, adapting to the worldwide market. Central figures like Zhang Yimou (*Life, Huozhe*, 1994) and Chen Kaige (*Farewell to My Concubine, Bawang bieji*, 1993) have found ways of coping with censorship. Chen's *Temptress Moon* (*Fengyue*, 1996), again with actress Gong Li, avoided critical issues; the film, which is set in 1911, portrays a successful gigolo who seduces older women, against a background of Shanghai casinos and night-clubs. The Sixth Generation, with films like Wang Xiaoshuai's *Wintertime, Springtime*, which have been shown abroad but not in China, still has to make its mark.

Hong Kong: Belated Search for Regional Identity

It is astonishing that an international city like Hong Kong, which can justifiably pride itself in its long tradition of relatively unrestricted freedom of the press, has produced so few literary testimonies of self-contemplation. Only a handful of writers have reflected on their own situation and its evolvement in pre- and post-war Hong Kong — on the role of the colony during the years of exciting affluence that had emerged gradually after the precarious situation produced by the Cultural Revolution. In the main, the picture that the West has of Hong Kong has been generated through Western works and films like Richard Mason's *The World of Suzie Wong* (1957), Han Suyin's *A Many-splendoured Thing* (1952), or other commercially-oriented novels and television series like James Clavell's *Tai Pan* (1966). What we see in them is usually the world of British-Chinese big business and Hong Kong's glittering high society.

What Is Representative of Hong Kong Literature?

Literary scholars in Hong Kong have compiled a few surveys of Hong Kong's regional literature. But, instead of being historical accounts of fascinating local cultural developments, these studies seem more like appeals in chagrin for such a literature. In an accompanying climate of scholarly indifference, only Lo Wai-luen (Lu Weiluan) has spent years of painstaking reconstruction work to revive the memory of those Chinese writers who, like Yu Dafu, Xiao Hong or Zhang Ailing, had at some time passed through Hong Kong or lived in the colony for a period of time. We are told about literature *in* and *from* Hong Kong, but definitely not about Hong Kong literature! Only the last few years before the 1997 watershed have seen an unprecedented search for the roots of Hong Kong identity and a last-minute monumental documentary effort by William Tay (Zheng Shusen) and others to present and preserve what long ago should have been unearthed and critically re-evaluated from Hong Kong related literature and culture.

Shi Shuqing,[50] sister of Taiwanese authoress Li Ang, who lived in Hong Kong for over a decade with her British banker husband, has published excellent portraits of PRC writers of the 1980s in Taiwan's *China Times* (*Shibao*). However, her cycle of novellas about life in Hong Kong's upper stratum fails to go beyond the level of entertainment. In a trilogy of novels published since 1995, she has made a second attempt to portray Hong Kong in anticipation of the year 1997, before eventually moving back to Taiwan.

At the same time, we find the official Chinese side making last-ditch efforts, via middlemen and fellow-travellers, to establish some kind of

Chinese Hong Kong literature, acceptable from PRC standards. These include, for example, the activities of the journalist and writer Liu Yichang, and his journal *Hongkong Literature* (*Xianggang wenxue*), also the initiative of a group of Beijing-friendly local writers. Tolerated up to 1997 in a grey area, "immigrant" post-modernist PRC Chinese writers like Ma Jian, on the other hand, were publishing their works, e.g. in an oppositional literary journal *News From Literature and the Arts* (*Wenyibao*, 1995–1996), disrespectfully appropriating the name of the official national PRC literary journal. Xi Xi, more urbane and sophisticated than most writers in the realm of "Cultural China," has ultimately found more readers in Taiwan than in Hong Kong where the media have clearly failed to take her seriously as a local author and cultural symbol of the city.

The restless 1990s have tempted young scholars to reject the idea of defining a so-called Hong Kong identity through such undistinguished literature. These intellectuals prefer to pursue the concept of popular culture,[51] which they believe can define and express the true nature of Hong Kong culture much more aptly. Popular culture embraces the media, television, film, the video industry, the national sport Karaoke, fashion, pop music, life-style in general, and much more, which together, they claim, give the city its unique identity. Taking this approach, intellectuals are finding vestiges of local post-modern instability and rootlessness, evidence of dissent and critical inquiry, in clear contrast to the enforced adaptation indispensable for all PRC Chinese over decades. Likewise, these scholars find themselves confronted in Hong Kong with a pre-emptive cultural submissiveness towards the new rulers, who they fear, will be under orders from Beijing.

Dangers for the Film Industry, Expectations from China after 1997

The development of the Hong Kong film industry in recent years shows the extent to which uncertainty about political and cultural status, issues of regional cultural identity, have driven Hong Kong's writers, artists and specialists of the popular film industry into the arms of China with high, and somewhat naive, expectations. Since 1995, a heated debate has flared up in Hong Kong cinema circles about the "death of the Hong Kong film."[52] Following the crisis year 1993, the industry which until then had gone from one success to another, declined so rapidly that its demise seemed virtually inevitable. Up to that point, Hong Kong had produced well over 100 films a year for commercial audiences. In the 1970s, *wuxia* films with the kungfu hero, Li Xiaolong, had been box-office successes, and the 1980s had seen a continuation of such successes with new thematical orientations and subject-clichés. But, even then, the film industry of this city with its six million population had generated only one-third of its revenues on the Hong Kong market itself. The remainder had derived from the markets in Korea, Taiwan, Southeast Asia and even the Chinese communities in North America. Meanwhile, these markets have partially collapsed under the onslaught of the supranational Hollywood film and its global strategies; at the same time, the anaemic slapstick mentality of parts of the Hong Kong cinema, furthermore, has estranged the audiences.

In 1995, after the Taiwanese government had virtually given up its former censorship and control of films, only 11 of Taipei's 114 cinemas were showing Taiwan films, the others were presenting Western, mainly Hollywood, movies. While the Hollywood film was reaching only 20% of Hong Kong's cinema goers in 1990, the share had more than doubled by 1995. A number of reasons can be cited for the "demise of the Hong Kong film": The expansion of the video market into almost every family home and the increase of electronic media as alternative forms of entertainment. The quality of the Hong Kong film deteriorated further, as outsiders became involved, who regarded investment in the industry more as a kind of big gamble than a form of popular art; brutality in the films increased, and the standards fell to an all-time low; even the Hong Kong mafia were rumoured to have a hand in the business. Films, like Wong Kar-wai's *Fallen Angels* (*Duoluo tianshi*, 1995) shown at the Berlin film festival in 1996, may be exceptions. Wang presented in this follow-up to his *Chungking Express*, a Wang Shuo-type protagonist, who is coerced into an affair with his female boss in a busy guesthouse atmosphere. Thus, directors like Wu Siyuan came to the conclusion that the only hope for the Hong Kong film was to orientate products towards the market on the Chinese mainland. If this could be achieved, Hong Kong's specialists in mass taste and its marketing professionals with their knowledge of effective distribution systems would displace the unsophisticated mainland operators, who still believed that financially China's film industry depended primarily on the sale of film copies. The hope for business success in China, many specialists argued, was considered to be the only possible breakthrough for the Hong Kong cinema industry.

Taiwan's uncertainties with respect to its cultural identity remain of a different nature. In contrast to Hong Kong, the island's democracy still has a slight chance — albeit jeopardized both from outside and inside — to move towards a more stable cultural consciousness and to establish an unchallenged local Taiwanese identity.

Other Forms of Regionalism in Jeopardy: Taiwan's Literature and Film

I would now like to reflect on some key aspects of these two related genres. Taiwan's literature[53] is noteworthy both in terms of artistic value and from the viewpoint of cultural policy, because of the particular forms and special ways in which it has developed over almost a century, in contrast to the other Chinese regional and provincial literatures. Taiwan's writers have been primarily motivated by the spirit of revolt against foreign rule; occasionally, however, we also find a touch of melancholic self-limitation and a pre-occupation with the central question of Taiwan's damaged identity.

Taiwan's New Literature originated in the early 1920s, after rather marginal and insignificant classical-literary-language beginnings in the 17th century in this southern haven of immigrants or, as it later became, the outermost province of the last imperial Manchu dynasty. Politically, the New Literature was moulded and often distorted by increasing repression under Japanese colonial rule and, subsequently, by the mainland Chinese occupation mentality of the early Kuomintang regime. It was not until the end of the 1980s, when the democratization process started in earnest on Taiwan, that the literature of the colonial period could be rediscovered or "excavated," as it were. It is only since that time that forces have been mobilized in an effort to "come to terms with the past" and has attempted to define Taiwan's vacillating identity for the 1990s. Politically and culturally, there are two opposing positions: while one side is striving for gradually increasing independence, the other continues to see Taiwan in the context of China; and, these positions appear so irreconcilable that no compromise seems likely or even conceivable. This underlying tension between "Taiwan consciousness," Taiwanese nativism or regionalism on the one hand, and "China consciousness" on the other, has in any case prevented the creation of a balanced platform from which Taiwanese scholars might have presented the long-awaited literary history of Taiwan, as a cornerstone of the new cultural identity. In times of "nation building,"[54] e.g., as during the first few years of the German empire under

Bismarck, the public has longed for a solid foundation of cultural identity. The fact that attempts in this direction have been made in Taiwan for three decades now and that such an identity-creating work for the field of literature has so far not be presented must be taken in itself as symptomatic of Taiwan's inner crisis in the closing years of the 20th century.

In the PRC, surprisingly, Taiwan literature was being brought to the reader during the last decade. Whilst this "presentation" was dictated by the regime, it was nevertheless handled with astonishing foresight by the PRC scholars entrusted with the job. In the last few years, they have published several literary history surveys which — as relations between Beijing and Taipei showed signs of relaxing — have even found their way into Taiwanese bookstores in both the original and as reprints.

Taiwanese Authors of the Japanese Period Rediscovered

I would now like to consider some of Taiwan's most important authors from the Japanese period who did not really come to be known until the 1990s and who are now gaining increasing recognition by literary scholars in the West. A detailed knowledge of their biographies and their ideas is vital to an understanding and a characterization of Taiwanese regionalism.

Chen Xugu (1891–1965), like Cai Qiutong, b. 1900, wrote short stories giving a satirical account of the arrogance of the Japanese colonials, especially the role of the Japanese policeman on Taiwan and the often slavish servility of many Taiwanese. Yang Shouyu (1905–1959), a close friend of Lai He,[55] the most significant author of the time, was a very prolific narrator in the Japanese period, who also gained a reputation as a poet. Among the subjects of his many stories were episodes in the lives of the lower social strata, the street trader, the out-of-work, and Taiwanese women. Wang Shilang, b. 1908, was a member of prominent literary groups in Taiwan and for a time edited *Taiwan's New Literature* (*Taiwan xin wenxue*),[56] the journal founded by Yang Kui, the second most important author of the period. After 1946, Wang was an influential journalist. He is probably best known for his short story *Night Rain* (*Yeyu*) which describes the breakup of a family following an unsuccessful strike by printing workers.

Zhang Wenhuan (1909–1978) wrote very stirring novels and short stories. He attended middle school and university in Japan, where he was co-founder of the journal *Formosa* which aimed at creating "a genuine Taiwanese literature." Zhang wrote only in Japanese, and one of his short novels became very popular with Japanese readers. Long Yingzong,[57] b. 1911, belonged to the group of authors who were increasingly influenced by Japan. It is thus no coincidence that he and Zhang Wenhuan represented Taiwan at the notorious First Conference on the Literature of Greater East Asia in Tokyo, in November 1942. The Japanese government used this conference to consolidate Japan's cultural supremacy in the colonies and in newly acquired territories by honouring collaboration-inclined authors. Finally, one of the most talented writers of the Japanese period was the author and literary critic, Lü Heruo (1914–1947), from Taichung (Taizhong).

Anti-communist Narrative Writing of the 1950s

So far we have looked at a number of authors from the Japanese period who, along with the most prominent representatives like physician Lai He or leftist activist Yang Kui, who tragically spent much of his life in the prisons of the Japanese and, especially, the KMT, have been recently brought to light again by the major cultural "excavation efforts." At the same time, the literature that emerged after 1949 has also been "revisited" in recent years. Younger literary critics have found that the literature of the 1950s and early 1960s needs to be re-examined, re-evaluated and reinterpreted.

Indeed, a kind of nostalgia for the four post-war decades appears to permeate society in the mid-1990s, and publications in this mood, e.g., from the China Times Press under feature editor Yang Ze, present a new and enlightening interpretation of the past. The writers of the Japanese period whom I mentioned earlier were isolated or ousted from the literary stage after 1945, and the direction was now determined by young mainlander intellectuals, supporters of the KMT. They, in turn, were required by the party to present a literature of strict ideological subordination and militant anti-Communism.

Jiang Gui[58] (1908–1980) was one of the most prominent representatives of anti-Communist narrative literature in Taiwan during the 1950s. Jiang's biography is available in English, as also is his best known novel *Whirlwind* (*Xuanfeng*, 1957). Zhu Xining,[59] b. 1926 in Shandong, is another intellectual and popular writer who came to prominence from the camp of the KMT military. Peng Ge,[60] b. 1926, a versatile journalist, was active in Taiwan in the service of the KMT and for many years worked as editor-in-chief of the official KMT *Central Daily News* (*Zhongyang ribao*). Peng published more than two dozen non-fiction works, translations, narrative prose and essays. Pan Renmu, b. 1920, who wrote in post-war Taiwan, was one of the most popular woman writers of this group of authors.

Taiwanese Modernism

During the late 1950s and early 1960s, a group of young writers in Taiwan, most of them belonging to the second generation of mainland immigrants, was deeply influenced by modern Western literature. Their models were Camus and Sartre, Faulkner and Joyce. It is important to remember that at this time Taiwan was a "cultural desert," cut adrift from both the new Chinese traditions of the 1930s and from literary developments on the mainland. Some of these writers left Taiwan and emigrated to the United States and elsewhere in order to retain their intellectual freedom. Because they have continued to influence literary circles in Taiwan and have also influenced writing on the mainland since the late 1970s, they are sometimes referred to as "semi-emigrants." The best known of them is Bai Xianyong, who portrayed the uprooted military and administrative élite of the KMT in Taiwan (*People from Taipei, Taibei ren*, 1971). Another is Wang Wenxin, author of the two modernist novels *Family Catastrophe* (*Jiabian*, 1972) and *Backed Against the Sea* (*Beihai de ren*, 1981).[61] Meanwhile, such are the forces of cultural nativism, however, that these authors and intellectuals, who still typify Taiwanese literature abroad to a certain extent, now take second place behind the more important *xiangtu* writers for most nativist-inclined readers in Taiwan.

Authors of Nativist Literature

In the 1970s, local Taiwanese writers again joined together to form a group which was first and foremost opposed to the then dominant modernists, who had largely ignored Taiwanese reality, and also to the rigid KMT establishment. These writers achieved success with what became known as nativist or *xiangtu* literature, which evolved into the literary mainstream on Taiwan for the next years.

Li Qiao, b. 1934, spent 20 years teaching in rural Taiwan, staying well away from the northern "capital of the mainlanders." He authored a trilogy on the history of Taiwan and, in 1995, a fictionalized account of the February 1947 massacre of the local population by the KMT army. Yang

Qingchu,[62] b. 1940 in a village near Tainan, who worked at many jobs, both as a labourer and a white-collar worker, gained recognition as an unsophisticated writer of the working classes, recounting what he himself had experienced. Yang also established a cultural centre and a publishing company. Wang Tuo,[63] and Yang paid for their convictions with long prison sentences; they now no longer write but are both actively involved in cultural policy and general political issues.

Lin Huaimin,[64] b. 1947 in Chiayi, studied in Iowa and took up ballet in New York. He wrote numerous short stories about the search of Taiwan's youth for a new identity. A homosexual like Taiwan's above-mentioned fiction author Bai Xianyong, he established a modern Taiwanese ballet, the Yunmen Ensemble, with both a national and local Chinese repertoire. Lin Shuangbu,[65] b. 1952, who like Li Qiao opted for the life of teacher in rural Taiwan, away from the "polluted" city of Taipei, has been one of the most outspoken of the local Taiwanese authors. The productive Lin has documented his thoughts and creative ideas — written down often in great haste for journals and newspapers — in two dozen books. Radical nativist author Song Zelai,[66] b. 1952, has changed course many times. Following Oskar Spengler, he pessimistically forecast not only the downfall of the West, but also the downfall of East Asia; he then, for a decade, sought salvation in local Zen-forms of Buddhism, represented a "literature of human rights" and wrote a bestseller about the murderous environmental destruction on Taiwan. In 1996, he reentered the literature field as editor of a radical nativist journal *New Taiwanese Literature Quarterly* (*Taiwan xinwenxue jikan*), mercilessly attacking every literary production close to semi-official cultural viewpoints and introducing a host of young talents. Wu Jinfa,[67] b. 1954, a journalist from the idyllic village of Meinong near Gaoxing, has portrayed[68] the tormented search of the Taiwanese for an identity of their own in contrast to cultural elements that had been imposed on them, first by the late Chinese empire, then by the Japanese, and more recently by the KMT who had fled the mainland. Particularly noteworthy are Wu's keen psychological observation and his use of the narrative techniques of the "absurd." The second important theme of this radical author who sympathizes so compassionately with his fellow Taiwanese, is the history and culture of Taiwan's displaced aborigines.

Women's Literature on Taiwan

In the 1990s, certain themes and genres came to be of central interest.

Here, for the sake of example, we shall consider poetry and literary criticism, women's writings and popular literature. In the 1980s, many female writers came to the fore who were able to build on the foundations laid by their predecessors.

Lin Haiyin,[69] b. 1919, had studied in Beijing and worked there as a journalist before returning to Taiwan in 1948. Many of her writings on the subject of women and the family are based on her own experience of life on the mainland. This is particularly true of her autobiographical novel *Memories of Peking: Southside Stories* (*Chengnan jiushi*, 1960), which is available in English translation. As feature editor of the *United Daily* (*Lianhe bao*), she had a major influence on the literary scene in Taiwan for several years. Yu Lihua, b. 1931, emigrated from Taiwan to the United States. She pioneered the so-called "foreign students' literature," which in the 1960s reflected the often traumatic experiences of the Chinese from Taiwan. Authoress Ouyang Zi,[70] b. 1939, a "modernist," who in 1962 left Taiwan to settle in the US, was considered to excel at drawing psychological portraits, especially of women. Liao Huiying,[71] b. 1948, from Taichung, who pursued a career in business after graduating from university, has portrayed, in a series of short stories and more recently novels, the new type of modern Taiwanese woman, especially the problems of the independent business woman. Su Weizhen, b. 1954, is to be located in the camp of regime-friendly intellectuals, as she was educated at the Party Cadre Academy in the milieu of the army. She is one of a group of women writers who seek, stylistically, to emulate the precocious Shanghai authoress Zhang Ailing (b. 1921, died in self-sought US exile in 1995)[72] who in Taiwan had become something of a mythical literary paragon *in absentia*. Su has gained recognition with both short stories and novels; as editor of the feature section of the conservative *United Daily*, she has been able to influence Taiwan's literary scene considerably. Zhu Tianxin, b. 1958 as daughter of the army writer Zhu Xining, has portrayed in her narrative writings since the end of the 1980s female protagonists of a new youth who play an active part in defining their new role in society and whose attitude to sexuality is extremely liberal by any standards.

On the Development of Taiwanese Poetry

Like narrative prose — after regionally coloured classical *wenyan*-origins at the end of the Qing dynasty — Taiwanese poetry too has changed course many times, from the experiments in the spirit of China's May-Fourth, a style of modernism that was heavily influenced by the West and also by Japanese lyrical prototypes,[73] to a new and deeply committed Taiwanese poetry with a strong local flavour. Taiwan's mainland poets and writers paved the way for this development.

Ya Xuan, b. 1932, has risen to prominence as an experimental modernist who has influenced the literary climate in Taiwan not only through his own poetry but also, up to the mid-1990s, through his position as senior editor of the influential *United Daily* feature section. Luo Fu, b. 1928, is one of several poets and narrative writers to come from the military. At the end of the 1980s, he renewed contact with contemporary poets on the mainland through his journal *Creation* (*Chuangshiji*). His restless artistic self-consciousness propelled him to and fro between the pride he and his fellow poets felt as the real precursors of the obscure *menglongshi* poets in the PRC and the melancholic feeling that as representative of a *provincial literature* he and his peers would never receive adequate recognition either in China or elsewhere. In 1996, both Ya and Luo made arrangements for their retirement in Canada. Yu Guangzhong,[74] b. 1928, who came to Taiwan from southern China, made a lasting impression on the lyrical scene in the 1960s and 1970s. However, as a close supporter of the regime's cultural policy, he polemically opposed *xiangtu* literature, which lost him many young readers. An otherwise highly respected university teacher, he wrote a great deal of poetry and essays and acted as a translator and publisher with an international perspective. Yale University professor Zheng Chouyu, b. 1933, whose poetry is widely read, can, like Bai Xianyong, be seen as a representative of mainland writers who emigrated to the United States. Younger regional Taiwanese poets include the Kaohsiung physician Zheng Jiongming, b. 1948, and the versatile Li Minyong, b. 1947.[75] Li is a frequent contributor in the press, an eloquent spokesman of the opposition and an expert on cultural policy. He has written several volumes of poetry and essays and published impressive collections of social and political analysis.

Popular and Mass Literature

Right up until the 1960s, Taiwan had been very much a closed society. The mass literature which had spread through the island from Taipei, with its lachrymose pseudo-traditionalism and cynical disregard for suppression, had functioned as an expedient diverting attention from political dictatorship and the manifold social taboos. As Taiwan opened up increasingly in the 1980s, an all-pervading popular literature, which was influenced particularly by the US and by Japan and was very much in keeping with a noisy, volatile television culture, eventually created book products in a commercially successful aesthetic form. These developments, at the same time, largely displaced most serious attempts at creating literary works.

Guo Lianghui,[76] b. 1926, wrote countless sentimental love stories which also found their way to the mainland. With her apolitical accounts of life in the Sahara and other far-off places, San Mao[77] (1943–1991) caught the imagination of Taiwan's youth in the 1970s, who felt increasingly caged in on the island. Qiong Yao, b. 1938, authored about 50 maudlin best-selling novels about love and marriage. When her books became available in the PRC, her popularity with schoolchildren and students there was so overwhelming that a "Qiong Yao storm" swept over the mainland. Zhao Shuxia (Susie Chen),[78] b. 1931, who has settled in Switzerland, can be seen as one of the few popular Chinese writers living in Europe to have achieved some degree of success both in Taiwan and on the mainland with sentimental and patriotic subjects. A film has been based on her novel about courtesan Sai Jinhua[79] and her liaison with Count Waldersee, the Commander of the Allied troops which suppressed the Boxer Rebellion.

New Taiwanese Film and Literature

The authors who were at the centre of interest in the 1990s or those who have been evaluated in a new light — from a review of the colonial period and the revisited anti-communist novels of the 1950s to Taiwan's modernism and nativist (*bentu*) literature — reached only a limited readership. The literary critics we have mentioned have been well aware of this: poets too had opted by definition for an élitist domain. Women's literature on the other hand and, to an even greater degree, popular literature reached a broad section of the public. From the colonial period until the 1980s, many writers had chosen the role of social reformer, using literature as one of the few domains relatively neglected or tolerated by the regime. It was finally the film and the new media in general which gave them access to the wider public. Some writers could not resist this temptation. It is from this perspective that we shall look, in passing, at the Taiwanese film scene.

Film and literature in Taiwan have formed a very special symbiosis. As in the PRC since entering the reform period, many contemporary films have been based on literary texts. We almost have the impression that some writers have forsaken their original medium, that they have been consciously entrusting their "message" to the new medium, the film, or in some cases the television film. Whatever the reasons, many literary works which originally addressed only a limited readership were now beginning to reach a mass audience in this way.

The screening in 1983 of three stories by the satirist Huang Chunming was a significant milestone in the history of the Taiwanese cinema, with the three directors responsible for this co-production becoming leading figures in the New Taiwanese Film. Hou Hsiao-hsien (Hou Xiaoxian)'s filming of *The Sandwich Man* (*Erzi de da wanou*, 1983) was combined with two other titles *Xiao Ding's Cap* and *Bitter Apples* (*Pingguo de ziwei*), which were produced by Zeng Chuangxiang and Wan Ren. This production undisputably marked the birth of the New Taiwanese Film.

In the following years, Hou produced the films *A Summer at Grandpa's* (*Dongdong de jiaqi*, 1984), *Dust in the Wind* (*Shaonian Ye Anla*, 1986), *The Boys from Feng-kuei* (*Fenggui laide ren*, 1983), *The Time to Live and the Time to Die* (*Tongnian wangshi*, 1985), and *Daughter of the Nile* (*Niluohe nüer*, 1987); his later films were *A City of Sadness* (*Beiqing chengshi*, 1989), *Dust of Angels* (*Lianlian fengchen*, 1992), and *The Puppetmaster* (*Ximeng rensheng*, 1993), *Good Men, Good Women* (*Haonan, haonü*, 1995). Hou Hsiao-hsien's *Goodbye South, Goodbye* (*Zaijian nanguo zaijian*, 1996) shows hot and humid Taiwan from a new angle: from the milieu of a nightclub, a group of friends move on, to Shanghai, in the same business. The above trilogy and Hou's later films played a key role in the revolt of "Taiwanese consciousness" against KMT repression. They brought to a wide audience the message of *xiangtu* literature and created a new Taiwanese sense of pride and a new defiance. Films based on popular literature on the other hand, like, e.g., Qiong Yao's works, continued to portray politically innocent, familiar subjects.

In the 1950s, the only films that had been permitted by the KMT were propaganda films and anti-communist documentaries. The film in Mandarin was brimful of "false consciousness," most of the subjects treated were completely out of line with Taiwanese reality. Precursors of the New Film were works by the director King Hu (Hu Jinquan) who worked with Shaw Brothers in Hong Kong and who in 1967 settled in Taiwan where he achieved a major success with *Dragon Gate Inn* (*Longmen kezhan*, 1966).[80] This ahistoric nostalgia triggered off countless other martial art productions and kung fu films.

The 1980s saw the breakthrough of *xiangtu* literature and the spread of this consciousness via the big screen to the general public. One element of the new Taiwanese consciousness in these films was the use of regional language; the Hakka dialect was also used in some productions. In *The Time to Live and the Time to Die*, Hou, born in 1947 and himself a Hakka, mixed the different language worlds of the *kejia*, the Taiwan dialect and the standard Mandarin (Chinese) *guoyu*. In their films, Hou and his fellow directors were highly critical of the increasing industrialization, they attempted to return to their regional-national cultural roots, indeed to find a new identity. Another director, Edward Yang (Yang Dechang), focused on the increasing isolation of the individual in society and the moral degeneration in towns and cities in his films *Taipeh Story* (*Qingmei zhuma*, 1985) and *The Terrorizers* (*Kongbu fenzi*, 1986). Zhang Yi's *Yu Qingsao* (1984) bitterly attacked the repressive system of traditional ethics based on functionalized twisted Confucianism. The as yet intact family bonds in rural Taiwan were contrasted with the broken human relationships in the towns and cities, where the protagonists found themselves incapable of adapting.

Co-production between directors from China and Taiwan in the 1990s is based on rather special motives taking very flexible forms. In the PRC, artistic cooperation, e.g., between Taiwan, China, Europe and the US, has had far-reaching political consequences. The Chinese government is slowly losing its former absolute control over China's film industry. This can be a highly explosive situation — we have seen that the very foundations of East Germany were undermined not least by the influence of television and TV-films.The film directors of the fifth generation in China have used several ruses, e.g., cooperation with sponsors from other countries and from Taiwan, to escape the troublesome meddling and control by the Beijing government. A whole series of films could be quoted here which originated in such a "Chinese co-production" with Taiwan.

Other than these, most successful Taiwan-US co-productions have been the comedies by Ang Lee (Li An) *The Wedding Banquet* (*Xiyan*, 1993) and *Eat Drink Man Woman* (*Yin shi nan nü*, 1994), also his *Few Women, Few Profits* (*Shaonü xiaoyü*, 1995).

Assessing Cultural Regionalism in Taiwan

I would now like to attempt to assess the significance of Taiwanese literature and its development during the 1990s in the West, for a wider public, beyond the confines of China and Taiwan. It need not be stressed that literature, like the cinema, must be considered indispensable elements of the new Taiwanese consciousness for this island with its own particular colonial and post-colonial development. It will probably take two generations of Taiwanese scholars to "excavate" the country's cultural heritage after decades of forced obscurity and suppressed history, to define and establish a new Taiwanese identity.

The underlying tension mentioned earlier — whether Taiwan will eventually be returned, like Hong Kong in 1997, to the "empire," whether the island is currently evolving towards an independent state, or whether it is moving towards a more or less "orderly" relationship with a future China — this tension will have to be resolved one way or the other.

The problems of defining or redefining one's own personal and regional identity, which, in our case, also means breaking free of colonial consciousness and facing the post-colonial situation, have a more global significance. Catastrophic turns in the biographies of the leading figures in Taiwan's fight for cultural freedom, the psychological and physical annihilation of intellectuals through persecution and long terms of imprisonment, the elemental uneasiness from collaborating with the ruling groups of the day, the sensitive question as to how much opportunism is permissible before it irreparably damages one's character and integrity, all these are human experiences and challenges which we find the world over. Nor does life in exile (in our case Taiwanese in Japan, China, and the US) bring problems that are specific to Taiwan. The challenges facing the individual in exile are basically alike in all countries, they can and should therefore be treated from a comparative perspective.

The significance of the Taiwan paradigm, indeed the essence of Taiwan's regional literary development, from a global perspective lies in such common elements, in similar challenges, and in comparable responses, both on the individual level and seen from the perspective of a vigorous, creative local society.

The different cultural manifestations of regional development in China, Hong Kong and Taiwan, as mapped out above, as well as the equally challenging realities of "Cultural China" in Southeast Asia and, more marginally in North America, incorporate the broadest range of theoretical possibilities of cultural interaction. But, the music seems to me less in effectively constructing theoretical models of "Greater China" explaining the complex interaction between the many different regions of "Cultural China." More attracting is the interplay of the unpredictable actual forces of rejuvenation and adaption, from post-colonial premises, to a globalized cultural situation, as shown above for 1996 and the preceding years. China is often not adequately aware that the old pose of cultural unity and superiority, even in a more moderate modern disguise, tends to create strong anxieties among regional partners. The pressures from the centre and the consequences of protest and conformism in cities, regions, and in the heart of individuals, are virulent enough to trigger further tragedies; likewise, such interaction may surprise the world with fascinating new cultural products, activities and visions.

Notes

Author's note: The following information is meant as exemplary reference for further reading. I mention basically English translations and some important scholarly work. See also Kam Louie and Louise Edwards (eds) *Bibliography of English Translations and Critiques of Contemporary Chinese Fiction 1945–1992* (Taipei: Centre for Chinese Studies, 1993); and "Further Reading" in Bonnie S. McDougall and Kam Louie, *The Literature of China in the Twentieth Century*, (London: Hurst, 1997, forthcoming).

1. Harvard Professor Tu Wei-ming first expanded an interview in the Hong Kong journal *Jiushi niandai* (The Nineties), June 1990, pp. 60–61 into the 1994 text "Cultural China: The Periphery as the Centre," in the collection of articles *The Living Tree: The Changing Meaning of Being Chinese Today* (Cambridge, Mass.: Harvard University Press, 1994), pp. 1–34, as a kind of introduction to this fascinating probe into contemporary forms of Chinese cultural identity. I use in this report only the narrower definition of the term, coined on three levels by Tu for China, Hong Kong and Taiwan — Chinese cultural elements in Southeast Asia — and on a third level for the impact of a community of intellectuals analysing and explaining China to an international audience. My perspective omits the meta-Chinese vision of strong elements of a global Chinese contemporary culture, reserves Chinese cultural presence in Southeast Asia for separate treatment by specialists of this area and confines itself to the East Asian context.
2. See, for example, Chen Xiaoming, *Shengyu de xingxiang — jiushi niandai de wenxue xushi yu wenhua weiji* (Residual Images — Literary Narratives of the 1990s and the Cultural Crisis) (Leiden: 1996), unpublished manuscript, 155 pages; preface International Institute for Asian Studies, Leiden, October 1996. Chen, like other members of the group of younger critics, complains in the preface to this book that the literary establishment has done its utmost to marginalize and isolate them from their potential Chinese audience.
3. See, for example, the presentation in encyclopaedic form of the literature of

the Republican period edited by a group of European scholars: N. G. D. Malmquist (ed.), *A Selective Guide to Chinese Literature 1900–1949* (Leiden: E. J. Brill, 1989), 4 vols., sponsored and initiated by the European Science Foundation.

4. Liu E, *The Travels of Lao Ts'an*, trans. Harold Shadick (Ithaca, NY: Cornell, 1952).
5. See Perry Link, *Mandarin Ducks and Butterflies: Popular Fiction in Early Twentieth-Century Chinese Cities* (Berkeley: University of California Press, 1981).
6. See references in William H. Nienhauser ed., *The Indiana Companion to Traditional Chinese Literature* (Taipei: Southern Materials Center, 1986); a new edition has been in preparation since 1996.
7. Yang Lian and Gao Xingjian, "Piaobo shi women huodele shenmo? Yang Lian han Gao Xingjian de duihua" (What Did We Gain from "Floating"? A Dialogue between Yang Lian and Gao Xingjian), October 1993 in *Renjing guihua* (Human Views — Devilish Words) (Beijing: Zhongyang bianyi publishers, 1994), pp. 293–327.
8. At least three dozen anthologies, especially of prose and poetry, which documented this literary reawakening became available in translation in the West. See H. Martin, Jeffrey Kinkley (eds), *Modern Chinese Writers. Self-Portrayals* (Armonk, NY: M. E. Sharpe, 1992), pp. 351–52; see also Kam Louie, *Bibliography* (see Author's note) and Bonnie S. McDougall, *The Literature of China* (see Author's note). In Germany alone, to mention one angle of the European development, more than 100 book translations from this period were produced. Periodicals like *Modern Chinese Literature* (Boulder, Colorado), have provided an overview of developments.
9. Zhang Jie, *Leaden Wings*, trans. Gladys Yang (London: Virago Press, 1987); also as *Heavy Wings*, trans. Howard Goldblatt (New York: Grove Weidenfeld, 1989).
10. Zhang Xinxin and Sang Ye, *Chinese Profiles* (Beijing: Chinese Literature, 1986); and *Chinese Lives*, trans. W. J. F. Jenner (New York: Pantheon, 1987).
11. Dai Houying, *Stones of the Wall*, trans. Frances Wood (London: Michael Joseph, 1985).
12. See also H. Martin, Jeffrey Kinkley (eds) (Note 8), pp. 20–25; and "The Blood-Stained Magnolia," *Chinese Literature*, April 1980, pp. 3–57.
13. Yang Jiang, *Ganxiao liuji* (Memories from Party School) (Beijing: 1981); see also *Yang Jiang zuopin ji* (Collected Writings by Yang Jiang) (Beijing: Zhongguo shehui kexue chubanshe, 1993), 3 vols.
14. For translations of Lu, Bai, Gu, Zong, Yang, Bei Dao, Acheng and Wang Anyi see Kam Louie, *Bibliography* (Author's Note).
15. Wang Meng, *Huodong bianrenxing* (trans. as Rare Talent Stupidity) (Beijing: 1987); the novel has been translated into Italian and German. See also

Selected Works of Wang Meng (Beijing: Foreign Languages Press, 1989), Vols. 1, 2.

16. On Liu Zaifu, see H. Martin, "'Men in the Crevice': Functions and Perspectives of Chinese Intellectuals versus the Authorities," paper, British Association of Chinese Studies 1996 conference, Cambridge, September 1996.
17. In Europe, for example, examples of such painting styles were shown in 1993 at highly acclaimed exhibitions in Berlin and again during 1996 in Bonn and Cologne.
18. On Cui Jian, see Andrew F. Jones, *Like a Knife: Ideology and Genre in Contemporary Chinese Popular Music* (Ithaca, NY: Cornell East Asia Series, 1992). Cp. also P. Link, R. Madsen, P. G. Pickowicz, *Unofficial China: Popular Culture and Thought in the People's Republic* (Boulder: Westview Press, 1989); and Wu Dingbo (ed.), *Handbook of Chinese Popular Culture* (New York: Greenwood Press, 1994).
19. See *Su Xiaokang, Wang Luxiang: Deathsong of the River — A Readers Guide to the Chinese TV Series Heshang*, trans. R. W. Bodman (Ithaca, NY: Cornell East Asia Series, 1992); and Christina Neder, *Fluβelegie: Chinas Identitätskrise. Die Debatte um die chinesische Fernsehserie Heshang 1988–1994* (River Elegy: China's Identity Crisis. The Debate about the Chinese Television Series Heshang 1988–1994) (Dortmund: Projekt Verlag, 1996), edition Cathay, Vol. 20.
20. Zhao Zhenkai (Bei Dao), *Waves*, trans. Bonnie S. McDougall (Hongkong: The Chinese University Press, 1985).
21. See Gao Xingjian's drama *Zhoumo sichongzou* (A Quartet at the Weekend), (Hong Kong: Tianyuan shuwu, 1996), with a bibliography of his plays, and other writings and a survey of international performances.
22. Gao Xingjian, *La montagne de l'âme*, trans. Noel and Liliane Dutrait (La Tour d'Aigues: Éditions de l'aube, 1995). The novel was published as *Lingshan*, 1990.
23. See Mo Yan, *Explosions and Other Stories*, trans. J. Wickeri (Hong Kong: Renditions, 1991), and *Red Sorghum: A Novel of China*, trans. Howard Goldblatt (New York: Viking, 1993). See also Mo Yan, *The Garlic Ballads*, trans. Howard Goldblatt (London: Hamish Hamilton, 1995).
24. On Can Xue, Liu Suola, Wang Anyi, Han Shaogong, Ye Zhaoyan, Duo Duo, Acheng, Mo Yan, Su Tong, Shi Tiesheng, Ge Fei, Sun Ganlu, and He Liwei see the mentioned bibliographies; "The Lost Boat" by Ge Fei is included in Henry Zhao (ed.), *The Lost Boat: Avant-garde Fiction from China* (London: Wellsweep, 1993), pp. 77–100. See Can Xue, *Dialogues in Paradise*, trans. Ronald Janssen (Evanston, IL: Northwestern University Press, 1989), and Can Xue, *Old Floating Cloud: Two Novellas*, trans. Ronald Janssen (Evanston, IL: Northwestern University Press, 1989).
25. "Xianshi yi zhong" translated in *Lost Boat* (Note 24), pp. 145–84. See Su

Tong, *Raise the Red Lantern: Three Novellas*, trans. Michael Duke (New York: William Morrow, 1993).

See the anthologies of *avant-garde* literature in Henry Zhao (ed.), *The Lost Boat ...*; and Henry Zhao (ed.), *UnderSky UnderGround, Chinese Writing Today* (London: Wellsweep, 1994), with stories by the authors Yu Hua and Ge Fei; see also Yu Hua, *The Past and the Punishments: Eight Stories*, trans. Andrew F. Jones (Honolulu: University of Hawaii Press, 1996).

For partial Wang Shuo translations, see *New Ghosts, Old Dreams, Chinese Rebel Voices* (New York: Times Books, 1992); on the *engagé* tendencies among writers during the preceding years, see also G. Barmé (ed.), *Seeds of Fire: Chinese Voices of Conscience* (New York: Hill & Wang, 1988). The novel *Living Dangerously* has been translated into German as Wang Shuo, *Herzklopfen heiβt das Spiel, Roman*, trans. Sabine Peschel (Zürich: Diogenes, 1995).

A collection of Li Rui translations into German is *Trügerische Heirat. Erzählungen vom Lande* (Doubtful Marriage, Stories from the Countryside), trans. Ines Gründel, Reiner Müller, et al. (Dortmund: Projekt Verlag, 1994), series *Arcus Chinatexte*, Vol. 3.

Cp. Duo Duo, *Looking Out from Death*, trans. Gregory Lee and John Cayley (London: 1989).

26. Information from colleague Eva Müller.
27. On Wang Shuo see the above mentioned novel and Gérémie Barmé, "Wang Shuo and *Liumang* (Hooligan) Culture," *The Australian Journal of Chinese Affairs*, No. 28 (July 1992), pp. 23–64.
28. For stories by Zhang Chengzhi in translation, see the above bibliographies and the anthology *UnderSky ...* (Note 25); also Zhang Chengzhi, *The Black Steed* (Beijing: Chinese Literature, 1990). A critical study of Zhang's fiction including "Xinlingshi" (History of the Soul) is Zhong Weiguang, "Weidao de Zhang Chengzhi, shundao de Wang Shuo" (Apologist Zhang Chengzhi, Easy-going Wang Shuo), *Beijing zhi chun* (Beijing Spring), June 1996, pp. 54–60.
29. Several international publishers, among them Krüger Verlag, Frankfurt, have prepared a translation of two novels and also selected stories by Hong Ying, b. 1962, living in London; the mentioned story is included in Hong Ying, *Xuanji zhi qiao* (Bridge of Abstruse Coincidence) (Kunming: Yunnan People's Publishing House, 1995).
30. The earlier mentioned two exhibitions of this "anti-art" staged in Berlin and Bonn provoked angry commentaries on Beijing television. See the catalogues Jochen Noth et al. (eds), *China Avantgarde* (Berlin: Edition Braus 1993); Dieter Ronte et al. (eds), *China, Zeitgenössische Malerei* (China, Contemporary Painting) (Cologne: Dumont 1996); and H. Kotzenberg (ed.), *Chinesische Tuschmalerei im 20. Jahrhundert* (Chinese Ink Paintings of the 20th century) (Munich, New York: Prestel, 1996).

31. See W. Draguhn and G. Schucher (eds), *Das neue Selbstbewußtsein in Asien: eine Herausforderung?* (The New Self-awareness in Asia: A Challenge?) (Hamburg: 1995), papers from a symposium in Berlin by the German Association of Asian Studies (Mitteilungen No. 257). In the literary field, Henry Zhao's attitude is a good example. For the emphasis on "cultural studies" in Asian literary criticism, cp. Wimal Dissanayake, "Cultural Studies: The Challenges Ahead For Asian Scholars," *Comparative Literature & Culture*, Hong Kong, No. 1 (September 1996), pp. 2–19.
32. Chen Xiaoming works at the Academy of Social Sciences in Beijing. His Ph.D. dissertation is *Jiegou de zongyi: lishi, huayu yu zhuti* (The Traces of Deconstruction: History, Discourse and Theme) (Beijing: Zhongguo shehui kexue chubanshe, 1994); a competent survey of the *Avant-garde* school is Chen Xiaoming, *Wubian de tiaozhan* (Unlimited Challenge) (Changchun: Shidai wenyi chubanshe, 1993).
33. Chen Pingyuan, professor at Beijing University, compiled a history of early modern narrative literature (1989), a book on the *wuxia* popular novels (1992) and several theoretical studies on the historiography of China's prose literature (1988, 1993).
34. See Henry Zhao (ed.), *The Lost Boat. Avant-garde Fiction from China* (London: Wellsweep, 1993), a good survey is the study of Zhao Yiheng, *The Need for Solitude* (*Biyao de gudu*), (Hong Kong: Tiandi Publishers, 1995); cp. his study *The Uneasy Narrator, Chinese Fiction from the Traditional to the Modern* (London: Oxford University Press, 1995).
35. The two volumes each on Late Qing, the Republican period and on PRC history in *The Cambridge History of China*, translated into Chinese, are widely circulated; the PRC history especially has had a strong impact in China.
36. See Henry Zhao ed., *UnderSky* … (Note 25), "*Sensing the Shift — New Wave Literature and Chinese Culture*," pp. 155–68, and the introduction to *Lost Boat* …, pp. 9–18.
37. We may include among such PRC scholars Kang Liu, Tang Xiaobin, Lu Tonglin, Lydia H. Liu and several others. See, for example, Liu Kang and Xiaobing Tang (eds), *Politics, Ideology and Literary Discourse in Modern China* (Durham, London: Duke University Press, 1993), also Lu Tonglin, *Gender and Sexuality in Twentieth-Century Chinese Literature and Society* (New York: State University of New York Press, 1993); Lu Tonglin, *Misogyny, Cultural Nihilism and Oppositional Politics, Contemporary Chinese Experimental Fiction* (Stanford: Stanford University Press, 1995). Cp. also Lydia H. Liu, *Translingual Practice: Literature, National Culture, and Translated Modernity, China 1900–1937* (Stanford: Stanford University Press, 1996).
38. Cp. Karl Eimermacher, *Russland, Wohin Eilst Du? Perestrojka und Kultur* (Russia, Where Are You Heading? Perestrojka and Culture) (Dortmund:

Projekt Verlag, 1996), 2 vols, part 5 in a series of analyses and documentation of Soviet cultural policy from 1917 up to 1995; for China, see Merle Goldman, *China's Intellectuals, Advice and Dissent* (Cambridge, Mass.: Harvard University Press, 1981) and also Merle Goldman, *Sowing the Seeds of Democracy in China: Political Reform in the Deng Xiaoping Era* (Cambridge, Mass.: Harvard University Press, 1994).

39. He Yuhuai, *Cycles of Repression and Relaxation: Politico-Literary Events in China 1976–1989* (Bochum: Brockmeyer, 1992), series Chinathemen, European Project on China's Modernisation, Vol. VI.
    H. Martin (Ma Hanmao) and Qi Mo (eds), *Dalu dangdai mingren pingzhuan, gongmin shehui de kaichuang zhe* (Biographies of Famous Cultural Personalities from China Mainland — Creators of a Civil Society) (Taipei: Zhengzhong shuju, 1995).
40. See, for example, *Cheng Ming*, No. 6 (1996), pp. 86–87, Huai Bing; Huai Ling in *Cheng Ming*, No. 8 (1996), pp. 83–84; *Cheng Ming*, No. 9 (1996), pp. 82–83, again by Huai Bing. The well-known Hong Kong critic, Ji Fuhua (Bi Hua), under his pseudonym Huai Bing offers an interpretation of "improvements of the literary situation," questioned by his anonymous critic. The 1996 developments clearly prove Ji too accommodating or even completely wrong in his interpretative efforts; he admits this in *Cheng Ming*, No. 12 (1996), pp. 82–83.
41. The novel *Feidu* (Rotten City) (Beijing: Beijing chubanshe, 1993); there have been commentaries on the book in the West, but no translation so far. The new work is Jia Pingwa, *Tumen* (Doors of the Earth) (Shenyang: Chunfeng wenyi, 1996).
42. On the two congresses, see *People's Daily*, 17, 18, 21 December 1996; Jiang Zemin's speech is carried in the 17 December issue. Sketchy reports are in Cheng Ming, No. 2 (1997), pp. 84–85, by the critic Huai Bing and by exile writer Kong Jiesheng on Jiang Zemin's programmatic talk, pp. 86–89. For other background on ousted authors and on intrigues against Bai Hua in Shanghai, see p. 32. Cp. also *Jiushi niandai* (The Nineties), No. 1 (1997), pp. 16–17.
43. See *Cheng Ming*, No. 12 (1996), pp. 82–89; and *Kaifang*, No. 12 (1996), pp. 16, and 90–91. On the preparatory debates of the writers' congress, see Howard Goldblatt (ed.), *Chinese Literature for the 1980s* (Armonk, NY: M. E. Sharpe, 1982); on the 1984 congress, Merle Goldman, *Sowing the Seeds of Democracy in China* (Cambridge, Mass.; Harvard University Press, 1994), pp. 137–50.
44. See *People's Daily*, 25 October 1996, with the indirect attacks on Wang Meng; *International Herald Tribune*, 27 November 1996 on Wang Shuo; *Asiaweek*, 22 November 1996, pp. 42–44 with excerpts of an interview with Mo Yan.

45. Li Zehou and Liu Zaifu, *Gaobie geming* (A Farewell to Revolution) (Hong Kong: Tiandi Publishers, 1996).
46. *Zhongguo zuojia*, No. 3 (July 1996).
47. Gao Xingjian, "The Voice of the Individual," pp. 71–81 (Paris, 4 April 1993) in *The Stockholm Journal of East Asian Studies*, Vol. 6, 1995. Gao maintains that by being forced into exile Chinese intellectuals experienced a kind of awakening, they arrived at new conclusions as for example the bitter condemnation of blind patriotism.
    Zhongguo keyi shuo bu! — lengzhan hou shidai de zhengzhi yu qinggan jueze (China Can Say No! — Options for Politics and Emotions in the Post-Cold War Period) (Beijing: Zhonghua gongshang lianhe chubanshe, 1996).
48. See Chen Kaige, *Autobiographie. Kinder des Drachen. Eine Jugend in der Kulturrevolution* (Autobiography: Children of the Dragon, A Childhood during the Cultural Revolution), trans. Stefan and Hu Chun Kramer with Ch. Hammer (Leipzig: Kiepenheuer, 1994), Vol. 2 of the series *Arcus Chinatexte* of the Richard-Wilhelm Translation Centre.
49. See Stefan Kramer, *Schattenbilder. Filmgeschichte Chinas und die Avantgarde der 80er und 90er Jahre* (Shadow Images: A film History of China and the *Avant-garde* of the 1980s and 1990s) (Dortmund: Projekt Verlag, 1996), published in the series edition Cathay, Vol. 23.
50. Two volumes of the trilogy by Shi Shuqing have been published as *Xianggang sanbuqu* (Hong Kong Trilogy) (Hong Kong: 1995), for comment see the Hong Kong monthly *Mingbao yuekan* (Ming Pao Monthly), November 1995, pp. 88 ff.
51. On regional identity, see Shi Wenhong et al., *Xianggang puji wenhua yanjiu* (Studies on Hong Kong Popular Culture) (Hong Kong: Sanlian Publishers, 1993). From the viewpoint of the Chinese society of Hong Kong, with its individual, social, economic, political and legal values, a pioneer effort of a new definition has been Lau Siu-kai, Kuan Hsin-Chi, *The Ethos of the Hong Kong Chinese* (Hong Kong: The Chinese University Press, 1988). On identity, see also Lo Fu, *Xianggang wenhua manyou* (A Survey of Hong Kong Culture) (Hong Kong: Zhonghua Publishers, 1993); and Liang Chengjun, (ed.), *Xianggang de liuxing wenhua* (Hong Kong's Popular Culture) (Hong Kong: Sanlian Publishers, 1993). See also the journal *Xianggang wenhua yanjiu* (Hong Kong Cultural Studies Bulletin), No. 6 (Winter 1996), with several articles on the role of Chinese and Hong Kong intellectuals. Cp. from the Chinese angle: Tu Wei-ming (Note 1).
52. The November 1995 issue of the prominent cultural journal *Mingbao yuekan* devoted a series of articles to this debate.
53. The following is a much abbreviated version of H. Martin, *Taiwan Literature — Postcolonial Options*, *Chinabilder* (China Perspectives), Vol. 3, (Dortmund: Projekt Verlag, 1996), pp. 177–210. See. E. Sandschneider, H.

Martin (eds), *Interdisciplinary Aspects of Research on Taiwan in Germany* (Dortmund: Projekt Verlag, 1994); the volume, referred to below as SM, includes a comprehensive bibliography of studies and translations. On the history of Taiwan literature, see H. Martin, "The History of Taiwanese Literature: Towards Cultural-Political Identity. Views from Taiwan, China, Japan and the West," *Hanxue yanjiu* (Chinese Studies), June 1996, Taipei, pp. 1–51. On film, see Stefan Kramer, *Schattenbilder …* (Note 49), and Ellen Widmer and David Der-wei Wang (eds), *From May Fourth to June Fourth: Fiction and Film in Twentieth Century China* (Cambridge, Mass.: Harvard University Press, 1993); see also Rey Chow, *Primitive Passions: Visuality, Sexuality, Ethnography, and Contemporary Chinese Cinema* (New York: Columbia University Press, 1995); and William Tay, "The Ideology of Initiation: The Films of Hou Hsiao-hsien," in *New Chinese Cinemas*, edited by Nick Browne (Cambridge, Mass.: Cambridge University Press, 1994), pp. 151–59.

54. On nation building, see a study by Michael Hanamura in SM (Note 53).
55. See SM, on the Taiwanese writer Lai He.
56. See SM, on Yang Kui.
57. See SM, on Long Yingzong.
58. See T. A. Ross, *Chiang Kuei* (New York: Twayne, 1974), and Jiang Gui, *The Whirlwind*, trans. Timothy A. Ross (San Francisco: Chinese Materials Center, 1977).
59. On Zhu Xining, see for example Chi Pang-yuan et al., *An Anthology of Contemporary Chinese Literature, Taiwan: 1949–1974* (Taipei: National Institute for Compilation and Translation, 1975), Vol. II, *Short Stories.*
60. See Peng Ko, *Black Tears, Stories of War-Torn China*, trans. Nancy Ing introduction by C. T. Hsia (Taipei: Chinese Materials Center, 1986).
61. S. Wang Wen-hsing, *Backed Against the Sea*, trans. Edward Gunn (Ithaca, NY: Cornell East Asia Series, 1993); and Wang Wen Hsing, *Family Catastrophe: A Modernist Novel*, trans. Susan Wan Dolling (Honolulu: Hawaii University Press, 1995). See also the study by Yvonne Songsheng Chang, *Modernism and the Nativist Resistance: Contemporary Chinese Fiction from Taiwan* (Durham-London: Duke University Press, 1993).
62. See SM (Note 53), on the stories of the Taiwanese writer Yang Qingchu. Cp. the *Selected Stories of Yang Ch'ing-ch'u*, trans. Thomas B. Gold (Taipei: Diyi Publishers, 1983).
63. See SM, a study on Taiwanese author Wang Tuo.
64. On the theme of homosexuality, see Bai Xianyong, *Crystal Boys*, trans. Howard Goldblatt (San Francisco: Gay Sunshine Press, 1989), and Michael Schütte, *Hurensühne, Bai Xianyong und sein Roman* Niezi (*1983*) (Bastards, Bai Xianyong and His Novel *Niezi* (1983) (Bochum: 1995), unpublished MA-thesis, Ruhr-University.

65. See also H. Martin and Jeffrey Kinkley (eds), *Modern Chinese Writers: Self-Portrayals* (Armonk, NY: M.E. Sharpe, 1992).
66. See H. Martin (ed.), *Modern Chinese Writers. Self-Portrayals*, and SM (Note 53), on Song Zelai. See also his autobiographical record of the years 1980–1996, dated April 1996, in *Taiwan xinwenxue jikan* (New Taiwanese Literary Quarterly), No. 5 (1996), pp. 305–17; cp. the explosive attack from a *xiangtu* perspective: Song Zelai, "Dangqian wentan zhenbingshu" (A Diagnosis of the Contemporary Literary Scene), *Taiwan xinwenxue jikan* (New Taiwanese Literature Quarterly), No. 4 (1996), pp. 275–304.
67. See SM (Note 53), a study by Martina Mohr, on Taiwan consciousness, Wu Jinfa and the socio-cultural problematique of the Formosan aborigines.
68. Cp. Christa Gescher, *Taiwanesische Literatur zur japanischen Besatzungszeit: Der Schriftsteller Wu Zhuoliu und sein Roman* Waisenkinder Asiens (Taiwan Literature during the Japanese Occupation: The Writer Wu Zhuoliu and His Novel *Orphans of Asia*) (Bochum: PhD thesis, 1995).
    See also Wu Zhuoliu, *The Fig Tree: Memoirs of a Taiwanese Patriot 1900–1947*, trans. Duncan B. Hunter (Dortmund: Projekt Verlag, 1994), edition Cathay, Vol. 1.
69. S. Lin Haiyin, *Green Seaweed and Salted Eggs*, trans. Nancy Ing (Taipei: Heritage Press, 1963); and Lin Haiyin, *Memories of Peking* (*Chengnan jiushi*), trans. Nancy Ing et al. (Hong Kong: The Chinese University Press, 1992).
70. Carsten Hoefer, *Literarischer Modernismus in Taiwan. Ouyang Zis Kurzgeschichten* (Literary Modernism in Taiwan: The Short Stories of Ouyang Zi) (Dortmund: Projekt Verlag, 1994), edition Cathay, Vol. 14.
71. On Liao Huiying, see SM (Note 53).
72. See H. M., "Like a Film Abruptly Torn off: Tension and Despair in Zhang Ailing's Writing Experience," paper of the Bonn conference Melancholy and Society in China, in H. Martin, *China Perspectives* (Chinabilder), Vol. 1, pp. 311–42 (Dortmund: Projekt Verlag, 1996).
73. See Yvonne Songsheng Chang, *Modernism and the Nativist Resistance* (Note 61).
74. Cp. Yu Guangzhong, *Acres of Barbed Wire: To China in Daydreams and Nightmares* (Taipei: Meiya, 1991).
75. On Zheng Jiongming, Li Minyong and the poetry of other *bentu* authors, see *Taiwan shiku* (Thesaurus of Taiwanese Poetry) (Kaohsiung 1990).
76. See Guo Lianghui, *Taipei Women*, trans. Constantine Tung (Hong Kong: New Enterprise Company, 1983); cp. Yang Zhao, "Sishinian Taiwan dazhong wenxue xiaoshi" (Forty Years of Taiwanese Mass Literature: A Brief History), pp. 25–69, in *Wenxue, shehui yu lishi xiangxiang* (Images of Literature, Society and History) (Taipei: Lianhe wenxue chubanshe, 1995).
77. See SM (Note 53), a study on popular literature and San Mao.

78. On Zhao Shuxia, cp. the translation Chao Shu-hsia, *Traumspuren, Erzählungen* (Dream Vestiges: Short-stories) (Cologne: Kai Yeh Publ., 1987).
79. Cp. Stephan von Minden, *Die merkwürdige Geschichte der Sai Jinhua: Historisch-philologische Untersuchung zur Entstehung und Verbreitung einer Legende aus der Zeit des Boxeraufstandes* (The Strange Story of Sai Jinhua: Historic-philological Research into the Origins and Spread of a Legend from the Time of the Boxer Uprising) (Stuttgart: Franz Steiner, 1994).
80. See Jin Yong, *Fox Volant of the Snowy Mountain*, trans. Olivia Mok (Hong Kong: The Chinese University Press, 1993). On the sub-genre, cp. also Kai Portmann, "Der fliegende Fuchs vom Schneeberg," *Die Gattung des chinesischen Ritterromans (wuxia xiaoshuo) und der Erfolgsautor Jin Yong* ("The Flying Fox from Snow Mountain," The Genre of the Chinese Adventure Novel [*wuxia xiaoshuo*] and the Author Jin Yong) (Bochum: Brockmeyer, 1994), series Chinathemen, No. 77.

13

Does China Face an Unstable Future? On the Political Impact of Rapid Growth

Andrew G. Walder

The spectre of future social and political instability, even the collapse of communist party rule and regional disintegration, haunts many forecasts about China's future. Indeed, China's top leaders appear to take this possibility very seriously, especially in the wake of their own political crisis in the spring of 1989 and the subsequent collapse of ruling communist parties in Eastern Europe and the Soviet Union from the fall of 1989 to the summer of 1991. Scholarship on China over the past decade has repeatedly emphasized three trends that seem to portend instability or even collapse: the unmistakable rise of independent social forces; the inequality, corruption, and inflation said to be characteristic of "partial reform"; and the clear loosening of the former system of political control over the population, and of the subordination of local governments to the centre.

The central argument of this chapter is that it is easy to exaggerate the potential for an unstable China if we simply extrapolate these trends into the future, for these trends will become destabilizing only under special conditions. These conditions are well understood and easy to specify. But, they are in turn very difficult to predict, because they depend on short-term interactions among China's political élites about which we have limited information (and which would be difficult to predict even with perfect information) and because they also depend on the political interaction of China's élite with the outside world, which is of course only partly a product of domestic events. Rapid economic growth has set into motion enormous changes in Chinese society and in the organization of the regime itself; but, to understand whether instability shall result, we are ill-served by linear extrapolations from obvious social and political trends. We need to adopt a view of the future that is based on contingency and chance.

Ominous Trends? China's Rising "Potential" for Instability

There are a number of good reasons for believing that the potential for an unstable China has risen steadily since the death of Mao Zedong. The process of economic reform, the opening of China to foreign capital, information, and ideas, and the frenetic economic growth of the past 20 years have all transformed Chinese society, and the regime itself, in fundamental ways. Journalistic and scholarly accounts alike emphasize the extent to which reform and growth have unleashed new social forces beyond the control of the regime that portend an increasingly autonomous and potentially restive society. They also emphasize the perils of market-oriented reform, which brings into being new sources of instability and dissatisfaction: inflation, corruption, unemployment, mass migration, and a widening gap between rich and poor. And finally, it is equally clear that the regime is in the process of losing the kind of centralized control that it once enjoyed: local party organizations and work units no longer exercise the kind of control over citizens's lives that was true of the Mao era; and, there has been an unmistakable rise in the autonomy of regional authorities from the dictates of the centre. The rise of new social forces in an increasingly unstable social and economic environment in which the capacity of the regime to control citizens and local authorities is clearly on the decline: these are good reasons for suspecting that China may face an increasingly unstable future.

The Rise of Autonomous Social Forces

The changes wrought in Chinese society since the mid-1970s are nothing short of astounding, and most striking among these changes is the increased autonomy of ordinary citizens from the scrutiny and control of party-state officials and organizations. In the commune system, China's peasants were tied to land and locality by a form of agricultural organization that separated them from the harvest. Private plots and market sidelines severely restricted, peasants had no alternative to subsistence from the work points and grain rations allocated by their collective production teams. Migration from the village was effectively stemmed: household grain rations were cut if family members were not present to earn work points, and any migrants to other areas would face a draconian system of grain rationing and household registration that effectively denied migrants food and residence. Salaried jobs in commune and brigade factories were allocated within the collective structures by commune officials; work outside the village as temporary or contract labour was similarly organized by brigade officials.[1]

Urban citizens were similarly entrenched in overlapping institutions of surveillance and control centred on neighbourhoods and workplaces. Neighbourhood committees maintained household registers, administered rations for grain and other foodstuffs, and patrolled the streets to ensure that there were no unregistered residents. For much of the 1970s, they ensured that youths sent down to the countryside could not return.

Employees of China's famed "work units" usually expected to remain for all of their lives in institutions that often provided housing, and a wide range of services and benefits. Urban employees experienced regular political meetings and found their behaviour and political attitudes observed and evaluated by party officials and their agents. For long periods of time in the 1960s and 1970s, there was little time outside of working hours for leisure or other activities. Consumer goods were in short supply and rationed, and the consumer goods that were available were distributed through work units either in kind or in the form of ration coupons. Permission to travel to another city, to marry, and other things all required the written permission of work unit leaders.[2] While in recent years many have found it necessary to point out that the control exercised over citizens was never really *total*, it is nonetheless beyond dispute that, under Mao, Chinese citizens found themselves under much greater government scrutiny and control than in other types of regimes, and even in such socialist regimes as Poland and the USSR.

How different the China of today! Collective agriculture disappeared early in the 1980s; peasant households now farm their own plots and are free to engage in any agricultural sidelines or other businesses. Peasants migrate freely to other rural regions, small towns, and even larger cities in search of wage labour. Anywhere from 60 to 90 million of this "floating population" now live outside their home villages on at least a temporary basis. Grain and other foodstuffs are available freely on markets; suburban hotels and dormitories cater to the migrants from rural China, and no permanent registration is necessary.

In the cities, the controls formerly centred on neighbourhood and work unit are a pale shadow of their former selves. Rationing for grain, other foodstuffs and for consumer items is largely a thing of the past, along with the extreme consumer austerity of the Mao era. The household registration system is no longer enforced with the stringency of years past. The role of party organizations in work units, along with their control over rewards, has suffered a serious decline, and there is no longer any serious effort to organize political meetings or indoctrinate employees in the workplace. While many urban work units still supply a wide range of services and benefits to their employees, they are increasingly nothing more than places of employment.

What has emerged from the shell of Mao era social institutions is what many observers call an increasingly autonomous society. In the countryside, villagers are often observed to be increasingly assertive in their dealings with local cadres;[3] traditional kinship rituals and religious observance have been revived in a spectacular fashion; new religions such as Christianity and local millenarian movements have been on the rise, along with local secret societies. Many rural regions are developing chain patterns of migration to other regions, and on occasion establish identifiable communities in urban areas (such as the former "Zhejiang village" near Beijing). Ethnic identities, for example in Moslem communities, have been revived and local officials increasingly play the "ethnic card" in their dealings with higher levels of government.[4]

In the cities, the decline of neighbourhood and work unit organization has given way to the rise of increasingly autonomous and, often, organized spheres of social life outside the direct control of the party and government. A thriving retail sector of shops, restaurants, and entertainment establishments, much of it private, have come to rival neighbourhood and work unit as alternative locations for socializing and leisure time. There has emerged a whole range of clubs and associations centred on personal, professional, and intellectual interest. So long as these organizations do not have overt political programmes, they usually meet with relative indifference on the part of government. Many observers argue that this unmistakable rise of these unmonitored physical spaces and social spheres for citizen association and public life have created the foundations for an autonomous, increasingly organized, and potentially assertive urban society.[5]

Chinese society clearly is a very different place from what it was 20 years ago, and it is possible to summarize the trend of change as pointing towards a new balance of power between "state" and "society" that tips increasingly in favour of the latter. The carefully organized and closely monitored, orderly society of the Mao years is giving way increasingly to a disordered and seemingly chaotic new reality. There are, after all, vast new sectors of the population and economy that are completely outside the former structures of control. The massive "floating population" of rural migrants is viewed increasingly as a source of potential urban unrest, and their presence in streets and railway stations is a cause of discomfort and sometimes alarm for the government and permanent populations. The small scale private sector in urban areas, under-reported in official statistics, employs as many of 20% of the urban population, and the rural private sector is much larger. The rise of crime is unmistakable and widely lamented. Isolated strikes and other labour protests are reportedly on the rise, and rural riots and localized rebellions have been reported with increasing frequency.

These highly publicized trends lead many Chinese officials openly to worry about "chaos," and they lead many independent observers to note signs of potential instability that are too obvious to ignore. These fears and observations seemed to find their clearest expression in the massive protests of spring 1989 — easily the largest and most sustained protest movement of any communist regime in that year, if not the most successful. A vibrant student movement stimulated broad public support in Beijing's streets and neighbourhoods. As the government appeared to lose control of the city for much of May, protests spread to cities throughout the country, and in some cases to violent riots. While the protests were curtailed through ruthless military action on 3–4 June, many feel that the "Tiananmen movement" was but a foretaste of the social forces that lie dormant beneath the surface of China's increasingly autonomous and disordered society.

The Perils of "Partial Reform"

The main reason why an autonomous society is viewed as an ominous threat to political stability is a corresponding view of "partial reform" as an inevitable source of destabilizing economic trends. One strong undercurrent in writings about the Chinese economy, especially during the 1980s, is that a gradual strategy of partial reform through diffident "half measures" will serve only to exacerbate the problems typical of planned economies while postponing until an indefinite future tough decisions about employment, price reform, and losses in the state sector.[6]

There is a number of popular aphorisms, mostly of East European origin, that convey the view that partial reform can create potentially serious economic problems. Perhaps the most memorable is the one in which a reforming communist regime decrees a great change in traffic patterns by having vehicles switch from the left to the right hand side of the road. But, the government, worried about potential disruption of traffic during the transition, does not want to move too quickly and seeks a controlled and painless transition. Therefore, the government decrees that during the first week only trucks will make the switch and, if all goes well, passenger cars will follow suit the next week. The underlying idea is that an economy that is neither fully planned nor fully market will only combine the disadvantages of capitalism with those of socialism and enjoy the advantages of neither.[7]

Two features of partial reform are seen as potentially destabilizing. The first is corruption: partial reform leaves vast economic resources in the hands of government agencies at all levels; it provides these same officials with vast powers to regulate all economic enterprise, including private enterprise, and by leaving in place a dual price structure after partial reform it provides opportunities for arbitrage and personal enrichment. Corruption is thought to create instability in two ways. First, by diverting economic resources into unproductive consumption and by distorting economic decision making, it undermines the foundations for further investment and growth of incomes and employment. Secondly, corruption leads to widespread popular disgust with officialdom and to a decline in the legitimacy of the regime.[8] Public opinion polls during the 1980s repeatedly showed this to be a major source of popular concern, and disgust over official corruption is widely seen as a driving force behind the popular protests of 1989.[9]

The second feature, partial reform, is widely criticized for creating macroeconomic instability, the most important manifestation of which is price inflation. A distorted and partially reformed price structure, coupled with continuing bailouts for state-owned industry, means that state enterprises continue to run up unredeemed debt and drain ever larger subsidies from the state budget. Continued over-investment in unproductive activities by firms not held accountable for their actions leads to characteristic cycles of boom and bust, as run-away growth has to be curtailed by drastic periodic contractions of credit. At the high point of the expansion drive, consumer price inflation reaches very high levels; and during the inevitable credit crunch, large numbers of temporary workers in the citics (the floating population) and rural industrial workers are thrown out of work as production contracts. Price inflation and worsening budget deficits are the price of partial reform. Price inflation reached a peak of close to 30% (officially) in the months preceding the Tiananmen demonstrations, and it is widely seen as a major cause of popular unrest.[10]

The road ahead for partial reform is often seen as perilous. More than a decade of rapid growth has led to a rapid rise in living standards, but income growth is threatened by inflation. Rapid industrialization has been achieved, primarily by unleashing a vibrant rural industrial sector, but the state sector remains — bloated, subsidized, a worsening drain on the state budget and an underlying source of waste and inflation. Inflation and corruption have become important sources of popular discontent, despite the obvious advances of recent years. And yet, the most sensitive and difficult tasks of reform still lie ahead. A further freeing of prices to carry out a full price reform would lead to even more severe inflation in the short run, and the spectre of militant urban labour protests in response to needed cutbacks of state sector wages and employment (the Gdansk scenario) haunts efforts to stem the flow of red ink and budget deficits.

The Weakening of the Centralized Party-State

If an increasingly autonomous society and economic instability were not already cause enough for worry, some also see unmistakable signs that the centralized party-state of the Mao era is in an advanced state of decline. The signs of decline are seen in two distinct areas: in the degree of centralized control exercised by Beijing over regional and local governments, and in the declining capacity of work units and other social institutions of the Mao era to monitor and control the population.

The changing balance of power between centre and localities is a major theme in the large literature on central-local relations in China, in which one reigning generalization is that China's political system after Mao is evolving into a "fragmented authoritarianism."[11] This decline of the centre is exemplified and most clearly illustrated by the massive shift of control over budgetary revenues that has resulted from the fiscal reforms of the 1980s. During the decade after 1967, the centre had controlled an average of 50% of all government revenues, an amount equal to 20% of national income. During the decade after 1978, however, the centre's share of revenues dropped to 28%, of national income to 13%.[12] Moreover, extra-budgetary revenues, which are controlled almost completely by localities, rose from 31% of the size of the state budget in 1978 to 103% in 1991. This shift in fiscal resources is understandably viewed as a good indicator of changing power relationships within the Chinese state and, indeed, as a decline of the centre. When higher level authorities no longer monopolize the resources upon which lower level jurisdictions depend, relationships within the hierarchy are characterized less by authoritative command and more by bargaining and negotiation.[13]

A second symptom of decline in the Mao-era state is the increasing inability and unwillingness of urban work units and village governments to monitor citizens and shoulder the tasks of political control. When the entire population was encapsulated within communes and work units, subject to close political monitoring and periodic political campaigns, and had little opportunity to earn incomes outside of this structure, the regime had an unrivalled capacity to stem collective protest before it had the opportunity to get underway. Now, vast sectors of the population — the migratory "floating population" and the large household and private sector — are completely outside this former network of organization.[14] Village governments no longer have the leverage over peasant households that control over grain and all income opportunities used to afford them.[15] Urban work units, increasingly preoccupied with earning incomes for their employees in a competitive economy, are no longer interested in paying the price of political surveillance, and the party's apparatus of control and reward has withered away.[16]

These mechanisms of control, which served to restrict the frequency and scope of popular protest in years past, were completely ineffective in stemming the massive popular response to the student movement in the spring of 1989. Indeed, there is strong evidence that state work units themselves became important centres for organization and protest in their own right.[17] More tellingly, however, *after* the military crackdown in early June, work units could not easily be induced to carry out the prescribed tasks of ferreting out and punishing those who had been involved. Instead, it is widely reported that work units — both in the academic and industrial worlds — made every effort to protect their employees and to dull the impulses towards persecution from above.[18] This is a remarkable change from 20 years ago, when such impulses from above could lead to fearsome political campaigns. Instead, most of the efforts at persecution fell to public security forces, which appear to have operated independently, as police forces, with little cooperation from work units in the cities. The crackdown in 1989, as draconian as it was, in fact illustrated a little-remarked transformation in the capacity of the Chinese state to enforce political control. No longer able to call upon the organized apparatus of surveillance and control characteristic of communist regimes, China now relies on the army and the police to maintain order. It has evolved into a more conventional authoritarian regime in which the military plays a central role.

Looming Instability or Evolution towards "Normality"?

These three trends — the increasing autonomy of large sectors of the population, the corruption, inflation and fiscal worries characteristic of transitional economies, and the decline of the highly centralized regime of the Mao years — all appear to point towards a potentially unstable future. The fact that more conservative party officials in China warn constantly about the necessity to stem social and political decay in order to avert political collapse and chaos serves to reinforce this suspicion. In my view, however, there is a strong tendency by some to exaggerate the implications of these trends. Employing a form of tunnel vision in which one's view is firmly on the Maoist past rather than on other developing and transitional economies, many observers misinterpret the significance of these trends. From a broader perspective, these same trends could just as easily be viewed as an evolution towards a more "normal" set of social and political arrangements.

A Society Spinning Out of Control?

It is beyond dispute that Chinese society has become much more fluid, chaotic, and much less effectively monitored and organized by rural and urban institutions than at any time in the Mao years. But, it is far from clear that this fact has important implications for China's political stability. To those who recall the austere and relatively well ordered society of the Mao years, China today must seem a society spinning out of control (though they forget the massive political upheavals of the Mao years). A less dramatic and entirely valid interpretation is that Chinese society is simply becoming more like other developing economies and is still not unusually chaotic compared to most of them.

Take, for example, the massive "floating population" of some 60 to 90 million rural residents who migrate for long periods to work in industry and on construction sites in China's rapidly developing rural and urban regions along the coast. The numbers, to be sure, are mind-boggling; these people jam the railways during the New Year's holidays and often sleep in public places. But, it is hard to see these migrants as a social problem of unusual severity. These people for the most part are not destitute. China's decollectivization divided land in a highly egalitarian fashion to all residents of villages. Virtually all of these migrants have land to till in their home villages. A far more severe problem is experienced by third-world countries in which large portions of the rural population are landless, and migrant permanently to large cities to live in poverty and squalor in shanty towns. No matter how chaotic things seem in China today, Shanghai is not

Mexico City, Rio de Janiero or Calcutta. Moreover, even if these rural masses were to become destitute in the future and settle in massive urban slums, it is far from clear that they would threaten the political order. Urban slums dwellers and migrant populations present difficult social problems, but they are difficult to organize and rarely fuel coherent political movements.

The same thing could be said about the often reported upsurges in industrial strikes and local riots in rural areas. True, these things appear to be on the rise, and they probably occur with greater frequency today than in most periods during the Mao era. However, strikes and riots are fairly normal events in any society; their occurrence may in fact serve to solve local disputes. No one has yet shown that China's rates of collective disputes are high by international standards. There is no reason to assume that they are like the first stirrings of a long-dormant volcano that now threatens to wreak havoc on the Chinese political landscape. Without coordination and organization, strikes and riots will remain just that, strikes and riots. And, even in the political eruption of 1989, urban workers showed only limited signs of organization and labour militancy.[19]

Finally, the evidence that Chinese society is developing greater autonomy and self-organization (leaving aside the debates about whether China is developing a *genuine* "civil society") in itself holds no particular implications for China's future instability. There is no known relationship between levels of autonomy and self-organization in a society and the stability of its political system. It could just as easily be argued that the evolution of a more autonomous society is something that could lay a foundation for future stability. There is little reason to assume that citizens shall use their autonomy to challenge political authorities; they might just as easily retreat into economic pursuits or private lives.

How Perilous Is "Partial Reform"?

One could plausibly argue that the perils of "partial reform" have been similarly exaggerated, and that their implications for China's future stability far from clear. First, the idea that "partial reform" is a uniquely flawed strategy is hard to accept given China's 15 years of rapid economic progress. The critique of partial reform seems increasingly odd, because there is no plausible alternative, except on paper, to gradual reform. And, it is hard to argue that such countries as Poland, which went the farthest in implementing plans for rapid monetary stabilization and privatization, have had more favourable economic outcomes than China. Could China's economic performance of the past 15 years really have been improved by embracing plans for rapid "full" reform implemented fitfully by Russia, Poland, and other transitional economies in recent years? It is hard to believe that such a reform scenario would not have caused much greater political instability in China than any of the worst scenarios conjured up by critics of partial reform.[20]

Let us turn to the three widely noted flaws of partial reform: corruption, inflation and macroeconomic stability, and crippling state sector debt. Corruption, to be sure, is an undeniably serious phenomenon in China, and it is without doubt a source of popular dissatisfaction. But, how serious is it as an economic and political problem? Clearly, it has not been so serious as to curtail foreign and domestic capital investment. China's rapid growth rates show that the incentives to invest are not being dulled by a rapacious officialdom. China is not the "kleptocracy" that one sees in Zaire or Nigeria. China's still predominantly public asset ownership, to be sure, creates conflicts of interest and opportunities for enrichment that are different in nature from the more familiar bribes and kickbacks of corruption elsewhere. However, to a certain extent, the opportunities for officials to earn incomes in a market-oriented economy help ensure that officials will not block or obstruct market reform, but instead embrace it. Public outrage alone is unlikely to have a large political impact; more important would be levels of corruption that impair the government's ability to perform its basic functions. There are few indications that corruption has reached this degree of severity.

Secondly, inflation: has China's record of inflation and macroeconomic instability really been all that bad? By international standards, the official inflation rates of 20–30% that have occurred when China's economy has "overheated," even if they underestimate real inflation rates by a wide mark, simply are not very high. In recent years, Russia, Poland, Hungary and other countries have had much higher rates of inflation. While the rapid growth in real incomes was stalled during the inflationary bout of the late 1980s, real income growth has resumed apace. Periodically slashing the supply of credit has been a somewhat clumsy, but effective, way of reducing inflationary pressures. In recent years, critics of partial reform have had to make room for writers outside the China field, who see China's incremental approach to fiscal reform and monetary liberalization an effective model from which the former communist regimes could profitably learn.[21]

Finally, is China's massive and still largely unreformed state sector really a hopeless drain on the state treasury and a sure cause of future inflation, budget deficits and macroeconomic instability? To be sure, further changes, including the systematic closure of hopeless plants and industries, will be hard to avoid. But, there are reasons to believe that the problems in this sector are not so severe or as intractable as they are sometimes portrayed.[22] True, there are massive accounting losses in state industry, but many money losing firms are still net contributors to the state treasury, as sizeable turnover and value-added taxes are paid before the base for income taxes is determined. Similarly, China's social welfare and pension system off-loads these massive costs onto state firms, where they are accounted for as costs of production. Many of these losses are an artefact of China's fiscal and welfare systems. In addition, some analysts interpret the losses of state enterprises as a sign that they are increasingly being subjected to strong competitive pressures from other sectors of the economy — the private, collective, and foreign-invested sectors — which now make up more than half of all industrial production. Profit rates have fallen and converged across sectors of the economy; and, some analysts have found that the stagnating factor productivity of state firms in the Mao years has been reversed and has improved at an accelerating rate in the post-Mao years.[23] Barry Naughton has recently argued that state sector losses are not a major source of macroeconomic instability in China — subsidies to this sector have fallen as a percentage of the budget since the mid-1980s, and their size is today a small percentage of gross domestic product.[24] Even if China's growth rates moderate somewhat in years ahead, sustained economic growth will make the inevitable restructuring of this shrinking sector considerably less painful than in any of the other transitional economies.

Political Disintegration or Gradual Evolution?

Lastly, what about the unmistakable signs of decline in the centre's domination of regions and localities, and in the system of grassroots controls upon which the Maoist regime depended for mass mobilization and political control? Don't these clear trends represent the decline of the Chinese state's capacity to govern? In my opinion, it is far from clear that these trends represent a decline in the capacity of the Chinese state to govern. What they *do* clearly represent is a decline of the kind of centralized party state characteristic of China during the Mao era, and which had historical parallels in the Soviet Union of Stalin, the Vietnam of Ho Chi-minh, and the North Korea of Kim Il-sung. It is not necessary for a Chinese state to be highly centralized or to have it exercise draconian grassroots controls in places of work in order for it to govern effectively.

Signs of an obvious decline in the centralization and grassroots control of the Chinese communist regime do not therefore portend political collapse. True, regional and local officials now control far more resources than they did in the past, and they are better able to act independently and resist directives from above that counter their local interests. True, ordinary citizens now have a greater capacity for self-organization and sustained collective action than in years past. These are simply signs that China's polity is becoming more like those of other nations, in which there is considerable give and take among state officials and agencies, and among local leaders and citizens. Whether this evolving form of politics will spin out of control and result in the disintegration of the state apparatus, as in the USSR in the summer of 1991, or whether ordinary citizens will form a powerful people's movement to challenge the regime, as in Poland in 1980, is not something that can be predicted based on the evolving structure of China's polity. To be sure, the potential is there, but whether it results in massive protest, the collapse of the Communist Party, or the disintegration of the Chinese state, is something that depends on processes that are far more short-term and contingent than the long term evolutionary trends that I have discussed here.

Politics Matter: Forecasts Based on Contingency and Chance

Many discussions of China's future appear to assume implicitly that prospects for political instability can be divined from trends in the structure of state and society. In a recent exchange in *Foreign Policy*, Jack Goldstone argues that China's demographic and environmental problems, and the trends outlined earlier in this essay, make China structurally very similar to earlier historical empires on the eve of their collapse, and he confidently concludes that the question is not whether, but how soon, China will collapse.[25] Yasheng Huang argues vigorously the opposite position, and provides considerable evidence for the proposition that China's state structures are still sound and that they have not been so weakened by decentralization and fiscal reform as to result in a serious loss of central control.[26]

While I share Huang's scepticism about confident predictions of China's collapse, I believe that both authors overestimate the extent to which political events can be predicted from structural conditions. I would like to emphasize instead that political instability — including social unrest — has *political* causes. When I say political causes, I mean specifically the extent to which conflict among political élites is resolvable with existing political institutions, and the extent to which that conflict is contained within the élite itself. When such conflicts are revealed outside the circle of top leaders, and when factions among these leaders reach out to other members of the state apparatus — regional and local leaders, editors of newspapers, regional military commanders and public security bureaus, and so forth — that is when the stage is set for political instability. When, in turn, these national or local élites seek to mobilize sectors of the population — especially workers and students — the stage is set for more broad-based social instability.

I am *not* making the commonplace point that such a split among élites provides an opportunity for protest "from below." This is a common caveat in both "society centred" analyses of protests as well as "state centred" emphases on state crisis as a facilitating condition for popular protest. I am making a very different point: that large scale protest "from below" is usually the result of an interaction between national and local élite factions in a situation where élite consensus and the discipline of the state apparatus cannot be maintained. Rather than protest "from below" seizing opportunities presented by a fragmented élite, I am arguing that broadly organized protest in society is *caused by* the interaction between divided élites and social groups. Without this élite split and resulting interaction, protest "from below" remains sporadic, isolated, and largely inconsequential for national stability. In other words, the large scale popular protests that so many appear to see as a potential source of political instability are a *symptom*, not a *cause*, of the instability of national political institutions.

I have arrived at this position largely by observing Chinese political history after 1949. Those who argue that a decline of state control over society, or of the central state's control over local government, has large implications for future political instability should recall that the Mao years themselves were subject to an unusually high degree of popular protest and political turmoil. With the possible exception of Poland, China has experienced more political turmoil and popular unrest than any other communist regime in this century. The Hundred Flowers period in the spring of 1957, the Cultural Revolution period of 1966–1968, and the last years of Mao's life (1974–1976), all were periods of urban protest and popular political mobilization. In each of these rounds of unrest, divisions among China's élite and in some cases factional conflict among them were central to the origins and the expansion of protest.

The student and worker protests of the Hundred Flowers period were the result of a divisive party rectification campaign during which citizens were urged for months to criticize local party officials before they finally began to respond, making local officials uncertain how, or whether, to respond. When workers and students began to engage in surprisingly active forms of collective action, and when local party officials began themselves to join in the criticism, and when in turn protest turned more fundamentally to higher levels of the party leadership and its imposition of a Soviet style system, the party élite closed ranks and crushed all signs of opposition in the ensuing anti-Rightist campaign.

The Cultural Revolution itself was of course initiated as an internal purge during which students and workers were eventually mobilized alternately to attack, and to defend, local power holders. That mobilized students and workers often took positions and pursued interests antithetical to either élite faction does not change the fact that their protests were a symptom, not a cause, of the collapse of China's political institutions initiated from the very top.[27]

And finally, the widespread regional strife that often took the form of street protests and coordinated general strikes were an expression of the jockeying for power of local and national élite factions in anticipation of the death of Mao.[28] In none of these cases, scholars have continually reminded us, were workers and students acting as mere tools of political leaders — they had interests and minds of their own, and often turned these opportunities to their own purposes. But, the fact remains that in no case could these protests have ever reached the size and degree of coordination — and the political impact — that they had, had it not been for the crucial interaction with political élites, who were key political actors in their own right.

What Were the Lessons of 1989?

But what about 1989? Didn't this show that things are different now? The political events of April–June 1989 in Beijing and scores of other Chinese cities, which are remembered under the misnomer "Tiananmen protests," were in many ways unprecedented. While there had been widespread political protest and turmoil during the Mao years, the nation's capital had never been paralyzed by independent popular protests — which in this case *did* originate completely independently of élite encouragement; in no instance, except during the self-inflicted collapse of regional governments in the late 1960s, had the Chinese government found it impossible to control the streets of a major city, much less the nation's capital, for such a long period; in no previous protest had such large numbers of ordinary citizens from all walks of life occupied a central square in defiance of government threats; and, while the army had been implicated in decades past in a number of attacks against civilian populations, both armed and unarmed (especially during the late 1960s), there had never since 1949 been an event quite like the bloodletting of 3–4 June.

During and shortly after these events, observers penned a common narrative that attributed them to the rise of a nascent "civil society" in China under the impact of economic growth and reform. A newly autonomous society struggling to free itself of remaining restraints, buffeted by the economic hardships of partial reform (in particular by inflation rates not seen since 1949), disgusted by the official corruption bred by a half reformed economy, itself a symptom of the loss of control by work units over the population and the growing weakness of the party centre — these were seen by many as the lessons of 1989. Chinese society had revealed itself as now much more capable of coordinated protest and common purpose than before; partial reform had bred deep-seated political dissatisfactions despite rapid growth in incomes and living standards; and the state had shown itself too weak to control these protests except through the most brutal means. Viewed from this perspective, 1989 indicated a potentially unstable future for China, which seemed even more certain after the spectacular collapses of communist regimes in Eastern Europe later that same year, and the collapse of the USSR less than two years later. The trend of history seems clear. Is China, then, the last and largest communist domino?

I view the arguments I have just outlined as a fundamental misreading of the lessons of 1989 and their implications for China's political future. While I have myself argued that the events of 1989 in China were politically unprecedented and that they reflected changes in the structure of Chinese society and state organizations during the 1980s, the mechanisms whereby popular protest expanded into a movement of large political import remained fundamentally the same as in past decades. The "Tiananmen protests" was emphatically *not* a case where an autonomous protest movement from below rose up to challenge and incapacitate a communist regime; where an increasingly autonomous "society" challenged an increasingly defensive "state." That interpretation is a myth that has more to do with intellectual fashions among western social scientists and historians than with events in China (or, except for Poland, in Eastern Europe, for that matter).

Instead, "Tiananmen" is a classic case in which nascent protests interact with a divided élite and party-state apparatus to create a wave of protests much larger and more politically consequential than could otherwise have occurred. Recall the timing of these events. In late April, a surprisingly strident student movement takes to the streets and meets with friendly crowds along the routes of their marches; the initial response is party editorial labelling the student movement as counter-revolutionary and threatening severe consequences — while General Secretary Zhao Ziyang is in Korea. After Zhao returns, the editorial line is moderated visibly, and then Zhao makes public statements indicating a clear split in the leadership over the issue. From that point, there appears to be two governments; one taking a hard line against "turmoil" and threatening severe consequences and another seeking accommodation, dialogue, and warning against the use of force.

It is at this stage that individuals and organizations within the state apparatus swing into action and in so doing expand the scale and significance of the movement far beyond the activities of university students. Crucial in this respect was a rebellion among newspaper reporters and editors, which resulted in a mass media divided over how to interpret the movement — both Central Television and *People's Daily*, among others, by the second week of May carried extensive and highly sympathetic coverage of the protests and especially of the student hunger strike. It has often been remarked that the student's use of street theatre — especially the hunger strike — was a shrewd political tactic that resonated strongly with China's popular culture and that was a major cause of the movement's growth.[29] While this is undoubtedly true, it should be kept firmly in mind that this political theatre would have played to an empty house had it not been given lavish national television and print coverage. Also crucial in expanding the scope of the protests and in further incapacitating the government's ability to act decisively to stem the protests was the open defection of key organizations and leaders from the party's official hard line — by university presidents, retired marshalls, the All China Federation of Trade Unions, the Women's Federation, and others, all of whom made public statements urging dialogue or who made donations to the hunger strikers. Those members of the state apparatus who did not actively take a political role stood inert, unwilling to commit to a course of action that was not sanctioned by a clear central authority. Chinese citizens reading the papers and watching television could have rightly concluded that support for the student hunger strikers was a patriotic duty viewed favourably by much of China's political leadership. Even after ordinary citizens flocked into the streets to block martial law troops during the third week of May — extending China's sense of political crisis — the mass media continued to undermine martial law orders for an additional several days.[30]

Tiananmen therefore demonstrates yet again the potent interaction of a divided leadership and state apparatus with impulses for protest from below. What the result would have been in 1989 in the absence of this élite split and the defection of the mass media is suggested by the remarkable but now largely forgotten national wave of pro-democracy protests by university students at the very end of 1986. In this case, there was again an élite split over how to respond to the student demonstrations, but this split was not made public, nor did political leaders or organizations in the state apparatus attempt to mobilize popular support. Hu Yaobang and other leading advocates of political reform were simply purged. Despite having sprung up in dozens of cities throughout China over a period of several weeks, the student marches were firmly shut down by local security forces.

The lesson of 1989, and the central point of this chapter, is that serious political and social instability will occur in China only if élite strife cannot be contained within the élite itself, and if one or more factions attempts to mobilize parts of the population to rally in its support. When this occurs, China's vast apparatus of government itself becomes a contentious polity of political actors — newspaper and television editors, state enterprise managers, heads of ministries, bureaus, and local governments, leaders of various police and military units. When this vast apparatus itself becomes an arena of contention, and when it uses its considerable resources, the results can indeed be explosive. In the absence of this particular form of élite conflict, it is unlikely that the social trends of recent years will translate into political instability — social problems, perhaps, but not political by threatening ones. It is in fact hard to give much credence to analyses that emphasize Chinese society's "potential" for mobilization and unrest, since that level, whatever it is, was certainly there in 1957, 1966–1968, 1974–1976, and 1989 — virtually every decade since 1949. While it may seem odd for a sociologist to make this argument, social trends themselves are unlikely to be important determinants of China's political stability. The extensive evolution of China's political and economic institutions in the past two decades means that China's political problems are no longer analogous to those of the stagnant and unreformed late communist regimes of the 1980s. China is an evolving East Asian authoritarian regime undergoing a rapid economic transformation. Does China face an unstable future? Does Indonesia?

Notes

1. See William L. Parish and Martin K. Whyte, *Village and Family in Contemporary China* (Chicago: University of Chicago Press, 1978); and Jean C. Oi, *State and Peasant in Contemporary China: The Political Economy of Village Government* (Berkeley: University of California Press, 1989).
2. See Martin K. Whyte, *Small Groups and Political Rituals in China* (Berkeley: University of California Press, 1974); Martin K. Whyte and William L. Parish, *Urban Life in Contemporary China* (Chicago: University of Chicago Press, 1984); Gail Henderson and Myron S. Cohen, *The Chinese Hospital: A Socialist Work Unit* (New Haven: Yale University Press, 1985); and Andrew G. Walder, *Communist Neo-Traditionalism: Work and Authority in Chinese Industry* (Berkeley: University of California Press, 1986).
3. See Yun-xiang Yan, "Everyday Power Relations: Changes in a North China Village," in *The Waning of the Communist State: Economic Origins of Political Decline in China and Hungary*, edited by Andrew G. Walder (Berkeley: University of California Press, 1995), pp. 215–41.
4. Dru Gladney, "Economy and Ethnicity: The Revitalization of a Muslim Minority in Southeastern China," in Walder (ed.) (Note 3), pp. 242–66.
5. See Deborah Davis et al. (eds), *Urban Spaces in Contemporary China* (Cambridge: Cambridge University Press, 1995).
6. See the summary of these views in Andrew G. Walder, "China's Transitional Economy: Interpreting Its Significance," *The China Quarterly*, No. 144 (December 1995), pp. 963–79.
7. See Steven Goldstein's masterful overview of the political science literature on the contradictions of reform in communist regimes: "China in Transition: The Political Foundations of Incremental Reform," *The China Quarterly*, No. 144 (December 1995), pp. 1105–31.

8. See Kathleen Hartford's excellent presentation of this argument: "The Political Economy behind Beijing Spring, 1989," in *The Chinese People's Movement: Perspectives on Spring 1989*, edited by Tony Saich (Armonk, NY: M. E. Sharpe, 1990), pp. 50–82.
9. See the considerable evidence presented in Shaoguang Wang, "Deng Xiaoping's Reform and the Chinese Workers' Participation in the Protest Movement of 1989," *Research in Political Economy*, No. 13 (1992), pp. 163–97.
10. See Wang, "Deng Xiaoping's Reforms" (Note 9) and Hartford, "The Political Economy of Beijing Spring" (Note 8).
11. See Kenneth Lieberthal, "Fragmented Authoritarianism," in *Bureaucracy, Politics, and Decision Making in Post-Mao China*, edited by Kenneth Lieberthal and David M. Lampton (Berkeley: University of California Press, 1992); and Jae Ho Chung, "Studies of Central Provincial Relations in the People's Republic of China: A Mid-Term Appraisal," *The China Quarterly*, No. 142 (September 1995).
12. Shaoguang Wang, "The Rise of the Regions: Fiscal Reform and the Decline of Central State Capacity in China," in Walder (ed.) (Note 3), pp. 87–113 and Table 4.3, p. 104.
13. See Andrew G. Walder, "The Quiet Revolution from Within: Economic Reform as a Source of Political Decline," in Walder (ed.) (Note 13), pp. 1–24.
14. See Dorothy J. Solinger, *China's Transients and the State: A Form of Civil Society?*, USC Seminar Series No. 1 (Hong Kong: Hong Kong Institute of Asia-Pacific Studies, The Chinese University of Hong Kong, 1991).
15. Oi, *State and Peasant in Contemporary China* (Note 1), pp. 183–98.
16. Andrew G. Walder, "Workers, Managers, and the State: The Reform Era and China's Political Crisis of 1989," *The China Quarterly*, No. 127 (September 1991), pp.
17. Ibid.
18. Ibid.
19. Andrew G. Walder and Gong Xiaoxia, "Workers in the Tiananmen Protests: The Politics of the Beijing Autonomous Workers' Federation," *The Australian Journal of Chinese Affairs*, No. 29 (January 1993), pp. 1–29.
20. See Louis Putterman, "The Role of Ownership and Property Rights in China's Economic Transition," *The China Quarterly*, No. 144 (December 1995), pp. 1047–65, and Peter Nolan and Robert F. Ash, "China's Economy on the Eve of Reform," ibid., pp. 980–98.
21. See Ronald I. McKinnon, "Spontaneous Order on the Road Back from Socialism: An Asian Perspective," *The American Economic Review*, Vol. 80 (May 1992), pp. 31–36.
22. See, for example, Gary H. Jefferson and Thomas G. Rawski, "Enterprise Reform in Chinese Industry," *The Journal of Economic Perspectives*, Vol. 8

(Spring 1994), pp. 47–70, and Thomas G. Rawski, "Chinese Industrial Reform: Accomplishments, Prospects, and Implications," *American Economic Review*, Vol. 84 (May 1994), pp. 271–75.

23. See Barry Naughton, "Implications of the State Monopoly over Industry and Its Relaxation," *Modern China*, Vol. 18, No. 1 (January 1992), pp. 14–41, and Naughton, *Growing Out of the Plan: Chinese Economic Reform, 1978–1993* (New York: Cambridge University Press, 1995).
24. See Barry Naughton, "China's Macroeconomy in Transition," *The China Quarterly*, No. 144 (December 1995), pp. 1083–104.
25. Jack A. Goldstone, "The Coming Chinese Collapse," *Foreign Policy*, No. 99 (Summer 1995), pp. 35–52.
26. Yasheng Huang, "Why China Will Not Collapse," *Foreign Policy*, No. 99 (Summer 1995), pp. 54–63.
27. Hong Yung Lee, *The Politics of the Chinese Cultural Revolution* (Berkeley: University of California Press, 1978).
28. Keith Forster, *Rebellion and Factionalism in a Chinese Province, Zhejiang, 1966–76* (Armonk, NY: M.E. Sharpe, 1990).
29. Joseph W. Esherick and Jeffrey Wasserstrom, "Acting Out Democracy: Political Theater in Modern China," *The Journal of Asian Studies*, Vol. 49, No. 3 (November 1990), pp. 835–65.
30. For a more detailed argument along these lines, see Andrew G. Walder, "Collective Protest and the Waning of the Communist State: Reflections on 1989, From the Perspective of Beijing," in *Contention, Repertoires and Political Opportunities: The Past and Future of Collective Action. Essays in Honor of Charles Tilly*, edited by Leslie Page Moch, Michael Hanagan, and Wayne Te Brake (forthcoming).

14

Legal Disputes and the Debate about Legitimate Norms

Isabelle Thireau and Hua Linshan

This chapter deals with one main component in the transformation process of Chinese society — legal reforms — and the new opportunities they provide for an interpretation of what constitutes a reasonable or appropriate behaviour under particular circumstances. Recent studies, written by Chinese or Western scholars, have focused on major issues such as the creation of legal institutions, the production of a growing number of laws covering various realms of social and economic life, and the interplay between the available means to settle disputes: mediation, arbitration or litigation.[1] Grounded worries have been expressed regarding, for instance, the difficulty with enforcing legal decisions or the control exerted by local governments and the Chinese Communist Party upon legal instances.[2] If those are fundamental questions, the topic we want to address in this chapter is slightly different. We would like to stress the part played by the discussions and deliberations carried out within the courts in the development of new norms and principles in Chinese society. As a matter of fact, courts can be considered as one among other few spaces in China where people are today given the opportunity to argue about what is right and what is wrong. Different interpretations of the same situation are provided in such venues, and various principles justifying people's decisions and actions are confronted. Arguments are expressed by the parties to the conflict and their representatives whose legitimacy, validity or relevance are evaluated and, eventually, rejected or reinforced. Agreements may be reached that illustrate a specific way to classify and combine principles stemming from the law but, also, from other resources inherited from traditional practices, collectivist distribution of rights and duties or specific usages born out of the economic reforms. If courts are one of the public spaces in China where discussions are held and agreements eventually reached, they differ nonetheless from other spaces, such as village assemblies, because of the explicit claim made upon those who participate in court sessions to justify their point of view by relying on collectively acknowledged principles, or in other words, to *jiang daoli*, and to relate their particular situation to more general concepts. This necessity, although present in the other spaces for discussion, is even stronger within the tribunals where, for instance, the resort to violence or to open menaces is precluded. A second distinction is that legal principles are bound to play a much more important role within legal institutions than outside of them.

Such an approach, of course, does not claim that genuine discussions between equals are a hallmark of today's Chinese society. Opposing views are often exchanged, and agreements reached, under a particular balance of power, as is the case in economic disputes involving local governments' interests. Criminal affairs bear the stamp of the ongoing campaigns, while those involving political issues must be readily dismissed as moments when different perspectives are confronted and discussed. The use of personal relationships to settle legal conflicts can certainly be observed. But, to emphasize only these situations tends to obscure the fact that, in many civil cases, the national as well as the local governments have no interests at stake other than to maintain social order and to find a solution to disputes. A discussion occurs, therefore, between the parties, their representatives and the judge, which is not eclipsed by the overwhelming authority of legal specialists and legal principles, nor by the interference of the local administration. In the course of this discussion, and under many institutional constraints, different perspectives are expressed concerning the more appropriate way to behave in given circumstances, and thresholds are tentatively designated to distinguish between acceptable and non-acceptable attitudes.

The concern about the need for new moral values in China usually focuses on the role that government or different élites might play, without considering the daily issues discussed by ordinary people and the solutions provided which actually amount to making choices as far as ethics are concerned. These choices, by contributing to the emergence of broad shared understandings, influence the type of social link being established within Chinese society and, consequently, the reaction of society's members towards the State and its representatives. Courts are precisely one of the places contributing to the emergence of broad shared understandings out of the necessity to provide concrete solutions to ongoing conflicts. As such, court sessions witness discussions concerning legitimate components of what can be regarded as practical reason.[3]

Our study relies on a preliminary analysis of legal disputes held in a basic level court. The data used come from 130 out of 230 court cases recorded during a few weeks in 1995 in a basic civil court of a medium-size city, located in a hinterland province.[4] Each case begins with an introduction of the parties to the conflict, including their representatives and, then, reproduces the discussion held between the plaintiff and the defendant, aiming at establishing the facts. Then comes the debate process, usually followed by a conciliation attempt during which the judge plays the part of a mediator. If no agreement can be reached, a judgement is delivered.

The ambition of the present contribution is rather limited. Follow-up publications, relying on a more extensive and detailed analysis of the present data, will hopefully place the cases observed back into the more general background of the Chinese legal system and will try to assess differences, such as those existing between plaintiffs and defendants, or rural and urban inhabitants. Our present aim is only to highlight the importance of the court as a place where individuals cannot but make explicit references to principles they consider legitimate to defend their own interests. The courts offer, therefore, an important field of observation for the researcher who is trying to understand changing norms in China, and they should not be dismissed as places where the debates are overwhelmingly influenced by the party, local governments, and their officers.

We will begin first with an analysis of the different types of disputes observed and show how they usually relate to rather ordinary facts of daily life that do not threaten local leaders' interests and require their interference. We will then pursue with a description of the identity of the parties to the conflict and their representatives, and we will stress the dominant part played during the debates by the plaintiffs and the defendants — as opposed to the legal specialists — that is, ordinary citizens, with their various resources and perspectives. With this information in mind, we will discuss the main principles mobilized by the participants and, finally, offer a preliminary analysis of the content of the agreements or judgements that put a formal end to the legal disputes. Unable to discuss in a detailed way, in the scope of this chapter, how agreements are reached and judgements pronounced, we will mainly point out the variety of principles mobilized by the actors present in the court and the tendency, often manifested, to combine various arguments and perspectives rather than stress the strict application of a rule, such as a legal disposition.

Table 1. Types of Disputes Analysed

Rights over houses and commercial spaces	50
Compensation for physical or material loss	30
Debts	26
Divorce and custody	16
Conflicts between neighbours	7
Unpaid salaries	3
Consumers complaints	4
Demands to put an end to a parent-child relationship	2
Demand to put an end to a contractual relationship	1
Worker dismissal	1

The Nature of the Legal Disputes Analysed

A brief description of the type of interests mobilized during the legal disputes may provide a first way to understand the debate going on in the courts and to appreciate the relative degree of autonomy enjoyed by the parties to the conflict as far as the intervention of local governments and collectives is concerned.

Each of the two first categories actually encompasses rather different issues. The first one, for instance, involves 11 conflicts concerned with inheritance or property rights to private houses and flats, 10 initiated by owners who have not been paid the rent they are entitled to, 9 by owners who want to move out the current tenants, 6 reflect disagreements about the right to use a public housing, 5 about the right to use a commercial space and 3 about the right to use a private accommodation. The remaining 6 cases express the views of individuals who had bought new flats and argue that the seller did not respect the contract, failing for instance to finish the construction in due time.

The legal disputes of the second category involve suits filed by persons who argue that their property, their reputation or themselves, physically or psychologically, have been damaged and who ask, therefore, for compensation. Situations encountered here vary a lot, including, for instance, events as different as violent confrontations between relatives, gossips between colleagues and unintended injuries committed by a neighbour.

The above classification provides only rough indications. As a matter of fact, it relies on the official label assigned to each case at the beginning of a session, and other designations might have been sometimes more accurate. In other words, many uncertainties still prevail in the identification of the dispute in legal terms and their belonging to a specific category. For instance, affairs officially labelled as related to debts cover a wide variety of situations, ranging from rather simple issues involving two individuals to much more complex economic disputes, such as questioning the validity of verbal agreements or the lack of quality control mechanisms. In one case for instance, a person acknowledged as a private merchant but who, later on, states that the merchandise he sold came from his work-unit, sells for RMB58,156 of sea products to a shop owner, who has allegedly remitted only RMB3,500. The defendant argues that he paid back much more than this small amount, although no written document was handed to him, and that part of the products could not be sold because of their poor quality.... In another debt case, the problem is actually one of use of a commercial space: the shop at stake has actually four different tenants, three unknown to the owner, mutually linked by various types of contracts ranging from formal renting to a "internal responsibility contract" system. Different qualifications of the dispute can also emerge during the court sessions, when underlying objectives are confronted to the initial motive of the legal dispute: for instance, a case described as one where a father wants to put an end to the kinship tie existing between himself and his daughter, actually reveals a confrontation between the two family members regarding the use of the public housing accommodation assigned by a work-unit. It could, therefore, have been classified also as a dispute over the right to use a public flat.

The brief description of the different types of disputes encountered supports our assumption that the government, national or local, will not directly interfere in the resolution process of the disputes frequently encountered by the civil courts. These disputes, as opposed to those coming to public attention through the media, bear no overt influence on the interests of those in a position of authority nor can they be systematically linked to specific ongoing propaganda campaigns. The parties to the conflict, their representatives and the judge are, therefore, going to enjoy a rather extended autonomy to mobilize various resources and assign responsibilities. They will do so by dealing with issues which may look rather simple and not highly sensitive but which actually have been the focus of successive transformations during the previous decades, such as property, inheritance or contractual relationships. It will, thus, be left to those present in the courts, to their interpretation of the law and not to an external power, to make a choice or establish a compromise between opposing interests, such as the traditional right of a woman to come back and live with her native family when her marriage faces difficulties and the legal right of a father to decide who should be able to live in the public house assigned to him by his work-unit and to eventually refuse his daughter to come back and live with him.

The Identity of the Parties to the Legal Disputes

A first way to capture the identity of those whose perspectives will be analysed later is to look at the way individuals and institutions (although represented by individuals) are distributed among the parties to the conflict.

The cases in which the plaintiff and the defendant are both individuals representing only themselves are, as shown in Table 2, the more numerous, and this would have been even more the case if we had integrated 63 cases of divorce that we chose to put aside at this stage. Most discussions are, therefore, going to be held, as far as our sample is concerned, between persons whose perspectives are not shaped by the internal rules nor by the specific interests of a work-unit. These individuals are bound to mobilize various resources, available to them according to their specific experience, to their current position and to the relationship existing with the other party, and as relevant as possible to the interests they want to defend.[5]

The knowledge and the position held by the various parties to the dispute can be partly understood through an important element of the identity: the declared professional activity. Without mentioning the exhaustive list of the occupations performed, let us focus on the main groups that can be distinguished among the parties of the 92 cases involving only individuals. Those who declare to be active or retired members of the "employee and worker" or *zhigong* category form the majority (58 on the side of the plaintiffs, thereafter P, and 64 on the side of the defendants, or D). The second group is composed of people who are unemployed or "waiting for a job" (9P and 25D), followed by that of the private merchants (9P and 10D). We can then mention for both sides 11 teachers, 8 cadres, 5 peasants, 3 students, 2 managers, 2 accountants, one actor, one driver, one soldier, one journalist. Besides the better knowledge of the various parties to the disputes provided by this information, a knowledge that could be confronted to the arguments produced in a further analysis, cautious to avoid simple and straightforward deterministic conclusions, two remarks can be made here. Firstly, when these professional activities are confronted with the disputes' accounts, a discrepancy emerges between the official activity and the one effectively pursued, to which the legal suit is linked. In other words, people who qualify themselves as peasants, workers, teachers

Table 2. Distribution between Individuals and Institutions (Societies, Municipal Departments, Banks, etc.)

Total: 130

	Defendant	
Plaintiff	Individuals	Institutions
Individuals	92	10
Institutions	16	12

or unemployed are in fact often engaged in all kinds of economic transactions, more or less informal and temporary. Someone who introduces himself as a peasant is actually going to head a construction team; another one who claims to be a worker is running a commercial space under the responsibility system; a declared employer is playing the part of a regular intermediary between given factories and shopkeepers; a cadre manages in fact a society; a teacher has established a partnership with a society ... not to speak of much more individual agreements and activities. Only the group of private merchants and that of managers bear identities directly linked to the new environment born out of the economic reforms.

We can suppose that most individuals engaged in informal economic ties will lack any comprehensive knowledge of the legal rules, incomplete and even contradictory as they may be, regarding the economic activities they participate into, meaning that they will often rely on principles other than legal to support their actions. Moreover, the discrepancy between the official status linked to the former social system which based people's identity and, we will argue, their moral status on their links with a given work-unit, and the informal activity performed, has a few consequences. It illustrates the decreasing power of regulation exerted by work-units. But, more importantly for the topic here discussed, the discrepancy attests to the existence of a space for interpersonal relationships and transactions, whose lack of legitimacy prevents the development of broadly shared principles and conventions, and whose uncertainties account for the numerous disputes and conflicts. Secondly, the important percentage of unemployed people among those targeted by legal suits may provide a partial explanation for some of the legal disputes linked to the incapacity expressed by given individuals to pay back their debts or to move out from a low-rent accommodation. It may also account for the involvement in illegal economic transactions. The group of concern here is actually not only that of the officially unemployed, many people characterized as members of the "employees and workers" category facing actually important financial difficulties due to their work-unit economic failure.

What about gender distribution? Since we cannot deal, in this short chapter, with the differences that may emerge between men and women as far as issues such as the choice of arguments or the attitude towards agreement versus adjudication are concerned, let us state briefly that 96 women (49P and 47D) and 159 men (65P and 94D) are present during the 130 cases analysed, excluding those standing in the tribunal as representatives of different institutions, who are all male. Once more, the picture would have been quite different if we had included the 63 remaining divorce cases, most divorce demands being raised by women.

Another element concerning the parties to the conflict, and bound to influence the court sessions, regards the past relationships existing between the plaintiff and the defendant. Many of them had actually been friends, neighbours or colleagues, but we would like to stress here the importance of kinship ties. As a matter of fact, out of the 92 cases mentioned above, 34 witness the confrontation between close relatives: parents and children, brothers and sisters, step-parents and step-children, uncles and nephews. Such a situation deserves further analysis, but it indicates the pressures imposed on the family by competing systems of distribution of rights and duties. A relative lack of means of regulation when family disputes arise seems to be pointed out by the fact that violence is often present. The data analysed show that at least in 21 out of the 130 cases under study, resort to violence is mentioned in the description of the facts leading to the legal dispute, which is often a family dispute. The level of hostility between the parties sometimes causes the intervention of mediation agencies, a situation which influences also the debate and the capacity to reach an agreement, the court appearing in such cases as the last resort. Actually, 25 out of the 130 disputes were brought in the court because of the failure of prior mediation attempts, the identity of the 26 mediators involved comprising, for instance, the elders of the large family, the members of a police station, the heads of the work-unit or a consumers' committee.

This is a very rapid sketch of the identity of the parties to the various legal disputes we review. As the data show, it is mostly individuals, and not institutions through their representatives, who are going to express their views inside the walls of the court and who are going to do so by relying on the interpretation, reformulation, combination of resources coming from different periods of the last decades of Chinese history. But, the characteristics of the debate going on in the courts can be shaped actually mostly by the legal specialists standing by the parties rather than by the parties themselves. To what extent is the rhetoric of law very present in the tribunals, limiting the broader social debate about legitimate norms analysed in this chapter? To answer this question, let us pursue our description by looking at who stands by these individuals in the court, help them articulate their ideas and provide them eventually with legal knowledge.

As a matter of fact, in appraising the debates carried on in the basic level court under study, it is necessary to know who are the participants to the discussions, besides the judge and the two parties standing in opposition in the legal dispute. The identity of the official representatives (*weituo dailiren*) and the amount and the nature of their intervention cannot but influence the type of arguments mobilized and the issue of the dispute.

As far as our data are concerned, the picture which emerges has the following characteristics.

As far as the last category shown in Table 3 is concerned, situations may vary a lot: one party may be accompanied by a lawyer and the other by a citizen less qualified in legal knowledge, while in other cases — and they are quite numerous — both parties may have required assistance both from a lawyer and from a friend or a relative. The majority of the disputes (58.5%) is, therefore, debated in the court without the presence of lawyers. This first indication allows us to expect the discussions and arguments not to be heavily influenced by legal knowledge and concepts.[6]

A more detailed comparison between the two types of representatives shows that the legal representatives are less numerous than the non-legal ones: 87 versus 97 for a total of at least 260 parties, being entitled to assign one or more persons to assist them throughout the whole process. It shows also a clear discrepancy in the distribution of these representatives between plaintiffs and defendants. Individuals or institutions who chose to resort to legal means to solve a conflict are supported by 58 lawyers and 59 ordinary representatives, while the defendants are counselled by 29 lawyers and 38 friends or relatives.

Before trying to discuss this information, let us describe the identity of those numerous representatives who are going to assist the parties, provide them with given perspectives and concepts in order to justify their claims, but who are not introduced as lawyers. We find among them, first of all, a group of 30 persons belonging to the category of "employees and workers," then 20 retired cadres, 18 persons only characterized by their kinship tie with the party concerned, 13 cadres, 7 managers, 2 retired

Table 3. Number and Nature of Parties' Representatives

(Total cases: 130)

Presence of representatives other than lawyers (for one or both parties)	39
Absence of lawyers and other representatives. Parties defend themselves.	37
Presence of lawyers only (for one or both parties)	27
Joint presence of lawyers and other representatives	27

employees, one member of the local Public Security Bureau, one Party secretary, one researcher, one journalist and 3 persons for whom the only indication provided is their name. Three groups can thus be broadly delineated: one composed of individuals whose assistance has been required because of their social status, such as retired cadres and, to a lesser extent, active and retired employees; a second group formed of individuals who are present to assist members of their kinship network, and a third one composed of employees, cadres or managers defending the interests of the institution to which they belong.

This information confirms the active participation of the parties directly concerned in the process of description and interpretation of the facts addressed. It supports our claim that courts offer one among other settings where it is possible to analyse the various principles that are mobilized by ordinary Chinese people to assign a meaning to a given situation, the institutional constraints influencing this interpretation process, and the content of the agreements that they will find acceptable.

If the number of lawyers involved is relatively small, this should not come as a surprise since, although the profession has been growing rapidly, the shortage of Chinese lawyers is widely recognized, with a current estimate of one lawyer for 15,000 inhabitants.[7] And the term "lawyer" used to designate the legal experts representing some of the parties may in fact be assigned to persons possessing very different qualifications. But, the fact that most people prefer to require the assistance of other members of the society or no assistance at all rather than hire the services of a lawyer is also linked to their unwillingness or incapacity to pay the needed fees, to which the expenses linked to the legal proceedings must be added.

Given the important part played by representatives lacking official expertise in legal affairs, it may be necessary to add a few remarks concerning the nature of their intervention. First, the idea, already mentioned,

Table 4. Distribution of Representatives between Plaintiffs and Defendants

	Plaintiffs	Defendants
Lawyers	38	19
Lawyers and other representatives	14	6
Other representatives	38	26
None	40	79
Total	130	130

that social positions linked to the pre-reform period still command more consideration than those linked to the economic reforms when it comes to public venues and discussions, is reinforced by the choice of retired cadres or employees to assist the parties. No manager and no private merchant for instance, having no personal interest at stake, is called to accompany and counsel a plaintiff or defendant in the court. Moreover, the idea that the retired cadres, by their presence, seem to play a fundamental part to assess the morality of the party concerned rather than participate actively in the debate is supported by the fact that most of them remain silent throughout the proceedings. As a matter of fact, the analysis of the sessions shows that the type of intervention of such representatives may be broadly divided into four categories: those who remain silent, those who are going to make one or two brief interventions, repeating for instance some of the facts stated by the party, summarizing his claims or presenting the written proofs to the judge, and those who are very active during the discussion, speaking on behalf of the party, adding new claims, rejecting or accepting conciliation. We decided to distinguish a fourth group, composed of those individuals who, whatever the length of their intervention, make explicit references to given laws. Our estimation, the aim of which is only to provide rough indications, is that the first group represents about 27% of the total, the second one 42%, the third one 27% and the last one 3%. In the first group, we find a great majority of those who possess no kinship ties or institutional links with the parties, adding to the feeling that they bring their moral caution rather than their knowledge to the persons they assist. Of course, another hypothesis would be that the implicit support offered by these cadres is linked to the power and the connections they enjoy, their explicit intervention being therefore unnecessary.

A surprising finding is that, when such an analysis is done regarding lawyers' intervention, the results are much the same: 27% remain silent, 43% make brief remarks, 25% are quite active, and 4% only make explicit reference to legal texts or procedures. The main difference between both types of representatives is that lawyers belonging to the second and third group rely more often than their non-specialized counterparts on an implicit knowledge of law. For instance, a lawyer is going to argue that "this conflict is actually about a transfer of agreement, the party which is sued has transferred to us the responsibility, assigned to him by society X, to complete a given part of the construction project, but he did so without gaining approval of society X. The contract signed between us and the defendant is therefore not valid, and the defendant must bear full responsibility for the inconvenience caused to us, and not the society X."[8] While an example of direct reference to the law would be illustrated, for instance, by a lawyer representing an insurance company which refuses to compensate a client for the loss of his car, and who indicates:

> We do not intend to pay, because the plaintiff did not provide enough evidence. He must give us proofs regarding the fact that both the car and the driver have disappeared; for instance, he must show us the driver's licence. The inquiry made by the Public Security did not reach the conclusion that the car had really disappeared. According to Articles 21 and 24 of the Insurance Law, we do not need to pay any money. If necessary, we can provide to the court the documents, written rules and laws concerning such kind of problem.[9]

A much more thorough study, using more diversified and representative data, would be required to reach some conclusions as far as the degree of specialization of lawyers' intervention is concerned. Nonetheless, the information gathered here seems to point to the low level of expertise mobilized by the lawyers during the 130 cases observed and to the qualitative differences of the services offered to the clients: some appear to bring most of all their moral caution to the party at stake, much like a retired cadre would do, while others actively defend the rights of their client. If this situation can easily be explained by the recent development of lawyers' training and the resulting uneven qualifications possessed, one cannot but raise the question of the nature of the current social expectations regarding lawyers: is their legal expertise the main element at stake, or their capacity to express in a more articulated way the claims of their clients, or the moral caution they bring to plaintiffs and defendants? The fact that 27% of them remain silent suggests that their sole presence, and the expenses implied, are sometimes considered to warrant the veracity of the facts narrated by their clients and the legitimacy of their actions.

Moreover, lawyers — and, in this respect, their attitude is very similar to that of other types of representatives — are quite eager to express their concern for moral issues that may be in accordance with the law or not but that are not going to be coined in legal terms. Trying to solve a conflict between a father and his children, a lawyer says for instance: "As a lawyer, I feel entitled to tell you, that there is nothing under the sky which does not come from the parents...."[10] The influence of the moral discourse and concerns on Chinese lawyers and judges, their cultural origin and their influence on the application of the law, should be stressed in further legal studies in order to provide a more cautious and accurate explanation of the influence of legal knowledge in China.

Finally, one cannot but notice the different choices made by plaintiffs and defendants. Various explanations can be suggested as mere hypothesis for a further questioning of the sources. The fact that defendants do not require, in most cases, the support of lawyers can be explained by their unwillingness to increase their financial burden. But, they actually often refuse other forms of support and stand alone in the court, a situation that may be linked to the implicit recognition that the facts addressed are difficult to negate, or to the desire to give as little publicity as possible to what is still considered to be a shameful event.

The disputes at stake have shown that the government or the local administration are not bound to influence heavily the court sessions. If privileged ties with influential cadres can be mobilized by some parties, the central and local governments are not going to intervene directly to solve disputes concerning debts, property rights or divorce applications. They will do so indirectly by enacting given legal documents, leaving some autonomy for the various actors in the court.

The important part played in civil courts by defendants and plaintiffs, standing in most cases alone in front of the judge or accompanied by members of the society not characterized by their legal expertise and by lawyers who are going to make a very uneven use of specialized knowledge, supports the idea that the debates are going to rely on various types of arguments, legal and non-legal, considered to be more or less legitimate. In other words, if one can resent the relative absence of legal expertise when observing the unfolding of court sessions, another perspective is to stress the wider debate about legitimate norms and practices that is actually held in the tribunals.

The Pragmatic Use of Different Resources Inherited from the Past

In what follows, we will describe different types of arguments and principles that are confronted in the court in order to delineate the broad spectrum of the discussions developed during legal disputes, without relating them to specific issues or social identities. It is also beyond the scope of the present chapter to establish distinctions between the attitudes of the parties, of their representatives and of the judges or to provide a detailed analysis of the argumentation process. Moreover, as we will mention possible relationships between different types of arguments, our attention will be directed not to the cases where the parties argue about the veracity of the facts ("this is not what happened") but to those where both parties agree about the facts while disagreeing about their qualification ("this is what happened, but it is or it is not an offence"), using thereby different principles to assign a meaning to the situation.[11] The cases where plaintiff and defendant agree about the facts in their interpretation but argue about the nature and the extent of the sanction, are very interesting since they support the search for a specific hierarchy between various norms, but they must be put aside as elements for further research.

Four broad types of arguments or practices mobilized by the participants during the discussions can be distinguished. Traditional principles the origin of which can be traced back to the pre-1949 period, collectivist principles or institutions characteristic of the years 1950–1978, legal principles, and finally usages the legitimacy of which is not articulated in general terms but which are born out of the economic reforms and which actually encompass given norms. Such an approach is adopted for the sake of clarity, and a more detailed and accurate analysis should discuss the cultural links or discontinuities existing between these four categories; as well, the approach should make distinctions between different components within what is now constituted as a single category, such as moral norms, political rules or institutional practices.

The following examples describe very briefly the way principles related to some of these four categories are going for instance to be opposed during the court sessions analysed.

A first broad type of situation encountered is when principles we call "collectivist" are confronted to other norms. Such principles can, for instance, be opposed to legal ones. In three cases in our sample, tenants requested to move out by the legal owners argue that they have been provided such an accommodation by their "advanced collectivist enterprise" which failed to offer them flats in a public housing. The cadres of these enterprises actually chose a few decades ago these accommodations for their workers, often paid the rent directly during a certain period, and then left this responsibility to the worker. The argument expressed by the tenants is that the collective, or society, is responsible for their housing accommodation. They are entitled to be assigned a lodging by their enterprise, or to be provided with a low rent accommodation. They cannot move out, therefore, if no other alternative, at least as cheap as the current one, is offered to them. All owners in the cases analysed are prompt to reply that their legal property rights must be protected and that they should not bear the responsibility to find another housing accommodation for the tenants. Nonetheless, the plaintiffs, their representatives and the judge usually agree that, if the dominant principle to solve those cases must be the defence of property rights as determined by law, one cannot ignore the existence of different rights and obligations the legitimacy of which was well established until 1978. These are going to be assigned the status of "practical difficulties" that should be taken into account during the resolution process. Therefore, a compromise is usually going to be found: tenants will have to leave, but the delays offered are much longer, running from 18 months to three years, than those generally assigned. Different principles stemming from some of the broad categories delineated above are actually often evaluated and classified according to the perceived degree of their legitimacy.

Legal disputes can also contribute to a common interpretation and reevaluation of the responsibilities assigned to organizations stemming from the collectivist system, such as the work-unit. Are the work-units extensions of the family, and can they assume the duties and responsibilities of the family in a society where the development of law requires a much clearer designation of rights and obligations? These are some of the questions addressed in the court. For instance, a young man has been seriously injured on the head when coming back home by a worker whose psychiatric problems are publicly known. He first files a suit against his assailant's mother to try to be reimbursed for more than RMB6,000 spent in medical fees, then drops the charge, the old peasant woman being unable to pay back the expense. He then turns to the work-unit of his assailant and asks it to bear the responsibility that the family is unable to assume. After a long debate, the work-unit of the disabled worker is recognized as having no legal obligation. The work-unit of the plaintiff, however, expresses its own moral obligation to reimburse the expenses of its employee. Through concrete and apparently minor disputes, it is actually the place assigned nowadays to the work-unit and, as a consequence, the rights and obligations of individuals and the new principles underlying the social link which are sometimes under discussion.

Legal provisions can also play an important part in assessing the responsibilities of collectives and providing protection to individuals. As a matter of fact, the development of the economic activities of the local administration often transforms persons under local government's administration into customers who are going eventually to defend their rights in the commercial field, thus contributing to limiting or, at least, challenging the arbitrary action of local administrative organs. For instance, in two cases, an administrative department of the municipality failed to deliver in due time newly built flats. The buyers claim that the existing contracts have not been respected, amounting to a breach of contract and that they should get their money back, plus some compensation. The argument put forward by the heads of both administrative services at stake is that they are dependent on other administrative services for many affairs, such as authorizations, money, choice of subcontractors.... They should not be held responsible for the delay since the administrative difficulties they face belong to the category of "irresistible forces," mentioned in the contract as a situation for which no one can be held accountable. If one judge seems sympathetic to the argument, the second one remains silent. But, in both cases the plaintiff's reaction is so vehement, stating that an expression such as "irresistible forces" can only be used to designate events like natural disasters and not to justify administrative intricacies or paralysis linked to competing interests, that the argument is abandoned. The responsibility of those who officially sold the flats are recognized as a basis for further discussion and, eventually, for an acceptable compromise. Other examples show how the combined use by the administration of market mechanisms and political authority, for instance when political power is used to perform an economic transaction on terms favourable to the administration's interests, may eventually be denounced on legal terms by plaintiffs. Relationships between local authorities and individuals are actually debated during such cases, and limits to arbitrary practices of the administration are tentatively assigned, using arguments and words carefully chosen under existing institutional constraints.

But collectivist principles, supported by legal documents, can also be confronted to traditional standards. This is the case for instance when, as already mentioned, a married daughter argues about her right to "come back to her native family" (*hui niangjia*), and to stay with her father in the public housing assigned to him by his work-unit, while the father claims that he enjoys the legal right to decide who can live under his roof. In this particular case, the daughter's claim will be defeated as not relevant to an urban context. It should be noted, nonetheless, that the judge has been trying actually to assess the quality of the relationship between the father and the daughter. It is only when he is convinced that hostility has reached such a level that they cannot live together, that he will reject the traditional argument as not valid, his main objective being to bring an end to the dispute. In three other disputes, daughters-in-law who apply to stay with their parents-in-law after the death of their husband are also confronted to the official rules regarding flats provided to one family member by work-units. They oppose the demand made by their husband's parents that they should move out by stressing the fact that, for instance, "my child is still a child of X family, although his father is dead"[12] or that "if my sister-in-law, married and with a child, is allowed to stay with them, how can they reject the wife and daughter of their son?"[13] In all these cases, the final decision will comfort the wishes of the parents-in-law. One judge will follow the others and mobilize the law as the dominant principle and interpret it as supporting the attitude of the older generation, while offering a compromise inspired by a rather traditional practice: the wife should move out but be allowed to leave her child with the husband's family. These cases show more pointedly how legal principles may sometimes be used to oppose traditional usages but also actually to comfort traditional practices.

A second broad type of situation is illustrated by the different relationships that can be established between principles that, as a matter of simplification, we call "traditional," and other arguments. We saw above examples of conflict between traditional and collectivist principles. But, we can pick up examples where traditional and legal principles are mobilized during the same dispute, whatever their relationship is. As a matter of fact, these two categories of arguments may sometimes overlap. For instance, the legal necessity for children to provide their parents with economic support, if needed, is usually interpreted by the parties, their representatives and the judge as an element of filial piety and is articulated both in traditional and legal terms. But, legal and traditional concepts may also stand in opposition. In one case, which runs over three sessions, a woman argues with the two daughters of her second husband, who just passed away, about the way to divide the family property. She rejects an oral agreement established previously with her step-daughters stating that she would keep half of the property, the rest being divided between the two sisters. Arguing that she ignored her legal rights at that time, she claims that half of the property should be considered as joint property of the couple belonging now to herself, while the other half should be divided between the various heirs, including herself. Later on, she indicates that the two daughters she had from her first marriage have been financially supported by her second husband during a few years, and they should, therefore, be considered as heirs to his property. This interpretation is rejected by the daughters of her second husband who claim that, according to "common practice," no kinship ties exist between their father and the daughters born out of the first marriage of their step-mother. The judge will support the plaintiff's claims, offering somehow a compromise that we will mention later.

In the case described above, an important element of the conflict is the existence of an informal agreement to which everyone should stick according to the two defendants. The traditional strength assigned to oral commitments is actually often contradicted by the attention paid by the judges to written agreements and documents. Facts considered for further discussion are often those which have a written basis, explaining the anger of an old man and his appeal for a "court of morality" amounting to a rejection, on moral grounds, of the court judging his case.

In other cases, the requirements of the law officially preclude given traditional concepts which are, nonetheless, allowed in the court. For instance, the idea that a correct understanding of an individual's action must rely on an evaluation of his moral qualities or, in other words, that the meaning of an act cannot be separated from the identity of the person who performs it, a traditional concept used also by the Chinese Communist Party, is sometimes mobilized by the parties in legal disputes. One party will thus argue that his or her opponent's behaviour, as far as the issue at stake is concerned, cannot be considered as correct since he has regularly committed offences in the past. The offences described can be coined in traditional terms, as is the case for instance when the low moral standards of a man are proved by the fact that he lost his wife's ashes, making it very difficult for his daughters to perform the ancestors' cult. But, they can also be coined in terms reminiscent of political struggles or campaigns: a woman supports her description of the defendant as a bad person by saying: "During the Cultural Revolution, he was even a commander of a rebel organization."[14] It should be pointed out that, if the judges usually do not stop the parties from expressing their views, they do not rely, at least explicitly, on this information to produce a judgement but use them to press the parties during the conciliation process.

Legal disputes may also be influenced by the discrepancy existing between official legal provisions on the one hand and, on the other hand, social practices born out of the specific institutional and administrative constraints under which the economic reforms are being carried out. These practices may actually have indirect links to collectivist or traditional principles, but the important point is that their legitimacy is not discussed, since this would often require to address sensitive issues regarding the present political and economic system. We are dealing here, for instance, with conventions established to anchor mutual expectations and support economic transactions under current uncertainties. Such a convention may be the acknowledged practice (at least in the region administered by the court under study), acknowledging that the mere exhibition of a property document concerning real estate, even if it does not carry the proper name on it, demonstrates some links between the person who can exhibit the document and the property at stake, allowing the first one to rent the second one. (Many cases indeed illustrate the fact that a property, such as a car or a house, may change hands very quickly and be sold six or seven times in a few months, the name of the initial owner being kept on the property documents.) This practice is recognized in our sample by the parties to the dispute as well as by the judge, the debate concerning merely the sanction that should be administered to an individual who took advantage of this usage to rent out a shop that he was actually running for a society, which had rented it from the owner. Other examples may be, for instance, the practice, for a given unit, to participate only nominally in a given project which is actually run by another organization, or *gua mingzi*, making it difficult to assess legal responsibilities when a problem arises. Or, the well-known practice of registering as public a property which is actually private. The parties, their representatives and the judge never question these usages in our sample, despite their violation of legal norms, but accept them as facts born out of the specific current situation, and this must be taken into account in the settlement of the dispute. If the law is rather silent here, it is not because of the perceived relevance and legitimacy of other arguments, rather it is the impossibility of applying the law without denouncing given contradictions and irregularities linked to the present system.

Many different perspectives could be used to analyse the data collected. However, we would like to make only a few points related to the topic discussed. First of all, legal norms are only one among the resources mobilized by the different participants to the discussions, whatever their status. The description of the facts and the conciliation attempt are often centred on non-legal arguments, even if lawyers and judges are relatively more inclined to mobilize the law. The reasons for such a situation are manifold and we will not discuss them here, stressing only the fact that the observation of court sessions is relevant not only to observing the way law is interpreted and applied, but to understanding more broadly social members' perception of what is wrong and what is right, of what can be justified and what is unacceptable under given circumstances. A second point, related to some general features of the social debate held in the courts rather than to their formal content as far as norms are concerned, is that each of the four categories delineated does not form a coherent and systematic body of knowledge that is rejected or adopted as a whole. According to the circumstances and the dispute at stake, individuals are going to consider as legitimate principles or conventions coming from one or more of the four broad categories delineated. In other words, people make choices within the heritage left to them. The third point is that the relationships established between arguments coming from these four broad categories are quite varied: they may overlap and be used to reinforce a claim, they may support a gradation of responsibilities, be combined to offer a compromise or be opposed to stress a specific choice. The choices made are nonetheless shaped by institutional constraints: some arguments just cannot be expressed.

Whatever the diversity of the principles and the related practices mobilized, the efforts of the various persons standing in the court are in most cases shaped by their desire to establish facts and to provide relevant arguments. If participants to the discussion do not usually care about assigning a specific qualification to their arguments, one third of the parties involved indicate that they are not speaking only from the point of view of particular interests. They will argue that their arguments encompass a more general perspective and can be viewed as reasonable (*heli*), and, in fewer cases, as normal (*zhengdang*), in conformity with human feelings (*heqing*), or legal (*hefa*). The quest for reasonable and normal arguments is an important element of the debate about legitimate norms, since it makes an explicit reference to shared understandings and common principles. As such, it offers a suggestion for a further analysis of the source. A first answer concerning the emergence of broad shared understandings can nonetheless be found in the analysis of the agreements considered to be reasonable or acceptable by the parties, and of the judgements produced if such an agreement fails. To what extent the settlement of legal disputes relies on legal principles, and to what extent the agreements and judgements reached reflect wider social concerns and contribute to the creation of new practices? These are the questions to which a very preliminary answer is now going to be provided.

The Settlement of the Disputes

Out of the 130 disputes analysed, 50 come to an end through the establishment of a conciliation agreement or *tiaojie xieyi*, 60 require the production of a judgement, 16 suits are withdrawn and 4 are considered as null and void. Table 5 provides rough estimations about the content of the settlement of the various disputes, the extent of the compromises established varying a lot according to the cases.

A high number of disputes are thus settled through an agreement. The court sessions are actually dominated by the efforts made by the judge, and sometimes the parties' representatives, to reach such type of settlement. The debates do not really aim to find out who is right and who is wrong according to the law, but to recognize what are the facts and the legitimate principles, legal or not, relevant to a settlement of the dispute. Judges act as mediators during most part of the sessions, avoiding for instance to label given situations or practices as illegal, and preferring qualifications, such as correct or reasonable. They resort to mediation techniques, such as trying to find out what are the underlying interests of the parties in case both of them are actually different and can be accommodated, or trying to compensate a loss in one area by a gain in another one. They do use legal procedures, but in order to help the mediation process and establish an account of the facts that can be accepted by both parties as a basis for further discussion. For instance, oral agreements made between the parties in the absence of any testimony, or written agreements the documents concerning which cannot be exhibited, are rejected as having no legal status. Elements which have no explicit connection with the dispute are put aside. Judges will eventually mention the type of legal judgement that could be produced to settle the ongoing dispute, but they do so to push for an agreement. In other words, they use their future role of arbitrator, if an agreement fails to be reached, in order to facilitate the mediation process.

Table 5. Legal Dispute Settlement

	Conciliation	Judgement
Plaintiff wins	19	30
Compromise	31	27
Defendant wins	—	3
Total	50	60

Their position of authority is actually recognized by some parties who will argue that they accept the conciliation attempt to show consideration to the judge and not out of their concern or trust for their opponent.

The cases are very rare when, at the end of the debate, the judge declares that the hostile attitude of both parties and the extent of their disagreement make any conciliation attempt useless. Most of the times, the judge will offer this possibility to the parties and press them to adopt such a conciliatory attitude, using quite traditional arguments such as: "You have to excuse and understand each other,"[15] "Each of you has demonstrated sincerity until now, so it should be easy to reach an agreement,"[16] "Let us forget about the details; what is the point to being so serious about this matter?,"[17] "If both of you make a concession, this affair can be solved very easily ..."[18] or "Let us take harmony as the rule."[19] To accept a compromise is still highly valued, as the analysis of court sessions reveals, making it sometimes difficult for the parties to reject such an offer. "You are willing to try to reconcile your views. This is a very good thing,"[20] often compliments the representative of the law.

To force the agreement, the judge, besides the moral appeal for a conciliatory move described above, may indicate the bad consequences that could result for both parties in case a judgement should be delivered. Those consequences can directly stem from the content of the judgement and its legal dispositions, as already mentioned above; but, in many cases, the judge will point out the damage a judgement and, in a particular case, any judgement, will cause to the relationship between the plaintiff and the defendant. The pressure for an agreement is indeed the greatest when the parties to the dispute are linked by kinship or friendship ties, happen to be neighbours or are colleagues of the same work-unit. "You are still members of the same family,"[21] "You are bound to see each other everyday since you are neighbours; you may need to help each other later; better try to reach an agreement ..."[22] often argues the judge. In one case, the two parties — a father and his daughter — rejecting any conciliation attempt, the judge even refuses to judge, explaining that "according to the law, the problem is very clear and I know what judgement I should pronounce. What I worry about is that, by doing so, I cannot but harm the relationship between both of you, and I refuse to do so. You just go back home, think about it, and we will meet next week to see what can be done."[23]

The reasons why the judges encourage the establishment of such agreements are manifold and difficult to assess here, but one should mention briefly, besides the part played by the positive value attached to the search for an agreement, the influence of institutional constraints, such as the difficulties met in the enforcement of legal decisions as well as the system of evaluation of judges' performance.

In most agreements, law plays a rather secondary part. Agreements offer the parties a wider room for manoeuvre, allowing them to play a more active part in the interpretation of the facts and the resolution process. For instance, in some cases, defendants are going to argue that they have no legal responsibility to pay an alleged compensation to the plaintiff, although a legal decision might have decided otherwise, but that they agree to do so out of moral or human considerations.

Compromises are usually based on a combination of different arguments, legal and not legal, expressed by the various participants. The following example illustrates this point, but many other cases could have been chosen. A father, aged 77, claims that his wife and his son have taken away part of his property. In 1951, he was sent to a labour camp for "historical reasons" and decided with his wife to sell out a property covering some 1,000 square metres. Later on, with his agreement his wife used that amount of money to buy two small buildings. In 1981, released, he comes back to live with his family, remarries with his wife who had divorced while he was in the labour camp, and decides to sell one of the buildings. In June 1994, a written agreement is established, rejected now by the plaintiff, giving this building to one of his sons in exchange for a RMB 80,000 compensation for the father. The building is worth RMB 350,000 according to third party estimations. The plaintiff is willing to give back the RMB 80,000 and recover the building, a common property of the couple. He argues that his son is only interested in using this place to do business and shows no filial piety towards him, although he tried his best to send money back home when he was in the labour camp. His son does not show him the respect he is entitled to and, therefore, he wants his house back. The mother, it should be added, stands by her son.

To encourage them to reach an agreement, the judge points out the fact that, legally speaking, the father still has time to deny the past agreement, since official procedures have not been done to put the property under his son's name. Moreover, he is also entitled to respect and to a fair treatment. Nonetheless, the father should take into account the fact that they are all members of the same family and that his wife had agreed to remarry with him after his return from the labour camp, a "difficult and courageous" gesture. None of the children would be happy if they divorced again, and everyone should make a concession, without calculating too strictly the losses and the gains. "Within the family, feelings are more important than money." After a brief discussion, the plaintiff agrees to recognize the former agreement, provided an additional sum of RMB 50,000 be later given to him.[24]

Besides the various principles recognized as legitimate to interpret the situations, most agreements take also into consideration the concrete circumstances of the parties to the conflict, that is, what type of compromise they are in the material capacity to accept. Agreements related to debts typically involve compromises, such as the surrender of the interests due or the extension of the period required for the payment of the debt. Disputes between owners and tenants often end, for instance with the owner offering a longer time than previously requested for the tenant to move out or paying an acceptable compensation when expenses had been done on the internal decoration of restaurants or commercial spaces that have to transfer elsewhere. Since defendants are unable to bargain in case of a judgement, they usually support the search for an agreement, while plaintiffs have to be convinced by the judge to do so. Conciliation agreements, nonetheless, do not always imply that the defendant has to make a concession. The defendant may just agree to the claims expressed by the other party and accept the sanction imposed, whatever its content.

If judges favour conciliation, they may yet reject an agreement when too much discrepancy exists between the result of the bargaining process and existing legal provisions. Such a situation can be observed in one case only of our sample, where a father demands his married daughter, who has just moved back with him, to move out, his one room flat being too small, he argues, to accommodate his daughter, his son-in-law and his grandson. Relationships, apparently, are not very good between them. As the defendants refuse to do so, the plaintiff offers to give them a monthly allowance of RMB 300 if they leave. The agreement is about to be concluded when the judge intervenes and, without justifying his position, indicates that a legal decision will be later transmitted to the parties. The judgement will actually require the daughter to leave without any compensation.[25]

However, in many cases, the parties are going to fail to reach an agreement. The plaintiff may refuse beforehand any conciliatory move, feeling that his rights are clearly established and that a judgement will assess them more completely than an agreement, or he may refuse the conditions offered by the defendant during the conciliation attempt. The relationship between both parties may also be such that a discussion to find common terms is impossible. "You say that I should forgive and understand you, and go for the conciliation," replies a plaintiff to the head of a municipal bureau in charge of housing affairs who had not respected the official delay in building a flat that she had bought, "but forgiveness and understanding are for people who have feelings for each other. We are not talking about feelings here, we are talking about a contract."[26]

Defendants are sometimes the ones who refuse conciliation. They can do so for various reasons, but one of them should be mentioned here: because they are not in the position to bargain and are unable for instance to pay their debts, whatever the facilities offered for the payment. "We cannot reconcile our views, I just cannot pay,"[27] puts a defendant bluntly, thus indicating his preference for a jugment that, by all means, will not be enforced easily. Such an attitude suggests that individuals may feel more committed to respect decisions they have personally agreed upon, as compared to compliance with a legal decision. This would partly explain the emphasis placed on agreements by legal institutions.

If agreements are not bound to make explicit references to the law, legal decisions are in the majority of the cases supported by the mention of a specific legal provision, although sometimes they will just read as follows: "Wang XX owes Chen XX RMB500, that should be paid back to Chen immediately after the judgement. Wang is also to pay the legal fees, that is, RMB 150."[28]

The application of the law may lead to a judgement supporting the demands of the plaintiff, but also to the assessment of the shared legal responsibility of both parties. In one case for instance, a woman criticizes one of her colleagues, saying that he should be called "Xia the Impure," alluding to malpractices she thinks he has committed at work. Xia asks her to stop, but she repeats her remark; some pushing occurs, and she falls down. She asks for Xia to pay RMB 400 for medical fees. The judgement will nonetheless read as follows: "… We believe that the physical rights of the citizens should be protected by the law. Xia overreacted, and he was the first to touch and push the plaintiff, who fell. His behaviour is wrong. He must bear the civil responsibility and pay a compensation. But, the plaintiff began the quarrel, she called Xia all kinds of names in front of other colleagues, and did not stop when the defendant asked her to do so. She therefore initiated the dispute and must bear some responsibility for it. According to Articles 119 and 134 of the General Rules of the Civil Law of the People's Republic of China, we decide that Xia should pay RMB 90 to the plaintiff. He must pay this sum in a delay of ten days following the judgement. As far as the legal fees are concerned, Xia must pay RMB 90 and the plaintiff the remaining RMB 60."[29]

But, judgements can also be based on a compromise between legal principles and other considerations, the judge relying on various arguments considered by him to be reasonable and legitimate. Such an example can be found for instance in a case, already mentioned before, where a woman argues about her property and inheritance rights with the two daughters of her second husband. According to the judge, five heirs can be acknowledged in this case: the woman, her own two daughters from a first marriage, and the two daughters of her second husband. The legal decision divides the property according to the law but assigns a wider share to one of the daughters of the deceased, on the grounds that "she is a student doing research. Her father supported her studies, and she should be allowed more money than the other heirs in order to pursue her education."

In other words, judges are going to use different means, ranging from moral persuasion to decisions supported by legal documents, in order to achieve what is considered officially as their main objective: to put an end to ongoing disputes and protect social order. The rhetoric of the law is going to be one among the possible resources mobilized by the judge, who is often going to resort to traditional principles shaping the intervention of mediators in China: emphasis on the consequences of the various solutions available to the parties, integration of specific elements of the situation such as the relationship existing between the parties in the resolution process, etc. As far as the plaintiffs' and defendants' behaviour is concerned, a rather mixed situation can be observed where, on the one hand, agreements are reached linked to the emphasis put on justice by conciliation, search for common benefits and mutual concessions, and, on the other hand, judgements are produced linked to the rejection, by some parties, of the above concepts and the quest for a clear assessment of rights and responsibilities.

Conclusion

The historical ruptures Chinese society has been confronted with during the last decades have contributed to the current uncertainties in the realm of social norms, uncertainties which explain that the law is sometimes welcomed as an instrument that will at least support the emergence of a prevailing interpretation of situations. But, these historical ruptures have also, paradoxically, introduced a certain plurality of principles and values, illustrated by the courts' proceedings. The parties to the conflict and the legal representatives mobilize various types of arguments, argue about their legitimacy, and use them to interpret the law or to support an agreement. If such a situation may not be very different from the one witnessed in Western courts, the extended margin of freedom encountered within the Chinese courts, as far as the application of the law is concerned, is nonetheless supported by factors specific to the present situation of the Chinese society. On the one hand, legal structures and expertise have been developing recently and are in a transitional stage, at a moment when principles stemming from different periods of recent Chinese history regain some legitimacy. On the other hand, the concept, stemming from Chinese cultural tradition, that agreement between the parties is better than adjudication by the judge, and that a good judgement takes into account, as much as possible, the different perspectives expressed as well as arguments other than the legal ones (moral principles or past relationships between the parties), accounts for the overt integration of factors other than the law in the settlement of legal disputes. In other words, if political reasons explain the subordinate part played by legal provisions and procedures in China, such as those clearly delineated by Jean-Pierre Cabestan in a recent article, the traditional perception, reinforced by the current situation, that laws are first of all a governmental instrument and not a reflection of ongoing social debates about norms, rights and obligations, contributes also to its subordination.[30]

Despite the institutional constraints exerted, despite the rather secondary place still occupied by legal institutions in China, this margin of freedom enables a broader discussion about legitimate norms and principles within civil courts and, thus, offers an important venue for a debate which is denied any existence on a more organized and public level. If such debate can be observed, much more informally, in villagers' discussions or workers' complaints, it is provided in courts with the support of much needed arbiters, procedures and provisions, that can eventually contribute to the legitimization process of given principles and practices.

Notes

1. Suzanne Ogden, *China's Unresolved Issues: Politics, Development and Culture* (Englewood Cliffs: Prentice Hall, 1995).

2. In November 1995, *The China Quarterly* dedicated its 141st issue to the development of legal institutions and legal documents in China.
3. As a matter of fact, the debate analysed here is not actually a public debate about social norms as such, stimulated by given groups of the society, but it is constituted by the multiple discussions arising out of disputes concerning various issues. The need of the parties to the dispute to justify their claims and eventually reach a solution offers an important opportunity to observe the principles mobilized and the arguments exchanged regarding their respective legitimacy under concrete circumstances.
4. Of the remaining 100 cases, 63 concern divorce applications, and we put them aside for a further and more systematic analysis, although 12 divorce cases are included in the present sample.
5. This issue is discussed more systematically in the introduction written by Bernard Lepetit to the collective book entitled *Les formes de l'expérience* (The Forms of Experience) (Paris: Albin Michel, 1993) as well as in the very stimulating contribution by Simona Cerutti published in the same volume under the title "Normes et pratiques, ou de la légitimité de leur opposition" (Norms and Practices: Of the Legitimacy of Their Opposition) pp. 127–50.
6. The percentage of cases involving lawyers is actually quite high, if we compare it with the official statistics showing that in 1995 lawyers were present in only 11% of the total civil cases recorded. *China Daily*, 13 January 1996. Even when taking the divorce cases into account, which are often carried out without lawyers, 30 of the cases recorded witness the intervention of lawyers.
7. "Lawyers: A Profession in Flux," *China News Analysis*, 15 February 1996, 10 pages.
8. Case 27.
9. Case 3.
10. Case 123.
11. Sebastien MacEvoy, *L'invention défensive. Poétique, linguistique, droit* (The Defensive Invention: Poetics, Linguistics, Law) (Paris: Métailie, 1995).
12. Case 41.
13. Case 110.
14. Case 35.
15. Case 13.
16. Case 41.
17. Case 128.
18. Case 44.
19. Hua Linshan and Isabelle Thireau discuss in *Enquête sociologique sur la Chine, 1911–1949* (Sociological Study on China, 1911–1949) (Paris: Presses universitaires de France, 1996) the principles underlying the settlement of local disputes in Taishan county, Guangdong province, before 1949.
20. Case 7.

21. Case 17.
22. Case 2.
23. Case 22.
24. Case 34.
25. Case 15.
26. Case 37.
27. Case 73.
28. Case 53.
29. Case 91.
30. Jean-Pierre Cabestan, "Chine: un Etat de lois sans état de droit" (China: A State of Laws without a State of Right), *Revue tiers monde*, Vol. 37, No. 147, July–September 1996, pp. 649–68.

Index

Note: Roman numerals refer to the pages of "Chronology"; the Arabic numerals to the pages of the main text.

Prepared by Maurice Brosseau